MIAMI
The American Crossroad

A Centennial Journey
1896-1996

ARVA MOORE PARKS   GREGORY W. BUSH

with

Laura Pincus

Institute for Public History
University of Miami
Coral Gables, Florida

SIMON & SCHUSTER
CUSTOM PUBLISHING

ISBN 0–536–59693-X

BA 96211

 SIMON & SCHUSTER CUSTOM PUBLISHING

160 Gould St./Needham Heights, MA 02194
Simon & Schuster Education Group

TABLE OF CONTENTS

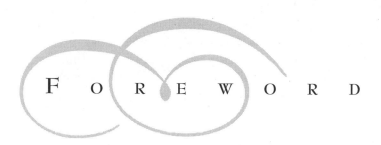

FOREWORD

Nobody can tell now, exactly, why Rome and Paris and London began, or what made them endure and grow great. It is as if there were places and times in which human activity becomes a whirlpool which gathers force not only from man's courage and ambitions and high hopes but from the very tides of disaster and human foolishness which otherwise disperse them. Such cities seem to grow in spite of people, by some power of the whirlpool itself, which puts to work good and bad, fineness and cheapness, everything, so long as it has fibre and force and the quality of aliveness that makes life. Something like that, it seems to me, has happened here in South Florida, under the sun and the hurricane, on sand and pineland between the changeless Everglades and the unchanging sea. Miami has been building itself with all the tough thrust and vigor of a tropic organism. I doubt if it will be complete or the whirlpool slack, in a long time because its strength is that nothing human is foreign to it, or will be.

MARJORY STONEMAN DOUGLAS

Looking backwards at age 106, Marjory Stoneman Douglas, older than the City of Miami, is one of the area's most revered residents. In 1941, she wrote this Foreword in the Depression era Works Progress Administration's Guide to Miami. Her words, prophetic at the time, still ring true today. She received the Presidential Medal of Freedom in 1993 for her tireless efforts to awaken people to the importance of protecting our fragile environment. (Michael Carlebach)

ACKNOWLEDGEMENTS

This book would not have been possible without the financial support of the following individuals, foundations and institutions. First and foremost is Prentice Hall who believed in the project from the beginning and contributed 22,000 books to the Dade County Public Schools. David Zarowin at Prentice Hall and Hal Hawkins at Simon and Schuster Custom Publishing have believed in the idea of a companion local history text in the American history curriculum. Their companies' gift insures that in the future young Miamians will learn about their hometown.

This project has been further enhanced by the generous support of the Ethel and W. George Kennedy Foundation that purchased copies of the reader for Dade's private schools and set up a prize for secondary school local history teaching. Initial funding came from Dean Ross Murfin of the College of Arts and Science and Provost Luis Glaser of the University of Miami. Other pre-publication expenses were underwritten by the Charles N. and Eleanor Knight Leigh Foundation, the Dade County Council of Arts and Sciences, Jean and Bill Soman and the Schulevitz Foundation. Historic preservation grant assistance was provided by the Bureau of Historic Preservation, Division of Historical Resources, Florida Department of State assisted by the Historic Preservation Advisory Council. We are grateful for the faith each had in what we were trying to do and for their generous support to make our dream a reality.

Miami: The American Crossroad is the fruit of the collaborative effort of its editors and a number of talented and public spirited individuals who care about the history of their community. It could not have been done without their help. Henry Green, an important force in the early stages of this book, helped organize the research and secured grants for the project. He also provided useful commentary. Christine Ardalan, the research coordinator for the first year, put an enormous amount of time into the project. Graham Andrew spent hundreds of hours researching and editing. Laura Pincus' research, writing and editing skills advanced her from research assistant to full collaborator. Their high standards of research can be seen throughout the book.

Several readers spent a great deal of time closely examining the manuscript to correct errors and improve the writing style. As always, Howard Kleinberg was an invaluable resource and friend who was always willing to assist us in every way. William Straight played an important role, made numerous editorial suggestions and provided valuable background information. Larry Wiggins was always eager to help. Other readers who gave useful suggestions were Jesus Mendez, Howard Wade, Dorothy Jenkins Fields, Paul Blaney, and Ray Mohl. Don Spivey, Chair of the University of Miami's History Department, offered us an invaluable critique and strong support from the beginning and through some difficult periods. His dedication to promoting public history in South Florida is having an impact.

We especially want to thank all the authors whose original contributions help flesh out perspectives on our past. Their names are included with the accounts they wrote. Many others helped in a variety of ways from locating photographs and documents to sharing their memories and materials. They include: Alfred Browning Parker, Garth Reeves, Alyce Robertson, Evelyn Wilde Mayerson, Betty Fleming, Bob Lafferty, Gregory Parks, Sol Lichter, Teresa Gillan, John Walker, William Carey, Eugenia Thomas, Thelma Gibson, Carita Vonk, Tammy Klinger, Anne Streeter, John O. Brown, Louisa Borecky and Stephanie Kirby.

We are especially grateful to photographers, John Gillan, Steven Brooke, Michael Carlebach and Martin Berman who allowed us the use of their wonderful images. *The Miami Herald* and publisher David Lawrence have been supportive of local history efforts and made its photographic collection available to us. Robb Parks worked many hours on photographic reproduction and Daniel Oria of Photo Pro went out of his way to help us meet deadlines.

A number of University of Miami students volunteered in local archives to find original documents for this project, notably Aldo Regalado, Raisa

Martinez, Edelyn de Varona, Erin Mayerson, Bryan Cooper and Monique Hofkin.

We also gratefully acknowledge the contributions of Raisa Martinez, Carolina Amram, Lisa Edmunds and Luis Castro. Judith Busch, Jesus Sanchez Reyes, Nuria Santizo and Lenny Del Granado helped with administrative facets of this project.

Local archivists who helped include: Becky Smith and Dawn Hugh of the Historical Association of Southern Florida, Sam Boldrick and George Faust of the Miami-Dade Main Library, Bill Whiting of the *Miami Herald* Library, Esperanza de Varona, Bill Brown and John McMin of the University of Miami's Special Collections and Dorothy Fields of the Black Archives.

To the families of those involved with this book, notably Bob McCabe, Will Sekoff, Paula Bush, Carmen Alvarez and Bach Ardalan—we appreciate your support and patience.

School Superintendent Octavio Visideo, School Board Chair Betsy Kaplan, Social Science Coordinator Paul Hanson and Social Studies Specialist Dorothy Fields all helped support this book within the Dade County School system.

Regina Daugherty was our backbone and right hand putting in many hours of special effort to finish the project. Preston Scanlon and Will Sekoff provided invaluable editing and production help. The wonderful book and cover design came from the extraordinary creative talents of Jim Kitchens.

In 1887 pioneer photographer Ralph M. Munroe captured what he described as South Florida's first community gathering—a Christmas party at the Bay View House in Coconut Grove. The men, women and children shown here included almost everyone (except Seminole Indians) who lived in what is now Greater Miami. The Bay View House, later the Peacock Inn, once stood in today's Peacock Park where Miamians still gather for special events. (Ralph Munroe)

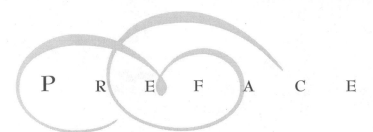

P R E F A C E

"Debates over the nature of the past are not merely textbook exercises for our students, demonstrating the difficult task of obtaining the truth. They are (consciously or not) public debates over values and developments that count in culture. It makes a difference how you view the past. . . ."

> *Warren Susman*
> *Culture as History, 1984*

History does not contain a fixed set of facts, a limited body of knowledge or a one dimensional view of the world. It involves a continuing struggle for deeper meaning through fresh insight and interpretation. By seeking new evidence in unusual and often obscure primary sources, we gain new perspectives—see more clearly and in depth—as well as acquire valuable information for others to consider. As we move beyond simplistic assumptions, ask questions, exchange and debate ideas, we develop a greater understanding of the human condition—past as well as present.

This view of history makes it more than a twice-told tale. It is the attempt to place the story of people in action—all kinds of people—in perspective. People yearn to be more than passive spectators in a large arena. They want to be part of the action and seek authentic experiences rather than accept what others interpret as reality.

What we have tried to do here is not simply re-tell history in our own words or as seen through our eyes. What we present is a compilation of many works by a diverse group of people who have participated in the journey to Miami's Centennial. It is their opinion, their point of view, about their time that we record. Many of the documents selected have never been printed before, or come from rare sources not previously available to the general public. They include letters, diaries, interviews and speeches as well as printed government documents and newspaper and magazine accounts. We are grateful for the people who wrote their reminiscences just for this book, or allowed us to tape record and transcribe their words.

We do not agree with every writer's point of view. In fact, we sought many different perspectives and opinions and often debated among ourselves on what to include. We tried to select documents that would pique interest and curiosity and stimulate thought, reading, research and especially dialogue and debate. We have left the documents as we found them which explains some of the grammatical inconsistencies that you will notice.

Although celebration of the City of Miami's Centennial prompted the writing of this book, when we use the word Miami, we use it in its broadest sense—Greater Miami and all of Dade County. The same is true when we use the term America.

The documents are arranged into seven chronological chapters and an epilogue. Each chapter includes a brief overview to help the reader view the documents in the context of the time and within the broader themes of American history. Each document has an introductory paragraph that gives the reader an insight into the source, the writer(s) background and ties the work into both the local and national/international picture. We have also included sidebars on "Living History" that encourage readers to know and visit our historic sites so that they can experience history first hand.

"Seeing is of course very much a matter of verbalization," wrote naturalist Annie Dillard in her book *Pilgrim of Tinker Creek*. "Unless I call attention to what passes before my eyes, I simply won't see it. It is, as Ruskin says, 'not merely unnoticed, but in the full, clear sense of the word, unseen.' "

The documents, and the people who wrote them, call for our attention. What is seen, is up to each reader. We hope the documents that we have selected will show that Miami's history is dazzling in its accomplishment, its variety of humanity, its color and expressions of hope and joy, tragedy, greed and suffering. We have gained a new awareness from the documents, from the selection process and from the many people who helped us make the book reflect all facets of our community. We hope that our readers will have this same experience. Above all else, we hope we have stimulated interest in reinvigorating and redefining Miami's as a community. Awareness and knowledge of the past are the first steps toward understanding and developing a pride in people—a pride in place. It is this pride that in turn, builds community.

GREGORY W. BUSH   ARVA MOORE PARKS

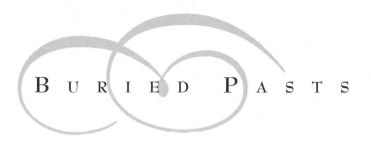

BURIED PASTS

chapter
one

1

"It is probably time we settled down. It is probably time we looked around us instead of looking ahead. We have no business, any longer, in being impatient with history. . . . History was part of the baggage we threw overboard when we launched ourselves into the New World. . . . Plunging into the future through a landscape that had no history, we did both the country some harm along with some good. Neither the country nor the society we built out of it can be healthy until we stop raiding and running, and learn to be quiet part of the time, and acquire the sense not of ownership but of belonging."

    Wallace Stegner
    Where the Bluebird Sings
    to the Lemonade Springs, 1992

In 1884, Ralph Munroe, the Miami area's earliest photographer, captured this beautiful picture of the mouth of the Miami River. Twelve years later, the new City of Miami would rise on these shores. (Ralph Munroe)

We can never completely conquer the land on which we live. Nature always returns to remind us that our view of conquest is an illusion. Nowhere is this more clearly seen than in the history of the Biscayne Bay region of South Florida where the shifting sands of time seem so unpredictable, like the weather. Until a century ago, South Florida's unique mixture of land and water, its climate and geographical distance from large population centers kept it largely isolated from the wider world. As a result, this lush, sub-tropical wilderness, with abundant public land for homesteading, was largely overlooked as wagonloads of men, women and children headed toward a new life in the American West. As the western frontier days were drawing to a close, South Florida remained an inaccessible wilderness where only a handful of adventuresome souls had carved out their place in the sun.

Our Earliest People

According to archaeologists, South Florida's first people arrived more than 12,000 years ago (the Paleo-Indian period). They probably crossed the land bridge from Asia through Alaska 40,000 years earlier and as time passed, followed the warmth of the sun southward. What we know about them comes from the work of archeologists who have uncovered numerous artifacts from early human communities throughout South Florida. Our earliest written documents describing the native people come from the Spanish, who arrived in the early 16th Century. Unfortunately, these accounts reflect a Spanish point of view and do not tell us what the native people thought about themselves.

From both archaeological and historical accounts, we know that the natives utilized the bounty of the land and the sea. They constructed tools from shells and stone; there was no metal embedded in the limestone. To survive the climate, most moved from place to place—from Biscayne Bay to the Keys or up the coast.

European Arrivals

In 1513, more than 100 years before the Pilgrims landed in New England, a Spaniard named Juan Ponce De León led an expedition that first sighted the Florida coast. He stepped ashore somewhere between today's St. Augustine and Jacksonville and claimed the land for Spain. Three months later, he sailed into Biscayne Bay and wrote in his journal, "reached Chequescha," the first name recorded for the Miami area.

During the next 40 years, other Spaniards tried to explore and settle Florida but soon gave up for more lucrative colonies in Peru, Mexico and the Caribbean.

Then in 1562, the French established Fort Caroline, near what is now Jacksonville, stimulating rivalry for the control of Florida. The King of Spain dispatched Pedro Menéndez de Avilés to remove the French and establish a Spanish settlement in their place. Menéndez not only annihilated the French colony, he established St. Augustine in 1565, which became the first permanent European settlement in what is now the United States. The King rewarded him by making him *adelantado* (governor) of Florida which at the time included all the land from today's Florida to Nova Scotia and from the Atlantic to the Mississippi.

After Menéndez became governor, he set about to establish other settlements and missions in Florida. One of these was a 1567 mission and settlement on the Miami River. He learned about the area from d' Escalante Fontaneda, who had been shipwrecked off Florida when he was 13 years old and wandered among the native peoples for 17 years. After Menéndez rescued him off Florida's southwest coast, he helped Menéndez secure a tenuous alliance with South Florida's native leader, Chief Carlos, who convinced Menéndez to marry his sister. This union gave Menéndez an advantage over other would-be Spanish conquistadors. He succeeded where all the previous explorers failed and was the first Spanish leader to have an on-going relationship with the native people.

Menéndez chose Brother Francisco Villareal, a Jesuit priest, to be the leader of the proposed settlement and mission on the Miami River that they called Tequesta, the name of the village chief. Natives helped the Spanish build a stockade containing 28 rather plain houses. The mission was abandoned a few years later after the Tequestas grew angry at Spanish abuses and demanded that they leave. This and two other attempts at settlement failed, but the Spanish remained allied with South Florida's native people against the British who increasingly threatened Spanish Florida.

Pedro Menéndez de Avilés founded St. Augustine in 1565—the first permanent settlement in what became the United States. Two years later, he founded a mission at Tequesta on the Miami River.

By the 18th Century, Creek Indians from Georgia, Alabama and the Carolinas, threatened by advancing English settlement, moved south into Florida. They were joined by runaway slaves who found sanctuary with the Indians who were soon known as Seminoles, from the Spanish *cimmarones*, meaning renegade.

Although it is estimated that more than 200,000 native people lived in Florida when the Spanish arrived, European disease, Spanish and Seminole conquests and inter-tribal warfare reduced both their power and numbers. By the 1750s, most of South Florida's original inhabitants vanished. When England took over Florida in 1763, all but a handful of the remaining people left with the Spanish for Havana rather than live under British rule.

During the Second Spanish Period, 1784-1821, when Spain regained control of Florida after the American Revolution, the King of Spain gave several land grants to the Bahamian squatters who had come to South Florida during the British Period. They became South Florida's first permanent non-native residents.

∽ Bloody Red, White And Blue

The United States gained control of Florida from Spain in the Adams-Onis Treaty of 1821. The treaty established a set of legal structures over the land including a territorial government and a commission to settle land titles. As a result, Bahamians Rebecca Egan and her son James were granted 640 acres each, Rebecca on the south bank and James on the north bank of the Miami River. Just south of the Rebecca Egan donation, Bahamians Jonathan Lewis and his sister-in-law Mary also received 640 acres each. All the rest of the land on the mainland of what would later become Miami was public land owned by the United States government.

In the early 1830s, a South Carolina transplant to Key West named Richard Fitzpatrick purchased the four grants in the Miami area and brought in a group of African slaves to provide the labor for his planned cotton plantation. In 1836, as head of Florida's territorial legislature, Fitzpatrick established Dade County. It was named after Army Major Francis Langhorne Dade who, along with 105 of his men, was killed during an Seminole ambush in central Florida known as "The Dade Massacre." A few months later, the Seminoles attacked the settlement in what is now Fort Lauderdale and they burned the Cape Florida Lighthouse on Key Biscayne. Fitzpatrick abandoned his plantation and removed his slaves to Key West to keep them from joining the Seminoles.

In response to the burning of the lighthouse and increasing conflict with the Indians, the Army established a fort on Fitzpatrick's land at the mouth of the Miami River in 1838 and named it after Navy Commander Alexander Dallas. Fort Dallas was used and abandoned by the government several times until it was closed twenty years later when both the Indians and the U.S. Army stopped fighting.

In 1843, during one of the relative periods of calm, Richard Fitzpatrick sold his vast holdings to his nephew William F. English. English laid out a village named Miami on the south bank of the Miami River and sold some lots on a street he called Porpoise Street. He built a plantation house for himself and quarters for his slaves on the north bank.

Florida became a state in 1845 and the Dade County seat was moved to Miami a year earlier. This period of optimism and growth was short lived. When hostilities resumed with the Seminoles in 1849, English left for the California Gold Rush to seek funds to build his city. The army re-opened and quartered troops in English's home and in his slave quarters. They also added a group of wooden buildings to the site. William English never returned to Miami. He died in California and his dreams for Miami died with him. When the Seminole Wars ended in 1857, Fort Dallas closed and the planned village of Miami faded into memory.

Homesteaders And Carpetbaggers

During the Civil War (1861-1865), Florida joined the Confederacy. Despite secession, the Union Navy never lost control of Key West and blockaded much of South Florida, including the Biscayne Bay region. Although area residents were far from the sounds of battle, the abandoned buildings at Fort Dallas became the home of a motley group of castoffs from both sides. Federal gunboats patrolled the area looking for blockade runners and on one occasion, burned down a suspected Confederate spy's home and store as a lesson to other would-be Southern sympathizers.

During Reconstruction, which followed the war, the Biscayne Bay region attracted several new types of residents: so called carpetbaggers from the north as well as homesteaders. They came to take advantage of the state government that was under northern control and the vast amounts of public land offered under the Homestead Law of 1862. The most daring and unscrupulous adventurer on the Miami River scene was William H. Gleason, originally from New York state. Gleason arrived in 1866 and was soon embroiled in state politics and unsuccessful attempts to control the land at the mouth of the Miami River. He also took over the dormant Dade County government and appointed his men, including African American homesteaders Andrew Price and Octavius Aimer, to public office.

Despite this flurry of activity, South Florida was still a very isolated and undeveloped region. In fact, in 1876, the U.S. Government built a series of Houses of Refuge along the Florida coast to help those who were shipwrecked on the most uninhabited shores. House of Refuge number five was built on what is now Miami Beach near 71st Street. For many years, it was the lone structure on the ocean beach.

In the 1880s, three New Jersey residents Henry B. Lum, Ezra Osborn and Elnathan T. Field bought all the available land along the coast from Jupiter to Key Biscayne to grow coconuts. They abandoned their efforts after rabbits and rats ate the young trees.

Communities On The Bay

Two Cleveland families—the Brickells and the Sturtevants—came to Miami in 1870. William and Mary Brickell opened an Indian trading post on the south side of the Miami River. They traded cloth, liquor and other goods for egret feathers and alligator hides. Joining the Brickells were Ephriam T. and Frances Sturtevant. Shortly after their arrival, however, the Sturtevants had a serious falling out with the Brickells and moved north to what is now Miami Shores where Gleason operated a post office named Biscayne. In the years to come, both of these families would have a significant impact on Miami's future.

Several miles south of the Miami River, a small settlement called Cocoanut Grove (the spelling was changed to Coconut in 1919) began attracting residents by the 1870s and 1880s. The first settlers came from the Bahamas and made their living as lighthouse keepers and fishermen. They were joined by an educated group of northerners and Europeans who were attracted to the wilderness. One of these was a New York boat designer named Ralph Middleton Munroe who had first visited the area in 1877. By 1891, he built the Barnacle, one of the area's oldest houses still in existence. Munroe brought others with him and helped talk Charles and Isabella Peacock, immigrants from England who had been residing in Fort Dallas, to open a small hotel there. The Peacock's Bay View House, that was later known as the Peacock Inn, became Miami's first tourist resort. The first tourists arrived in 1886.

A valuable sense of community developed in the Grove, seen in the creation of the Union Chapel in 1891 on land donated by Munroe, a place where whites and blacks, many from the Bahamas, worshipped together. By 1895, the Grove also had a school, library, woman's club and yacht club as well as an established business street. A nearby community of predominately black Bahamians called Kebo, grew up around what is now Charles Avenue. It too had churches, clubs and fraternal organizations.

On the Five miles south of the Grove was the Town of Cutler, near today's Cutler Road and 168th Street. William Fuzzard cut a wagon road through the

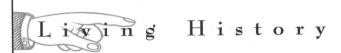

Living History

The Barnacle
3485 Main Highway
Coconut Grove

Ralph Munroe discovered South Florida in 1877. His first and lasting impression was that of a "sea-lover's eager appreciation of a sailor's paradise." Munroe returned in 1881 with his young bride, gravely ill with tuberculosis, in a futile attempt to restore her to health. Her grave, quietly lying on a spot beside the Coconut Grove Library, is the oldest marked grave in Miami.

But even this tragedy did not dim his enthusiasm for the bay. In 1884, he convinced the Charles Peacock family to build a hotel on the bayfront in what is now Peacock Park. He helped them in this venture and promptly became their number one guest, bringing many of his northern friends with him.

It is not surprising that the first thing Munroe did after he decided to move to the Grove was to build a boathouse. The second floor of the boathouse served as his first real home in South Florida and also became the first home of the Biscayne Bay Yacht Club which he co-founded in 1887 and served as commodore for the first 22 years of its existence. The 1926 Hurricane destroyed the original boathouse but Munroe rebuilt it almost exactly as it was.

In 1891, he built his home, the Barnacle, high on the ridge over-looking his beloved Biscayne Bay. Originally, the Barnacle was a one-story cottage built off the ground on oil-treated posts to prevent termite damage. Munroe's strong ideas of adapting his home to the environment were demonstrated in the wide piazza built on three sides of the house to provide both shade from the tropic sun and protection from the frequent showers.

In 1908, the Barnacle needed an addition. Munroe had remarried and had two children, Wirth and Patty. He decided the easiest solution was to raise the entire house on stilts and build a new first floor underneath. A few years later, he added a library wing.

Ralph Munroe spent a life-time trying to keep the beauty of the Grove and the bay as he found it. When he died in 1933, a major city had grown up around him. But at the Barnacle, he had successfully held the line. Hidden behind a dense tropical hammock, the Barnacle survived, just yards from busy Main Highway. It is no surprise that his daughter Patty Catlow and the his son's widow, Mary Munroe chose to sell the house to the State of Florida in 1973 rather than develop the property. Today, the Barnacle is a State Historic Site, open to the public.

dense tropical hammock to connect Cutler to Coconut Grove. Cutler too had a small hotel known as the Richmond Inn and a business street.

Another settlement called Lemon City developed on Biscayne Bay five miles north of the Miami River. It had three business streets by 1895, a real estate office and a bustling dock. Like Coconut Grove, Lemon City also had a school, church and other community institutions. It became the first community to be connected to the outside world when a road was cleared from Lantana to Lemon City in 1892 and a stagecoach began weekly operations.

Although South Florida remained isolated and almost forgotten, other cities in Florida, like Key West, Jacksonville and Tampa were developing rapidly. The most important factor in Florida's development was the railroad. Although Florida had only 550 miles of rails in 1881, by the end of the decade, more than 2,500 miles of railroad track had been laid. Rail magnate Henry B. Plant was the dominant railroad builder to

Tampa where he created the luxurious Tampa Bay Hotel that quickly became a popular gathering place for the rich.

Most of the East Coast development came from the investments and organizing efforts of Henry Flagler, partner of oil baron John D. Rockefeller in the Standard Oil Corporation. Flagler created the Florida East Coast Railroad in conjunction with a series of hotels that began in St. Augustine in 1888 and by 1894 had reached Palm Beach. Although the railroad was inching its way toward the Miami River, it was still outside the area of development. As the 1890s began, what today we call Greater Miami had a population of less than 100 people while the future City of Miami itself had less than 20.

∽ A Woman With Vision

This was soon to change. In 1891, Ephriam Sturtevant's daughter, Julia Tuttle, a Cleveland widow, purchased a 640 acre tract on the north bank of the Miami River and moved to the area with her two grown children. Tuttle had first come to visit her father on Biscayne Bay in 1875 when she was only 26 years old.

She, like her parents, believed that South Florida had great potential as the site of a major new city. This is not surprising considering the fact that her family had come to the Western Reserve of Ohio in the early 1800s and had watched Cleveland grow into a major city.

Tuttle was both a visionary and a land speculator. Beginning in 1892, she spent several years trying to convince fellow Clevelander, Henry Flagler, to bring his railroad to Miami, even offering him half her land as an inducement. Following the terrible freezes of 1894-95, that spared the Miami area, he finally took her up on her offer. (William and Mary Brickell sweetened the pot by adding large parcels of their land into the deal.) Within a year, Flagler's workmen were laying tracks between Palm Beach and Miami.

Once the railroad arrived, the modern world descended on the area with a rush. Few had any interest in the past or the generations of people, both native and immigrant, who had once lived here. The newcomers, like those who came before them and those who followed, were interested in the new life they came to build for themselves in their adopted land. As a result of their insensitivity, very little of South Florida's early history is visible today.

———※◇※———

In the Beginning

Robert S. Carr
The Early People

Robert Carr is the Dade County archaeologist. He became interested in archaeology as a child growing up in Miami. He received his Master's Degree from Florida State University and became Dade County's first archaeologist in 1978. He has written numerous books and articles on Dade County's unique archaeological history. Through Carr's efforts, much new information about Miami's past and its native people has been uncovered.

Prior to Miami's written history, before the arrival of the Seminoles and the pioneer settlers, the land teemed with life—a 100,000 year legacy of a land above the sea. At that time, vast grassy savannas existed where the Everglades stands today. Animals such as mammoth, bison, horse, camel, and sloth roamed freely, an integral part of the food chain that supported jaguar, dire wolf, and panther. In the sky were condor and cara-cara, feasting on the daily losers in a world of

serene beauty that was built on the survival of the strongest and healthiest.

Only man, deer, dogs, and other small mammals, reptiles, and birds emerged as the evolutionary victors after the great natural disaster 11,000 years ago that broke the diverse web of life. Over a period of centuries, some unknown force caused the glaciers and Arctic ice to melt—flooding the oceans with water and raising sea levels by 300 feet. Rainfall increased causing Florida's dry savannas to be flooded, killing grasses and trees. Animals died by the millions.

Evidence of this epic natural event is hidden beneath the dirt throughout North and South America. Miami's chapter of this global disaster was discovered by accident when John and Wanda Simmons climbed into a large solution hole in Cutler Ridge looking for wood to use for carving knife handles. The smooth small "twig" they picked up from the dirt seemed too hard and polished to be wood. When carefully examined, it was found to be the fossil tooth of an extinct horse.

In 1985, the Metro-Dade Historical Preservation Division directed an archaeological investigation of the solution hole that was conducted by the Ar-

Dade County archeologist Bob Carr examines pre-historic animal and human remains at a South Dade site. They provide vivid testament to the human activity on the shores of Biscayne Bay 10,000 years ago. (Bob Carr)

chaeological and Historical Conservancy. Within several days of excavation, the archaeological team began to uncover human teeth, artifacts and burnt rocks—all evidence that man had lived and died inside it.

Miami's earliest chapter of human adaptation emerged from these diggings. Radiocarbon dates of 10,620 + 120 years were secured from two samples of charcoal. A variety of artifacts made from bone and stone provide a dramatic glimpse into a culture that predates the Tequesta by at least 8,000 years. Some of the artifacts demonstrate trade or migrations from central Florida. Large limestone rocks stacked carefully beneath a ledge represent South Florida's earliest house. Pieces of marine shell and shark teeth indicate one of the earliest known examples of marine exploitation and fishing in North America.

The Cutler Fossil Site provides the first hands-on immersion into a distant past, unknown and forgotten—a flicker of the human flame that once smoldered deep within solution-hole caves with a promise of things to come. Archaeologists call these ancient people Paleo-Indians, or old Indians, simply because they predate any tribal name—either written or passed on by word of mouth to their ancestors.

Life and death pressed on here. At least five individuals were buried within the sediments, includ-

ing a single skull placed beneath a small mound of rocks and the bones of a baby laying deep within the wet mud. The child was a life lost too soon, and a handful of hickory nuts were strewn around the body providing food for her spirit.

Miami's boom and bustle were still a hundred centuries away. A thousand hurricanes would come and go. Biscayne Bay would emerge in 5,000 years. The rumble of the railroad, the iron mammoth, would someday conquer the Atlantic Coastal Ridge with bellowing sounds and its unnatural smoke, and with it came the new users of the land—those who thought they owned it, those who sold it and those who cleared it to stretch a quilt of roads and homes across this final American frontier.

The Cutler Fossil Site whispers above the noise and clutter of Miami's megalopolis to remind each of us that we are all connected to a distant past. There is a debt we owe to our human ancestors we best not forget, and that perhaps it is not we and our scientific brushes that uncover and reveal the past, but that the past uncovers us. We are self-discovered with each upturned stone and brown bone that mirrors each of us.

Source: Robert S. Carr, "The Cutler Fossil Site" (unpublished manuscript, Miami, Florida, 1996).

The Spanish Describe the Native People

Hernando d' Escalante Fontaneda
First Recorded History, c1575

Hernando d' Escalante Fontaneda was shipwrecked on Florida's shores when he was 13 years old. He spent the next 17 years living with the Indians until he was rescued by Pedro Menéndez de Avilés in 1566. His knowledge and associations helped Menéndez in his historic meeting with the South Florida Indians. Even though his memoirs were not written until 1575, his knowledge of the native people stands alone as the most complete and earliest eye-witness account of South Florida's native people.

Toward the north of the Martires and near a place of the Indians called Tequesta, situate[d] on the bank of a river which extends into the country the distance of fifteen leagues, and issues from another lake of fresh water, which is said by some Indians who have traversed it more than I to be an arm of the Lake of Mayaimi. . . . They have bread of roots [comptie], which is the common food the greater part of the time and because of the lake, which rises in some seasons so high that the roots cannot be reached in consequence of the water, they are for some time without eating this bread. Fish is plenty and very good. There is another root, like the truffle over here, which is sweet and there are other different roots of many kinds; but when there is hunting, either deer or birds, they prefer to eat meat of fowl. I will also mention that in the rivers of fresh water are infinite quantities of eels, very savory and enormous trout. The eels are nearly the size of a man, thick as the thigh and some of them are smaller. The Indians also eat lagartos [alligators], and snakes, and animals like rats, which live in the lake, fresh-water tortoises, and many more disgusting reptiles which, if we were to continue enumerating, we should never be through.

These Indians occupy a very rocky and a very marshy country. They have no product of mines or things that we have in this part of the world. The men go naked, and the women in a shawl made of a kind of palm-leaf, split and woven. They are subjects of Carlos and pay him tribute of . . . food and roots, the skins of deer, and other articles.

Source: Hernando d'Escalante Fontaneda, *Memoir of Hernando d'Escalante Fontaneda*, (c1575) trans. by Buckingham Smith, ed. by David O. True (Coral Gables: University of Miami Press, 1944) pp. 27-28.

Juan Lopez de Velasco
The Village of Tequesta, 1569

Juan Lopez de Velasco was a Spanish geographer who visited Florida in 1571. In the following excerpt, attributed to him, he writes about the native people and their culture. Hernando d'Escalante Fontaneda may have given these notes to him prior to his voyage.

The Indians of Tequesta . . . extending from the Martires to the Canaveral, have a custom when the Cacique [tribal chief] dies, his body is disjointed, and the larger bones from his body taken out. They are placed in a large box and carried to the house of the Cacique where every Indian from the town goes to see and adore them, believing them to be their Gods.

In winter all the Indians go out to sea in their canoes, to hunt for sea cows [Manatees]. One of their number carries three stakes fastened to his girdle, and a rope on his arm. When he discovers a sea cow he throws his rope around his neck, and as the animal sinks under the water, the Indian drives a stake through one of its nostrils, and no matter how much it may dive, the Indian never loses it, because he goes on its back. After it has been killed, they cut open its head and take out two large bones, which they place in the coffin with the bodies of their dead and worship them.

Source: "Notes and Annotations of the Cosmographer Lopez de Velasco, 1569," Abby Brooks Collection, Manuscript Division, Library of Congress, Washington D.C.

In 1564, artist Jacques Le Moyne came to Florida with the French who built Fort Caroline near today's Jacksonville. His drawings, though stylized, provide the earliest known likeness of Florida's native people.

The Missions at Tequesta

Brother Francisco Villareal
A Mission in the Wilderness, 1568

In March 1567, Pedro Menéndez de Avilés sent a Jesuit priest to establish a mission on the north bank of the Miami River in an effort to Christianize the people they called Tequesta Indians. The following letter was written by Brother Villareal to his superior telling him of the difficulties of life on the Miami River.

I and the others have constantly remained healthy, glory be to God, which helps us endure with little difficulty some of the burdens of the land that otherwise would seem insufferable. I am referring to the three or more months of mosquitoes we have endured, in which I passed some nights and days without being able to sleep for an hour; and in addition to that we also had some days when we were without food. And because you have heard a great deal about this over there, I shall not expand on it except to say that our sleep during all that time was around the fire and immersed in clouds of smoke, as one could not survive in any other way. . . .

I teach the doctrina to the children in the house of the chief, where there are many adults present, who, I believe also learn it, even though they do not recite it as do the children; the chief told me that he is grasping it. . . .

In reference to your reverence's instructions that I should try to make the Indians love me, I have tried to some degree; and to that end, I brought a little corn.

Source: Letter of Brother Francisco de Villareal to Father Rogel, January 23, 1568, quoted in Felix Zubillaga, *Monumenta Antiquae Floridae* (Rome: Monumenta Historixca Societatis Iesu, 1946), trans. by John Hann, pp. 235-40.

Father Juan Rogel
Soldiers Doom Mission, 1568

Two months after Brother Villareal wrote his letter from Tequesta, the mission was abandoned after fighting broke out between the Indians and the Spanish soldiers. Father Juan Rogel expressed his disappointment in the actions of the Spanish soldiers that had ruined any prospects for a successful mission and settlement.

For it is thus that wherever we Spanish are, [we are] so proud and unrestrained that we try to trample everything underfoot, and thus the soldiers of that fort began to treat the natives in the same way [they would have] if they had conquered them by war, subjecting them to grievous insults and mistreatments; because of which, when the Indians could endure it no longer, they first warned them that they should leave, [saying] that this was not a good land for settling; and when they were not able to settle it by warnings, they decided to kill those whom they could, among the Spaniards and set fire to their own houses and village and so they did.

Source: Letter of Father Juan Rogel to Father Francisco Borgia, July 25, 1568, quoted in Felix Zubillaga, *Monumenta Antiquae Floridae* (Rome: Monumenta Historica Societatis Iesu, 1946), trans. by John Hann, p. 321.

Father Joseph Maria Monaco and
Joseph Xavier Alaña
The Pueblo de Santa Maria de Loreto, 1743

In 1711, more than 2,000 South Florida Indians, threatened by the southern migration of the Seminoles, asked for asylum in Cuba. All but 70 died of diseases in Cuba for which they had no immunity and the rest returned to Florida. Another boatlift in 1734 also failed and the Cubans decided to help them in Florida rather than bring them to Havana. Thus in 1743, the Spanish once again returned to the Miami River and built a mission/settlement they called Santa Maria de Loreto. The Indians were hostile and the Spanish quickly gave up the effort and destroyed the village. In the following document, the two priests in charge of the mission characterize the cultural differences between the Spanish and the Indians.

At the mouth of the said River we found a village [of] these [Indians] without huts in which there lived clustered together up to one hundred and eighty people between men, women, and children, who made up about one-half of this number. . . .

The reception which they gave us was very cold, and, finally, after having taken all the foodstuffs destined for them, with intolerables they openly declared their displeasure over our coming, to the point of denying repeatedly that in Havana they had begged for priests to make them Christians. . . . But, in their mouth this matter of becoming Christian has no other meaning except receiving the Sacramental Water with these conditions; that without their working, the King our Lord will be obligated to support them and clothe them . . . despite the fact that both the men and the women walk about naked except for [covering] what is most necessary; and he is to furnish them with rum, alleging the precedent of Florida; they are to be allowed to maintain the superstitions that they are full of; and, lastly, punishment is not to be used in the teaching of the children, and the latter was the first condition which the chief proposed to us in the name of all. It is a cause for amazement; for the affection that they have for their sons reaches the extremity of suffering blows from them and burning and cutting themselves voluntarily in order to demonstrate their sorrow over the same thing having happened by accident to the son, without ever receiving any sign of reverence from the latter. Their bold proposal of these conditions derives from their being convinced that in allowing our religion to enter in any fashion, they are doing us so great a favor that they went so far as to say to us, that, if we wished to build a Church in their village, we would have to pay a tax to the Indians, and that, if Spaniards were to come here to settle, they would have to pay tribute to the chief for the lands, which belong to him, not to the King of Spain. . . .

The errors, idolatries, and superstitions of these people are among the most brutal, but what is surprising is the very tenacious attachment with which they maintain all this and the ridicule they direct toward beliefs contrary to theirs and the arguments [they are based on]. Let us look at the idols. The principal one is a small board with the image of a fish and other figures like tongues. They have [now] hidden this, because one day one of us stepped on it experimentally, in an effort to remove their fear of the calamities which they expected would follow the least contempt toward it, and, we have slight hope of taking it from them without violence. The other idol, which is the God of Cemetery, the theater of their most frequent superstitions was a crudity of a bird carved . . . which in the matter of hideousness did justice to the original, and which we burned, after breaking it into pieces along with the hut which they had for a church, when it seemed to us that it could be done without a riot on the part of the Indians, as we had an armed galley hovering over them, which was there in passing, coming from Florida; so it did succeed, though not without many signs of grief, and even moans and tears from the women. . . .

These tiny little tribes fight constantly and they are shrinking, as is testified to by the remembrance of the greater number there was twenty years ago, so that if they are left to their barbarous ways, they will have disappeared in a few years, whether on account of the Skirmishes, or on account of the Rum that they will drink until they burst, or on account of the children that they kill, or on account of those whom the small pox carries off for the lack of a remedy, and, finally, whether on account of those who perish at the hands of the Uchises, [Seminoles] in which case [not legible] from the advantages these few Indians bring to our Nation, not only because of the aversion they maintain toward the English, but also because of the devotion toward ours, even though it is only based on interest.

Source: Letter and Enclosures, Governor of Cuba to the King, September 28, 1743, trans. by John Hann, Archivo General de Indias-Seville 58—2—10/15, (Gainesville: P. K. Younge Library of Florida History, University of Florida).

The British Take Over

William Gerard De Brahm
The Cape Florida Society, 1773

When the Seven Years War ended in 1763 (Americans called it the French and Indian War), the Treaty of Paris gave Florida to Great Britain ending 250 years of Spanish rule. The first order of business for the British was to survey the land and then entice settlers to the area. In 1764, Governor James Grant of East Florida appointed William Gerard De Brahm surveyor general to carefully survey and map the entire east coast of Florida.

The following document is a portion of DeBrahm's report to Lord Dartmouth who planned a 6,000 acre settlement on his 40,000 acre grant in what is today South Dade County. It was meant to serve as a guide to the area. To the best of our knowledge, the area was never settled during this brief British Period.

You will perhaps meet at your arrival with persons on the spot or in other parts, if you should tuch any, who will endeavour to prepossess your minds with many prejudices in reguard to climate, soil, insects, wild beasts, tempests, Indians, french and Spanish wars believe me, that the persons you will meet with in any part of America never have ben on the spot, or if they have ben, they never took proper pains nor inclined to inquire minutely so as to form a fair Judgement of the place; . . . as to wild beasts (:Bears, panters, Basilisks and crocodills which are the only offensive one:) they are never known to have hurt a person, unless when they being attaqued, was obliged to defend them selves, they all will flye at the Sight of a human species, except Basilisks (:rattlesnakes:) they cannot flye, but when a person comes near them, they will give warning with ratteling their tales, which is equal to the noise of the mounting of a watch, at which noise one may Stand of. crocodilles in deed will attaque a person but not otherwise than in the water. as to tempests you will certainly see more of them in that place, than in any other you have ben, as you will be situated open to the Gulf of Sandwich [Biscayne Bay] within and the Florida Stream without the Sound of Darmouth, in which stream the winds between North and East have great powers and cause turbulations of disagreable effects but only to those on the stream in Vessels, and not to you on Shore in your houses, whereby your minds at first will be affected, until you became acquainted and familiar to it, when your aprehensions will be much less to what they can be in hurranganes on Shore. as to Indians, you will find them in your first setting out rather friendly and usefull, if any in their way of hunting (:being unlimitted:) Should come near you, they will endeavour to gain your accquaintance and friendship by Supplying you with Venison, of which they will make practice, provided you present them with a little Corn, Rice or salt (:by no means let them know you have stronger liquor than water:). . . . the Indians will not brake out into War, nor be jealous about your settlement, nor even complain of it out of a political pretence, provided the Governor is required to send invitations to the head men of the Seminolskees (:Indians, which live in small Tribes and have built Towns to the West and South of St. Augustin:) these headmen may easily be informed and satisfied, that His Majesty has thought it necessary a Settlement Should be made at Cape Florida by His Subjects to give assistance and relieve to so many distressed, which yearly Suffer Shipwrack on or near that place. a present of few coats, some Weastcoats, Blankets, Shirts, guns, powder and Balls to the value of 50 pound Sterling distributed among the headmen (:which are about six or seven:) will make the Settlement at Cape Florida an object, if not agreeable, at least indifferent to these Barbarians.

Source: William Gerard De Brahm, "Information and Recommendations to the Cape Florida Society," with cover letter to Lord Dartmouth, May 4, 1773, quoted in Roland E. Chardon, "The Cape Florida Society," *Tequesta* XXXV (1975), pp. 31-36.

South Florida Attracts All Kinds

The Good Samaritan of the Cape Florida Settlement, 1817

Following the American Revolution, the Treaty of Paris gave Florida back to the Spanish. During this Second Spanish Period (1783-1821), a small group of Bahamians settled on the Miami River and along the bluffs of Biscayne Bay. They called themselves the Cape Florida Settlement. They traveled to Nassau for special occasions like christenings and weddings. Often, notices of these events appeared in the Bahamian newspaper. They published the following under "Ship News" in The Nassau Royal Gazette. *This document demonstrates that from the beginning, South Florida's geography influenced its diversity.*

Having observed in the course of long experience that several masters of vessels, who had the misfortune to be cast away on the Martyrs [Keys] and the Coasts of Florida, ignorant of the existence [sic] of any settlement at Cape Florida, have attempted to proceed to the Northward in their boats, deprived of every sustenance, we feel it incumbent upon me to inform such as may hereafter experience a like misfortune, that if they pass to the North side of Key Biscayne, they will find the entrance of Boca Ratones [Indian Creek], through which they can safely go with their boats and they will see the Houses in front on the mainland.

In case of Shipwreck to the northward of Boca Ratones, at the distance of two miles there from, they will perceive mangroves thinly scattered, from where the houses may be seen; and in this situation on making a signal with fire or otherwise, they will obtain assistance.

If it should happen to the Southward of New River they may proceed southwardly along the Beach where they will meet every four miles, posts fixed in the ground, on which is an inscription in English, French and Spanish indicating where Wells of fresh water have been purposely dug.

Source: "Inhabitants of Cape Florida Addressed to Mariners Passing Through the Gulf of Florida," *Nassau Royal Gazette*, January 11, 1817.

Conflict on the New Frontier

John Thompson
The Burning of Cape Florida Lighthouse, 1836

John Thompson was the Keeper of the Cape Florida Lighthouse when the Indians attacked in July 1836. His black assistant Aaron Carter was killed but Thompson miraculously escaped death and was rescued by the Navy from his perch on the top of the tower. With the stairs burned out, the sailors fired a ramrod with a line attached. This permitted a heavy line and two sailors to be hoisted to the top by means of a pully to help him on his descent via the line. After this experience, he became a sort of celebrity and frequently lectured on the subject.

On the 23d of July last, about 4:00 P.M., as I was going from the kitchen to the dwelling house, I discovered a large body of Indians within twenty yards of me, back of the kitchen. I ran for the lighthouse, and called out to the old negro man that was with me to run, for the Indians were near; at that moment they discharged a volley of rifle balls which cut my clothes and hat, and perforated the door in many places. We got in and as I was turning the key the savages had hold of the door. I stationed the negro at the door, with orders to let me know if they attempted to break in; I then took me three muskets, which were loaded with ball and buckshot, and went to the second window. Seeing a large body of them opposite the dwelling house, I discharged my muskets in succession among them, which put them in some confusion; they then for the second time, began their horrid yells and in a minute no sash or glass was left at the window, for they vented their rage at that spot. I fired at them from some of the other windows and from the top of the house; in fact, I fired whenever I could get an Indian for a mark. I kept them from the house until dark.

They then poured in a heavy fire at all the windows and lantern; that was the time they set fire to the door and window even with the ground. The window was boarded up with plank and filled up with stone inside; but the flames spread fast; being fed with yellow pine wood. Their balls had perforated the tin tanks of oil, consisting of two hundred and twenty-five gallons. My bedding, clothing, and in fact everything I had, was soaked in oil. I stopped at the door until driven away by the flames. I then took a keg of gunpowder, my balls and one musket to the top of the house, then went below, and began to cut away the stairs about half-way up from the bottom. I had difficulty in getting the old negro up the space I had already cut; but the flames now drove me from my labor, and I retreated to the top of the house. I covered over the scuttle that leads to the lantern which kept the fire from me for some time; at last the awful moment arrived, the crackling of flames burnt around me, the savages at the same time began their hellish yells. My poor old negro looked at me with tears in his eyes, but he could not speak. We went out of the lantern and lay down on the edge of the platform, two feet wide; the lantern now was full of flames, and lamps and glasses bursting and flying in all directions, my clothing on fire, and to move from the place where I was would be instant death from their rifles. My flesh was roasting, and to put an end to my horrible suffering, I got up, threw the keg of gunpowder down the scuttle—instantly it exploded, and shook the tower from top to the bottom. It had not the desired effect of blowing me into eternity, but it threw down the stairs and all the wooden work near the top of the house; it damped the fire for a moment, but it soon blazed as fierce as ever; the negro man said he was wounded, which was the last word he spoke.

By this time I had received some wounds myself; and finding no chance for my life, for I was roasting alive, I took the determination to jump off. I got up, went outside the iron railing, recommending my soul to God, and was on the point of going head foremost on the rocks below, when something dictated to me to return and lie down again. I did so, and in two minutes the fire fell to the bottom of the house. It is a remarkable circumstance that not one ball struck me when I stood up outside the railing, although they were flying all around me like hailstones. I found the old Negro man dead, being shot in several places, and literally roasted. A few minutes after the fire fell a stiff breeze sprung up from the southward, which was a great blessing to me. I had to lie where I was, for I could not walk, having received six rifle balls, three in each foot. The Indians, thinking me dead, left the lighthouse and set fire to the dwelling house, kitchen and other outhouses, and began to carry off their plunder to the beach. . . .

Source: "Light Keeper's Own Account of Attack by Indians on Florida Light in 1836," *Miami Metropolis*, June 23, 1916.

Henry E. Perrine
Escape from Indian Key, 1840

Henry E. Perrine was the son of Dr. Henry Perrine who, in 1838, was granted a full township of land in South Dade, providing he put a settler on each of the 36 sections and introduce tropical plants. The Seminole War kept him from completing his project and he was killed by the Indians on Indian Key in 1840. The following account, written by Henry E. Perrine in 1885, describes the harrowing attack and his miraculous escape with his mother and sisters. In 1876, young Perrine came back to South Florida in an effort to settle what he called Perrineville. Within a year, he gave up on the South Florida wilderness and returned to New York.

In relating this story of our escape, I shall give you my own personal recollections as to nearly every incident connected with it, for although I was only a few months over thirteen years of age, you can well imagine that the impressions made upon my mind could not easily be effaced. . . .

About two o'clock on the morning of August 7th, 1840, my parents and sisters were awakened by the sound of rifles and muskets, the fall of glass from the broken windows, and the yells of savages. They hastened to the head of stairs, but as they were about to descend discovered that I was not with them. I was lying peacefully asleep on a mattress on the floor, in the southeast corner of the hall, unconscious of danger. My sister Hester came back and wakened me, saying in a whisper "come, don't make any noise!" As I heard the continuous yelling of the Indians, which sounded alarmingly near, without fully comprehending the cause, I said "what is it? what is it?" She replied "the Indians! come, and be very quiet." As the Indians seemed to be engaged in attacking the houses

some distance away, father said he would go upstairs and see what he could do; doubtless intending to get his Colt's rifle, which was good for sixteen shots, and also some of the old style Allen's "pepper-box" six barreled pistols, and prepare for defense. . . . We all sat down on the floor in our night-clothes, and I laid my head in mother's lap. I can remember the thoughts which passed through my mind; I had read Indian stories many times, and I said to myself "can it be that I am really being one of the actors in such a story?" and "must it be that pretty soon I will be killed?" Then I thought of my dearly loved grandmother far away at the North, and I said to mother, "we will never see grandma again," for I could see no sure way of escape.

Very soon after this we heard the Indians pounding and battering the doors of buildings near us, and as it was evident that our house must soon be attacked, we raised the trap-door to descend into the water beneath, I leading the way in the darkness. My sister Sarah had been confined to her bed for two weeks previous to that time, only having sat up long enough to have her bed made the day before. As she put her foot into the water she involuntarily shrank back, thus leaving a mark upon the step, which might have caused our discovery had not father, shortly after our descent, come down into the bathroom, and after closing the trap-door drew a chest of seeds over; thus completely hiding our place of retreat; saving our lives by the sacrifice of his own. . . .

We cautiously found our way through the water around the wall, and feeling along the outer wall, came to the passage-way leading to the turtle crawl. I was rejoiced to find that the extreme high tide, called the spring tide, had not yet appeared, as that would have effectually cut off all hope for us by filling the passage-way completely to the top. As it was there was a space left of about a foot between the surface of the water and the planks above so that when we crouched down and made our way to the farther end, we sat down on the marly bottom with the water reaching our necks.

For some little time after our entrance the chilliness of the air and water was such as to make my teeth chatter like one with the ague, and we feared that I might be heard; but after a while the chill passed off. I cannot tell now how soon or how long it was before we heard the Indians come leaping upon the wharf and upon the space directly over our heads. . . .

We could hear them in the pantry dashing the crockery to pieces upon the floor; accompanying each act of wanton destruction with similar demonstrations of joy. A voice was heard saying in English, "they are all hid; the old man upstairs." In a few minutes after this we heard a prolonged sound as of the battering against a heavy door, apparently in the upper part of the house; and then, as that ceased, there was a loud chorus of yells which doubtless proclaimed to our listening and affrighted ears the death of my father. . . . For a long time after this we could hear the savages dragging the plunder obtained from the house over our heads, and loading it into boats alongside the wharf. At one time, about day-break, the turtles in the "crawl" under the wharf splashed the water with their flippers,

and one of the Indians raised a plank and looked down to ascertain the cause. Providentially he was satisfied with the short inspection and did not look towards the end, where in breathless suspense behind the piles we sat concealed, for our night-clothes showing white beyond might have betrayed us. Oh! how slowly and wearily passed the hours as we longed and prayed for day; for we thought that surely they would leave before sunrise.

Source: Henry Perrine, *A True Story of Some Eventful Years in Grandpa's Life* (Buffalo, New York: E. H. Hutchinson, 1885), pp. 52-57.

The Village of Miami

Master Edward C. Anderson, USN
Miami, 1844

Edward Clifford Anderson, scion of an old and distinguished Savannah, Georgia family, served on the U.S.S. General Taylor. The Taylor, a coastal steamer, surveyed the waters of the Florida Territory for ten months in 1844. The following is excerpted from Anderson's diary, as he arrived at the Miami River for an overnight stop.

A senator of Florida, Mr. Wm. F. English is the chief cook & bottle washer of the establishment, he is lame of a leg and intends flooding the United States & Key West with Coonti & sugar or whatever else his productive plantation that is to be will produce. Mr. E. is a Colonel of course, as are all the natives of this region. The settlers are "armed occupants," so called, receiving from Government a certain quantity of land as a grant. They are very sanguine of establishing eventually a flourishing settlement & have laid out a town & city yet to be built. I have no idea however that the Miami will ever be much more than it is for there are but few facilities and no capital either at present or in prospect. The soil along the bank of the river is a strata of limestone which merges itself at a little distance back into pine barren land. I have never in all my travels met with such an immense number of horseflies & other insects as are to be found here.

Source: W. Stanley Hoole, ed., *The Florida Territory in 1844: The Diary of Master Edward C. Anderson* (Alabama: University of Alabama Press, 1977), pp. 36-37.

Rose Wagner Richards
Miami's First Industry, 1858

Rose Wagner Richards came to Miami in February 1858 from Charleston, South Carolina. Her father William had run a store for the military at Fort Dallas during the Third Seminole War. Her reminiscences, published in The Miami News in 1903, give an extraordinary eyewitness account of frontier living. The excerpt below describes Miami's first industry—the manufacture of comptie starch. The Ferguson factory was on the Miami River near today's 12th Avenue. (Ferguson had an earlier factory up the river at the Falls, just west of today's 27th Avenue that was abandoned during the war.) The comptie starch industry remained in Miami until the 1920s when most of the wild comptie was exhausted and civilization moved in on the pineland where the comptie once flourished.

The writer will now describe the industries in which the people then living here were interested; (1858) and which, in fact, for many years after, was the principal means by which they lived. Starch made from the roots of a plant growing wild on the pine land, and very plentifully, called Comptie, Coontie, or West Indian Arrow-Root. Starch-making from the roots of this plant gave employment to all who were not otherwise employed.

The two principal factories were those of Captain Sinclair and Mr. George Ferguson. Mr. Ferguson's factory or mill, was situated on the south side of the Miami river about two miles up, and where now stand a number of large cocoanut trees to mark the place.

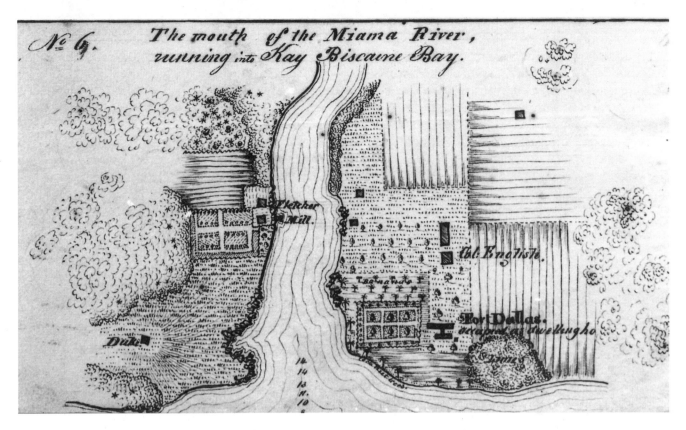

This 1849 U.S. Coast Survey map shows the beginning of Col. William English's "Village of Miami." It included the original 1838 Fort Dallas buildings as well as English's home and slave quarters. (National Archives)

He also had a pair of burrs for grinding corn into meal for himself or any one else having any to grind. He also kept a store in which was kept the Post-Office already referred to, and once a month the mail boat from Key West would bring what news there was from the outside world—never much, but eagerly looked for.

He having the whole territory south of the river to gather the roots from, and having the help to dry them and the conveniences for working them into starch, enabled him to make large shipments to such places where a market was to be had.

The other factory, the one owned by Captain Sinclair, was built on what is now known as Wagner's Creek, and was worked by steam. With sufficient help and also a large territory to gather from, being anywhere from the Miami River to Little River, and from the bay, back to the Everglades, an immense amount of starch was made here also. There was at this time a schooner named *Joshua Skinner*, owned by Mr. Frederick Filer, of Key West, which was bringing the mail and also freight and passengers to this place. Captain Samuel Filer, now of Buena Vista was her Captain, and

Mr. Henry Filer, now of Lemon City, was also one of the crew.

The schooner would leave Key West on the eighth day of each month, and leave Miami on the twenty-fifth of every month, this giving the boat a great deal of time in other pursuits, such as going to wrecks, which occurred occasionally on the reefs.

Source: Mrs. Adam Richards, "Reminiscences of the Early Days of Miami," *Miami News*, 1903. (See Agnew Welsh Notebook XXXVI, Miami-Dade Public Library.)

John Wood
Miami, 1865

One month after the end of the Civil War, John Wood and Confederate General John Breckenridge came ashore at Fort Dallas to seek assistance in their escape to Cuba. Miami's isolated location made it a known hide-out for a variety of unsavory characters. Prior to Breckenridge's arrival, federal troops had already been in Miami looking for Confederate President Jefferson Davis. The following is excerpted from a book by Wood on Civil War escapes.

The old barracks [Fort Dallas] were in sight as we slowly worked our way against the current. Located in a small clearing, with cocoanut-trees in the foreground, the white buildings made, with a backing of deep green, a very pretty picture. We approached cautiously, not knowing with what reception we should meet. As we neared the small wharf, we found waiting some twenty or thirty men, "of all colors, from the pale Yankee to the ebony Congo, all armed: a more motley and villainous-looking crew never trod the deck of one of Captain Kidd's ships. We saw at once with whom we had to deal—deserters from the army and navy of both sides, a mixture of Spaniards and Cubans, outlaws and renegades."

Source: John Taylor Wood, "The Escape of General Breckenridge," *Famous Adventures and Prison Escapes of Civil War* (New York. Century, 1893), pp. 52-57.

J. W. Ewan
Christmas with the Seminoles, 1874

J.W. Ewan came to Miami from South Carolina in 1874 to manage the property owned by the Biscayne Bay Company on the north bank of the Miami River. He operated an Indian trading post at Fort Dallas and served in the Florida Legislature. He also homesteaded in Coconut Grove. Many newcomers lived temporarily at his house, on land that later became the property of naturalist David Fairchild. While serving as postmaster, he changed the spelling of Miami to "Maama." He was fondly known as "The Duke of Dade." Here he recalls the native people of the 1870s.

I had met a few of the Indians from time to time during the fall and winter of 1874, but on Christmas Eve quite an assembly of them had met at Brickell's Point, with a view of celebrating the "White Man's Christmas". . . .

It was about 7 p.m., when a party of us crossed the river from Fort Dallas and landed about half way between Brickell's Point and what was then known as the Barnes' place. We saw about thirty Indians, of all sizes, from babes at the breast to "Old Halleck," about 90 years of age. We were formally introduced to the grown men, among them Key West Billy, Billy Sunshine, Miami Doctor, Miami Jimmie, Cypress Tommie, Johnnie Jumper, Big Mouth Tiger, Young Tiger Tail, etc.

The men were grouped around their sof-kee kettle, eating supper. The women stood by to serve them and replenish their lightwood fires . . . Sof-kee is a combination of coontie starch and green corn, making a course gruel. A large brass kettle stood in the center of each group and one large spoon was used to dip with, a wooden spoon made of cypress, with a very long handle. This single spoon was shared by all. They were also eating young alligator tails, terrapin and garfish barbecued to which were added sweet potatoes and bananas. Coffee was also served and occasionally a cork was drawn from a quart bottle and whiskey offered. . . .

We were offered eatables and partook of terrapin cooked in the shell, venison, sweet potatoes and bananas. After the men had finished eating the squaws and pickaninnies, as they called their children, feasted the men grouping themselves and talking over their adventures. . . . As the glow increased, dancing commenced . . . Miami Doctor, to whom I was talking, had gathered me to his bosom—he is over 6 feet tall; my feet were off the ground and I was wriggling in space. The men were all dancing and singing, the chant was their music. When the Doctor got out of breath, I was "landed"; he gave me a withering glance and said: "White man dance good; Indian all the same; ungah.". . .

The night was growing old, clouds had risen, and at 12 o'clock quite a heavy shower came on. The squaws and younger Indians had cut brush and palmetto leaves, and made quite a substantial shelter. So all the elderly people present, red and white, were sheltered. The Seminoles are a thoughtful and kind people to their aged and young, manifesting the greatest love and affection for them. . . .

The show over, a final dance was held, interspersed with the Seminole rallying call and war whoop. As the day star rose, we shook hands all around; they asked us to come to their Christmas, or "Green Corn Dance," and we parted that Christmas morn, having been hospitably entertained by the Seminoles.

Source: J. W. Ewan, "The Seminole's Christmas," *Miami Metropolis*, March 15, 1901, p. 6.

Living History

Charles Avenue, formerly called "Evangelist Street," was the site of Kebo, the first black settlement on the South Florida mainland. In the early days, its residents came almost exclusively from the Bahamas. Most of the early families were related and came from the island of Eleuthera via Key West. It was these black settlers who planted many of the Grove's tropical trees and plants and taught the Easterners how to live in the sub-tropical wilderness.

Charles Avenue's first resident was Mariah Brown who came to work at the Peacock Inn in 1884. Her home is still standing at 3298 Charles Avenue. The area's most important developer was Ebenezer Woodberry Franklin Stirrup, who built over 100 homes in the area. Stirrup believed that each man should have his own home, so he sold or rented his homes for very little money. His home, located at 3243 Charles Avenue, was built with Florida pine in 1897 and survives as a historic landmark today.

Kebo also had thriving religious and civic organizations. St Agnes Baptist Church, now

The Charles Avenue cemetery. (John Gillan)

Macedonia Baptist Church was the first black church on the South Florida mainland as well as the first Baptist church in the area. Several denominations built a common cemetery. The Methodist Church housed the first school and the Odd Fellows Hall housed a library and literary society. Many prominent Miamians trace their roots to these first families of Coconut Grove.

Almost all of the early settlers of Kebo were from the Bahamas. (Ralph Munroe)

Making Miami Home

George W. Parsons
Frontier Tragedy, 1874

George W. Parsons, the son of a doctor, came to South Florida from New York City in November, 1873 when he was 24 years old. He lived here for about a year and a half and left a remarkable diary of his adventure. At first he planned on making South Florida his permanent home but difficult living conditions forced him to change his mind. His description of the death of William and Mary Brickell's 11 year old daughter Emma is especially poignant.

Friday April 3rd, 1874

Mr. Brickell's child died this PM & while he was away too at Key West. Hers was a strange disease. She was in the habit of bathing frequently & walking to the house in her wet clothes & this practice was probably the cause of her death. She was seized with a nervous twitching about the eyes & face & then her joints would stiffen & she seemed to suffer a great deal, saying she wanted to die. She seemed an especial favorite of her fathers & to the last called for him. A boat was dispatched for Dr. Potter but was not very far on its journey when the death occurred. Col W & I went over in the evening for his mother & I offered my services which were accepted. No one seemed to know what to do & I was ignorant too but did what I thought to be right & had the satisfaction to hear afterwards from the Dr. that I did all that could have been done. First took the body with Wagner's help from the death room which was very warm into the parlor, placed it on several boards, opened all the windows to have plenty of air, kept all lights out of the room & @ intervals through the night bathed the face with spirits always leaving a cloth wet with some on the face. Mrs. Whitner made a shroud for the little form & that work occupied a considerable portion of the night. I [of] course did not get any sleep, not even a wink. . . .

Saturday April 4th, 1874

The doctor was needed although the child was dead for another was coming to life, a remarkable coincidence & already Mrs. B. was confined. It was premature brought on by trouble & excitement although not far from the natural time & both mother & child were doing well upon Mr. B.'s arrival. He would not bury tonight although I urged it as much as I thought proper.

Source: George W. Parsons, "Diary 1873-1875" (unpublished manuscript, Library of Florida History, University of Florida).

Frances Leonard Sturtevant
"Life in Dade County," 1876

Frances Leonard Sturtevant was the mother of Julia Tuttle. She came to South Florida from Cleveland with her husband Ephriam in 1870 and settled in what they called Biscayne that later became Miami Shores. Before her marriage, she taught Indians in Tallahassee. Julia Tuttle often visited her parents before moving here herself in 1891. The following document comes from The Semi-Tropical Magazine *that promoted Florida and encouraged immigration from other parts of the United States.*

Our people tend to gravitate independently, which is not surprising. One would need to be endowed with the gift of tongues, as of old, to address each in his vernacular, yet most understand enough of English to express themselves intelligibly. A few of the descendants of the fearless class who remained through the Indian troubles, under the armed occupation arrangement, are still here. Refugees, from some of the more northern of the Southern States. Yankees constitute a very small minority. Russia, Sweden, Norway, Denmark, England, Scotland, Ireland, Germany, Prussia, Spain, Italy and France, with the Islands adjacent to each are all laid under contribution. The Bahamas, St. Domingo, Cuba, China and Mexico help to make up the medley. Most acquire sufficient mechanical skill to build and repair their boats and construct their own dwellings. When inclined to seek a new location the majority of them can readily transfer their worldly possessions to the boat and have ample room for the family during the transit. . . .

Our male, is largely in excess of our female population. . . . Our isolation, the sparseness of our population, with our mild climate, constitute the charm in this mode of life; as civilization advances it will become a thing of the past.

Source: Mrs. E. T. Sturtevant, "Life in Dade County," The Semi-Tropical II (April, 1876), p. 204.

Ralph Middleton Munroe
The "Simple and Genuine Life," 1877

Ralph Munroe was a young single man looking for adventure when he came to South Florida in 1877. He returned in 1881 with his young, ill wife, who died and was buried here. After that tragedy, he returned each winter until he made Coconut Grove his permanent home in 1886. In the 1930s, he wrote The Commodore's

Seminoles frequently came to Coconut Grove to trade. Coconut Grove's front door was the dock at Charles and Isabella Peacock's Bay View House, later the Peacock Inn. It stood in what is today's Peacock Park. (Ralph Munroe)

Story that recalled his remarkable life on the bay. His influence on Coconut Grove can still be seen at his home, The Barnacle, now a State of Florida Historic Site. The following document comes from his book.

My favorable impression of Biscayne Bay was both deep and lasting. Undoubtedly the first element in this was the incomparable climate. Along with this, and in some measure a part of it, was the sea-lover's eager appreciation of this sailor's paradise, in which calms, storms, fogs, ice, and many other marine hazards were either unknown or rare. There was also a keen fascination in the varied humanity drawn to the wilderness. Both virtues and frailties are attracted by

the chances of pioneer adventure, and the handful of Biscayne settlers in 1877 included a wider variety of character and history than many a Northern town. Their isolation and mutual dependence brought out their peculiarities in high relief, while at the same time it touched them with a warmth of friendship and service unknown in large communities. This close touch with those of simple and genuine life . . . helped to establish Biscayne Bay permanently in my affections.

Source: Ralph Middleton Munroe and Vincent Gilpin, *The Commodore's Story* (New York: Ives Washburn Publisher, 1930), pp. 103-4.

Kirk Munroe
"The Forgotten Remnant," 1889

At the 1893 Chicago World's Fair, 10,000 American children voted Kirk Munroe the most popular author of children's books in America. He wrote 36 books and hundreds of magazine articles, many with South Florida themes. He and his wife Mary Barr moved to Coconut Grove in 1886 and he lived there until his death in 1930. Both of the Munroes left their imprint on Coconut Grove. The Munroes' sympathy for the Seminole Indians was deep and enduring and they were two of the few white people that the Indians trusted.

Their ever-present fear is that an attempt will be made to remove them to the Indian Territory; and so strong is their attachment to their warm, sunny, Everglades homes, that they declare they will fight rather than submit to expatriation. This fear renders them shy of all white men, and especially of those whom they suspect of being in any way connected with Government. The land-grabbers and cowboys of south Florida are making constant efforts to promote a cause for such removal or extermination, and probably, in course of time, they will be successful. These efforts often take the form of insults or open aggression; but are generally confined to the concocting of tales of threatened Seminole outbreaks or outrages, that always find a ready circulation through the newspaper press of both South and North.

The Indians themselves are rapidly killing off the deer and alligators from their hunting grounds, while the plume birds are disappearing like morning dew before the white bird-butchers, who, in the employ of Northern millinery houses, infest the coasts of south Florida, and ruthlessly destroy old birds and young, eggs and nests, wherever they find them. White settlers are crowding the Seminoles away from their old-time haunts; their choicest lands are being seized upon by speculators. Their future offers no brighter prospect than that of many another tribe long since blotted from existence, and, unless some attention is given to their condition, another chapter of our Indian history will be sealed with injustice and murder. Some of the Indian fields, upon which they are most dependent for their food supplies, have already been homesteaded by white land-grabbers, who, when asked to show proofs of occupation and improvement, point to the work of the Indians and claim it as their own. . . .

Today these Florida Seminoles are peaceful, industrious, and self-supporting. Civilization has already gained a hold upon them, and each successive year finds them living more and more as white men live. If they could only be assured the inalienable rights guaranteed by our Constitution—the possession of life and property, and the pursuit of happiness—they would soon work out their own salvation, and prove themselves as worthy members of society. . . . The mere recognition by the Government of these Indians as human beings possessed of human rights, as well as of human failings, would be the taking of one step toward the creation of a century of honor that should, in some measure, efface the memory of the "Century of Dishonor" just closed.

Source: Kirk Munroe, "A Forgotten Remnant," *Scribner's* VII (March, 1890), pp. 315-317.

Emma Gilpin
A Visit to Miami, 1890

In March 1890, the John R. Gilpin family of Philadelphia, who were avid sailors, "discovered" Palm Beach—an obscure outpost town. There was no road southward, and pioneers could only reach Biscayne Bay by sailboat or by walking down the beach. Early in April 1890, the family sailed down to Biscayne Bay. In this excerpt from her diary, Mrs. Gilpin recounts her impression of the area. In later years, the Gilpins spent every winter in Coconut Grove. Her son Vincent collaborated with Ralph Munroe in writing The Commodore's Story.

Friday, April 11th, 1890

Along the shore was to be seen the same sand beach, and the large pine trees, coming closer and closer to the shore. The human interests were the lone mail-carrier from Lake Worth, who carries the mail down the beach, a distance of 60 miles, once a week, and the three "Houses of Refuge" built by the U.S. government for the relief of ship-wrecked persons on this beach. A surf-boat is housed ready for any necessary use. As we passed the second the stripes and stars were strung up as a greeting. The Narres [Norris] Cut was reached by noon, and we had made the outside trip in less than 10 hours—9.55,—the shortest trip on record. We entered [Biscayne] Bay, and found it large,—40 miles long and 4 or 5 wide. All are quieted at once, and enjoy the sail across the bay, 6 or 7 miles, to "Lemon City," which we find [to be] a store, dock, and several houses built back among the pines. . . . To my delight I saw the dock was full of Indians, with them were their squaws,

papooses, and canoes full of camping outfit. They had been hunting deer, and were selling out and laying in stores for a fishing trip up Snake Creek, 25 miles above. They had sold out their trophies before we came, but I went among them at once and asked for deer-skins, horns, and alligator hides, but they had none. . . . The Hill party want to photograph the Indians, but the women positively refused, though the men and children always are pleased to be "pictured." Found the man I spoke with was Robert Osceola, a descendant of the old chief, and himself a young chief, with quite the prettiest young squaw among them for himself. The squaws were dressed in blue calicoes, trimmed with red white and yellow ruffles or bands. How they make them is the marvel . . . They all look very strong and muscular. It is said the developement of their [bodies] is owing to the continued use of the canoe, which is a dug-out of cypress, 20 to 30 feet long, which they propel by polling or paddling. The canoes contain all that is necessary for living on their nomadic expeditions from point to point,—camp-kit, dogs, chickens, terrapin, vermin and children. . . . Their word is thoroughly reliable, and they come when they say they will. . . .

Saturday, April 12th, 1890
        After breakfast sail for the outside peninsula so that Mr. Dewey could see the House of Refuge keeper about his taxes. Boat too small to take anyone else. In half an hour they return with Mr. Peacock and Den-

nis, two keepers, in a Govt. life-boat. They come aboard, and we ask them about the crocodile pond, but he says the crocodiles would not appear [on] such a cold day. . . . We sailed back to Lemon City, where we again landed and Mailed some letters . . . for the beach-walker to take back to Lake Worth on Monday morning . . . walked back in the pines, and came across a settlement made by a German, Matthaus—saw the mother and 6 children. She was a bright little woman, and ready to show us everything about their 3-year-old establishment—fine pineapples, cotton plants, avocado pears, etc. They manufacture the Comptie starch used for puddings; the root grows everywhere through the woods, and they dig, wash, grind, strain, soak, ferment, dry and ship the whitened starch when finished, and it helps to make a living. . . . They ship egg-plants and tomatoes to New York via Key West, with varying success. . . .

Monday, April 14th, 1890
(Cocoanut Grove, Bay Biscayne)
        We move off, and sail lazily up to Miami over the transparent waters of the bay, and over the bottom gardens of sea-weeds with sponges and toad-fish now and then. . . . We are several hours getting up to Brickell's dock. Anchor and group to meet Mr. Brickell, who entertains us with vivid accounts of his visits to Japan and Australia. . . . Mr. B. is a character in this neighborhood. Owns all the bay-front near by, and holds it at enormous prices. Has

a northern house here,—made at the north, and brought down in sections, and put up, but now going to decay. Large piazza overlooking the bay,—large rooms, French windows to floor, bay windows at both ends,—fine walnut railed stairway,—old trees around. His warehouse is at the dock,—store near the house; hundreds of alligator skins in the warehouse being packed for New York, killed by the Indians. . . . Go up on the front piazza of the new warehouse, and take in the magnificent view of the whole bay with its outside islands, reefs, shoals, cuts and light-houses. On this warm day we can imagine nothing more charming than this location for a whole season, where one could catch every breeze that blows, and command innumerable pictures of grand beauty over towards the ocean, and those of quiet beauty on the other side, up the Miami River. Opposite is the site of Fort Dallas, built in 1845 by the United States Government during the Indian war. The cocoa palms are oldest of all we have seen, so old as to be broken down frequently by the Atlantic gales. This is the favorite point for beauty on the whole bay, but is owned with such uncertain title that no man is willing to buy it, though all want it.

Source: Emma Gilpin, "Diary of Mrs. John R. Gilpin," 1890

Mary Barr Munroe
"Pioneer Women"

Mary Barr Monroe was born in 1852 in Glasgow, Scotland. When she was two years old, the family emigrated to America, arriving in Galveston, Texas, in 1854. After Mary's father died of yellow fever in 1854, the Barr family moved to New York. Her mother, Amelia Barr, became a world famous novelist. Mary married Kirk Munroe, a famous author of boys books, in 1883. Shortly after their marriage, they moved to the wilderness of Coconut Grove, where they built a home they called "The Scrububs." While in the area, (1886-1923) Mrs. Munroe fought for the preservation of its wildlife, helped found the Housekeepers Club for women and was a legendary community leader. She was also one of the leaders in early efforts to save the Everglades. Her early account of life in Coconut Grove, first published in The Miami Metropolis, *provides unusual insight into the women of the era.*

Pioneer life, as we know, is always hardest on a woman, but one of the wonderful things about it is a woman's ever willingness to follow the man of her choice. Old or young, the wilderness has no terrors for her like being left behind or having Him go alone.

I wonder how many women in Dade County today would have come here of their own will, or from choice. In many cases the men have come first and such glorious accounts of wonderful weather, delicious fruits, and the ease and freedom of a life in the wilderness (all too true) has tempted many a woman, who came rejoicing so, at the joy of her man, that she has never murmured at her thousand and one little trials that beset the pioneer woman's life day and night causing many a tear and backward glance for the comforts of a civilized home.

I know one woman who wore a sun bonnet all day both in and out of the house for the first month she was at Cocoanut Grove so that her husband should not see her crying. Today she is very happy in the home he gave her as we all are after a few months of "settling down," but it is hard for a man to realize what it means to a woman to give up family, friends, church, doctor and a comfortable house and sleep in a tent, while the first house is being built, which is usually spoken of as the future packing house, or chicken house, when the groves come into bearing. They do not realize the fear the women have at finding out that crawling creatures of the earth are so near to them, or the pain that comes with the hardening of soft hands in doing the daily housework of pioneer life. No, and women will seldom let them know. So the men are not to blame.

The great loneliness of the early days seems always to be the thing remembered by the women; they longed for other women from the great outside world. I do not think anyone ever had differences in those days and they all seemed to have been good cooks, and when one remembers that most of that work was done out of doors over wood fires it is interesting to hear of the dinners these pioneer women prepared for families and guests. There are wonderful stories of Johnny cake, "sweet and plenty of it," stewed venison, ash baked sweet potatoes, boiled Seminole squash, corn pones, roast wild hog, and wild turkey, coontie pudding, and coontie pancake, Indian Sofkie, Gypsy Stew, Reef Bean soup, turtle fry, and fried chicken. . . .

Pioneer days are wonderful days, and there is one thing certain, they bring out all there is in a man and woman. They teach forbearance, on a big scale, and there is another wonderful thing, no one ever regrets them.

The Housekeeper's Club had a junior club called the "Pine Needles." In 1895, the Pine Needles organized the Miami area's first library. The girls are dressed for their "broom drill" that they performed for community functions. (Ralph Munroe)

There is a big recompense someway for women are just as ready today to go into the wilderness to do without the comforts of life. In fact to learn life all over again as they ever were, and Dade county Florida has had, and has her share of these brave-hearted women, and her men are proud of them.

Source: Mary Barr Monroe, "Pioneer Women of Dade County," *Miami Metropolis*, July 3, 1909, p. 3.

The Housekeeper's Club 1892

Six pioneer women, including Flora McFarlane, Mary Barr Munroe and Isabella Peacock, founded the Housekeeper's Club of Coconut Grove in February 1891. The club met every Thursday from three to five and sought to bring together the mothers and housekeepers of the "little settlement" of Coconut Grove. The members got to know each other, exchanged ideas on subjects such as cooking and homesteading, and raised money for area improvements. The club had a wonderful mix of women from all walks of life and had a great influence on the development of Coconut Grove. An article on the club, and the women's lifestyle in a yet undeveloped region, appeared in Harper's Bazaar *in 1892.*

It is to these women and their club—a housekeeper's club—that I wish to introduce my read-

ers. A woman's working club in every sense of the word, with an attending membership of twenty and a correspondence membership of ten, the latter residents of New York, Boston, San Francisco, Brooklyn, Staten Island and Key West.

To most of the women born and brought up on the keys of the reef or in Key West, and of English parentage—for the majority of the settlers came originally from the Bahamas—the experience of belonging to a society, however simple, for *women only*, was a novelty. Although "our club" is now a frequent and proud expression among them, and one member, in talking it over with her husband, assured him that the "by-laws of her club were as well made and just as binding as those concocted in the capitol at Tallahassee."

And so they are to the faithful band of women who gather every Thursday afternoon in the little Sunday school building, and join heart and hand in helping each other to enjoy and improve the two hours a week rescued from their household cares. For nearly every member is a mother, not of one, but in several cases of eight and ten children, with no one to assist in the daily and hourly work attending such a household, so that the first rule made and rigidly enforced, "No babies allowed at the meetings," is a genuine relief, and gives time and freedom for much that would be otherwise impossible.

Sometimes the children are taken to a neighboring house, ten or twelve little tots from one to three years old, and a husband or eldest son volunteers to oversee those that are able to walk, in which case, as it draws near closing time, one little head after another will be seen coming, Indian file, along the narrow path, all of them bareheaded or nearly so, in search of mamma and generally in great glee of having escaped. Of course there follows a grand baby show.

The originator of the club is its president, Miss Flora McFarlane, of New Jersey, a woman who has proved herself in every way capable for the life she intends leading, having homesteaded a hundred and fifty acres of government land, which she has gone bravely to work to clear and improve.

Source: "A Housekeepers' Club," *Harper's Bazaar* XXV (April 16, 1892).

Building a House that Lasts
1892

Caleb and Henrietta Trapp and their son Harlan came to Coconut Grove from Iowa in 1887. The Trapps settled on the bluff in Coconut Grove and lived for about a year in a palmetto shack like the Seminole Indians. Caleb and his son Harlan decided to build a home out of rock that they hewed from the cliff with chisels and hatchets. They quarried the rock carefully, creating a series of rock steps sixty feet wide in the process. The double walls of the house were completed on December 28, 1889. Henrietta Trapp, the Grove's first school teacher, was known for keeping a lantern glowing in her upstairs bedroom at night to aid mariners as they came into the Coconut Grove mooring. Their home, which was remodeled and enlarged in 1926-27, still stands at 2521 South Bayshore Drive.

One of the land-marks of Biscayne Bay is the "rock house" built by Caleb Trapp, Esq., a gentleman over seventy years old. He hewed out of the solid rock bluff blocks of stone and built a two story house that will be a monument to his industry for centuries to come, unless some vandal hands secure the property and removes the rock house to make room for one of the gaudy and cheap tinsel structures so fashionable in English speaking countries. We ought all at the earliest moment possible emulate the noble example of Mr. Trapp and build entirely of the beautiful white rock so easily worked and so everlasting. When we contrast our wooden towns and villages with the solid stone and tile built towns of Spanish America, it makes us look cheap, tawdry and temporary. . . . How much we could learn from our Latin neighbors if we were not so conceited.

Source: "Notes From Our Neighbors," *Tropical Sun* (Juno, Florida), April 21, 1892.

Julia Tuttle
Asking a Friend for Help, 1892

Julia Tuttle, who moved to Miami in November 1891, quickly became involved in her adopted hometown. Her family had been friends of the Rockefellers in Cleveland and she frequently wrote John D. Rockefeller for advice as well as contributions to a variety of causes. In the following letter, she seeks his assistance in building a Baptist church in the area. Although Rockefeller sent some money, Mrs. Tuttle returned it after the minister gave up and left the area. Miami got its first Baptist Church in 1896.

Fort Dallas—Miami
Dade C. Fla.
May 3, 1892

Dear Mr. Rockefeller—

I have so far carried out my plans that I am living in Florida. We have all enjoyed our winter here very much and think we shall stay most of the summer.

Of course in this new country we have found many things to do and many ways in which we could lend a helping hand to the people. The young people have been helping in Sunday School and union church work.

A few days since one of the good people came to me with a subscription paper to raise funds to build a Baptist church—I gladly put my name down for what I felt able to do but I see they will have a hard time to get money enough to finish the little church. They have a lot for the church and one for a parsonage which has been given and the church will cost about $800.00 I think—I should not think of asking this for any but your own denomination but I know how deep your interest is in the work of your own church and I really think there are few places where a little help would do more good or be more thoroughly appreciated than right here in South Florida.

I was sorry to miss seeing Mrs. Rockefeller and yourself last summer but you were both away when I called . . . I trust you are all well—you will soon be going to Forest Hill which is I think the most charming country home I have ever seen—I hope some day we may see you all here for I too am going to have a beautiful home. With kind regards to all, I am yours

Sincerely,

Julia D. Tuttle

Source: Letter, Julia Tuttle to John D. Rockefeller, May 3, 1892, Record Group l, Incoming Correspondence, Office, MS Box 47 (Office l879-1994), Rockefeller Archive Center, North Tarrytown, N.Y.

Rockefeller Responds

May 21st, 1892
Mrs. Julia D. Tuttle
Fort Dallas, Miami, Dade Co., Fla.

Dear Madam:
    Your letter, of the 3rd inst., is received. We are glad to know you are enjoying the new home. Enclosed please find my check, to your order for $50xx for the little Baptist Church you refer to.

Yours Truly,

John D. Rockefeller

Source: Letter, John D. Rockefeller to Julia D. Tuttle, May 21, 1892, Letterbook Volume 31, p. 223, Rockefeller Archive Center, North Tarrytown, N.Y.

Carting Away the Past

John Sewell
Clearing the Land, 1896

When John Sewell, Henry Flagler's foreman, arrived in Miami in March 1896, he discovered that the land chosen for Flagler's Royal Palm Hotel was covered with a huge "mountain-like" Indian burial mound. His first order of business was to clear the site. In the following account from his personal memoirs, Sewell describes how he and his workers buried the remains of Miami's first people "under a fine residence." Today, the First Union Financial Center and part of the Dupont Plaza parking lot cover this singular historic ground.

Among the landmarks of Miami that I found here was an Indian mound near the bay south of 14th Street and near the northeast corner of the proposed site for the Royal Palm Hotel. This stood up like a small mountain from the bay, looking west, and many writers have estimated it to have been eighty or ninety feet high. Probably the top of the trees on this mound were sixty feet above the water, but the earth and rock were only about twenty feet or not over twenty-five feet above the water level. There were large trees growing on top of the mound and it was about one hundred feet long by seventy-five feet wide. To make room for the hotel veranda this mound had to be moved and I had to take it down. There were two or three graves on top of the mound, where the dead had been buried, but we could not find out whose bones they were nor anything connected with them. I put these bones in barrels and stored them away. Then proceeded to haul the soil out and screen it to help make a lawn later. The rock I filled in near the bay to help make the boulevard around the hotel and near the center of the mound, on the natural level of the ground, I began to find Indian skeletons and altogether I took out between fifty and sixty skulls. I preserved all the bones and stored them away in barrels and gave away a great many of the skeletons to anyone that wanted them. Then stored the bones in my tool house for future reference, where they remained until the hotel was completed at the end of the year. As my tool house had to be torn down, I took about four of my most trusted negroes and hauled all of these skeletons out near by where there was a big hole in the ground, about twelve feet deep, and dumped the bones in it, then filled the hole up with sand and instructed the negroes to forget this burial and whereabouts of same—and I suppose they did. I have never heard anything outside of this burial ground. There is fine residence now standing over the bones—and the things that the owners don't know will never hurt them. And the Indians' bones are now resting in peace. I found nothing else of importance in the mound except a few beads and Indian trinkets.

Source: John Sewell, *Miami Memoirs*, A New Pictorial Edition of John Sewell's Own Story (1933), ed. by Arva Moore Parks (Miami: Arva Parks & Co., 1987), pp. 57, 59.

In March 1896, John Sewell, Flagler's construction boss, (in short sleeves) stood by as his 12 workers carted away the bones from the Tequesta Indian burial mound at the mouth of the Miami River to make way for the Royal Palm Hotel. The men, that Sewell called "his black artillery" are (in no certain order) A. W. Brown, Philip Bowman, Jim Hawkins, Warren Merridy, Richard Mangrom, Romeo Fashaw, Scipio Coleman, Sam Anderson, Davie Heartly, J. B. Brown, William Collier and Joe Thompson. The white men in the background are J. E. Lummus, C. T. McCrimmon, T. L. Townley and E. G. Sewell. (J.N. Chamberlain)

THE INSTANT CITY
1896-1915

chapter
2
two

"*A quick-grown city, founded and built by the living generation, lacked monuments from the past. It was overwhelmed by its imaginary present greatness and its debt to the future. . . . New World cities depended on new-formed loyalties and enthusiasms, shallow-rooted, easily transplanted. . . . Old World cities often outgrew their walls; but Upstart towns had none. Their key idea from their beginning was less defense or preservation (for their was nothing yet to preserve) than growth. They measured themselves, not by their ability to keep out invaders, but by their power to attract immigrants. The American identification of life with progress was rooted here.*"

Daniel Boorstin
The Americans:
The National Experience, 1965

Henry Flagler's grand 400 room Royal Palm Hotel, with its 600 foot verandah, was the young city's reason for being. It not only dominated the skyline, but the city's economic and social life.

Miami was an "instant city" created by the arrival of the railroad, the expanding market for winter fruits and vegetables, the availability of land and the growing popularity of winter resorts for the new leisure class. The engineer, the investor and the promoter were pivotal figures in this new era. They built railroads, constructed highways, developed land and carved new communities out of the wilderness. Although the Flagler organization clearly dominated the region, a broader array of residents, from housewives and mothers, to store owners, saloon keepers, laborers and homesteaders, helped define the city's unique, diverse and ever-changing character.

∞ The City That Was Never A Town

By early 1896, as workers hacked their way through the palmetto and Dade County pine to bring the railroad into Miami, prospective small businessmen and workmen arrived seeking new homes, new lives and new opportunities. Many who had lost everything in the 1894-95 freeze, saw Miami as a place to start their lives over. Most lived in tents and hastily constructed shacks because there was little available lodging. In fact, a floating hotel on the river, Julia Tuttle's half-finished Miami Hotel and a few basic storefronts were the only signs that a city was in the making.

Flagler's work crew arrived on March 2nd to clear the spot for his luxury Royal Palm Hotel and lay out the streets. John Sewell, an energetic and domineering man, who was elected the city's third mayor and later wrote a book chronicling Miami's history, was the foreman. Once work began on the hotel, change came with dizzying speed.

On April 13, Flagler and his party arrived on a special train and two days later several hundred people cheered the arrival of the first official train connecting Miami to the rest of the United States. By May, Miami had a newspaper—*The Miami Metropolis*, a bank, a group of stores and several churches. In the first issue of the *Metropolis*, the paper editorialized for incorporation hoping this added status would help sell the area.

On July 28, 1896 at 2:00 pm, eligible voters gathered in a room over the Lobby Pool Hall on today's South Miami Avenue just north of the river, to incorporate. Three hundred and forty-four men, one third of them black, voted in the first election that created the City of Miami. (Women were not allowed to vote.) Sewell, eager to have Miami incorporated as a city and not a town, used his black workers, that he referred to as his "Black Artillery," to swell the electorate to over 300, the legal requirement for city status. He also made sure that Flagler's men would control the infant city's first governing body. Even though more than a third of the registered voters were black, and blacks were the primary work force in the new city, they were segregated by law into a small area of town west of the white area that was designated "Colored Town." Although the principal property owners, Julia Tuttle and Henry Flagler were from the north, they followed the southern practice of segregation when they planned their new city. Soon after Miami's incorporation, blacks were kept from voting in local elections.

Miami quickly became known as "The Magic City" because, as early residents liked to brag, it grew from a wilderness to a full-blown city "as if by magic." But despite its city status, Miami retained the aura of a frontier boom town. Residents were predominantly male and came mostly from other parts of Florida and neighboring southern states. Unlike other southern cities, a sizable minority came from the north and a variety of foreign countries.

Miami was a rough and tumble place where institutions like the police, the courts and the schools were almost non-existent. Even though Julia Tuttle and Henry Flagler had forbidden the sale of alcohol within the city limits (allowing it only for guests at the Royal Palm) a thriving vice district called North Miami quickly grew up just beyond the city borders near today's N.E. 11th Street. Saloons, gambling dives and houses of prostitution flourished in full view of the new city that prided itself on its "morality."

Henry Flagler's magnificent Royal Palm Hotel dominated the small, dusty settlement. In fact, as Marjory Stoneman Douglas once wrote, the Royal Palm was the city's "whole reason for being" even though it was only open during the season—January to March. Located at the mouth of the Miami River and painted bright yellow, it was 700 feet long, had 350 guest rooms, 200 bathrooms and an additional 100 rooms for maids and hotel staff. The main dining room seated over 500, and there were separate dining rooms for maids and children, and others for black as well as white servants. The hotel featured a 578-foot long verandah overlooking the bay, a grand ballroom and the area's first (salt water) swimming pool.

Winter guests took long leisurely boat rides up the Miami River to exotic attractions like "the falls" and the mysterious Everglades, viewed from the vantage of the Everglades Tower. They visited other attractions like the "Devil's Punch Bowl, "a mysterious basin carved in the rock just south of today's Rickenbacker Causeway and the natural bridge at Arch Creek. They fished the bountiful waters of Biscayne Bay with renowned local guides like Captain Charlie Thompson and they strolled through the Royal Palm gardens, marveling at the varied species of tropical fruits and flowers. Famous visitors, who were often friends of Flagler's, included such titans of industry as John Jacob Astor, Andrew Carnegie and John D. Rockefeller who arrived in their private railroad cars or on opulent yachts. These American capitalists fueled the vision of Julia Tuttle and Henry Flagler, yet Miami was not simply their territory. During the off season, it reverted back to the local populace who spent most of the year in frantic preparation for the next season.

∽ Building Community

Even though the city was strictly segregated by law, and most locals rarely set foot inside the Royal Palm Hotel, early Miamians felt a sense of pride in the city they were building, despite the fact that most were not able to participate in all that it offered. They often spoke and wrote about what they called the "Miami Spirit" that grew through shared sacrifice and struggle.

It was not an easy time. A disastrous Christmas night fire in 1896 destroyed the new downtown which the merchants quickly rebuilt on what later became Flagler Street. A terrible freeze in 1897 destroyed most of the farmer's crops. In the summer of 1898, during the Spanish-American-Cuban War, the U.S. government stationed 7,500 troops in Miami even though the city only had 2,500 residents. Although Flagler had lobbied Washington officials for the troop encampment (and the federal funding that went with it), the soldier's behavior grew ugly. Many of the men resented being used as cheap labor to improve the value of Flagler's land. Bored and miserable in the summer heat, the soldiers (many from other southern states) constantly harassed the black community who resided just west of the military camp. At one point conditions got so bad that blacks had to flee to Coconut Grove for protection.

A severe outbreak of both typhoid fever and measles in the military camp decimated the troops and frightened Miamians. The following year a yellow fever epidemic led to a rigid quarantine that brought business to a standstill for several months. Fortunately, only 14 people died but hundreds were stricken.

Only primitive medical facilities existed in the early days. While one of the earliest physicians in the area had been a woman, Dr. Eleanor Galt Simmons, Dr. James Jackson was clearly the most prominent early Miami physician. He worked for the FEC railroad but tirelessly attended to patients throughout the region. He was so beloved that when he died in 1924, downtown stores closed during his funeral, flags flew at half-mast and the city hospital was renamed in his honor.

Business, religious and social organizations and novel forms of entertainment helped define community life. Merchants chartered a Board of Trade in 1907 that later became the Chamber of Commerce. *The Miami Metropolis* was a sounding board of local opinion and, along with Flagler's *Florida Homeseeker*, the primary promoter of the region's economic growth.

Early entertainment included baseball games and ferry trips to what would become Miami Beach. Church, school and club socials were also well attended. By the first decade of the new century, nickelodeons and movie theaters, many of which were open air, became popular. Special events like the Mid-Winter Agricultural Fair and Fourth of July parades were eagerly awaited community events as well as promotional tools to attract tourists and new residents.

Most new residents were devout church goers. Different denominations first held services in a community tent where ministers took turns delivering sermons. Flagler, a religious man, gave a free church lot to most of the larger denominations in both the white and black communities. He financed the Presbyterian Church building as well, because he was a Presbyterian. In the absence of a synagogue, some Jewish residents attended Christian Sunday Schools where they studied the Old Testament. Most of the religious bodies supported the temperance movement, especially after the city became "wet" following Julia Tuttle's death in 1898. Carrie Nation, a national temperance leader known for destroying saloons with her ax, came to Miami in 1908 and held a major rally. After a series of "wet-dry" elections, Miami voted itself "dry" in 1913, not to be (officially) overturned until 1933.

∞ Redesigning The Land

By the first decade of the 20th Century, residential, commercial and agricultural lands were becoming increasingly valuable. Calls to "reclaim" the Everglades and transform it into "black gold" (wealth from the rich, black muck agricultural land) became popular. In 1901, Governor William Sherman Jennings began a crusade to reclaim the Everglades from the land developers. First, using the courts and the U.S. Government, he wrestled more than two million acres away from individuals and corporations. They had been given large grants of land in the Everglades in return for building railroads and canals—most of which were never completed Thanks to Governor Jennings, a large chunk of the Everglades reverted back to the state. Governor Napoleon Bonaparte Broward followed Jennings and started the drainage process in November 1905 with the dredging of the New River Canal in Fort Lauderdale.

By 1913, the Miami Canal (on the right) was completed and the Miami River (on the left) came to a dead end at the dynamited falls. Prior to draining, all the land west of the bridge, now 27th Avenue, was Everglades. (SPA)

That same year, crowds of Miamians went to what would later become Miami Beach to watch the dredge dig through the last piece of earth that separated the ocean from the bay. The opening of Government Cut created Fisher Island and was seen as another step toward creating a much needed deep water port for the young city.

Serious reclamation began in Miami in 1909 when the State of Florida sliced through the rim of the glades, just west of today's 27th Avenue, and blew up the Miami River falls to begin construction of the Miami Canal. For days, after the dikes were removed and the canal opened, the Everglades water rushed through the canal and out into the sea killing fish and muddying the clear waters of the Miami River and Biscayne Bay forever.

Few Miamians, like most other Floridians, questioned the advisability of drainage. Most were caught up in the enthusiasm of development and had little understanding of the value of the Everglades except as potential real estate. Ironically, in 1906, Governor Jennings' wife, May Mann Jennings, launched the ultimately successful effort to preserve the Royal Palm Hammock which was the beginning of the Everglades Park movement.

As the city grew, pressure to extend "Colored Town's" boundaries caused conflict between the races as blacks struggled against heightening forms of segregation and overcrowded living conditions. Florida laws, similar to laws throughout the South, became increasingly restrictive due to whites reasserting their power after the end of Reconstruction. The poll tax and white primaries made it almost impossible for blacks to vote. New laws, known as "Jim Crow" laws, forbade blacks and whites from attending the same schools, traveling in the same railway cars, or drinking from the same water fountains. By law, the definition of Negro, "colored person," "mulatto" or "persons of color" was very specific. "Every person having one-eighth or more of African or Negro blood" was so classified. (This law was repealed in 1968).

∞ Moving On

While engineers reconfigured chunks of the mainland, Henry Flagler, spurred by the planned construction of the Panama Canal, busily embarked on his greatest venture—the Overseas Railroad to Key West. By 1904, his railroad reached Homestead, opening up new agricultural markets at stops along the way like Kendall, Perrine, Peters and Goulds. By this time,

Flagler also succeeded in clearing up the disputed title of the old Perrine Grant that included 320,000 acres of South Dade real estate. The U.S. Government gave the grant to Henry Perrine in 1838 for tropical plant introduction. After the Indians killed him on Indian Key in 1840, the conditions of the grant were never satisfied. In 1897, Flagler, working with the Perrine heirs and the so called "Squatters Union," a group of individuals who had been living on the land, used his influence to settle the long dispute with the federal government. In return, he received 1/4 of the land and a right-of-way for the railroad. This opened up much of South Dade for development.

From 1905-1912, what newspapers and politicians called "Flagler's Folly" pushed south and west toward Key West despite mosquito-infested summers and three devastating hurricanes. New settlements, primarily agricultural, grew up around the railroad stations. When the railroad reached Key West in 1912, what had been "Flagler's Folly" suddenly was hailed as one of history's greatest engineering feats—"the Eighth Wonder of the World."

From the time of Miami's incorporation, Flagler wielded enormous control over the city and little happened that he did not influence one way or the other. From the local docks, streets, city council and water system, the Flagler system ran Miami like it was its own personal business. No one disputed the fact that Miami benefited enormously from Flagler's presence. Increasingly, however, locals resented the predominance of the Flagler organization and by the time of Flagler's death in 1913, some had organized against his control of shipping and the port as well as the railroad.

Until 1904, *The Miami Metropolis*, was firmly under the influence of Flagler and editorially supported his point of view. After S. Bobo Dean took over as managing editor in 1904, the paper became increasingly critical of Flagler. In response, Flagler money helped launch *The Miami Herald* in 1910, under the editorship of Frank Stoneman. This move gave the city two strong newspapers with differing points of view. The rivalry continued until 1988, when *The Miami News*, formerly *The Metropolis*, folded.

∞ The End Of An Era

Much of the "magic" behind Miami's fast growth came from Flagler's money and tourist dollars. The hard work of local residents, however, as well as the widespread use of new technology also helped de-

Living History

Station Agent's House, 1904
Florida Pioneer Museum
826 Krome Avenue
Florida City, Florida

Henry Flagler's team of civil engineers, led by William Krome, began surveying South Dade in the early 20th Century to determine the path of the Florida East Coast Railroad as it snaked through an unbroken wilderness on the way to Key West. One of the early railroad buildings, the Station Agent's House, was built in Homestead in 1904. It was typical of many of the railroad buildings that housed FEC station agents. The house was moved to its present location in Florida City in 1964 and became the Florida Pio-

(Larry Wiggins)

neer Museum. Twelve years later, the Homestead Depot was also moved to Florida City. The depot was severely damaged by Hurricane Andrew but has been reconstructed. The wooden caboose and house have also been restored returning the Florida Pioneer Museum to its pre-Andrew appearance.

velopment. In 1911, bolstered by a strong spirit of accomplishment, city leaders planned a week-long series of events to celebrate Miami's 15th birthday. Besides an automobile parade and track and field events, the highlight of the celebration was Miamians first glimpse of an airplane flight. Promoters brought in a Wright Brothers' plane (by train) and turned Flagler's golf grounds, now the Metro Justice Complex, into a flying field. One of its excited passengers was E. G. Sewell, who along with his brother John Sewell had owned the area's earliest shoe store back in 1896. Sewell organized the 15th anniversary event to bring greater attention to Miami. In the years that followed, he became Miami's most visible promoter and helped the area emerge as the nation's pre-eminent winter playground.

After Flagler's death in 1913, from what was described as "old age and exhaustion," Miami entered a new era as other major developers and city builders emerged on the scene. One of these men was Carl Graham Fisher. Fisher came to Miami in 1910, fresh from making his fortune in Prest-O-Lite, the first practical automobile headlight. He watched L. T. Highleyman create "Point View," off today's Brickell Avenue, from former mangroves and bay bottom and

invested in the project. Next, he joined John Collins, who was busy building a bridge across Biscayne Bay to his spit of oceanfront land that he called Ocean Beach. With Fisher's capital, imagination and promotional skills, Collins' determination and the work of the Lummus brothers, who also invested in the bridge, the new City of Miami Beach was incorporated by 1915.

By the time the Collins bridge was completed to the island in 1913, Carl Fisher was already dreaming of a national highway to Miami. In October 1915, more than 1,000 Miamians joined in the grand celebration to welcome him and his Dixie Highway Pathfinders into Miami after a 16 day trip from Chicago. That same year, Captain James E. Jaudon began promoting the Tamiami Trail across the Everglades to connect Miami with Tampa.

By 1915, much of the infrastructure was in place that would launch the area toward further growth and development. Miamians, eager to grow and prosper, paid little attention to future consequences of their disregard for the natural and built environment. Instead, they turned the future over to anyone and everyone who promised paradise and profit. "Instant cities," after all, lacked memory and their founders gave little thought to anything but the present.

Pioneer Visions

E. V. Blackman
Interview with Julia Tuttle, 1896

E. V. Blackman, a New Yorker by birth, came to Miami from Lake County, Florida after the 1895 freeze where he had been a citrus grower and Methodist minister. He organized Miami's First Methodist Episcopal Church in 1896 while also serving as a newspaper correspondent for Henry Flagler and editor of Flagler's Florida East Coast Homeseeker. *In 1897, he brought Miami its first convention, the tobacco growers, and organized the Mid-Winter Fair—the first county fair in Florida. He is also credited with giving Miami the nickname: "The Magic City." He died in 1921. In his book,* Miami and Dade County Florida, *he described an early meeting he had with Julia Tuttle.*

Soon after I came to Miami I made the acquaintance of the late Mrs. Julia D. Tuttle, who impressed me as being a woman of great foresight, a woman who could at all hazards carry out her plans, although many of her plans reached far into the future of Miami and Dade County. Many of her plans have been more than carried out, and while some of them have not yet materialized, who knows but that they will be carried out in full before many years roll around;

in fact, her highest aspirations may have been but slight visions of what the future of Miami will eventually be.

Many thought Mrs. Tuttle a dreamer—a chaser of shadows—but the passing years have proven beyond question that she was a woman of great foresight, a woman who had visions of the future that others were not permitted to see. I remember one evening, in the latter part of 1896, Mrs. Tuttle sent me a note inviting me to come to her home. It was a pleasure for me to grant her request. On my arrival at her home, she said: "I have a new inspiration regarding the future of Miami and I want to tell it to you, for I know that you will remember it and some time use it." We were seated in her living room, she occupying a large settee on the south side of the room. "Now," she said, "I want to talk to you, and don't laugh at my predictions, for I feel sure they will all come true. All these years I have had but one thought and that is to see Miami grow to one of the largest, if not the largest, city in all the southland. I have had many discouragements—discouragements that perhaps to one of a different temperament might have proven fatal—but the one thought and belief that at some future time these dreams of Miami's greatness would prove true has urged me on during all these years. No sacrifice on my part has been neglected to assist in bringing about my convictions of what Miami will eventually be—one of the greatest and most important cities, financially, com-

Julia Tuttle and Henry Flagler are considered the founders of Miami. (HASF)

mercially and residential, as well as the most important deep water port in all the southland. How many years will pass before this becomes true is, to me, yet a mystery. I can now only get a glimpse of the far future, but I want to tell you what I see will be the condition ten years hence." She then gave a description of what she saw in her farsightedness, or vision, of what Miami would be ten years hence. To me it seemed like the dream of a real dreamer. There were then many buildings under process of construction. The great Royal Palm Hotel was beginning to form shape; its foundations were completed and the frame of the superstructure was being placed in position. The late Joseph A. McDonald, who had faith in the future of Miami as the coming city of the southland, was building the Biscayne Bay Hotel; Mr. Flagler was erecting cottages on 13th and 14th streets, the street improvements had commenced, and Mr. Flagler was dredging a channel from the Miami River to Cape Florida. On every hand improvements were being carried on, indicating a permanency and the rapid building up of the city. Mrs. Tuttle said that in ten years Miami would have a resident population of more than ten thousand people. She then went on and described many of the buildings that she saw in her vision, the beautiful streets, the great rows of business blocks and the beautiful homes. I said to Mrs. Tuttle: "You have a very active and far reaching imagination. You surely do not mean to say

that within ten years all this development will be brought about." She replied most emphatically that she believed even greater developments would be made during the coming ten years. Mrs. Tuttle's vision did not all come true within the time stated. In 1906 there was a permanent population of between three and four thousand, but the buildings, both business and residential, had more than kept pace with Mrs. Tuttle's vision. . . .

Mrs. Tuttle had equally bright visions regarding the port of Miami. Along this line she said: "It will not be many years hence when Miami will be the most important port on the Atlantic Coast in the South. The time will come when the harbor and its approach will be dredged to a depth that will allow the deep sea—going vessels to anchor. Not only will this bring in the coastwise steamers, whose captains now cast longing eyes toward Miami as they pass, but the South American vessels will finally ply between their home ports and Miami, and Miami will become the great center of the South American trade. Vessels from all ports of the world will call at Miami, making Miami the greatest commercial center in all the south land. This may seem far-fetched to you, but as surely as the sun rises and sets all of this will come true." Again, we ask, was this a day dream or was it vision or inspiration?

Source: E. V. Blackman, *Miami and Dade County, Florida* (Washington: Victor Rainbolt, 1921), pp. 58-59.

Building a City

John Sewell
Building the Royal Palm Hotel, 1896

John Sewell, Flagler's foreman arrived in Miami on March 3, 1896. Two weeks later, he supervised the clearing for the Royal Palm Hotel that he said "started Miami." He was proud of his role and the role of his African American workers. He kept up with them through the years and reassembled them to ride on a float celebrating Miami's 15th Birthday. Sewell served as the third mayor of Miami and was a charter member of the Baptist Church. His home, Halisee Hall, that he built facing Flagler's golf course, is now part of the Jackson Memorial Hospital Complex and still stands amidst the many hospital buildings. He died in 1939, six years after he published his memoirs. In this document, Sewell describes the ground breaking of the Royal Palm Hotel.

Among the arrivals was J. E. Lummus, who had been here before and had arranged with Mrs. Tuttle to put up a store building for him on her property on Avenue D near the Miami River. He was going into the mercantile business and having a general store. Mr. C. T. McCrimmon came about that time. He was going into the contracting business. Then came T. L. Townley. He was going into the drug business. So these and myself and brother, E. G., made a party of five that kind of ran together. About that time Mr. J. N. Chamberlain, a photographer, arrived as he had arranged to rent a studio in the Royal Palm Casino when it was built and wanted to see the site for the proposed city.

He had his camera with him and wanted to take the picture of the first work breaking ground for the Royal Palm. I invited the boys all down to get in the picture. Mr. Chamberlain took the picture of the work, including the twelve negro men that I had brought with me and the five white men of the party.

That picture has gone all over this country, showing the starting of Miami. On the third of March 1921, I had another picture made on the same ground by the same photographer and three of the same men, J. E. Lummus, E. G. Sewell and myself, making a quarter of a century between the two pictures. I had some made at the same place on the fifteenth anniversary, which showed nearly all the white men and some of the negro men. But at this time, twenty-five years afterwards, the negro men that are living are scattered. I know the whereabouts of only five of them, while all of the white men are living except Mr. C. T. McCrimmon. Mr. Townley is living in Oklahoma. The others live in Miami. Three of the negroes still live in Miami, Rich Mangrom, Jim Hawkins, and Warren Merridy. Rev. A. W. Brown lives in Ft. Lauderdale, Fla. He bears the distinction of throwing the first shovel of dirt starting to make Miami a city. He was my leader of the gang. Joe Thompson, the fifth one, lives at Deerfield, Florida. All the living seem to be doing well and are prosperous. I prize the pictures very much indeed, all made by the same photographer, reaching over a period of twenty-five years; and Mr. Chamberlain was not a young man when he took the first one in March 1896. The white men in this picture were all on the waiting list when this picture was taken, except myself, as I had a job, and the other boys were my guests. But the whole bunch soon got into business, and each made good in his particular line of business.

Source: John Sewell, *Miami Memoirs*, A New Pictorial Edition of John Sewell's Own Story (1933), ed. by Arva Moore Parks (Miami: Arva Parks & Co., 1987), pp. 43-44.

John Sewell
A Religious Gathering, 1896

John Sewell was a religious man and believed that every town needed a strong group of churches. His humorous account of the future city's first church service, held in the Presbyterian tent with an Episcopal bishop and a ragtag congregation, paints a vivid picture of the difficulties of trying to bring religion into a frontier-style town.

About the third Sunday after my arrival here I received a note from Miss Fannie Tuttle, daughter of Mrs. Julia D. Tuttle, and a young lady at that time. She wanted me to go with her in her launch to Lemon City to hear some Episcopal bishop preach and she was going to bring the bishop back with her and he would preach in the Congregational tent that after-noon. She stated in the note that, if I could not go, she would like to borrow my light rowboat, called the May, as she feared the water was so low in the bay that her launch could not get to the dock at Lemon City. I wrote her in reply I was sorry that I could not go, but she was welcome to the May, and I would hear the bishop that afternoon in the tent. About 3:30 that afternoon I strolled over to the tent. I found the bishop sitting on the preacher's stand, also Mrs. Plass was at the organ, and Miss Tuttle and the bishop's secretary were sitting in the choir seats—only four in the tent. The bishop rose and said that "we have a preacher, an organist and a choir, and one for a congregation and that we had better begin the service." I rose and asked him if he was going to preach and he answered in the affirma-tive. I told him just to wait a few minutes and I would get him a congregation, for there was no use of his wasting a sermon on me. He said that he was afraid to let me go for fear I would not come back. Miss Tuttle assured him that I would come back and he agreed to wait.

First thing that I did was to go over on Avenue D where there was a pool room with a crowd of men playing pool. (I will state that there were pool rooms and cold drink stands strung along on Avenue D near the Miami River within a week after my arrival here.) I told the men that ran this pool room to close up the pool room right then and for the whole bunch to go across the street to the gospel tent, as there was a preacher over there who wanted to preach and had no congregation and that I was not going to have a preacher come to Miami and go away and say that he could not get a congregation to preach to. So they closed the pool room and the men began to file out and go over to the tent. I went to the cold drink stands and gave them the same spiel. So they closed up shop and went to church. Then I went to our quarters in the Miami Hotel, where a great many of us were kind of camping then, and went up and down the halls giv-ing them the same spiel that there was a preacher here who wanted to preach and nobody to preach to. Some of the men were asleep in their rooms on their cots, as we didn't have beds then. Some of the men that were asleep on their cots didn't take to the idea of getting up and going to church. Those of that class I turned their cots over and spilled them out on the floor and the shock waked them enough to know that I meant business. So they quietly dressed themselves and went to church, a regular stream leaving the hotel for the tent. Among those in the bunch were J. E. Lummus, E. G. Sewell, C. T. McCrimmon, T. L. Townely and L. C. Oliver, that I remember. Altogether I sent between twenty five and forty out of the hotel. Then I went around to the tents and shacks looking for a congregation, and sent all that I found to the tent. I finally ran across a couple of ladies walking up the railroad grade, as the railroad track had not reached Miami then. I asked them if they would mind going to the gospel tent to hear this bishop preach as he wanted to preach and I was trying to muster him up a congregation. They said they would be glad to go. I think one of these ladies was Mrs. A. B. Weaver and the other a Mrs. Campbell. At this time this was a city of men—very few ladies. After sending these two ladies on to church, all the woods around seemed deserted, and I decided that I had gotten everybody over to the tent and went back to the tent myself. There I found the tent full and all singing, and it sounded good, and I finally found space on a bench for a seat and the bishop started to preach. About the time that I got my seat and had heard about a dozen words of his sermon, I heard the steam boat whistle blow for a landing at the foot of Avenue D. I had to leave the tent and go down and put my men to work unloading the boat as we were bringing lumber and material for the Royal Palm Hotel on boats from Ft. Lauderdale, which was the terminal of the railroad at that time, and I had to unload boats as quickly as possible to keep them going. But I got the bishop a fine congregation by thrashing out the highways and byways, even if I did not get to hear his sermon myself. Of course, at that time I was very near law in Miami. I had no trouble in closing the pool rooms and cold drink stands, as the proprietors were willing to do anything I asked.

Source: John Sewell, *Miami Memoirs*, A Pictorial Edition of John Sewell's Own Story (1933), ed. by Arva Moore Parks (Miami: Arva Parks & Co., 1987), pp. 121-123.

The Miami Metropolis
Calling for Incorporation, 1896

Miami's first newspaper was The Miami Metropolis, *owned by the Flagler's lawyer Walter S. Graham. The first issue, on May 15, 1896, had ten pages that extolled the virtues of the "coming Metropolis" of Miami. In 1923, Ohio governor and 1920 presidential candidate, James Cox, purchased* The Metropolis *and changed its name to* The Miami Daily News. The Miami News *folded on December 31, 1988.*

We should take steps to incorporate the town of Miami without delay. There will be 1,500 people before the 1st of July and while the absence of saloons has a great deal to do with insuring the peace of the town, still it is necessary to incorporate and organize a good, strong municipal government as soon as possible.

The steps should be taken carefully. It should not be left to the haphazard judgment of the man, or men, upon whom the drawing up of an advertisement of notice of incorporation should fall, to exercise his own sweet will as to the location of the town boundaries and the amount of territory the municipality should embrace. We ought to incorporate so as to be able to frame and enforce such ordinances as are necessary.

Sanitary matters should be looked after. The removal of excrement and all kinds of disease—producing products at stated intervals should be rigidly insisted upon. No use to put clauses in the contracts and deeds to insure a model town if nuisances can be committed in and about the business center and dead fish be deposited without stint on the river shore about the city dock. An ounce of prevention in prohibiting houses of ill fame from getting a foothold is worth a ton of Parkhurstism [Parkhurst led an investigation of corruption in New York City] after they are well rooted. Indecent bathing should be prohibited within the town limits and Sunday should be well observed.

For these and many other reasons the town should be incorporated before August 1st. Why not call a meeting and appoint a committee to take the matter in hand and, above all, try to get a decent set of officers for the first year? They will be more needed then than at any future time. We know that the holder of a municipal office gets little, if any pay, not much honor and an abundance of abuse. But our best business men should be willing to serve for a year or two at least, so as to get the town established on a proper basis.

Source: "Incorporate at Once," *Miami Metropolis*, May 15, 1896.

Isidor Cohen
Remembering Miami's Early Days

Isidor Cohen arrived in Miami in 1896 and was one of the city's first merchants and Jewish residents. Here, on the occasion of Miami's 25th anniversary, he recalls the city's earliest days. His diary entries and comments describe the city, trace the actions of city founders at the time of incorporation and question the influence of Henry Flagler on Miami. His reference to Lightburn [sic] refers to A. C. Lightbourn who was the principal leader of the black community during this era. Cohen became a

Black workers were critically important in building the new City of Miami. On July 28, 1896, they joined the assembly upstairs in the Lobby Pool Hall (building with lightning rod) and helped incorporate the City of Miami. (J. N. Chamberlain)

very successful merchant and was active in the founding of Miami's first Jewish congregation. In 1925, he wrote and published Historical Sketches and Sidelights of Miami, Florida, *a vivid account of Miami's early days.*

First part of June, 1896: There is some talk about incorporating this place. *The Metropolis* claims that we have enough citizens to become incorporated as a city. I wonder what this corporation paper is up to. There is a rumor that either J. A. McDonald or his son-in-law, John B. Reilly, will be made the first mayor. The railroad bunch is certainly taking control of politics in this neck of the woods. . . .

Last part of July, 1896: This is now the city of Miami. We are duly incorporated and we expect to beat Key West in population in a very short time. We are almost up to West Palm Beach right now. The slate—made up by John Sewell and the rest of the railroad bunch—has been duly elected, as follows: John B. Reilly, mayor: councilmen—Joseph A. McDonald, Dan Cosgrove, W. S. Graham, W. M. Brown, Fred S. Morse, F. T. Budge, and E. L. Brady. There were quite a number of negroes at the incorporation meeting. A darky named Lightburn delivered the best speech. Some people favored naming the city "Flagler," but the opposition was too strong, and the name 'Miami' has been adopted, after the name of the river.

In the fall of 1896 Miami had the appearance of a prosperous little town: and North Miami beginning at the north line of First street, was firmly established as the worst seat of iniquity imaginable. In that place Dr. Jackson had acquired his remarkable surgical skill, as scarcely a day passed without the doctor be being summoned to probe for bullets in the anatomies of the habitues of the late notorious district. Business that fall was pretty good, and our merchant princes were preparing for the approaching tourist season. . . .

Source: "Miami—Rough, Uninviting, 25 Years Ago," *Miami Metropolis*, July 28, 1921, p. 4.

Lula Lummus
"The Few Comforts of Civilization," 1896

Lula Lummus, who was born near Tallahassee, came to Miami from Sanford, Florida a short time before the first train arrived. She joined her husband J. N. who, along with his brother J. E., opened a grocery in the new city. They spent their first days in Miami at Julia Tuttle's half-finished Hotel Miami that J. N. Lummus later managed. She was a founder of Trinity Episcopal Church and her husband became the first mayor of Miami Beach. She died in Miami in 1947. The following account describes the thrill of being a part of creating a new city.

Miami—May 1896

We now live at Miami, Fla., the terminus of the East Coast Railroad. I feel like I am in another world, but the novelty is fascinating and interesting. Miami is situated on the Miami River and beautiful Biscayne Bay. It is decidedly a "boom" town. This place is only a few months old and has a population of several hundred people.

Everything is crude and we have few comforts of civilization, but I'm enjoying living near to nature's heart. Twenty business houses are going up, and in a few years everyone predicts this place will be equal to Tampa. Boats run three times per week from Key West, and crowds arrive on every train to see the much talked of place.

I had the thrill of my life when I stood and watched the first train come in! All rejoiced to see that important mark of civilization. . . .

Sitting on the hotel veranda, looking over the surrounding country, you can see dozens of tents where refined people live. Men are here from every state, almost, looking for work, or to invest, and make this their future home. It seems strange to me that only white men are employed as mechanics. . . .

Mr. Flagler is having the ground prepared for his new hotel. It will be built on a point facing the bay.

Mrs. Julia Tuttle's home, with its well kept lawns and lovely tropical flowers and luscious fruits, shows what can be done here in Dixie land! The old Fort Dallas within her grounds is of much interest to sightseers. It is a picturesque sight crumbling away and covered with beautiful ivy.

Source: Mrs. J. N. [Lula] Lummus, "May 1896," *Sanford Chronicle*, May, 1896.

Florida's Jim Crow Laws

Soon after Reconstruction ended, Southern states passed what were called "Jim Crow" laws. Named for a character in a minstrel show, the term Jim Crow described laws that required racial segregation in public facilities. The Supreme Court signaled its approval of such laws in the 1896 decision of Plessy v. Ferguson whereby segregated facilities were permitted as long as they were "separate but equal." Other laws strengthened legal segregation throughout Florida. The following document is Florida's 1895 school segregation law.

Be it enacted by the Legislature of the State of Florida. Section l. It shall be a penal offense for any individual, body of individuals, corporation or association to conduct within this State any school of any grade, public, private or parochial wherein white persons and negroes shall be instructed or boarded within the same building, or taught in the same class, or at the same time by the same teachers.

Source: The Acts and Resolutions Adopted by the Legislature of Florida, Florida State Archives, Tallahassee, Florida, quoted in Raymond M. Hyser and J. Christ Arndt, *Voices of the American Past: Documents in U.S. History Volume II* (Orlando: Harcourt Brace College Publishers, 1995), p. 69.

Miami's First Public Schools, 1898

The City of Miami's first public schools—one white and one black—opened on October 12, 1896 even though the county superintendent was disappointed in the lack of community interest and remarked that he certainly did not want to force a school on anyone. Despite the white school's location in a rented storefront near the piney woods, 38 children showed up the first day. Within a month, enrollment swelled to 79. Most of the students were newcomers who had never laid eyes on each other until the first day of school. The first white high school graduation did not occur until 1904. The black public school opened in a church with Mrs. A. C. Lightbourn as the teacher. In July 1897, her husband, A. C. Lightbourn, superintendent of the black schools, convinced the School Board to appropriate money for a school building. Henry Flagler gave the land for the white school and Julia Tuttle gave the land for the black school. There was no recognized 12th grade education for blacks, however, until Booker T. Washington High School opened in 1927. The following document comes from The East Florida Homeseeker, a Flagler magazine article was clearly written from the white point of view when it spoke of "ample" schools for both blacks and whites. This reflected the inherent inequality of the "separate but equal" doctrine that was established in 1896 and ruled unconstitutional in 1954.

Three years ago Prof. R. E. McDonald was employed to open the first public school in Miami. The board secured an empty store building, near the corner of Avenue D and Eleventh street. In a few weeks it was found necessary to employ another teacher. Miss Amy Mann, of St. Augustine, was then employed by the Board of Public Instruction to take charge of the primary department. During the entire session the attendance increased, until many were turned away. The necessity for a public school building was so apparent that the matter was taken up by the city officials and other leading citizens. In a town that was in its infancy, to build a building that would be a credit to the city and at the same time give ample accommodations to the increasing number of pupils, was no small matter. The county was not able to purchase the grounds and erect such a building. The matter was canvassed, and it was decided to make an application for aid to Mr. Henry M. Flagler. Mr. Joseph A. McDonald was delighted to do this work. No sooner had he made the application, explaining the matter to Mr. Flagler, when, with his usual liberality, he [Flagler] subscribed $1,000 toward the enterprise. This gave the citizens and the board new courage, and the County Board of Instruction appropriated $500. Next came the Fort Dallas Land Company, with a donation of three lots in the most desirable portion of the city. The city then made an appropriation of $1,000, and the work was taken up, Mr. McDonald furnishing the plans. The building was erected and finished in time for the second year's term. It was apparent that two teachers were not sufficient. Miss Merritt was chosen for principal, and Mrs. Edith Hunter and Miss Mann as assistants. The term proved a most successful one, and long before the term ended each room was crowded. The third year opened with Miss Merritt in charge, assisted by Mrs. Hunter and Miss Jeannette Obenchain. It was soon apparent that another teacher would have to be employed, as the school population had increased so rapidly. Miss O'Neal was then secured as the fourth teacher. The enrollment has now reached 165. The course of study has been largely extended and now embraces all the branches that are taken up in the best graded schools of the country. From present indications the present school building will have to be enlarged before another term, to make room for the ever increasing number of pupils. The citizens of Miami have reason to be proud of its school, its teachers and its building. The population has increased far more rapidly than the most sanguine expected. In fact, at the time that the building of the house was being agitated, many thought that the proposed building was much too large. Time has proven the wisdom of Mr. McDonald in planning for a large building. Miami's graded school stands at the head of the list, not only in numbers, but in efficiency.

MIAMI'S COLORED SCHOOL

Not only have the children of the white people been furnished with ample school facilities, but the children of the colored people have been provided with ample educational advantages. The county donated $250, the city $150, and the Fort Dallas Land Company $100 toward erecting them a building. The late Mrs. Julia D. Tuttle donated a valuable lot on which to build. The school building is a credit to that portion of the city where it is located. Superintendent Merritt has taken the same pains to furnish them with the best grade of teachers that can be found. There is no county in the State that can boast of better school buildings or more efficient tutors than the county of Dade. Although the youngest in point of settlement as a whole, she has outstripped the older-settled counties in point of education.

Source: "Miami's Public School," *The Florida East Coast Homeseeker*, December, 1898, p. 9.

Growing Pains

Henry M. Flagler
Lobbying for a Troop Encampment, 1898

On February 7, 1898, the U. S. S. Maine was blown up in the Havana harbor, fueling the nation's entry into war with Spain. Flagler saw the war as a way to attract more people to Miami. Using his considerable political clout, he convinced the government to send troops to Miami in the middle of the summer. The following is his letter to Senator Platt that answers these concerns with an obvious promotional, less than truthful twist.

FLORIDA EAST COAST RAILWAY

President's Office
26 Broadway, N.Y.

Apr. 30'98

Dear Senator Platt,

This war with Spain may be a long one; it may be short. Regular troops are being sent to New Orleans, Mobile and Tampa. In other words in the Gulf sections that were infected with Yellow Fever last year. As far as I can learn from the newspapers, there has been no destination fixed for volunteers. I can hardly conceive it possible that the Government proposes to mobilize these volunteers in their separate States to await orders. It seems to me that they will send them South to be acclimated in the first place, and to be near at hand in the second. Troops sent to the Lower East Coast of Fla. would be put into a district which never has been infected, and would be entirely independent and isolated from the Gulf basis of operations, and yet so near the scene of action that they could be moved to the front just as quick as if at the present basis of operations. If located there, they will be on the Atlantic Coast, the healthiest summer point in the south. If it was thought best to locate a portion of them at St. Augustine, ample ground can be had for camping purposes. At St. A. we have an abundant supply of artesian water. It is true that it is strictly impregnated with lime, and might for a few days, be a laxative. In my judgment, Miami would be a preferable point for a large number of troops. You know something of the climate at Palm Beach. Miami is 68 miles further south. The climate is the same at Palm Beach. The strange part of it all is that the temperature during the summer months both at Miami and Palm Beach, will run from five to ten degrees lower than at

Jacksonville, Savannah, Charleston or other points 500, 600 and 700 miles further north. In one respect Miami is different from Palm Beach. The whole frontage on Biscayne Bay is limestone rock, covered with dense growth, principally of hard wood. At Miami, we have an inexhaustible supply of purest water. . . . I have built an iron water tower at Miami, 120 ft. in height. On the south side of the Miami River, across from the town, there is an unbroken stretch of five miles of bay front, most admirably adapted for camping purposes. A water pipe could very easily be extended to the camp, and thus an abundance of pure water be supplied. The drainage is excellent, and for the comfort of officers and men, they can depend upon the constant sea breeze. I don't believe there is a pleasanter location on the Atlantic Coast, south of Bar Harbor, to spend the summer in than at Miami. At my own expense, I have dredged a channel 12 ft. deep, up Biscayne Bay, from Cape Fla. a distance of about 8 miles. I am carrying a tri-weekly mail between Miami and Key West, with a side wheel steamer 286 ft. long, known as the "City of Key West". I also own the S. S. Miami, 240 ft. long on the water line, twin screw, built expressly for the trade between Miami and The Bahamas. In addition, I have another steamer (chartered) sailing under the Brazilian flag. Besides these, I have two stern wheel boats such as are used on the western rivers. With this fleet, we could put a large number of men into Key West at very short notice, or if the Government chose, she could send deep draft transports to the mouth of the Bay, and use our boats as transfer boats. . . . General Graham, in command of the Department of the Gulf, has been at Miami, and probably understands the situation thoroughly. I fancy however, that the best interests of the volunteer troops may require someone of greater influence than General Graham.

If you think it worth while to submit the facts as herein stated to the Government, and they are favorably acted upon, I shall feel that I have done the volunteer troops a good service.

With all good wishes, I am,

Very truly yours,

HM Flagler
President

Source: Letter, Henry M. Flagler to Senator T. C. Platt, April 30, 1898, National Archives Record Group 77.

J. K. Dorn
Miami During the Spanish American War, 1898

German born J. K. Dorn came to Miami when he was 20 years old from Winter Park, Florida soon after the 1895 freeze. He was an early owner of the Red Cross Pharmacy that later became J. Byrons Department Store. He was also a successful real estate developer and automobile dealer. He died in 1956. The following description was excerpted from a talk he gave to a joint Historical Association of Southern Florida and Miami Pioneers meeting on November 17, 1942.

In 1898 the war with Spain broke out. The *Maine* was wrecked in the harbor of Cuba, and of course all Miamians thought the war would be brought over to the Florida shores. In fact, we became so worried that we had the state build us a sand fort about a mile south of Brickell's Point, adjoining Commodore Roome's place. The state also sent us two 10-inch guns which we never used, but they were admired by all who saw them.

We had 7200 troops stationed in Miami and did they paint the town red! What we now call hot dog stands were all over the city. Townley Brothers, the only drug store, was doing a rushing business. In fact, they had six large barrels all connected at the top by a small pipe, all filled with water, made into lemonade, and it would take only a few hours to empty them.

One afternoon a couple of boys from Company L of Texas came out of Townley Brothers' store and walked over to what is now Budge's Hardware store. A big, burly Negro was coming down the sidewalk on what is now Miami Avenue. Two ladies were walking towards him. Instead of the negro stepping off the sidewalk and allowing the ladies to pass, he made the ladies get off and let him pass. This was too much for the boys from Texas. They grabbed this negro, gave him a good beating and started to string him up to a pine tree across the street. Some officers happened to come along just in time to prevent a tragedy, but the boys did string up the negro's shirt. The negro was taken back to colored town and everything was quiet until eight o'clock that night.

Negro town then was across the railroad tracks and Flagler Street, about 40 or 50 houses. That night Company L of Texas marched through colored town, pulled out their colts and shot out every kerosene lamp found burning. This caused a stampede of the colored people to Avenue G bridge on their way to Coconut Grove. Next morning our restaurants, hotels and stores were without help, so we sent a squad to Coconut Grove and promised them they would be protected, so they returned and by eleven o'clock were working again.

But that wasn't enough for the boys from Company L. The next night they marched north a mile, outside the city limits to a place where liquor was sold. Billy Woods was operating a saloon and he had a colored department. The boys went into the saloon and threw rocks at all the bottles standing on the counters. They were eventually quieted down and taken back to camp.

The troops caused so much trouble and dissension among the colored people that the people of Miami complained to the authorities and they were finally withdrawn from Miami and sent to Jacksonville and Tampa.

Source: J. K. Dorn, "Recollections of Early Miami," *Tequesta*, IX (1949), pp. 54-55.

Dr. Corrie Fowler
Battling "Yellow Jack," 1899

In the fall of 1899, yellow fever broke out in Miami. At the time, Miamians did not know that mosquitoes caused the dreaded disease and instead, believed that it was highly contagious. Because of this misconception, when someone became ill, a yellow flag was posted in front of their house and if someone died, all their personal belongings were burned. At first, Miamians fearful that yellow fever would kill the tourist season, tried to hide the outbreak from the general pubic. The public health official declared a quarantine anyway. Both Dr. Corrie Fowler and her husband Dr. Samuel Mills Fowler, were homeopathic physicians. They came to Miami in 1897 because Dr. Samuel Fowler was Henry Flagler's personal physician. The following year, their daughter, Corrie, married Julia Tuttle's son, Harry. The following account of the yellow fever epidemic and fire is derived from an unpublished manuscript written by Fae Cunningham MacArthur, Dr. Corrie Fowler's granddaughter.

In late summer of that year Grandmother and little Fae returned to Miami, leaving brother Mills in military school in Gainesville, Georgia. The family had sold their original home in Miami and there was no house available when they returned, so the young Tuttles, who were still honeymooning, wrote and invited them to move into the Miami Hotel, which was closed for the summer. . . . Also living at the hotel was

During the Spanish-American-Cuban War, locals came to the Royal Palm docks to view Spanish prisoners-of-war who were on their way to prison in Atlanta. Some Miamians bought buttons from their uniforms as souvenirs. (J.N. Chamberlain)

a Professor Hargroves—a dancing teacher, who had been permitted to give dancing lessons in the hotel's dining room. About this time Professor Hargroves boarded a South American banana boat which had put into port here, to buy fruit, and about ten days later [he] fell ill with yellow fever—the first case of the disease to make its appearance in Miami. An epidemic of the fever immediately swept the town, bringing on the now famous 'shotgun quarantine.' All the people who had been staying at the hotel or who had in any way contacted Mr. Hargroves, were taken aboard the old boat Biscayne to the middle of the Bay and held there for fifteen days. . . . Despite this precaution almost all those aboard came down with the fever. Among the few who did escape it was Mr. Dorn, and Mother. On their return to shore the hotel became a sort of hospital for the sick people who had been living there. The housekeeper for the hotel had her quarters on the third floor as did Grandmother. On the seventh day of Grandmother's illness—considered the crisis day, the housekeeper's oilstove exploded and set fire to the hotel. Grandmother's nurse had stepped into another patient's room—meanwhile the fire was raging outside Grandmother's door. She, too weak to

walk—frantic with fear but still preserving her physician's calm—bundled herself in a wool blanket—crawled to the stairway and rolled down the three flights with the flames leaping down the stairwell behind her. She managed to reach the porch and get into a chair. Men stood in the street and watched—afraid to come near because of the fever, but Sheriff John Frohock drafted three men to help him and they carried her, using the chair as a litter, to the Knapp Restaurant across the street. All the patients were rescued but the hotel was destroyed.

Source: Fae Cunningham MacArthur, "History of My Family in Florida," (unpublished manuscript, n.d.).

John C. Gramling
Building a Charity Hospital, 1908

John C. Gramling came to Miami from Alabama in 1898. He was a lawyer and served as Municipal and County Judge as well as State's Attorney. He was one of the prime movers behind the creation of Miami's first public hospital (excluding temporary emergency hospitals during the 1899 yellow fever epidemic.) He wrote the following history of the Miami Relief Association.

About the year 1908 the several forces in Miami joined in a community service on Thanksgiving day, and elected officers to what was then in existence, and known as the Miami Relief Association. Although I was not present at that meeting I was unanimously chosen as President of that association. I applied for and obtained a charter, not for profit, under the name of the Miami Relief Association, of which I was President, and fulfilled my duties to the best of my ability. I was Municipal Judge at that time.

North of what is now First Street, and Miami Avenue was practically nothing but old frame shacks, and I came in contact with people who were very ill, and some who died of various kinds of diseases, and surroundings of uninhabitable conditions. I solicited and obtained the free services of the physicians of Miami to wait on the destitute people. I believe that Dr. E. K. Jaudon and my brother, Dr. W. S. Gramling, were called on by me night and day more than any other of the physicians in Miami and they always responded to these calls gladly and willingly as though they were being paid for such services. In some instances I recall that Dr. P. T. Skaggs took charge of many calls and in a few of the cases Dr. Jackson. I recall sending to Dr. Huddleston some of them. However, Dr. Jaudon and I were of the opinion that if we had a charity hospital we could save the lives of many of these people.

In June of 1908 I obtained a charter for the Dade County Hospital Association with about fifteen Directors, and then went to Palm Beach and met Mr. Flagler and Mr. Parrott. Mr. Parrott was vice President of the Florida East Coast Railway, and told them of conditions in Miami and they agreed to give us two lots in Miami which we would select. We made selections time and time again, but there was opposition by the people living in the vicinity of the lots we selected, and it did not seem that we were progressing very much. However, I had pledged from the Carpenter's Union, labor sufficient to build a hospital and from the lumber yards . . . all of the physicians in Miami had pledged their services free, and the County had agreed to pay for every county patient $9.00, either for a month or less, and the City had agreed to pay for the city patients, but it seemed we could not get the lots on which to erect the building.

At this critical moment Mr. Frank B. Stoneman came to me and stated the Reverend Father Friend, who was the Catholic Priest in charge here at that time and T. W. Jackson, who was employed by the Florida East Coast Railway Company and C. W.

Schmidt, who owned and operated a restaurant in the building which is now known as the Roberts Hotel, had a meeting and that they had decided that this hospital must be built at once and that they were ready and willing to give their time and efforts to this work and thereupon we had a reorganization and Mr. Stoneman was elected President of the association and the five of us were elected as Directors.

We then purchased from P. Ullendorff, two lots on which now stands the American Legion Building, on the corner of Biscayne Boulevard and Seventh Street, at about $9,000 for the two lots and under very easy payments. We erected a small building and it was filled to overflowing before it was completed. I believe that Dr. E. K. Jaudon was the first physician who had charge of the hospital.

We raised money by public subscription for several years until we convinced the city and county that it was absolutely necessary to have a hospital because at the time we started to erect the hospital many people believed that we did not need a charity hospital because they were not aware of conditions at that time. When the expenses seemed to be beyond our power to raise we made a proposition to the city that we would deed them the property and let the city take it over with the understanding that it would always be operated as a charity hospital, and by a unanimous vote the city took over our burdens, and soon thereafter, probably a year or two, plans were prepared for the present hospital, which is now known as the Jackson Memorial Hospital. . . .

Just prior to the erection of the hospital, while I was municipal Judge and President of the Miami Relief Association, I was called out in "colored town" and I saw that in some buildings out there that things were in a deplorable condition. In one large building, I saw about five or six negroes, all of whom were supposed to die within a few days from different kinds of diseases, so I appealed to Mayor F. H. Wharton, who is now City Manager, and requested him to have erected on the lot adjoining the City Jail, which was then located in a small frame building on Southeast First Street near the Railroad, a tent, to house these sick negroes, as I was in fear of some kind of epidemic breaking out if some sanitary measures were not taken. Mr. Frank Hardee, who was then Chief of Police, together with Mayor Wharton, took charge of the situation immediately and erected the tent, which was quite a large affair, and put cots in it and had one portion for the women and one part for the men, and got some physicians in attendance on them, and to the best of my recollection, not a one of them died, but all were cured but those who were in the last stages of tuberculosis, and they were so patched up, that Mr. Wharton and I appealed to the Florida East Coast Railway for passes to get these people free passage from whence they came, and we procured many passes for both white and colored people to return to their homes, in order to clean up conditions in Miami.

Source: John C. Gramling, "The First Charity Hospital in Dade County, Florida," (unpublished manuscript, Miami, Florida, c1935).

Business is Booming

Mateo Encinosa
A New Industry for Miami

The Miami Metropolis published a special magazine section in 1901 that reviewed the progress of business, education and agriculture and highlighted the leading movers and shakers. One such businessman was Cuban born cigar manufacturer, M. Encinosa. The Cubans brought the cigar industry to Key West in 1867 where it flourished until labor unrest caused many manufacturers to relocate to Tampa at about the same time Miami was incorporated. The Metropolis encouraged the cigar industry which began with Luis Gonzalez who was profiled in the first issue of The Metropolis in May 1896. On July 30, two days after the City of Miami was incorporated, M. Encinosa and Company sent the first box of cigars out of their Miami factory. Although both Miami and Jacksonville had a few cigar factories and wished for more, Tampa quickly dominated the market for clear Havana cigars throughout the United States.

M. Encinosa & Co.
Cigar Manufacturers

He who ten years hence essays to write of Miami's industries will of necessity devote much space to her cigar factories. At present the industry of manufacturing cigars is in its infancy, though indeed a lusty and promising infant. Its chief representative is the factory of M. Encinosa & Co., which turns out as good "a smoke" as the most fastidious and critical devotee of the weed could wish. The leading brands manufactured are "Ever Faithful," "Tourist," and "Something New," and in their making neither expense of mate-

rial or careful workmanship is spared. The very best Cuban tobacco—and that means the very best tobacco in the world—used; while Mr. Encinosa, with many years of practical experience in the business, gives his closest personal attention to the production of a perfect cigar, whose reputation can be staked on the satisfaction it affords the purchaser.

Mr. Encinosa is a native of Bejucal, Cuba, where he was born in 1866. He came to Key West in 1873, and there learned the cigar business. He came to Miami last October, and bought out a small factory which was then in operation, and established his present business, which has flourished ever since like a green bay tree. The product of his factory is steadily gaining in popular favor, and a constantly increasing output is necessary to meet the growing demands of the trade. If conscientious effort to produce a first class article and unremitting attention to business count for anything, the business of this factory assuredly will grow into proportions that will make it a source of pride to the city.

Source: "M. Encinosa & Co," *The Illustrated Edition of Miami Metropolis*, October, 1901.

Ruby Padgett
A Prize Essay, 1904

The following essay was written by a 14-year-old school girl. It won the first prize offered by Professor R. E. Hall for the best essay on "Dade County and Its Resources, written by a pupil of the Dade County Public Schools in any grade up to the eighth." It was published in an early Miami City Directory. Ruby was the youngest in a family of five children. Her father was a farmer. The city directory lists the Padgett family as living at 222 Avenue D which would be in the neighborhood of today's 9th Street and North Miami Avenue.

DADE COUNTY AND ITS RESOURCES

Just a few years ago [Dade County] was a literal wilderness, unknown, unpeopled, and unavailable. The climate is delightful, the winters are mild, and the summers are pleasant. There is no place anywhere that is healthier than in Dade county. There is no place in the United States that is as desirable for an all-the-year round home as this county. The surface is very rocky and the rock is very useful in building roads and houses. . . .

The people who farm grow tomatoes, beans, celery, cabbages, cucumbers, eggplants, watermelons,

Irish potatoes, sweet potatoes, beets, onions, peppers, turnips, and lettuce. Tomato growing is carried on more extensively than any other vegetable product in Dade county, thousands of acres being planted each year. . . .

The principal fruits of Dade county are mangoes, avocado, pears, pineapples, guavas, sapodillas, oranges, grapefruit, bananas, limes, lemons, cocoanuts, grapes, pawpaws, maumee apples, kumquats, Tahiti limes, strawberries, sugar apples, peaches, Japanese plums, figs, Japan persimmons, and Catley guavas.

Much has been said within the last few years on the subject of fruit raising. Some take the position that oranges and grapefruit cannot be successfully grown in Dade county, especially in the more southern portion, where rock abounds; others have taken the position that this county will in the near future become the greatest citrus-growing county in the State.

Lumbering will in the near future become a very important industry. . . .

The largest city of Dade county is Miami. Perhaps there is no place along the line of the Florida East Coast that has enjoyed a more permanent prosperity than the city of Miami. The largest school of Dade county is in Miami. The educational advantages of Dade county are most excellent. In Miami there is a large school building with the very best of teachers. Over 400 scholars attend.

During the summer the county has built one of the finest steel bridges over the Miami river that is in the State.

A fine jail, made of Dade county rock, has been completed; also, the finest courthouse in the State has lately been finished. It is also built of rock.

Dredging by the Florida East Coast railway has been carried on for the deep water harbor. The making of Miami a deep waterport, where ships from all the world can enter is a very important factor in the building of the Magic City. When completed it will make Miami one of the most important commercial centers on the Atlantic coast. It is also expected that Miami will be made a very important naval center, which will add to its greatness as a commercial city. . . .

These are the principal resources of Dade County.

Ruby Padgett,

Aged Fourteen Years
7th Grade
Miami, Fla.

Source: *Official Directory of the City of Miami and Nearby Towns* (Miami: Allen R. Parrish, 1904), pp. 63-64.

Engineering the Land

G. Duncan Brossier
Creating Government Cut, 1905

From the beginning, Miami longed for a deepwater port. The first step toward this goal came on March 14, 1905 with the opening of Government Cut, which also created what would later be called Fisher Island. Spoil banks from the dredging marked the beginning of Dodge, Watson and Lummus Islands. A short time later, the Port of Miami moved to 6th Street from its original site on the Miami River. It remained there until 1964 when all operations moved to Dodge Island and the old port became Bicentennial Park. G. Duncan Brossier, who came to Miami in 1891, was a prominent Miami realtor and a leader in civic affairs.

On one summer's day in 1905 the entire populace of the City of Miami was called upon to celebrate the biggest factor in the development of Greater Miami. The occasion was the completing of the cut through the island from Biscayne Bay to the Atlantic Ocean. On that day the muddy waters of Biscayne Bay were destined to mingle with the turquoise blue of the Atlantic Ocean.

For several months, the P. Sanford Ross Dredging Company had been engaged in digging the channel from [the] Miami side of the bay to the ocean. They had proceeded far enough with their dredging operations that the honorable mayor of Miami, then John Sewell, declared a holiday for the purpose of witnessing this great event. The entire population of 3,500 people were present and it was a gala day.

There was a great deal of excitement, as with each dip of the dredge the workers would cut a few feet closer to the ocean. The people were lined up on both sides of the cut making merry, forecasting, prophesying what the completion of the channel would mean to Miami. Then, for some unknown reason, the dredging operation stopped—the dipper dug its nose in the sand and refused to budge. Something had gone wrong. When the superintendent of the dredge announced that he had experienced a breakdown, and that joining of these two waters would have to be postponed for another day, you can imagine the great disappointment to the patriarchs who had come so far, under such trying conditions, to witness this event.

However, John Sewell, the man who never had been found wanting in any crucial moment, came to the rescue. With a spade he began to dig and soon the sand was flying in every direction. In less than 30 minutes a little stream from the bay, following the line of the trench made by Mr. Sewell, joined the waters of the Atlantic Ocean. The current being very rapid and the pressure on the bay side rather strong, it was only a few hours until the cut widened from a foot to nearly ten feet, and the next day, those of us who visited the scene, found that the bay had cut a path through the island to a width over 500 feet.

And this was the beginning of Miami's harbor development!

Source: Capt. G. Duncan Brossier, quoted in, John Sewell, *Miami Memoirs, A New Pictorial Edition of John Sewell's Own Story* (1933), ed. by Arva Moore Parks (Miami: Arva Parks & Co., 1987), p. 191.

Hoyt Frazure
Draining the Everglades, 1909

Hoyt Frazure and his family moved to Miami from Kissimmee in 1905. They lived in Buena Vista, Allapattah and Miami while Hoyt was growing up. When he was a teenager, the family operated "The Frazure House," a boarding house on what is now Biscayne Boulevard and N. E. 1st Street. He later wrote his memoirs that were published by The Miami Herald. Frazure's description of "Draining the Everglades" provides an insight to the popular thinking of the day when it was perfectly acceptable to drain the wetlands and sell "land by the gallon."

It took a governor with a name like Napoleon Bonaparte Broward to drain the Everglades but not even he could do it in four years.

Albert W. Gilchrist, who became governor in 1909, completed the canal system that Governor Broward started.

When I was a boy I heard a lot about the "rich Everglades." Everybody was looking forward to seeing the vast wet area drained; when it would be opened to farming. People talked of the Everglades as though the area was going to be the "Promised Land."

All kinds of advertising and promotion schemes were worked up for selling the Everglades as the time approached when the drainage canals were to be opened. I think the best one I ever heard was that of the Tatum Brothers, prominent Miami real estate operators.

The Tatum Brothers—there were four, J. H., S. M., B. B. and J. R.—set up a bucket dredge on a barge and anchored it in the south fork of the Miami

River, at NW 22nd Avenue and about 11th Street. Then they put full page ads in *The Miami Herald* and in the old *Miami Metropolis* announcing that "The Tatum Brothers are Draining the Everglades."

I have good reason to remember the dredge—of seeing it bringing up buckets full of muck from the bottom of the shallow stream; of seeing the heavy black smoke boiling out of the smoke stack; of hearing the boiler blow off steam when the sweating Negro fireman put too much fat pine wood on the fire. . . .

The Tatum Brothers had a contract to sell a big chunk of land lying west of 22nd Avenue. At that time the country was swamp as far as you could see. When you stepped off the west side of the Avenue you were "overboard."

Looking west, you could see nothing but sawgrass and cypress. All the area where the Miami International Airport is now located was under water.

They cut up the swamp in five, 10 and 20-acre blocks and sold it off.

It might have been under water then but when the drainage of the Everglades was completed these "farms" would be "the most productive in the world." So the Tatum Brothers said.

At that time the Miami Canal was being dredged to Lake Okeechobee, but the public couldn't see any progress. A dam had been put in the canal at about where NW 36th Street is now to prevent drainage before the canal was completed. Otherwise, the canal would have drained and there wouldn't have been enough water left to float the dredge.

So the Tatum Brothers decided to provide the visual evidence that the Everglades really were being drained.

I don't want to give the idea that the Tatum Brothers were crooks. . . .

Although the scheme used by the Tatum Brothers might land you in jail now, in those days it was perfectly acceptable. The old law of trade—"Let the Buyer Beware"—was still pretty much the rule. . . .

The black earth brought up by the dredge dipper equaled the proverbial riches of the Nile valley. It must have made a favorable impression on buyers—and that was the idea. . . .

I remember hearing a man say:

"They just operate the dredge on the days that they put ads in the papers. One week they put the soil on the right bank and the next week they take it off the right bank and put it on the left bank.". . .

Within a few months after that the Miami Canal was completed to Lake Okeechobee. Then the dam was removed.

Water flowed like a torrent out of the canal and down the Miami River, and it continued to flow uncontrolled for weeks. The water level in the Everglades steadily dropped and the sawgrass country became so dry that a mule could walk across it without muck shoes. . . .

The opening of the Miami Canal made it possible to develop Hialeah, Miami Springs and Opa-Locka during the Boom.

But some people predicted that those who drained the Everglades would be sorry. During periods of drought the muck dried out and cracked open. Fires swept through the sawgrass and ignited the muck. Acrid smoke blew into Miami and our eyes smarted from the fumes.

Then, in wet years, the area was beset by floods; and people who had homes there had to use rowboats.

The last major floods occurred in 1947 and 1948, when the town, built in areas that one time was Everglades, went under water.

After that the Central and Southern Florida Flood Control District was organized and millions of dollars were spent by federal and state agencies to prevent disastrous floods and to protect South Florida from the effects of over-drainage.

I've often heard conservation-minded people decry the drainage of the Everglades and express the wish that we could return the original condition.

Looking back, I can agree that it would be idyllic; but the idea is far from being practical. A major part of Dade's population now lives in areas that once was under water for a good part of the year.

It's a highly complex subject that can be solved only by the best minds among engineers and scientists.

But I'm sure that pioneers will agree with me when I express the hope that we hasten along with a program of conservation and management that will provide some kind of balance between expanding developments and the rapid retreat of the natural scene.

Source: Hoyt Frazure as told to Nixon Smiley, "Memories of Old Miami," *Miami Herald*, 1969, pp. 17-18.

By 1908, Miami began to look more like a small, sedate southern town than a wild West boom town. Business shifted to Flagler Street and most of the original wooden buildings on Avenue D (Miami Avenue) were gone. (MN)

Sarah R. W. Palmer
Miami a City Beautiful, 1911

Sarah R. W. Palmer was the granddaughter of Dr. Henry Perrine who the Seminoles killed at Indian Key in 1840. Her mother, Hester, who was a young girl at the time, survived the Indian attack by hiding in a turtle kraal. Mrs. Palmer was one of the beneficiaries of the 1897 Perrine Grant settlement whereby the heirs of Dr. Perrine were awarded clear title to his 1838 grant that included an entire South Dade township. She came to Miami in the early years of the 20th Century and was interested in poetry, Florida history, horticulture and beautification. Her grandson, Perrine Palmer, Jr., served as mayor of Miami in the 1940s.

City of Magic and bewildering hours,
Of dreams of enchantment and beautiful flowers.
Land of whispering pine and of rustling palm,
Where Old Ocean soothes the rough waves to a calm,
As the swift flowing tide from Mexican seas
City of bright sunshine cooled by dim clouds,
Of lovers' entrancement when moonlight enshrouds.
Land of tradition of warriors strong,
Where gay plumaged birds fill the air with sweet song.
Old Ocean's cool kiss on thy River's warm mouth,
Proclaims thee, Miami, the Queen of the South.

Many opportunities for permanent beauty offer themselves to us Miamians, which if we fail in seizing now will be lost forever. Parks along the bay and river are necessities not requiring much argument; but do Miamians realize the value of a system of small parks throughout the city? Our climate being our most wonderful asset, we should utilize every device for its easy enjoyment. With the denuding of the hammocks incident to the rapid settling of this section, soon all trace of the marvelous tropical growths will disappear unless some plan of preservation of specimens is adopted. If the city would secure spaces for a small square or circle every five or ten blocks in all directions and would plant them with native trees from our hammocks, posterity could not have greater cause for gratitude. . . .

A beautiful landscape left as nature formed it calls forth emotions that the best railway cutting or embankment cannot arouse. . . . There is a charm in the old irregularities of elevation and the street lines that served the uses of the people faithfully and bear many charming historical records. Engineering skill has its place, but as the rules of grammar cannot give the last grace to discourse, so the engineer's lines cannot give the last and best graces to our streets and parks. . . . Excessive leveling is as bad as excessive seeking for straightness and right angles. . . . There is a tendency to overplant. Trees should be fewer and planted singly and by and by they will come to have characters of their own. The varieties should be labeled for public instruction. Walks should be first convenient. Superfluous toil kills beauty. Severe simplicity is best.

Source: "Miami A City Beautiful," *Miami Herald*, August 7, 1911, p. 3.

Living History

Coral Gables Merrick House
907 Coral Way
Coral Gables, Florida

(Bob McCabe)

In 1898, Solomon Merrick, a Congregational minister, and his 12-year-old son George came to Miami from Massachusetts. Merrick purchased a 640 acre homestead in the "Back Country" and he and his son began planting grapefruit trees. The following year, Mrs. Althea Merrick and the other Merrick children joined the family. At first they lived in a simple wooden house they called "Guavonia."

In 1906, as the family grapefruit groves began to bear, the Merrick family prospered and built a new house, designed by Mrs. Merrick, out of "coral rock," (oolithic limestone) that was quarried at what later became Venetian Pool. They named the house Coral Gables and their grapefruit plantation became known as the Coral Gables Plantation.

In 1921, George Merrick launched his planned subdivision named Coral Gables on his family's grove land. This was the beginning of what ultimately became the City of Coral Gables in 1925.

In 1976, the City of Coral Gables acquired the house from W.L. Philbrick who had purchased the house and founded the Merrick Manor Foundation in an effort to preserve it.

Today, "Coral Gables Merrick House" is restored and open to the public for tours and select events. It is filled with many period pieces, as well as Merrick family items.

Looking Ahead

The Florida Flower Magazine
Forseeing Miami's Future, 1911

The Florida Flower with a sub headline that read: "It Blossoms Weekly," was a weekly magazine published in Tampa, Florida. Its July 15, 1911 issue was devoted to Miami's 15th birthday celebration and contained some remarkable descriptive information about Miami and its people. Miami's dream to become a great Hemispheric City began at the time the city was founded and continued throughout its history.

MIAMI

In the Fifteenth Year of Progress—A Thriving and Optimistic Town—Destined to Become a Great Shipping Point—A Tropical Prosperous Place—The Los Angeles of the Atlantic Coast

Miami is now in the fifteenth year of progress, uninterrupted and satisfactory; a thriving and optimistic youngster; sturdy, alert, confident; looking into a bright and interesting future which will reach out over the Seven Seas.

The Florida Peninsula, instead of being the jumping-off place of the United States, is the gateway looking into the world, and Miami, her first city, is at the very entrance of a new lock, which will open into the rich commerce of South America, Australia, Europe and many islands of the sea. The key which will open it is intelligent publicity, such as will be distributed broadcast by *The Florida Flower Magazine.*

Miami in the future is destined to become a great shipping point. The harbor will accommodate ocean liners and freighters, and the cereals and products of the drained Everglades will be carried to many countries. In return, products from the tropics and the West Indies will pass through Miami on the way north, over the railroad extension from Key West, by aid of the Panama Canal. The far-seeing mind can easily discern the possibilities of the future and build upon them. . . .

Miami, without a doubt, is to be the Los Angeles of the Atlantic Coast. While considerable stress has been laid on her lands, fruits and garden truck, yet the climate is her greatest asset. Miami is a good summer town, being cool and comfortable, and her winter climate is of surpassing splendor and of health-giving properties.

A new trend of thought, too, is liberated in Miami—that of confidence and hope, twin builders of prosperity, material and spiritual success. Miami is fifteen years old and note her remarkable progress. It will be a safe guide to what she will be in the future.

Source: "Miami," *The Florida Flower: It Blossoms Weekly*, July 15, 1911, p. 1.

Technology and Transportation

Flying Into the Future, 1911

The highlight of Miami's 15th birthday celebration was the city's first airplane flight arranged by super promoter E. G. Sewell. Most of the town gathered at Flagler's golf links, now the Metro Justice Complex, to witness this historic event. The Wright Brothers' plane came in on the train and was towed to the golf grounds. The program called for "Birdman" Gill to fly four flights on two different days—July 20-21, 1911. During the fourth flight on the second day, E. G. Sewell went along and became the first Miamian to fly in a plane. The following accounts from The Miami Metropolis *and* The Miami Herald, *describe these history-making flights.*

Everybody who could, and its seemed that nearly everybody in Miami found time and opportunity to do so, turned out yesterday afternoon to see the demonstration of aerial navigation or the flying machine fly and every one of them came away satisfied.

It was a great exhibition and one that proved to the satisfaction of the most skeptical that the time is not far distant when the art of flying and the machines with which to do it will be so thoroughly perfected that travel through the air will become an every day occurrence.

There were fully five thousand persons on the aviation grounds—the golf grounds. They went by boat, by auto, by wheel and they all got there and filled the observation stand, crowded the field and blocked the roads with autos and other vehicles. It took a full company of militia to keep the field clear enough for the aviator to operate his machine. . . .

THE FIRST FLIGHT

The machine was brought out from the hangar promptly at 4 o'clock and after making a run of several yards on the ground, Gill started up in the air on his tour of inspection. After circling the aviation grounds several times and flying so as to make the figure "8," he descended to the hangar to prepare for the next feat. The crowd was very generous with applause for Gill's work.

ALTITUDE FLIGHT

The second ascent was altitude flight. The machine arose with the grace of a bird, and went soaring up in the air to a height of several hundred feet. Then the famous "spiral glide" was performed. Starting from an altitude of about 1,000 feet, the birdman came down in a spiral formation, long, graceful, circles being inscribed in the air. The feat is one of the most beautiful performed by any air pilot.

HAIR RAISING STUNT

But the hair-raising stunt is the "motor glide." From several hundred feet above the ground the motor is shut off and the airship appears to be falling to the earth. Everyone feels his heart and stop breathing in fear that the machine is going to smash on the ground; but it is only in the show. Just before the ground is reached, the machine is tilted upward again and rises from the earth.

Source: "Bird-Man Gill Made Grand Flights," *Miami Metropolis*, July 21, 1911, p. 1.

E.G. Sewell Takes Off

A fourth flight was made yesterday afternoon and Mr. Gill took Mr. E. G. Sewell as a passenger. The flight was not a sensational one, but the fact that a passenger was carried made it doubly interesting.

TELLS OF EXPERIENCE

In speaking about this "going up in the air," Mr. Sewell said:

"It was the finest ride I ever experienced, the breeze was fine; the scenery the greatest ever. The Everglades, the drainage canal, the city of Miami, Atlantic ocean and big steamers pass all being in plain view."

"We passed some birds and they had to duck to get out of our way. We went up about a thousand feet and the sensation was one I will never forget. However, there was never a moment of the time I was up that I did not enjoy it.". . .

To Mr. Sewell belongs the never-to-be-taken-away honor of being the first Miamian, in fact the first Dade county man to go up in the air and the first man in all Florida to go up in a Wright machine, for this is the first time a Wright machine has made a flight anywhere in this state.

Source: "Among Clouds Gill Climbed in Daring Flights," *Miami Herald*, July 22, 1911, p. 1.

The End of an Era

Henry Flagler
Passing of a Giant, 1913

A few days after Henry Flagler's 82nd birthday, the "Extension Special" left Miami for Key West across his Oversees Railroad. Ten thousand people greeted Flagler in Key West—bands played, whistles blew and children threw roses in his path. "We did it," he said with tears in his eyes, "now I can die in peace." A year later, the aging Flagler slipped and fell down the marble steps of his Palm Beach mansion. He never recovered from the fall. He died on May 20, 1913. The following article is an editorial that ran in The Miami Herald.

Just as the seeds of development which he planted are bursting into the full foliage, flower and fruitage of progress and prosperity the great developer of the East Coast of Florida is compelled to cease his activities and take his place in those silent halls prepared for all who live. . . .

While the generation of which Mr. Flagler came, has seen many men of great constructive ability, there were not many of them who achieved more for mankind than he. Beginning his creative work in this state after he had well passed middle life, he persisted in his plans of development until he had created an empire out of what was a barren and hopeless wilderness. With the far-seeing eye of the prophet, he saw in the East Coast of Florida the possibilities of opening up a new land where thousands of men and women could plant their farms and groves, build up their homes and develop communities into towns and cities filled with beautiful dwellings, stately churches and splendid schools. . . .

Passing judgment on his own work in building up and developing the East Coast, Mr. Flagler, himself said, "It is pleasant for me to believe that I have been able to give opportunity to a large number of men to make homes for themselves, who might not otherwise have had them." And, perhaps, no other statement could quite so well set forth the real object of Mr. Flagler in building his great road from Jacksonville to Key West. . . .

History gives credit to men who have gone out into the wilderness and have conquered it for civilization. We have glorified the pioneer who, axe in hand, has subdued the forests and the prairies and replaced them with farms and gardens, towns and cities. Mr. Flagler was a pioneer, endowed with all the courage and the hope and the vision of the pioneers who made America. His position was a peculiar one in that his pioneering was for others and he began it backed by the great wealth accumulated in his early manhood. But he commenced his task with all the disadvantages of his early pioneer prototype. He was advised by his associates not to spend his money in an enterprise doomed to failure. The cost of the great work, he saw would be enormous, and in the nature of things, could not yield, in his lifetime, any adequate returns. But he saw, and pushed forward, until the great work, greater than any one individual had ever undertaken, alone, had been accomplished.

Source: "The Master Builder," *Miami Herald*, May 23, 1913, p. 4.

Carl Fisher, created the concept of Dixie Highway to connect the mid-West to Miami. In October 1915, the Dixie Highway Pathfinders crossed the Buena Vista Arch near NE 40th Street and 2nd Avenue. (Alice Wood)

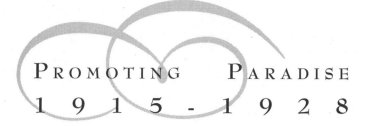

PROMOTING PARADISE
1915-1928

chapter three

"The sun and its fruits are certainly the first and the staying ingredient in The Great Florida Boom, which in the last five years has . . . crept over the country, invading houses, unsettling the settled, disturbing nest eggs, enriching advertising columns, employing the trained and untrained publicity men, enticing the rich, giving joy to the speculators of North and South and finally forcing over one hundred and ten millions of people to "Think of Florida."

> Ida M. Tarbell
> *"Florida and Then What?*
> *Impressions of the Boom"*
> McCalls Magazine, *May 1926*

Once Biscayne Boulevard was created, it became the street for hotels. During the Boom, four new hotels—the Alcazar, Everglades, Watson and Columbus and an addition to the McAllister went up at the same time.

With the death of Henry Flagler in 1913, Miami entered a new era. For the first time since its founding, the young city was on its own and the Flagler interests would no longer be the dominate force behind growth and development. Other factors also influenced this change in direction. The railroad lost its preeminent position after Carl Fisher created the Dixie Highway in 1915 and Henry Ford introduced the inexpensive mass-produced "Tin Lizzie." Now, many Americans could hop in their cars and drive to Miami. Fisher represented a new breed of leaders who viewed publicity and advertising as the key to South Florida's future. His promotional skills, along with other super salesmen like "Ev" Sewell, George Merrick and William Jennings Bryan, thrust the Miami area into national consciousness as a modern paradise. By the early 1920s, their advertising and marketing campaigns, combined with abundant land, new roads and the availability of the automobile, created a tourist and real estate boom that was unprecedented in American history. The Boom of the 1920s became a proper noun.

By 1925, Miami's population had grown from 30,000 in 1920 to more than 130,000 people. It also had a glamorous new identity as "America's Playground." Spectacles like polo games, speed boat races and horse races attracted an ever increasing number of pleasure-seeking tourists, as did nationally known jazz orchestras like Paul Whiteman and Jan Garber. Yet the endless hype, fun and frenetic real estate speculation were symptomatic of deeper problems. America's shaky financial structure relied more and more on the dreams and illusion of get-rich-quick schemes, publicity and advertising. For Miami, as well as the rest of the nation, it was only a matter of time until reality burst illusion's bubble and turned the dream into a nightmare.

∽ Slogans and Sacrifice

Once Miami boosters discovered the effects of advertising, not even America's entry into war could slow down the urge to sell Miami. While Miami had always had its boosters, "Ev" Sewell, who got his start as chairman of Miami's 15th birthday celebration, was clearly the leader of the parade. He launched Miami's first national advertising campaign in 1916 with the clever slogan: "Miami—Where Summer Spends the Winter." The response was so positive that local hotels and rooming houses could not handle the overflow crowd. (To ease the crunch, local preachers asked people to invite tourists into their homes.) Sewell also encouraged national figures like three time presidential candidate, William Jennings Bryan, to become a resident and local booster. A legendary orator, Bryan would draw more than 6,000 people to his Royal Palm Park Sunday School class that quickly became a tourist attraction. If it hadn't been for the war that America entered in April 1917, the Boom would have probably started in 1916.

Sewell, however, was not going to let a war slow the city's progress. Like Flagler during the Spanish-American-Cuban War, he saw the war as a new opportunity for Miami. By October 1917, he had convinced the Navy to open one of the nation's first flying schools at Dinner Key in Coconut Grove. Other military installations followed.

The presence of the "daring young men in their flying machines" bolstered the economy. Locals entertained the servicemen and provided them a home away from home. Thousands of young men registered for the draft and enlisted in the service. Others joined the Red Cross or supported local war bond drives. Sometimes, however, this patriotic zeal fueled by wartime propaganda went too far. Federal agencies like Herbert Hoover's Food Administration and George Creel's Committee on Public Information bombarded the public with patriotic messages. Federal sedition legislation undermined free speech. Anti-German hysteria forced locals with German backgrounds, notably baker John Seybold, to go to inordinate lengths to prove their patriotism. Some zealots even criticized the White Temple Methodist Church for performing the Messiah because composer Handel was German.

∽ Speed and Spectacle

On November 11, 1918, the Great War was over. Miamians celebrated with a parade down Flagler Street and, like the rest of the nation, eagerly returned to what President Harding called "normalcy." Miami's promoters, however, never looked back. They embarked on another advertising campaign. Capitalizing on a national mood of victory and self-righteousness, South Florida positioned itself as the nation's playground and land of opportunity.

"Ev" Sewell and the Miami Chamber of Commerce went to work to make the Naval Air Station a permanent facility. This effort almost started another war between the Chamber of Commerce and the people of Coconut Grove. Groveites incorporated as a town in 1919 in order to have more clout against the downtown developers.

By the early 1920s, thousands and thousands of people from all over the country sold their homes and businesses, packed up their belongings in the family car and began their hopeful trek to Florida via the Dixie Highway. One visitor reported that everyone in Miami lived, breathed and sold real estate and for a while, the city reportedly issued 60 new real estate licenses a day. As the mania progressed, residents placed "Not for Sale" signs on their lawns to keep speculators at bay.

A group of aggressive salesmen called "binder boys" flocked to Flagler Street to sell land to eager buyers. What they sold were "binders" or down-pay-

The most important promoter of Miami from its 15th anniversary celebration in 1911 until his death in 1940 was Ev Sewell (left) seen here with Miami publicity director Hamilton Wright. (SPA)

ments that would hold the land until full payment was made. The demand was so heavy, that often people could sell their binders for profit and the binders would turn over two or three times as the day progressed, with people making money on each sale and not even bothering to ever take possession of the land. It was not unusual for entire subdivisions to sell out in one day—many sight unseen.

George Merrick, a visionary and master salesman, sold a dream—"Where Your Castles in Spain are Made Real"—in his newly created Coral Gables subdivision, the first planned city in Florida. He hired William Jennings Bryan to give lectures at Venetian Pool on the joys of Coral Gables. Airplane designer Glenn Curtiss, in concert with James Bright, built Hialeah and Miami Springs. Curtiss also created the Moorish fantasy of Opa-Locka. Other romantically titled subdivisions, like Aladdin City and Fairlawn spread out across Dade County. While some of the subdivisions were built, it was not unusual to see advertising billboards, grandiose entrance gates, sidewalks, street signs and salesmen—yet not a single home under construction.

Downtown Miami filled with skyscrapers and lost its small town look. To deal with the growing me-tropolis that was spreading out in all directions, the city adopted the Chaille Plan. It divided the city into four sections with Flagler Street and Miami Avenue as the starting point. It also abolished the town council and adopted the progressive commission-manager form of government and then elected five bank presidents to the city commission.

Greater Miami was born in 1925 after a majority of electors voted to annex Lemon City, Allapattah, Silver Bluff, Little River and Coconut Grove into the City of Miami. A new architectural style called Mediterranean or Spanish Revival overtook the city. Before the Boom ended, South Florida sported not one but three replicas of Spain's famed Giralda Tower—*The Miami Daily News* building and the Roney Plaza and Biltmore Hotels. The glorious Olympia Theater, built by Paramount in 1926, created a grand air-conditioned movie palace with a Spanish "outdoor" courtyard complete with fake twinkling stars and gossamer clouds.

Miami Beach also flourished during the Boom under the leadership of Carl Fisher, the Lummus brothers and the family of John Collins. The Beach, in contrast to the more stuffy aura of Palm Beach, attracted wealthy northern industrialists with its glamour and

(John Gillan)

Living History

Opa-Locka City Hall
777 Sharazad Boulevard
Opa-Locka

Opa-Locka was originally named "Opatishawockalocka," from the Seminole word meaning "big island covered with many trees in the swamps." It was the inspiration of famous aviator Glenn Curtiss, who also developed Hialeah. Prompted by Curtiss' vision, Bernhardt Muller, a famous New York architect, wove the story of *The One Thousand and One Tales From the Arabian Nights* into his themed Boom-time city incorporated in 1926. The end of the Boom marked the end of Curtiss' work in Opa-Locka and the planned city was never completed. The remnants of these early days, however, provide one of the most fascinating architectural exhibits in Dade County. The city's Moorish motif is best seen in the Opa-Locka City Hall that was completed just weeks before the devastating 1926 Hurricane. It has recently been restored to its original splendor. Each year the City of Opa-Locka celebrates its heritage with an Arabian Nights Festival. Opa-Locka is the only incorporated city in Dade County where the majority of the citizens are African Americans.

fast life. Exclusive (though illegal) gambling clubs and pari-mutuel betting flourished and illicit liquor was always available. New hotels sprouted in Miami Beach, a winter "polo set" emerged, and exclusive, highly restricted social clubs opened.

"Restricted" was the euphemism of the day for excluding Jews. Carl Fisher and other hotel operators and developers on Miami Beach often excluded them from hotels and private clubs and prohibited them from buying property in certain areas. As a result, a Jewish enclave grew south of Lincoln Road that served as a point of demarcation between restricted and non-restricted Miami Beach.

When national prohibition became law in 1920, Miami, dry since 1913, was already awash in illegal booze. Its incredibly open coastline was an easy destination for the "rum-runners" who used high powered speedboats to bring liquor in from the Bahamas. Law enforcement was a joke, not only when it came to prohibition, but in other areas of vice like prostitution and gambling as well. In 1928, Al Capone, attracted to the wide-open land of opportunity, bought a house on Palm Island and shocked the town into realizing what it was becoming. While religious leaders decried the tolerance for "sin," they had little influence on stemming the ever-growing tide of illegal activities that many believed were necessary to keep the tourists happy.

Greater Miami promoters and developers used both speed and spectacle to lure tourists and would-be-buyers to the area. Fisher introduced polo to Miami Beach and held speed boat races off of Star Island. Glenn Curtiss and James Bright brought horse racing and jai-alai to Hialeah along with pari-mutuel betting, which at the time, was illegal. Fulford-by-The-Sea, now North Miami Beach, opened a speedway. Nearby, in today's North Miami, an enterprising promoter named Arthur Voetglin opened Pueblo Feliz (Joyful City) a Spanish village themed entertainment center. Coral Gables brought in world-class entertainers and celebrities and held elaborately themed parties and elegant affairs.

❧ Separate Worlds

Miami's frenetic Boom also impacted what was then called Colored Town. Increased need for labor lured black workers into the area. Colored Town became extremely overcrowded and any effort to expand the neighborhood was met with white opposition that sometimes turned violent. The 1920s brought a national resurgence of the Ku Klux Klan that promoted both white supremacy and nativism. Many local political leaders, as well as members of the police department, were known Klansmen. In this era, many accepted the Klan as a sort of white fraternity. The Klan

During the 1920s, the Ku Klux Klan experienced a nationwide revival. In Miami, KKK members participated in respectable events like the 1926 "Fiesta of the American Tropics" parade down Flagler Street. (Gleason Waite Romer, MDPL)

had a large headquarters building across from Ada Merritt Junior High School in today's Little Havana. The Klan marched in full regalia in local parades and even held an annual children's circus to raise money for local charities.

Despite this new image of respectability, the Klan continued to promote its old forms of intolerance. Following its 1915 revival, the Klan not only harassed blacks but threatened Catholics, Jews and immigrants as well. Members tarred and feathered several ministers, both white and black, who preached tolerance and equality, and drove them out of town. Simultaneously, thousands of black Miamians joined the black nationalist movement known as the United Negro Improvement Association under the leadership of Marcus Garvey. The UNIA frequently held solidarity marches and promoted black pride.

Despite the obstacles of segregation, what we today call Overtown flourished both economically and socially in this era. It was downtown for all of Greater Miami's black residents and had all the types of stores found in any major city. The influential Colored Board of Trade frequently petitioned elected officials on behalf of their community. Most of the time, their pleas fell on deaf ears. Because blacks had no place to swim, D. A. Dorsey purchased Fisher Island and planned to create a black resort there. It was not built, however, and Dorsey sold the land to industrialist W. K. Vanderbilt. One significant victory was the 1927 opening of Booker T. Washington Senior High—the first black high school in Miami. *The Miami Times*, founded in 1923, was not Miami's first black newspaper—*The Industrial Reporter* holds that honor—but the *Times* proved to be the strongest and most enduring. Besides a strong business and professional community, N.W. 2nd Avenue's flourishing night life made it the "Harlem of the South."

∞ Stormy Weather

By early 1926, the red-hot Boom was cooling. The railroad declared an embargo on building material as it tried to repair overburdened tracks. To make matters worse, a ship, the *Prinz Valdemar*, ran aground and flipped on its side in the harbor, blocking shipping for weeks. The inflated prices paid for land, the attempts by northern interests to discourage their customers from investing in Florida, and the lack of materials for new housing all led to the collapse of what the press called the "Florida Frenzy." The final blow came in the form of a killer hurricane that struck the area on September 17-18, 1926, killing 114 people and destroying much of South Florida. Unlike today, there was little advance warning before the storm devastated the city and its citizens.

Miami Mayor Ed Romfh downplayed the destruction, fearful that if word got out about how bad it really was, the upcoming tourist season would be ruined. Unfortunately, this stiff-upper-lip attitude stopped some much needed relief. During these desperate early days after the storm, Miamians pulled together to pick up the pieces of their lives and start over again. But all was not lost. Just two weeks after the Hurricane passed, the brand new University of Miami opened on schedule even though it had to move into a half-finished apartment-hotel that was located several miles from its Mediterranean-revival styled main campus, still under construction. For the next 20 years, the half-finished buildings remained skeletons as the university continued to operate out of the Anastasia and San Sebastian apartments, affectionately known as the "cardboard college" because the walls were so thin.

Despite everyone's optimistic rhetoric, Miami was soon in the midst of a deep depression ahead of the rest of the nation that was still on a stock-market roller-coaster ride. The few bright spots in the late 1920s included the opening of Biscayne Boulevard and the completion of Bayfront Park that was pumped out of bay bottom during the Boom. The Boulevard development, dubbed the "Fifth Avenue of the South," introduced a new style of architecture to the area that today is known as Art Deco. The Sears Building, with its large parking lot, was the ancestor of the shopping malls that lay three decades in the future.

When the Royal Palm Hotel closed for good in 1928, it marked the passing of an older era. By this time, new Boomtime skyscrapers and modern buildings had all but replaced the original city and in many ways another "instant city" emerged. That May, when Miami hosted the national Shrine convention, Miamians enjoyed one last gasp of fantasy before they faced the real world of depression. For one week, Bayfront Park and Biscayne Boulevard became "the Garden of Allah" complete with an Arabian bazaar, an ornate bandstand, assorted towering monoliths and a row of enormous Sphinx. A huge spotlight, advertised as the largest artificial "Aurora Borealis" ever built, lured Miamians to the unbelievable spectacle that was right out of the *Arabian Nights*. A three hour morning parade, which began at 29th Street and the Boulevard and ended at the "Garden of Allah," capped the week's special events. Banks, stores and even schools closed so no one would miss the extravaganza that drew a record 200,000 people.

In the years to come, Miami would have other booms and other parades. None, however, would ever come close to matching the spectacle of the Boom of the 1920s or the time when, for one week, "Miami became Mecca."

⟐

Two Miami's on the Brink of Change

Thelma Peters
Growing Up in Miami

Thelma Peterson Peters was a well known and highly honored teacher, historian and author. She wrote three books about Miami and hundreds of articles. She also taught at Miami Edison Senior High for 27 years and organized the first social studies department at Miami Dade Community College. In the following selection, she writes about her memories of downtown Miami from the time of her arrival in 1915 until the 1920s. Her account gives a vivid impression of the era between Flagler's death and the Boom of the 1920s. She died in 1996.

When we first came to Dade County in 1915, I was ten. We lived in a rented house in Buena Vista until Papa could build a house for us on 2nd Avenue near N.E. 30th Street. I attended the Buena Vista School, usually walking back and forth.

But Papa soon sold the new home and bought a thirteen-acre farm three miles north of Little River, part piney-woods, part glade-marl. Now we had to go all the way to Miami to shop. After we got the cow that meant every three days we had to have ice.

We always made the shopping trip as a family outing. We would park on Flagler Street and if Papa had business Mama would take my sister and me to the movies. In those days all movies were silent and there was no color. From time to time there were captions that advanced the story. And there was usually a piano player who interpreted the action of the screen— if there were galloping horses, she galloped; for a love scene, she played soft and low.

It was fun to be on Flagler Street. We often saw Seminole Indians in their colorful clothes. We would shop for groceries at a store along West Flagler, and we had a favorite ice cream store where we bought ice cream cones. Burdine's had our favorite Downtown restaurant. Our last stop was always at the ice

plant on N.E. 6th Street. Papa regularly got a hundred pounds of ice, cut in two pieces, so it was easier to handle with his ice tongs. We carried the ice on a rack attached to the back of our Model T Ford. We kids always got scraps of ice to suck on the way home.

I had often seen the Halcyon Hotel (on the site of the duPont Building) and marveled at the great columns and the little red-topped turrets, for I had been brought up on fairy tales and this hotel seemed just out of one. Once while shopping Downtown with my Aunt Nora, we went to the great Royal Palm Hotel for what she called a "walk-through." As it happened, this was the only time in my life I was in the Royal Palm. Then we headed back to Flagler. Aunt Nora noticed empty rockers on the porch of the Halcyon and insisted on going there for a rest. But I squirmed in my rocker, feeling we did not belong in such a ritzy place.

But I came to know the hotel. After I went as far as I could go in the little school at Arch Creek—that is, through the tenth grade, I had to make a choice as to where I would finish high school—at the Dade County Agricultural High School in Lemon City (now Miami Edison) or at Miami High School. Since the Lemon City School did not offer Latin, Mama insisted I go to Miami High. They arranged transportation for me with two students, Claude and Mabel Sparkman, who lived in North Miami and would take me as a passenger for one dollar a week.

At that time Miami High was on N.W. 2nd Avenue, quite near Downtown. As an entering junior, I joined several organizations so I had a better way to get acquainted. When one of my activities meant I had to stay after school, the Sparkmans went on home and I walked to Royal Palm Park where there was an Arthur Pryor band concert every day. I would sit in the area away from the bandshell and near the street so I could watch out for Mama, who would come to get me. . . .

In the spring of 1921, it was time for the Seniors to be entertained by the Juniors at the prom. The junior class president was Thomas Peters, whose father owned the Halcyon Hotel, so, as expected, the prom was held in the ballroom of the Halcyon. In my history class the teacher sat us alphabetically so I had come to be somewhat acquainted with Thomas Peters for my name was Peterson. I wrote a little play to be presented at the prom—it was called "The Country Cousin from Squashville," and I played the leading role—the Country Cousin. The butler in the play was played by Thomas, whom I would later marry. The play went over so well it got mention in the next day's newspaper. . . .

In 1926, I graduated from Brenau College and three months later got married. We had a fateful honeymoon in Bimini at a hotel also owned by my father-in-law. The great hurricane of 1926 struck Bimini before it hit Miami and the hotel was so badly damaged that it was never repaired. But we had managed to save ourselves by getting in a storage place under the kitchen. A couple of days after the blow a bootlegger got his boat repaired and made a run to Miami, passing the word along that we were safe. Eventually my father-in-law was able to rent a boat and pick us up. We were shocked at how badly Miami had been hit. Tom and I were glad for a chance to live at the Halcyon. We had a large room that included an alcove in one of the turrets. The desk was located in this alcove and I claimed the spot as my own. . . .

From my airy perch I could look down on the Olympia Theater, where we often went. I loved the decor and the mighty organ. From my perch I was getting a new perspective of Miami and feeling a kinship which I never lost. Only because a baby was coming did we move into a well-furnished home in Miami Shores, not far from where my family lived.

Source: Thelma Peters, "My Kinship with Downtown Miami," *City News*, Fall 1992, pp. 2-3.

Kelsey Leroy Pharr
Colored Town, 1915

Kelsey Leroy Pharr, who came to Miami from South Carolina, was an African American leader who was a successful businessman, podiatrist and funeral director. As head of the Colored Board of Trade, he often wrote articles for The Miami Metropolis *describing the businesses and social activities in "Colored Town," the name the Overtown community was called at the time. The Dade County School Board honored Mr. Pharr by naming Kelsey Pharr Elementary School after him.*

BOARD OF TRADE

The progressive spirit of the colored people of Miami is very significantly induced by the organization of the Colored Board of Trade. This organization arose out of the clearly realized necessity of federating and focalizing the commercial and civic concerns of the race. . . .

The Colored Board of Trade commands the enthusiastic support of strong men of the race and it is rendering a vital service for the larger good of Miami and Dade county. Though but recently organized, the Colored Board of Trade has won the respect and confidence of the commercial and civic bodies among the whites and in many helpful ways it co-operates with the Miami Chamber of Commerce. It is the clearing house for the best ideas of the race along lines of commercials and civic betterment. . . .

CIVIC

The civic life of the colored people in Dade county and the city of Miami is best judged by the following figures which have been gathered by the civic committee of the Colored Board of Trade. It is safe to say that these statistics are very reasonably stated. The committee was unable to obtain the exact figures for reason that very recently a state census has been taken and those figures are not to be published before a certain given date.

Approximately there are 7,000 colored people in Dade county, and their holdings in real estate and otherwise aggregate $800,000. There are in the city of Miami, approximately 5,450 negroes, and their holdings in real estate and personal property easily aggregate $500,000. We give here the names of several colored persons who have accomplished much in their chosen lines of endeavor and are comfortably situated for years to come: Geder Walker, J. H. Howard, D. A. Dorsey, Thomas O'Gars, E. W. F. Stirrup, H. S. Bragg, Nelson Thompson, S. J. Boyd, J. J. Hurd, Mrs. Ella Griffin, Mrs. Hattie Reddick, Mrs. Laura Gaskin, Dr. W. B. Sawyer, W. W. Wilson, Dr. S. M. Frazier, Israel Jones and others who have taken advantage of the wonderful opportunities which the county and sites have to offer.

BUSINESS

In the city of Miami, there are owned and controlled by race-loving negroes; 3 drug stores, 6 refreshment parlors, 1 theatre, 17 grocery stores, 4 meat markets, 5 fish markets, 9 barber shops, 2 bicycle shops, 7 boarding houses, 2 fruit stands, 17 hackmen, 9 draymen, 4 real estate offices, 11 restaurants, 4 lunch counters, 3 insurance companies, (one of which has it's home office in Miami), 1 saving association, 2 undertaking parlors, (the firm of Carter and Pharr, having the only licensed colored embalmers south of St. Augustine), 12 tailor shops and pressing clubs, and two expert cutters, 1 plumber, 1 printer, 1 blacksmith shop, 2 bakeries, 1 ice dealer, 14 dress makers, 5 shoeshine parlors, 1 milliner and dealer in notions, 1 furniture store, 1 carriage and automobile trimmer and painter, 3 hair emporiums, 2 upholsterers, 2 shoe-makers, 2 livery-men, and 7 stone, wood and painting contractors.

The oldest and most successful restaurant keepers are Mrs. Mary A. Houston and Mrs. Refoe. They have been in business here for 8 and 5 years respectively. The oldest barbers from point of service, are J. S. Stroman, H. R. Register and W. F. Thompson; 17 and 18 years respectively. The oldest grocerymen are J. W. Grace and Allen Stokes who are still in the business.

Probably the most successful business man in this part of the state, is Dana A. Dorsey. He came to Miami in 1897 when the city was in its infancy and engaged in truck farming. After several years in that profitable business he turned his attention to real estate, upon which he has built himself. He was the first to suggest and cause to be organized a Negro Savings Bank in the southern part of the state. In more recent years he has entered the mercantile world and has been successful in all the lines of business in which he has engaged. One of his greatest aims is to furnish employment for the youth of the race. D. A. Dorsey has been an ardent churchman and a patron of fraternal organizations. He has, with limited education, garnered a comfortable fortune and is without a doubt one of the wealthiest men in the country, regardless of color. . . .

The magnificent business block on Avenue G owned by J. H. Howard would be a credit to any city. . . . It is a stone building and always presents a splendid appearance because of the beautiful white material out of which it is finished. J. H. Howard was a grocer in this city for many years and by honest dealings with his fellowmen was successful. Later he launched into the real estate business and is now engaged in that line of work. He has been greatly assisted by his estimable wife in making the record which he has made.

Another splendid stone building on Avenue G which deserves special mention, is that owned by R. A. Powers, the pioneer furniture dealer of this section of the city. He came to Miami as an employee of a white furniture dealer and during the time of his service with him he conceived the idea of doing business for himself, and later opened a store of his own. In this line of work he has succeeded and the valuable property holdings, together with this splendid building which graces the business section of our town, are evidences of that success.

The Lyric Theatre is possibly the most beautiful and costly playhouse owned by colored people in all the Southland. To Geder Walker, Miami's colored citizens owe much gratitude for having provided so beautiful and commodious a building for their pleasure. It is equipped with everything that is needed for modern theatrical performances. It is now, and always has been, managed by competent negro men. Its moving picture machines are thoroughly understood by its well trained negro operators. The building is made of brown stone on the front and the sides are of the popular reinforced concrete. The interior compares favorable with the big theatres of metropolitan cities. Geder Walker is a marvelous example of what mother-wit can do in the business world. He has had little or no education, but is rated among the most substantial citizens of the county. In connection with the next door to the theatre, he operates a beautiful ice cream parlor and cafe.

Source: Kelsey L. Pharr, ed., Recording Secretary of the Board of the Colored Board of Trade, "Colored Town Section of the City of Miami is a Thriving Community . . ." *Miami Metropolis*, October 16, 1915, p. 46.

Roberta J. Thompson and Dorothy J. McKellar
Colored Town was Our Downtown

Roberta Johnson Thompson and Dorothy Johnson McKellar both are native Miamians who were born and raised in Overtown. Both were elementary school teachers in the Dade County Public Schools for more than 30 years. Mrs. Thompson also was a principal in Goulds. Mrs. McKellar's daughter, Dorothy Jenkins Fields, founder of the Black Archives, History and Research Foundation of South Florida, transcribed their comments.

In 1903, our parents, Ida Ellen (Roberts) and Sam D. Johnson, who were born in Harbour Island, Bahamas, moved to Miami from Key West. They had seven children: the first two, Samuel and Elaine, were born in Key West. The others of us: Roberta, Frederick, Dorothy, Kenneth and John were born in Miami. The original family home was located at 2nd Street and Florida Avenue in what was then known as Colored Town, now Overtown. When the city renamed the streets, ours changed to N.W. 10th Street and 1st Court. Known to old-timers as the Johnson Compound, it consisted of two houses and one office, an arrangement which accommodated the seven of us as well as our individual families.

Like many others, our parents were enticed to settle in Miami because of the weather and the anticipation of economic gain. It is believed that immigration laws encouraged Bahamian blacks to relocate to Miami. Islanders came from all over and many remained and became American citizens.

Living just around the corner from Avenue G (N.W. 2nd Avenue), we watched it turn from a dirt road to the major business street for blacks in South Florida. There were restaurants, variety stores, grocery stores, barber shops, beauty shops, tailor shops and furniture stores on 2nd Avenue and throughout the immediate area. In addition to regular shoe repair shops, there was also a black shoemaker who created and produced shoes, handbags and belts. Many dressmakers, milliners and tailors also conducted businesses directly out of their homes as well as from storefronts. Self-contained, Colored Town provided goods and services so that residents did not have to go out of the neighborhood to shop. Residents owned and operated their own businesses and hired a significant number of employees as well. On both weekdays and weekends, Overtown was bustling with shoppers, and those seeking dining and entertainment. Others just strolled with pride, up and down the streets.

It seemed to us that prior to the 1920s, many Bahamian and northern whites owned most of the Downtown businesses. They were always cordial and even the poorest of them employed black women as

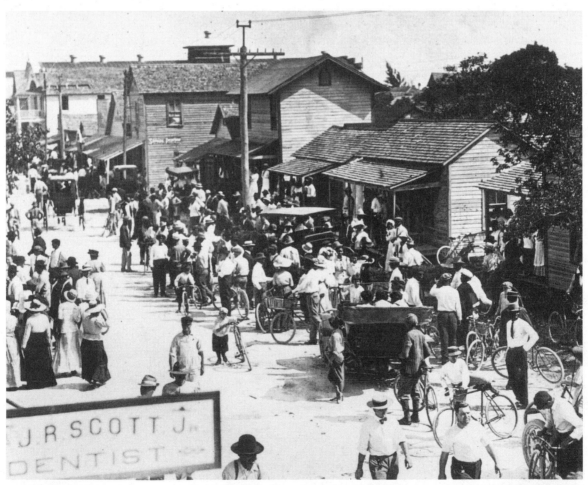

Avenue G (N. W. Second Avenue) was the heart of downtown Colored Town, now Overtown. Black residents from all over South Florida considered it their downtown. (Black Archives)

domestics and black men as helpers. Later, as more Southern whites opened businesses in Downtown, there was a lack of tolerance for us. We did not feel as welcomed.

While blacks were usually welcomed as shoppers, culture and entertainment was not available to us in Downtown Miami. It was definitely off limits. In fact, before night came, we walked very fast to return to our area in fear of being caught and punished, which was the rule not the exception.

Miami's white Downtown business and cultural/entertainment section was only six blocks south of us. Within walking distance, it was commonplace for children and adults to walk Downtown to shop. We remember walking to town on the railroad tracks to buy bread from the Seybold Bakery. There were several bakeries in our section, so this gave us a choice. We also shopped at Budge's and Railey's Hardware Stores and purchased anything we wanted. On occasion, our family purchased shoes from Sewell's Shoe Store on Flagler Street. Sometimes we were allowed to try them on as long as we wore protective coverings—socks on our feet and skull caps on our heads.

Numerous black men had good jobs as helpers in the stores and banks Downtown. Black women worked in Fort Dallas Park, a very wealthy white section on the Miami River adjacent to the Downtown business center. Our mother was a seamstress, and usually worked out of our home. On occasion however, she cleaned rooms or did a little laundry in Fort Dallas Park. Our Aunt Alice was one of the black women domestics who "kept house" for white families when they closed up for the summer. Sometimes, one of the Johnson girls would stay with Aunt Alice while she was housekeeping. We remember the beautiful gate at the entrance to Fort Dallas Park and one house, which had a large anchor and chain in the front.

Papa was a general helper for several well-known white families including Frank T. Budge, the hardware store proprietor, the Honorable William Jennings Bryan, and the Chaffees, cousins of John D. Rockefeller. He often took the older children to work with him. While he and our brothers worked out-of-doors at the Budge home, one sister, Roberta, played with Budge's daughter Helen. Sometimes they played downstairs in the yard near the pump house. Other times, they played upstairs in Helen's room with her dolls and playhouse. Later our father worked as a gardener planting flowers at Vizcaya. Our oldest brother, Samuel, fondly recalled learning math as he helped Papa plant flowers in geometric designs.

By the time we were young adults, Miami's Colored Town/Overtown had become the cradle of business, culture and entertainment for South Florida's black residents, visitors and tourists. We were all part of this dynamic community, that also included Jewish and Chinese merchants. Geared toward tourism, the area was alive and busy day and night as people came to enjoy the entertainment, partake of the exotic foods and listen to popular as well as gospel music. The repeat business brought by visitors and tourists, helped stabilize Overtown's economy. It also promoted pride in a people who were self-motivated and self-contained.

In addition to goods and services, there were several fine restaurants, a privately owned tennis court and several first-class hotels. One hotel, The Mary Elizabeth, had three floors, and was the tallest building in Overtown. It also was the first to have an elevator. It was a hangout for quite a few celebrities. Some of its notable guests [in later years] included: Supreme Court Justice Thurgood Marshall, Congressman Adam Clayton Powell, labor leader A. Phillip Randolph, and Dr. Mary McLeod Bethune, an advisor to President Franklin D. Roosevelt. W.E.B. DuBois, an internationally-known intellectual, author and journalist, vacationed here on his way to and from conferences in Cuba and the West Indies. Famous folklorist Zora Neale Hurston lived in Overtown and worked as a maid on Miami Beach.

Nearly all of the arts were available in Overtown. Because of South Florida's policy of strict segregation of the races, black entertainers who performed in Miami and on Miami Beach could not bed or board there after the show. As a result, they came to Overtown for the night. Sometimes they held jam sessions with local residents, jamming until daybreak. Luminaries like Count Bassie, Ella Fitzgerald, Cab Calloway, Josephine Baker, Billie Holiday, Sammy Davis, Jr., the Inkspots, Louie "Satchmo" Armstong, Nat "King" Cole, B.B. King, and Aretha Franklin were frequent performers in Overtown. Before the demise of what we called "Little Broadway" in the late 50s and early 60s, Clyde Killens, a local black entertainment promoter, brought some of the same stars, along with those who were just being discovered, to Miami to perform exclusively in Overtown.

Desegregation, urban renewal and construction of two expressways altered the character of the neighborhood and killed the once vibrant center of economic and cultural activity. The substantial black ownership of hotels, theaters, rooming houses, night clubs, stores and neighborhood markets declined. Before the decline and decay set in, we were one of the fortunate families who moved away.

Our oldest brother Samuel, Dr. S. H. Johnson, heard that the white Downtown business establishment had predicted and planned the demise of our area. As a result, he found an area in the suburbs which would provide houses and yard space for all of our families to live together in a compound, much as we had done in Overtown. In August 1948, we moved to what was platted as Glen Wood Heights, later called Brownsville. We still live there today. Brownsville, essentially a bedroom community, was one of many enclaves in Dade County that black families created to escape overcrowdedness and blight. From Brownsville, we re-

turned to Overtown and Downtown for business and shopping. Overtown's "Little Broadway" was still the only place we could go for education, culture and entertainment.

Although we lived in Brownsville, our heart and minds never left the educational and cultural hub we once knew. For the most part, we worked there everyday and like most families, returned nights and weekends until the area was destroyed. Overtown is no longer Downtown to us, but we continue to think of it as home.

Source: Roberta J. Thompson and Dorothy J. McKellar, "Colored Town/Overtown Was Downtown to Us," *City News*, Fall 1992, p. 3-4.

A City Goes to War

Students on the War, 1918

World War I started in Europe in August 1914 and the U.S. entered the war three years later. Americans, aware of the severity and depth of the conflicts, closely monitored the events oversees. As students concluded their school year in June 1917, fighting in the war and sacrificing their lives seemed a real possibility. Hazel Filer, a student at Miami High, wrote the following poem.

Loyalty

America is our native land,
For her we'll always fight,
For her the cry of all rings out,
"To Arms!" for man's own right.

For our own land, we'll always stand
And heed to every call,
Millions now are standing near
To help her, ere she fall.

Come now, stand by your President,
Fight 'till the fight is through,
Then we may all in peace surround
Our own Red, White, and Blue.

Hazel Filer

Source: *Miahi 1917* (Miami: The Hefty Press [1917]), p. 83.

African Americans Serve Their Country, 1918

During World War I, Miami's black community proudly fought for their country. Reflecting the segregated conditions in America, blacks were assigned to their own units. Undeterred by the separatism, most black Americans stood proud behind their soldiers. Here, a Colored Town parade, uniting most of the community, is held to send off the draftees. Despite their acts of valor in "the war to make the world safe for democracy," they returned to inequality at home.

With brass bands "fore and aft," and about 90 per cent of colored town represented in the parade, the negroes who entrained yesterday morning for Camp Dix, Wrightstown, N.J., were given a send-off that they will never forget. Sixty-five of the negroes were selected from Dade County registrants, one was inducted into the service and several others were transferred from other draft boards. On their way north this contingent [was] joined by other contingents from towns between here and Jacksonville.

All the negroes who left Miami yesterday morning were presented with comfort bags by the Southeastern Red Cross chapter. This was announced today by Mrs. R. D. Maxwell, chairman of the comfort bag committee.

The St. Agnes and Cocoanut Grove colored band provided the music for the parade. The men were under the charge of Lieutenants W.W. Wright, George B. Corney, Emil Q. Withers, who came to Miami to take the negroes north.

Source: "Colored Town Almost Depopulated Yesterday When Draftees Left," *Miami Metropolis*, clipping, c1918.

Hatred for the "Beast of Berlin," 1918

The government believed that public support of America's involvement in World War I was critical to securing victory. President Wilson's administration felt that its citizens had to believe in the "nobility" of their cause, and the evil intentions of Austria-Hungary, the Ottoman Empire and most importantly Germany. A Committee of Public Information, headed by George Creel, created the war propaganda which promoted these messages. Books, editorials, posters and motion pictures which portrayed the Kaiser as immoral and celebrated the allied armies were commonplace. The following document describes an audience viewing a wartime film in Miami.

Hundreds of people left the Paramount theater boiling mad with rage at Wilhelm II, the Hohenzollern monarch of Germany, yesterday afternoon and evening, after they had witnessed the wonderful seven-reel feature film, "The Kaiser—The Beast of Berlin."

The revolting brutality of the man that the American and allied armies are going to "get" before they end the present war was depicted in a horrible manner in the picture, and the big audience that filled the Paramount at each performance watched the brutal invasion of Belgium and the treatment of the Belgian non-combatants by the Kaiser's Hun hordes with tense faces. . . .

The audience was so excited that it arose to its feet when the American troops entered the war, and stood cheering when the allied armies, led by General Pershing, captured Berlin and sent the Kaiser to Belgium as a prisoner of King Albert.

Source: "Miami Deeply Moved By Beast of Berlin," *Miami Herald*, May 16, 1918, p. 2.

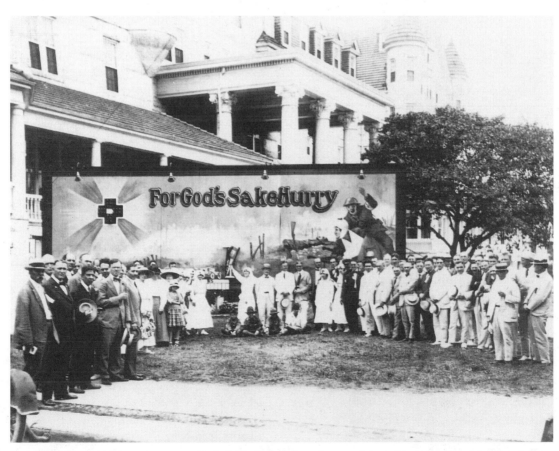

War bond drives and wartime propaganda kept the area hyped up in favor of war as this promotional photo illustrates. It was taken in front of the Halcyon Hotel that stood on the site of the present DuPont Building.

Return to Normalcy

Coconut Grove Takes on Miami
1918

During the war, Coconut Grove's Dinner Key Naval Air Station housed more than 1,300 men. The noise of their seaplanes disrupted the tranquillity of the neighborhood but Groveites tolerated the intrusion because of the need to support the war. When the war was coming to an end, however, and downtown promoters wanted to make the station permanent, many prominent Grove residents like James Deering, who owned Vizcaya, David Fairchild and Ralph Munroe, launched a campaign to remove it. Others, like E. G. Sewell and George Merrick, favored the permanent base and argued that the station enhanced Miami's economic condition and strategically protected the city. In what became one of the most controversial issues of the day, civic leaders fueled the debate by bombarding officials in Washington with their position. In the following documents, two points of view are shown. The first is from James Deering, owner of Vizcaya, written to his neighbor Secretary of State William Jennings Bryan. The second is a statement by the Miami Chamber of Commerce. Those opposed won the argument and the base was closed in 1919.

Asking a Neighbor to Help

December 16th, 1918

Dear Mr. Secretary,

I enclose two papers which as you will see are copies of affidavits. I write you as feeling under a sense of duty to a neighbor and a friend.

As you will see the lessee of the Busch house, adjoining yours, has not been able to continue living in the house and has abandoned it. It is my opinion without the slightest intentional exaggeration, an opinion confirmed by all interested, that the value of your property, Villa Serena, has shrunk one-half by the presence of the Naval Air Station at Dinner Key. Had this station been where it is before I bought or built here, I should never have considered my present location for a minute. What I say of your property is true of all the property in this vicinity. The case of course, is worse at Cocoanut Grove. . . .

It has been said in Washington that no one objects to the location of the station except a few millionaires. No one knows better than you how few millionaires are here and how thickly the small homes are scattered about of those people who have little else than their homes and their hands. So far from objecting to the use of the station during the war everyone has lent a helping hand in every way possible. I, for example, have given the use of one of the islands just off my house and have offered the use of a second. It is only when it is proposed to make this flying station permanent that the inhabitants protest in the name of their health, happiness and property. . . .

So far as the population here is concerned it is a case of those who live near you and me and the people of Cocoanut Grove, where the station is located, against some of the shopkeepers of Miami, who want the business growing out of the station. Morally, and, if it were a legal case, legally the latter have no right to a voice in the matter and no right to consideration. It is simply from this point of view a question of Cocoanut Grove, where the station is located, and those of us who live so near that our rights of property and happiness are involved. . . .

I am prepared and all those interested are prepared to take any amount of time and trouble involved in righting the mistake that has been made. I am sure that your love for Villa Serena and the very considerable property interest involved in it will make you feel as I do, that it is a duty to ourselves to leave no stone unturned in this matter.

I am very glad to know that even if you are not to live in your home this winter you are, as I understand it, nevertheless to be in Miami.

With kindest regards to Mrs. Bryan and yourself, I am always,

Yours very sincerely,
James Deering

Source: Letter, James Deering to William Jennings Bryan, December 16, 1918, file 0142-398B, Record Group 72, National Archives.

A Different Point of View

NOW, THEREFORE, be it Resolved by the Board of Directors of the said Chamber of Commerce that we hereby pledge ourselves and the members of said Chamber of Commerce generally to do all in our power that may properly be done in an effort to have said Dinner Key Naval Air Station made permanent.

Our reasons for taking this action are as follows:

First: Said Naval Air Station, as now completed, is ideally constructed and ideally located. As it appears to us, it would be a great waste of public property to have the same abandoned after the conclusion of the present war.

Second: It has been authoritatively shown that Miami offers to aeroplane operators a greater number of flying hours per annum than can any other school or station in the country.

Third: Its location on Biscayne Bay is particularly strategic for the purpose of patrolling the Florida Coast and for the protection of the Florida Straits.

Fourth: The location of the Station at Dinner Key has fortified the people of this community with a feeling of safety, as we recognize it as a great protection from possible bombardment from the Sea.

Fifth: It has had, and will have an interesting and educational influence among the people of Florida, and among the great number of northern visitors who annually spend their winters in this community.

Sixth: It has been of great advantage to Miami in a business way, and will continue to be so as long as any considerable number of men connected with the Navy are stationed there.

MIAMI CHAMBER OF COMMERCE

Guy W. Livingston.
E.G. Sewell

Source: Petition, "Miami Chamber of Commerce: Dinner Key Naval Base," February 6, 1919, file 0142-398, Record Group 72, National Archives.

Marjory Stoneman Douglas Fighting for Women's Rights

In 1920, the passage of the 19th amendment gave women the right to vote and culminated a long struggle for women's rights. National leaders like Elizabeth Cady Stanton and Susan B. Anthony, who were known as "suffragettes," led the fight for change. Florida had its own share of suffragettes including Miami's Marjory Stoneman Douglas. Despite their best efforts, the Florida Legislature refused to ratify the amendment. (It passed without their endorsement.) In 1969, the Florida Legislature finally ratified the amendment as a symbolic gesture in honor of the League of Women Voter's 50th anniversary. Here, excerpted from her autobiography, Mrs. Douglas recalls her eventful day in Tallahassee.

Mrs. Bryan [William Jennings Bryan's wife] was a devoted suffragist, and I got to work with her on that count. The women's suffrage amendment had been passed in some states, but hadn't gotten too far in Florida. In the spring of 1916, Mrs. Bryan enlisted me and Mrs. Frank Stranahan of Ft. Lauderdale, plus the widow of old Governor Napoleon Bonaparte Broward and the widow of another ex-governor, W.S. Jennings, to speak to the state legislature about ratifying the suffrage amendment. Mrs. Jennings I'd met before. In fact, the Jenningses of Jacksonville were the Jenningses of Bryan's middle name. There was some direct relation.

We went to Tallahassee by Pullman train. I remember the red dust of those red hills beyond the Suwannee seeping in around the joints of the Pullman car. In Tallahassee we stayed in the old Leon Hotel, which was full of lobbyists where you'd expect to see them, down in the lobby discussing politics all night long. Mrs. Broward was sick and had to stay in bed, but she'd go over and speak to the legislators and return to bed as soon as she got back. We'd sit on her bed and she'd tell about the days when her husband was governor and when he was running guns to Cuba in the Spanish American War. Mr. Broward was a canny old pirate, and he'd smuggled guns down the Florida coast. I liked Mrs. Broward and her stories even though my father was her husband's greatest enemy in the dredging of the Everglades.

Mrs. Jennings was younger than Mrs. Broward, and Mrs. Stranahan and I were younger still. All four of us spoke to a joint committee, wearing our best hats. It was a large room with men sitting around on two sides with their backs propped up against the walls and large brass spittoons between every other one of them. Talking to them was like talking to graven images. They never paid attention to us at all. They weren't even listening. This was my first taste of the politics of north Florida.

These were the so-called "wool-hat boys in the red hills beyond the Suwannee" and they ran the state. Because of them, Florida was the last state in the union to ratify the amendment. Even though our testimony was ignored, it was valuable for me to work with women who'd struggled in this political arena. It was a long time before you began to feel that the legislators from north Florida even knew there was a south Florida. That was also a thing I had to learn.

Source: Marjory Stoneman Douglas with John Rothchild, *Voice of the River* (Englewood, Florida: Pineapple Press, 1987), pp. 106-7.

Creating the Boom

William Jennings Bryan
On Building a Great City, 1920

William Jennings Bryan was a major leader of the Democratic Party from 1896 until his death in 1925. Elected to Congress in 1890, Bryan became known as a great orator. His speeches, especially those on the free coinage of silver and religion, became known across the country. He ran unsuccessfully for president in 1896, 1900 and 1908. Bryan moved to Miami in 1916 and became the city's most famous and enthusiastic land booster. His Royal Palm Park Sunday School Class drew upward of 6,000 people a week and became a popular tourist attraction. He went to work for George Merrick during the Boom and held lectures at Venetian Pool to attract buyers to Coral Gables. In a speech he gave to real estate agents in 1920, he revealed his image for the future of Miami.

"We must make Miami attractive for the middle class people, and make it possible for them to come here to live," declared William Jennings Bryan in addressing members of the Miami Realty Board at the weekly luncheon of that organization, yesterday, at the Chinese-American restaurant. It was the best attended luncheon ever enjoyed by the board.

Mr. Bryan said that while it was of great benefit to the city for millionaires to come here for their winter homes and that this class of people should be urged to come to Miami, it was necessary for the city to reach the middle class and for the city to make things attractive for these people, in order to become a greater city.

He urged that the city be made a clean city. "You cannot build a city by inviting the sporting element. The greatest advertisement you can have is to let it be known that Miami is peopled by folks who are interested in virtue and the higher things of life. Then when people come, you have nothing to be ashamed of," he said.

One of the greatest needs of the city is more parks. He urged that in every new subdivisions, a block or even half a block, be reserved for park purposes, and declared that it was better for the city to have ten one-block parks than one ten-block park, as the smaller parks would be more convenient.

URGE ESTABLISHMENT OF SCHOOLS

Mr. Bryan urged that a number of boarding schools be established here, as a means of attracting people to Miami. He said that many people who would otherwise come to Miami do not come because there are no boarding schools here, and said that by the establishment of such schools, the children could be sent here early in the school year and the parents could join them during the season. Another advantage of establishing such schools here would be making it possible for young people of Latin America to come here for their education, which would make possible more closer relations between the United States and Latin America, and would also help Miami in its trade-relations to Mexico, Cuba and other Latin American countries. . . .

DEEP WATER IS NEEDED

"Deep-water is something that Miami vitally needs," said Mr. Bryan. "The real estate men of Miami should get behind this problem and help get deep water."

He pointed out that while a railroad could be used by only the corporation owning the right of way, the harbor could be used by hundreds of different

Living History

Biltmore Hotel
1200 Anastasia Avenue
Coral Gables

On January 15, 1926, Coral Gables' $1,250,000 Biltmore Hotel opened. Designed by Schultze and Weaver, with 350 guests rooms, magnificent public spaces and the world's largest hotel swimming pool, the Biltmore was the final exclamation point of George Merrick's planned City of Coral Gables. By 1929, the Coral Gables Corporation was bankrupt and the hotel was sold.

The hotel remained open during the Depression by holding special events like water shows and tea dances for local residents. After World War II started, the government took over the hotel and made it an Army Air Force Hospital. Following the war, it became a Veterans Administration Hospital and continued in that role until 1968.

When the Veterans Administration left, the hotel was abandoned. In 1970, when citizens heard that the government had sold the property to a developer who had plans to tear it down, they led the fight for a bond referendum to fund purchasing the property. As it turned out, the federal government gave the hotel to the City in 1973.

The hotel remained in limbo for many years until the City of Coral Gables could figure out what to do with it. Again, citizens groups pushed for the city to encourage private developers to bid on the property. Finally in 1986, the beautifully restored hotel reopened. Today, it is in the midst of another new life with a new hotel operator who has added even more glamour. During the Summit of the Americas, the Biltmore received national attention as the site of the history-making state dinner.

Three time presidential candidate William Jennings Bryan came to Miami to live in 1916 and became a major booster of the area. His Sunday School class at Royal Palm Park was a major tourist attraction. (SPA)

companies, who would help solve the transportation problem.

Mr. Bryan pointed out the necessity of a deep water harbor in Miami as a means of development of the Everglades. The success of the Everglades development depends upon deep water to a large extent, in order that the produce of the Everglades could be transported at low rates.

He drew a comparison between the development of the Everglades and the irrigation of desert lands in the west. He said that irrigation had made possible the settlement of thousands of people on former desert lands and declared that none of these reclamation projects was as important as the Everglades project. He said that the draining of the Everglades would provide homes for thousands of people.

Source: "Must Make Magic City Attractive For Middle Class of People, Says W. J. Bryan, Addressing Realty Men," *Miami Herald,* November 25, 1920, p. 1.

George Merrick
Launching the Boom, 1921

George Merrick dropped out of college after his father died to manage the family's Coral Gables Plantation grapefruit groves. In addition to running a profitable agricultural business, he became a successful real estate developer in Miami and Coconut Grove. While he developed other properties, he completely planned his model Coral Gables subdivision, named after the family home, before the first lots were sold in November 1921. Merrick, with his national advertising and promotion campaign, turned a local real estate boom into a national phenomena. At one point the crowds were so heavy he had to build a tent city across from today's Coral Gables High School to accommodate them. When the Depression cost him his fortune and forced his ouster from his beloved Coral Gables, he ran a fishing camp in the Keys. His city planning ideas and his dream of "The City Beautiful" are still evident today and remain a legacy to his genius. He died in 1941 while serving as Postmaster of Miami. This article, appearing in The Miami Daily Tribune, *June 3, 1925, explored the nature of Merrick's character and his vision for Coral Gables.*

George Merrick's minutes are priceless things, every one of them counting for full "sixty seconds' worth of distance run," and he is also a very modest man. A photograph of him is a rarity, because he shuns the camera; an interview with him is even more rare, for personal publicity he does not court. . . .

DREAMER? Yes, and more—a dreamer with the faculty for surrounding himself with men to translate his dreams into practicality, into buildings, and lakes, and waterways, and beautiful landscapes, into flowers and shrubs and homes, and into churches, and schools and institutions of learning, and beaches and playgrounds, and cities!

And truly can it be said that his "vassals are the years"—for within four years he has built a city and is building it greater; he has transplanted the best of the Old World, the work and art and inspiration of centuries, into a concentrated New World city of miraculous age-old beauty, where in "lace of stone their spires stab the skies and with their golden crosses kiss the sun"—the perpetual glorious sunshine of Southern Florida, the place where the dreamer's dreams are made to come true. . . . .

WRITER, poet, dreamer, philosopher, lover of all things beautiful, creator, thinker, kindly, courteous, good-natured, gregarious human man—all of these can be applied to George Merrick without any touch of fulsome adulation. . . .

He will never stop until they lay him under six feet of earth, and this country may well hope that will be a long time yet. Coral Gables was not the beginning with him, nor will it be the end. He has dreams away beyond it—dreams of a well-founded city of at least a million souls, and of George Merrick turning a task laid aside, writing stories and the mystical poetry which find their wellsprings in his heart. . . .

"We have the greatest known architects in America at work upon the plans of this greater Coral Gables, which is Greater Miami," said Mr. Merrick. "We have adapted the Spanish architecture at points; but we chiefly adapted the Mediterranean type of architecture as best fitted by the comparison of climate and conditions, for the beauty of this country. Everything is designed to be in harmony. . . .

We have taken Flagler Street, bent it as a one hundred-foot road through Coral Gables, as Ponce de Leon Boulevard. We will take that street, really Flagler, and the car line to the university station, and then right on to Chapman Field, and also merging with the East and West Dixie Highways going south and with the Overseas Highway. Ultimately it will connect up with the eighty-acre amusement island, and we will run speed boat and taxis and ferries to Cape Florida. These may connect some time later with a possible electric railway to Miami Beach and Miami—belt and encircle the whole with a rapid transit electric and ferry system, and have one monumental city," he concluded.

"And after that?" inquired the writer.

"After that I may be able to sit down and do what I have always wanted to do," he said.

"Rest?" I asked. "No—write," he exclaimed with a passion of earnestness that seemed to come from his very soul.

That's the manner of man this George E. Merrick is.

Source: Vernon Knowles, "An Impression of George E. Merrick: Builder of the City of Coral Gables," *Miami Daily Tribune*, June 3, 1925.

Boomtime Frenzy

Frederick Louis Allen
Why the Boom Happened

Frederick Louis Allen wrote Only Yesterday *in 1931. His informal history described the carefree optimism of the 1920s and became an instant best-seller. In a chapter entitled "Home Sweet Florida," he painted a vivid picture of the Florida Boom and documented its role as a national and vital movement of the "Roaring Twenties."*

There was nothing languorous about the atmosphere of tropical Miami during that memorable summer and autumn of 1925. The whole city had become one frenzied real estate exchange. There were said to be 2,000 real-estate offices and 25,000 agents marketing house-lots or acreage. The shirt-sleeved crowds hurrying to and fro under the widely advertised Florida sun talked of binders and options and water-frontages and hundred-thousand-dollar profits; the city fathers had been forced to pass an ordinance forbidding the sale of property in the street, or even the showing of a map, to prevent inordinate traffic congestion. The warm air vibrated with the clatter of riveters, for the steel skeletons of skyscrapers were rising to give Miami a skyline appropriate to its metropolitan destiny. Motor-busses roared down Flagler Street, carrying "prospects" on free trips to watch dredges and steam-shovels converting the outlying mangrove swamps and the sandbars of the Bay of Biscayne into gorgeous Venetian cities for the American home-makers and pleasure-seekers of the future. The Dixie Highway was clogged with automobiles from every part of the country; a traveler caught in a traffic jam counted the license-plates of eighteen states among the sedans and flivvers waiting in line. Hotels were overcrowded. People were sleeping wherever they could lay their heads, in station waiting-rooms or in automobiles. . . .

How Miami grew! . . .

For this amazing boom, which had gradually been gathering headway for several years but had not become sensational until 1924, there were a number of causes. Let us list them categorically.

1. First of all, of course, the climate—Florida's unanswerable argument.

2. The accessibility of the state to the populous cities of the Northeast—an advantage which Southern California could not well deny.

3. The automobile, which was rapidly making America into a nation of nomads; teaching all manner of men and women to explore their country, and enabling even the small farmer, the summer-boarding-house keeper, and the garage man to pack their families into flivvers and tour southward from auto-camp to auto-camp for a winter of sunny leisure.

4. The abounding confidence engendered by Coolidge Prosperity, which persuaded the four-thousand-dollar-a-year salesman that in some magical way he too might tomorrow be able to buy a fine house and all the good things of earth.

5. A paradoxical, widespread, but only half-acknowledged revolt against the very urbanization and industrialization of the country, the very concentration upon work, the very routine and smoke and congestion and twentieth-century standardization of living upon which Coolidge Prosperity was based. These things might bring the American business man money, but to spend it he longed to escape from them—into the free sunshine of the remembered countryside, into the easy-going life and beauty of the European past, into some never-never land which combined American sport and comfort with Latin glamour— a Venice equipped with bathtubs and electric ice-boxes, a Seville provided with three eighteen-hole golf courses.

6. The example of Southern California, which had advertised its climate at the top of its lungs and

had prospered by so doing: why, argued the Floridians, couldn't Florida do likewise?

7. And finally, another result of Coolidge Prosperity: not only did John Jones expect that presently he might be able to afford a house at Boca Raton and a vacation-time of tarpon-fishing or polo, but he also was fed on stories of bold business enterprise and sudden wealth until he was ready to believe that the craziest real-estate development might be the gold-mine which would work this miracle for him.

Source: Frederick Lewis Allen, *Only Yesterday: An Informal History of the Nineteen-Twenties* (New York: Harper & Brothers, 1931), pp. 270-73.

T. H. Weigall
The Bedlam That Was Miami, 1925

T. H. Weigall was a British journalist who came to Miami in 1925 to seek his fortune. He ended up working as a publicist for George Merrick whom he greatly admired. After a year, and just before the 1926 Hurricane, he gave up on Florida and returned to London. His book, Boom in Paradise, *gives an outsider's view of one of Miami's most interesting eras. He describes the variety of people who were drawn to Miami by visions of riches awaiting them at the end of the rainbow. In the following excerpt, Weigall provides one of the best descriptions of "the frenzy that was Flagler Street" during the Boom .*

My first impression, as I wandered out into the blazing sunlight of that tropical afternoon into that bedlam that was Miami, was of utter confusion. Everywhere there was building going forward at express speed; and mingled with the perpetual screeching of the motor-horns a thousand automatic riveters poured out their deafening music, a thousand drills and hammers and winches added to the insane chorus. Everywhere there was dust. Hatless, coatless men rushed about the blazing streets, their arms full of papers, perspiration pouring from their foreheads. Every shop seemed to be combined with a real estate office; at every doorway crowds of young men were shouting and speechmaking, thrusting forward papers and proclaiming to heaven the unsurpassed chances which they were offering to make a fortune. One had been prepared for real estate madness; and here it was, in excelsis. Everybody in Miami was real estate mad. Towering office buildings, almost entirely occupied by "realtors," were the scenes of indescribable enthusiasm and confusion. Everywhere there was hand-shaking, back-slapping, and general boosting. Everyone I saw seemed to be shaking diagrams of "desirable subdivisions." Business men— a phenomenon surely never before known in the world's history—could be seen at all the little street corner cafes concluding what I felt sure to be big deals over a sarsaparilla or a sundae."

Source: T. H. Weigall, *Boom in Paradise* (New York: Alfred H. King, 1932), pp. 49-50.

America's Playground

T. H. Weigall
A Very "Wet" Miami

T. H. Weigall's vivid account of the Boom makes it clear why South Florida garnered the reputation as "the leakiest spot in America." Although Prohibition was the law of the land, few in tourist oriented Miami paid any attention to it. The lack of law enforcement and the city's proximity to the Bahamas made rum-running a lucrative and popular profession.

Every visitor to America comes back with his own version of the working or non-working of the prohibition laws. . . . Florida, from my own personal experience of it, was the wettest country I have ever known. The state legislature had definitely abandoned any attempt to enforce the provisions of the eighteenth amendment; and the united factors of a tropical climate, the proximity of areas where liquor of all sorts was obtainable at all hours and at the lowest prices, and the presence of a vast amount of ready cash in the hands of people eager to spend it, combined to render quite abortive the intermittent efforts of the federal agents. . . .

The price of a bottle of whiskey in Florida ranged from three dollars upwards, and a good brand of French champagne fetched about ten dollars. Curiously enough, one of the most prized luxuries was beer,

Living History

Olympia Theater (Gusman Center for the Performing Arts)
174 East Flagler Street
Miami

The 1920s was the era of the grand movie palaces. Lavishly designed, these theaters were more like mini-castles than contemporary movieplexes. Miami's Olympia Theater, located in the heart of downtown, was one of the most beautiful of the era.

A gala premiere on the night of February 18, 1926 marked the theater's opening. Costing over $1.5 million to build, the Olympia was the first structure in Miami to be air conditioned. Architect John Eberson created an "atmospheric design" for the Olympia—the illusion of being in an outdoor courtyard or garden. The high, arched ceiling looked like a cerulean blue sky with twinkling stars and artificial clouds. Vintage chandeliers lit up the lobby, and the "mighty Wurlitzer" pipe organ filled the cavernous auditorium with music.

Through the years, some of the greatest show business stars graced the Olympia's stage for its famous vaudeville shows that accompanied the movie attraction. Headliners like Desi Arnaz and Jackie Gleason performed at the Olympia when they were unknowns.

By the 1970's, the Olympia was a dilapidated structure with only a hint of its former splendor. In 1971, when it seemed as though the theater would be torn down, philanthropist Maurice Gusman bought it to save it from destruction. He hired architect Morris Lapidus to restore the aging beauty. After Gusman gave it to the City of Miami, it was re-named Gusman Center for the Performing Arts.

Today, the theater is used for performing arts including the Miami Film Festival and has been featured on American Movie Classics. In 1996, when budget cuts once again threatened its future, Miami's resident superstar, Sylvester Stallone, gave the city $50,000 to keep the theater open.

Thousands of "binder boys"—slick, knicker clad salesmen who sold "binders" or deposits on real estate—helped fuel the Boom. In this busy Flagler Street scene, a binder boy can be seen crossing the street in the lower left.

which fetched a dollar a bottle at the standard rates. Practically all of the hotels served these drinks quite openly, and indeed there was no particular need to conceal them. . . . In Miami there were at least two proper old-fashioned saloons, with polished counters, brass hand-rails and stocks of bottles ranged on wooden shelves behind the bar. One of them was within 200 yards of the central police station, and there was a constable on point duty directly opposite its entrance. A famous "beer-garden" on Miami Beach Island conducted most of its business on a wide verandah overlooking the main street, with only the flimsiest of bamboo sun-blinds to shield the glasses of iced Pilsener from the glare. . . .

The amount of drinking that went on all over Florida, especially in the larger towns, was simply astounding. I should say that during the boom there must have been more alcohol per head consumed in Florida than in any other country in the world.

Source: T. H. Weigall, *Boom in Paradise* (New York: Alfred H. King, 1932), pp. 176-79.

Kenneth Ballinger
"Ain't We Got Fun?" 1925

The song, "Ain't We Got Fun," was a popular song during the "Roaring Twenties." During the Boom, Miami garnered a national reputation as a fun-filled playground. Visitors and residents enjoyed everything from golf to alligator wrestling. Like the rest of the nation, Miamians were enthralled with the latest fads, foibles and fashions. Here, Kenneth Ballinger sampled the Miami-style fun.

The Coral Gables Country Club was a favorite with dancers, as Jan Garber and his orchestra made the moon over Coral Gables immortal. Tina and Ghirardy were a colorful dance team on the palm-fringed dance patio of the club that winter. Over at the Venetian pool was the younger Henry Coppinger wrestling an alligator. . . .

Ben Bernie and his "lads" played at the Wofford Hotel, whose owner, Mrs. Tatem Wofford, boasted she had opened the first hotel in Miami Beach in 1916. The great rambling Royal Palm Hotel began its twenty-ninth season New Year's Day with a ball described as "brilliant," but which we might consider somewhat stodgy. The Urmey Hotel, another aristocrat, started its season in December. Don Lanning was a hit at the Park Theater. Jimmie Hodges initiated his $75,000 "Follie" supper club in Hialeah, with Lew Hampton as the featured singer. Kid Canfield, the reformed gambler, delivered a well attended lecture on the evils of games of chance.

Much other amusement was available in Hialeah. By the middle of January the new $750,000 racing oval of the Miami Jockey club was ready to open. In the stables were such horses as Wise Counselor, who had defeated the French marvel Epinard, and In Memoriam, who had bowed to Zev. A crowd estimated at 17,000 packed the new clubhouse and grandstand for the opening January 15. . . .

The Spanish game of jai alai also drew good crowds in Hialeah, in the old fronton that was wrecked in 1926. Movies were being made in the Hialeah studios, leased to Pathe Exchange for the filming of "Black Caesar's Clan." They even had a balloon ascension and parachute drop in Holleman Park as part of the winter amusement.

Night golf with phosphorescent balls was being tried at Hollywood, where Gene Sarazen had taken up the duties of professional after losing the national pro title. The fourth miniature golf course in the United States was built in Hollywood to lead the spread of the craze which bloomed so suddenly and died so completely.

Source: Kenneth Ballinger, *Miami Million: The Dance of the Dollars in the Great Florida Land Boom of 1925* (Miami: The Franklin Press, 1936), pp. 47-8.

The Speedway at Fulford-By-The-Sea, 1926

Promotion of the Boom extended to Miami's subdivisions. M. C. Tebbets, developer of Fulford-By-The Sea (today's North Miami Beach), ranked as one of the master promoters of the era. Tebbets built a huge, million-dollar wooden raceway and planned a $300,000 race there. The event was held on Feb. 22, 1926, but was the only

contest ever held at the track. Like so many promoters of the Boom, Tebbets ended up bankrupt, and the 1926 Hurricane turned his racetrack into match sticks. Locals called Tebbets' one-race racetrack "Fulford's Folly."

PETER DE PAOLA WINS FIRST FULFORD AUTO CLASSIC

Smiling, debonair Peter De Paola, nephew of the famous Ralph De Palma and the 1925 racing champion of America, got a brilliant start for his 1926 campaign on the brick, board and dirt paths, by capturing first place in the inaugural race over the one and a quarter wooden bowl at Fulford Monday.

Driving his big Dusenberg, carefully never reckless but always up with the leaders, the little Italian was rewarded by having the machine come through the 30 mile grind without having to stop at the pits and in the starting time of 2:19:12:95 for an average of 120 miles per hour, better by 20 miles an hour than the old world's record of 109 miles hung up by Tommy Milton in Kansas City in 1922. . . .

When the Italian crossed the finish line after getting the checkered flag from Barney Oldfield, he circled the track once more and then came gliding into the pits, to be surrounded by a group of exultant friends. . . .

Only two upsets marred the serenity of the afternoon. Benny Hill brought the crowd to its feet in the early part of the afternoon when he blew a rear tire and turned a couple of figure "eights" on the far side of the track. Straightening out, Benny, to whom accidents are nothing new, brought his car in the pit and after getting a new tire, headed out again.

"Doc" Shattue pulled the other thrill, when his red boat slipped from the middle of the track, slid along the rail, but failed to go over. "Doc," also straightened out, came in—for a pair of goggles—and was off.

Veteran Tommy Milton never did get his car in shape for the race and although running quite a bit, could not keep up and finally had to wheel it from the tracks. Others who fell by the wayside included Zeke Meyers, Jerry Wonderich, Cooper's two entries, Dave Lewis, Peter Kreis.

Source: "Peter De Paola Wins First Fulford Auto Classic," *Miami Metropolis*, February 23, 1926.

—————>•◦•<—————

Blown Away

L.F. Reardon
"Unforgettable Horror," 1926

For eleven hours on September 17-18, 1926, South Florida faced its greatest test, as the killer hurricane blew through Miami and Miami Beach. At that time, hurricanes were not named nor did Miamians receive much warning as to its impending arrival. A huge tidal wave washed over Miami Beach and pushed Biscayne Bay up the Miami River creating a bore that forced the river over its shores. The devastation was even worse than what people living in South Dade experienced from Hurricane Andrew. L. F. Reardon was a Miami journalist who was living in Coral Gables. His vivid, eyewitness description captured both the horror of the storm and its desolate aftermath.

SATURDAY, SEPTEMBER 18

I have just come through Hell. Before placing the day and date at the head of the chronicle, I had to stop and think, cudgel my brain, ponder. I'm not normal. I'm not sure that I'm perfectly sane. My body feels as it would after ten rounds of fighting or three football games. Each foot weighs a ton, and my head is splitting. But we're all here at the Everglades Hotel— Deanie, Mark, Sheila and myself—and the storm has gone over to Alabama.

I must set this down now for I'm not sure how long my reason will last. My God, but I'm tired. I'll write it now while every minute's horror of those unforgettable ten hours stands out in my brain like a year in an inferno. . . .

The wind was rising. We locked all windows and barred the double doors leading from the sun parlor to the living room. We were not afraid at this time but considered that the house stands alone on high ground, unsheltered by close or adjoining buildings. . . . My first apprehension came when the rising gale tore the awning from the east window of my room, at the northern rear of the house, and whipped the iron weight bar through the glass. . . .

The gale had now reached a steady roar, but compared to what was to come, it was a gentle zephyr soughing through the palms. The walls trembled and there was a crash of glass downstairs. What to do—we could not see each other and had to shout to make ourselves heard. Would we stay in the house and take our chances, or go out into the storm? . . .

I pushed the family ahead of me down the corridor to the stairway. Taking one under each arm I went down, and we held a shouting consultation at the back door leading through the laundry to the garage. We would sit in the car so that if the house came down it would fall towards the south and away from us. . . .

We stayed in the car from two o'clock Saturday morning until seven o'clock. Five hours of torture expecting every moment to be buried under tons of stucco and Cuban tile or swept away entirely. . . .

The morning tempest subsided more slowly than that of the night and we returned for the second time into what was a home but now a scene of sickening desolation. Nothing was left. Those three words tell the story.

SUNDAY, SEPTEMBER 19

They're bringing in the dead from Hialeah. All night the ambulances have been screaming along Biscayne Boulevard and through the main streets. The injured are being taken to the McAllister Hotel which is being used as a base hospital. Martial law declared last night. You must have a pass to be in the streets after six o'clock in the evening. Reports have it Miami Beach has been washed completely away and the dead are decomposing in piles of thousands. Both causeways are wrecked and none can cross the Bay, we can only guess yet.

MONDAY, SEPTEMBER 20

The city is waking to the horrors of disaster. All of yesterday there was a spirit of hysterical joking, except among those actively engaged in relief work. Miami has met with perhaps the greatest catastrophe in the history of this country since the Johnstown flood and we might as well admit to the outside world. One reason for the prevailing levity Sunday among those who had not lost relatives in the titanic blast was the absence of any communication. Telephones and telegraphs are things of the past and future. Details were not to be had; none yet knew the facts. Candles flickered last night in homes and apartments. Bonfires illuminated the ruins of houses as the former occupants slept in the open and awoke this morning to renewed realization of their loss. . . .

Source: L. F. Reardon, *The Florida Hurricane and Disaster* (Miami: Miami Publishing Company, 1926), pp. 4-32.

Few were spared the devastating effects of the 1926 Hurricane. This family standing in front of their destroyed home, serves as a vivid reminder of the nature's force—a fact Miamians learned once again in 1992.

Myrette Burnett
Coming into a Catastrophe, 1926

When the 1926 Hurricane hit, Myrette Burnett, who came to Miami to teach at Miami High School, had just arrived in town and was staying temporarily at the Everglades Hotel. The following document is a letter she wrote to her family in Meridian, Mississippi on the Sunday after the tragedy. She described the conditions during what she believed to be two different storms. In reality, unknown to Miamians, a calm eye passed over the city during the middle of the fervor. After the storm, Ms. Burnett did teach at Miami High. She later married and raised a daughter in Miami Shores.

Dear Homefolks:

Miss Rosen and I are resting up in the Lounge Room of this hotel which overlooks Bay Biscayne. Ships, big ships, are across the way in Royal Palm Park. They were turned over and driven in by the hurricanes.

Let me say as briefly as I can that the hurricanes were fierce. News reports couldn't exaggerate how terrible it has been, the damage that has been done, and the horribleness of the situation. They can't exaggerate because the most superlative adjectives are too mild to describe the disaster. . . .

When we were taking our walk Friday night down Flagler street the storm had begun but we were ignorant of it. While I was taking my bath at 12:30 Friday night the wind was blowing terribly. We went to sleep about one. At two or two thirty we were awakened by windows crashing and the like. Lights were out; water was cut off; everything was black as night,

black night. Then vivid flashes of lightening would brighten the room. . . .

I kept lying on the bed awhile. Miss Rosen dressed; handed me my clothes. Then I dressed. We moved to my bathroom to keep away from glass. At last dawn came and with it gradually came the calm . . . we passed a Greek restaurant that served coffee toast and . . . cantaloupes. While we were there eating the second hurricane came. We sat there for safety. Just about 10 o'clock the worst came. We had to dash across the street to the Cinderella Ballroom for safety. And part of the ceiling of that fell in. They said that was the most substantial building because it was steel reinforced concrete. . . .

After that hurricane we went back to my room. . . . So we stayed there just a few minutes. Then went on the streets to see the wreckage. OK I don't believe there is a building that hasn't been damaged. We bought an extra. It stated that thousands of dollars of damage had been done but folks say millions have been ruined. . . .

I should be and I am glad to be alive and safe. It is fortunate that I had my room reserved and paid for.

The town is under martial law.

Will write later
Don't worry.

Love,
Myrt

Source: Letter, Myrette Burnette, September 1926, loaned by her daughter, Gloria Branham Burnam.

Founding of the University of Miami, 1926

When George Merrick dreamed of Coral Gables, he saw a "City Beautiful" of Mediterranean-style houses, lavish landscaping and even a university. That school, the University of Miami, opened its doors two weeks after the 1926 Hurricane even though it had to move into a half-finished apartment hotel next to today's Coral Gables Youth Center and abandon its main campus that was under construction. It was dubbed the "cardboard college" because the walls were so thin. With a senior class of just four, the first years were true pioneering and the university struggled to survive during the Depression. Today the University of Miami is recognized as a major research university. The following document was written by students and published in the first Ibis, *the university's yearbook.*

A Dreamer has his place in the realm of man, and without him a very uninteresting existence would be the lot of his fellow creatures. But a dreamer who repeatedly makes his dreams come true is a real boon, not only to his contemporaries, but to all the generations to follow. He is an example that many strive to follow, and a leader who is blazing a trail for those to come after him.

Having spent his boyhood days in a home that was surrounded by an unbroken wilderness of palmetto and pine, George E. Merrick visualized a city of beautiful homes, a community of high ideals and a center of education. His vision was made into reality, the beautiful city is known throughout the country. The climax of the realizations of his dreams came on the day [February 24, 1926] when the cornerstone of the University of Miami was laid. The ceremony was attended by more than seven thousand residents of Miami, Coral Gables, and surrounding sections. Included in the number present were men and women famous in the educational world, business and professional life, and one thousand school children.

Judge William E. Walsh, chairman of the Board of Regents presided at the exercises, and appropriate speeches were delivered by Frank B. Shutts, member of the Board of Regents, and Hamilton Holt, president of Rollins College. Mr. Merrick then told of his dreams of what had then become realities, and of the inspiration he had received many years before from his father, to whom the new building in dedicated. The cornerstone was laid by Frederick Zeigen, Secretary of the Board. This cornerstone laying marked the official beginning of one of the world's greatest institutions of learning.

The days following were filled with preliminary details. Bowman Foster Ashe, in the capacity of executive secretary, was busy every minute with conferences with architects, the compiling of the curricula, the purchasing of equipment, and the immense task of securing the best faculty possible. The success he experienced in his many and varied duties is recorded elsewhere. . . .

Construction was put under way at double speed, men were working day and night; roaring trucks were carrying material in a steady stream; all this bustle and energy was being put forth in an effort to complete the Anastasia Hotel in time to turn it into the temporary home of the new university. The University Building was under construction and could not possibly have been finished in time to begin classes in the fall, in spite of the greatest effort that could be made. So, on Friday, October 15, the doors of the Anastasia were opened to the first day of registration of a new institution of learning. . . .

Soon the exploding exhausts from trucks, hauling dirt and other materials for the completion of the patio, made it necessary for the professors to strain their voices in an effort to make themselves heard above the din. The patio was filled in, a smooth concrete floor laid, and a stage built in one corner for performances of the Conservatory and School of Dancing. The floor was lined off for a basketball court and bleachers were erected to accommodate the spectators.

Meanwhile the Art Department had been placing posters about town advertising the football games that were to be held at the temporary stadium. The stadium is situated adjacent to the University Building and was well filled at all the games by students and friends who witnessed an undefeated season by the Hurricanes. A student section of the stadium was built on one side of the field and the townspeople occupied the rest of the stadium on the other side.

The record achieved by the Hurricanes in spite of many handicaps will never be forgotten, and the University is now near the end of its first year with a record that equals that of the eleven. We have overcome just as many difficulties and borne up under just as many disappointments. We hope to begin the second year of our history in a building that will rival any structure on any campus in the country.

Source: *The Ibis* (Miami: Strange Printing Company [1927]), pp. 15-16.

GOVERNMENT EXPANDS
1928 - 1945

"Governments can err—Presidents do make mistakes, but the immortal Dante tells us that divine justice weighs the sins of the cold-blooded and the sins of the warm-hearted in different scales. Better the occasional faults of a government that lives in a spirit of charity than the consistent omissions of a government frozen in the ice of its own indifference. There is a mysterious cycle in human events. To some generations much is given. Of other generations much is expected. This generation of Americans has a rendezvous with destiny."

Franklin Delano Roosevelt, 1936

The Jungle Queen tourist boat cruises up the Miami River past the Granada Apartments, Miami's first condominium that sat on the site of today's Hyatt Hotel. The Dade County Courthouse, completed in 1928, is on the left.

In 1928, Dade County's new skyscraper courthouse opened. The elegant building, that also housed the City of Miami offices and both city and county jails, symbolized the optimism of both city and county government. Starting in 1933, however, city and county government influence took a back seat. During the Depression and World War II, the federal government became the driving force that transformed Miami from a small southern city into a dynamic modern metropolis.

Beyond modest help in developing the Port of Miami, there was little federal involvement in the early history of the City of Miami and only a narrowly defined group—primarily white males—held political power. Like much of the South, power was further defined by the Democratic Party that solidly controlled both state and local politics. Women, under the Constitution of the United States, did not have the right to vote until the Constitution was amended in 1920. In addition, Jim Crow laws made it largely impossible for blacks to vote.

Some major advances in voting rights, however, occurred in this era. Women won the right to vote. In 1937, under the leadership of Dade Senator Ernest R Graham, the state legislature repealed the poll tax, one of the mechanisms that limited black voting. In 1944, another anti-black measure, the White Primary, was declared unconstitutional by the United States Supreme Court.

Government programs and projects during the Depression and World War II had a lasting effect on Greater Miami. Many facilities built by New Deal agencies are still enjoyed today. WPA art and architecture are a part of our cultural and architectural heritage. Many World War II facilities, particularly airports, were turned over to local government following the war. Finally, wartime activities of the Navy and the Army Air Force further defined and supported Miami's future as a gateway city.

"Brother Can You Spare a Dime?"

By 1927, while the rest of the nation was still on a spending spree and a stock-market frenzy, Miami continued to fall deeper into depression. Banks failed, half-finished construction projects stalled, real estate values plummeted and many people, who had come during the heady days of the Boom, deserted the area. The hallmark Bank of Bay Biscayne and Sewell Brothers, two businesses that had been a part of the city since its founding, closed their doors. George Merrick (founder of Coral Gables) lost all his money and was so broke, he couldn't even afford to buy a tire for his automobile. He and his wife moved to the Keys where they ran a fishing camp. Miami and Coral Gables both defaulted on loans, and teacher's salaries were drastically reduced. Families saw their bread-winner out of work, their life-savings disappear in bank failures and their homes repossessed and sold for taxes on the courthouse steps.

One of the few bright spots in Miami's plummeting economy was the emergence of the aviation industry. Pan American Airways moved to Miami in 1928 and by the early 1930s, its "Flying Clippers" were arriving and leaving from their new terminal at Dinner Key. At about the same time, Eastern Airlines began flying from the old Pan American Field that eventually became part of today's vast Miami International Airport. To further promote Miami as an aviation center, the city inaugurated the All-American Air Maneuvers that attracted fliers from all over the world and huge crowds to the annual event.

"Anything to Please the Tourists"

From the time of the city's founding, Greater Miami's leaders had been pre-occupied with tourism and went to great lengths to keep the tourists happy. Miami adopted what was euphemistically called the "liberal policy." In practice it meant that law enforcement and community leaders would turn a blind-eye toward illicit activities like booze, gambling and prostitution. In short, if it was illegal, but fun, Miami had it.

Unfortunately, Miami's wide-open reputation not only attracted tourists, it also attracted a group of people Miamians didn't like. The most notorious of these was the infamous "Scarface" Al Capone who moved to Palm Island in 1928. The police and political establishment tried to run him out of town but his bevy of lawyers went to court to put a stop to the harassment. Capone stayed put until the federal government convicted him of income tax evasion in 1931

During the Depression, the Farm Security Administration hired photogaphers to educate Americans about the plight of the rural poor as seen here in this moving shot of Homestead migrant workers. (Marion Post Wolcott)

and hauled him off to a federal prison. By this time, however, the damage was done. Organized crime had taken over Miami's illegal fun and games.

When Doyle E. Carlton became Governor of Florida in 1929, he decided to crack down on Miami's booming, illegal pari-mutuel gambling industry. In this instance, however, the same people who tried to run Al Capone out of town, were horrified by Carlton's act. Most believed that the illegal horse and dog tracks, and the jai-alai frontons were harmless pastimes and a real boon to Miami's tourist economy. Following the Carlton crackdown, state representative Dan Chappell, bolstered by strong *Miami Herald* backing, succeeded in legalizing pari-mutuel gambling in Florida over Governor Carlton's veto. As additional revenue flowed into state and local coffers, the legislature went so far as to legalize slot machines as well. After one year of the slots, however, when they appeared in practically every store and restaurant in town, they became illegal once again.

Local leaders were willing to do just about anything to keep the tourists coming. They brought in professional publicists like Carl Byoir and Steve Hannigan who utilized promotional stunts and bathing beauties to attract attention to South Florida. In 1935, even the state tried to help by liberalizing their divorce laws to give out-of-staters yet another reason to come to Florida. Some ideas had more lasting value. In 1933, a group of civic leaders created the Palm Festival football game on New Year's Day to get the tourists in early. (When their money ran out they called on local gamblers to pay the visiting team's way home!) Two years later, it was re-named the Orange Bowl Festival and became one of South Florida's most enduring spectacles.

∞ A New Deal for Miami

Franklin Roosevelt and his promised "New Deal" swept Dade County in the pivotal election of 1932. Yet it was Roosevelt's trip through Miami that almost changed the course of history. In February 1933, President-Elect Roosevelt stopped in Miami while vacationing on his friend Vincent Astor's yacht. While addressing a crowd at Bayfront Park, Guiseppe Zangara, an unemployed brick-layer, attempted to assassinate Roosevelt. Zangara missed the president-elect, but hit four others and mortally wounded Mayor Anton Cermak of Chicago. Justice was swift in those days. Thirty-three days after the shocking event, Zangara was executed at Florida's Raiford Prison.

Federal money played a crucial role in reviving Miami's economy during the New Deal. Over 16,000 Miamians received direct assistance from the Federal Emergency Relief Agency but Roosevelt preferred work relief to simply dispensing cash to the needy. This philosophy was reflected in the New Deal's alphabet soup agencies that were instituted to put people to work.

The Civilian Conservation Corps (CCC) hired young men 18 to 25 to work in reforestation, in developing rural areas and in building parks. The CCC paid $30 a month and provided free housing in a camp that the men built themselves. Miami's CCC camp was in what was then a pine woods across from today's Dadeland Mall. Their most notable local projects included Greynolds and Matheson Hammock Parks and Fairchild Tropical Garden.

In 1935, Congress also created the Works Progress Administration (WPA) with the largest peace-time appropriation in U.S. history. The WPA's Federal Theater entertained depression-weary Miamians at the Miami High School Auditorium and at the Scottish Rite Temple. They held children's programs at the Bayfront Park Bandshell. The Federal Music Project hired unemployed musicians who performed symphonic productions and grand opera. Even writers, photographers and historians were put to work by the WPA. The WPA Guide to Miami helped spur tourism to the area. Historians compiled primary source documents and recorded oral histories including valuable testimonies from ex-slaves.

Artists worked out of a WPA warehouse in Coral Gables. They produced a variety of art objects—concrete fountains, bas-relief sculptures, murals—that were installed in public buildings. Some of their most notable works were done by muralists like Denman Fink. His historical piece in the central courtroom of the downtown Federal Building and in the lobby of the Miami High School Auditorium are still favorites. Charles Erdman's work in the Miami Beach Post Office is another legacy of the WPA that is still appreciated today.

A third New Deal agency, the Public Works Administration (PWA) was also active in Miami.

Thanks to the lobbying effort of Roddey Burdine (son of the founder of Burdine's Department Store) and City of Miami Recreation Director Earnie Seiler, the PWA built the 25,000 seat Orange Bowl Stadium.

The PWA also built several schools in the Miami area. Shenandoah Junior High and Coral Way Elementary were notable PWA projects. Public buildings included the Skaggs Building at Jackson Memorial Hospital and Coral Gables' old Police and Fire Station. Often the WPA and PWA worked together. Two good examples of this co-operation can be seen in the sculpture at the Coral Gables Police and Fire Station and the decorative tile work at Coral Way Elementary.

Beyond relief from unemployment, the New Deal created more enduring reforms. The Wagner Labor Relations Act, passed in 1935, initiated regular procedures for labor organization and the Wages and Hours Act (1938) established the nation's first minimum wage at 40 cents an hour.

The Social Security Act, also passed in 1935, provided a safety net for elderly Americans. This act made it possible for more senior citizens to retire and when retirement time came, many chose the Miami area. As a result, Miami and Miami Beach's elderly population grew.

These, and other New Deal policies, did not end the Depression but they certainly helped stimulate both the local and national economy. They also gave people a sense that the government was trying to do something about the crisis. Although Miami led the nation into the Depression, it was on its way out earlier than most other American cities. By 1935, greater numbers of tourists began returning to the area, leading to the construction of numerous new hotels. On Miami Beach, the curves and flourishes of a new style of architecture that today is know as Art Deco or Moderne style, began to offset the older architectural style of Mediterranean Revival. The following year, the romantic song: "Moon Over Miami," was number one on the popular radio show "Your Hit Parade."

∞ Intolerance Rules the Day

A large number of Jews moved to South Florida during the 1930s. Discrimination continued, particularly on Miami Beach which had the area's fastest growing Jewish population. In 1930, Baron de Hirsch Meyer became the first Jew elected to the Miami Beach City Commission. Another prominent member of the Jewish community, third-term commissioner Mitchell

Living History

The New Deal not only helped the nation out of Depression, it also produced a sort of cultural renaissance. Thousands of artists, designers, writers and builders found work through programs such as the Works Progress Administration and the Public Works Administration. All over the United States, the WPA left a legacy that is still visible today.

Many New Deal buildings reflected their own style—sometimes called Depression Moderne. One of the best examples in Greater Miami is the Miami Beach Post Office. With its Moderne forms and streamlined geometric designs, the Post Office at 1300 Washington Avenue captured the visual trends of the time. Designed by architect H. L. Cheney in 1937, the post office is a circular structure flanked by lower rectangular masses. Echoing the harsh economic times, its facade is unadorned, sparse and a bit somber.

Historical murals painted by WPA artist Charles Erdman recreated scenes of Florida history in the post office's lobby. The three murals show the meeting between native Americans and Ponce de Leon, the natives' battle with DeSoto and their confrontation with American army commanders. Murals were a popular art form in Depression era public buildings and many artists across America worked in this medium. In 1977, the post office was one of the first buildings to be restored in the newly created Art Deco District.

Wolfson, was elected Mayor by his fellow commissioners in 1943, a post he voluntarily gave up to join the army. Despite these political gains, many hotels and apartments as well as private clubs remained restricted to "Gentiles Only," especially north of Lincoln Road.

Miami's African American community continued to face even more serious problems, despite some assistance from New Deal programs. Thanks to the prodding of Father John Culmer, *The Miami Herald* published a series that exposed serious housing problems and festering social conditions in Miami's black community. In 1934, the federal government helped fund the Liberty Square low cost housing project. Completed in 1937, Liberty Square, run by James E. Scott in its early days, provided housing for families and was the new center for blacks in northern Dade County. (A few years later, a similar low-cost housing project for whites was built across from Edison High School.)

By the late 1930s, African Americans in Miami became more assertive of their rights due, in part, to national events. Mary McLeod Bethune, the President of Florida's Bethune-Cookman College, gained national influence as a spokesperson for blacks; Eleanor Roosevelt assisted the famous singer Marian Anderson to perform at the Lincoln Memorial after being denied the right to sing at the Hall of the Daughters of the American Revolution. Joe Louis defeated German Max Schmeling to become a national hero. Within the next 20 years, many of these national leaders would have an impact on Miami's struggle for black equality as well.

Despite the obstacles of segregation, black Miamians made gains in Miami's strictly segregated society. In 1936, Annie M. Coleman organized the Friendship Garden Club that was later renamed the Friendship Garden and Civic Club. As the years went by, the club's influence spread and Mrs. Coleman and her workers were able to get the white establishment to listen to some of their concerns. Blacks also increased their voting registration after the abolition of the poll tax. In early May 1939, blacks defied serious threats from the KKK and increased their participation in a Miami election from their standard 50 votes to more than a 1,000. In 1944, the City of Miami created a black police force. In May 1945, Otis Mundy led a protest at Baker's Haulover Beach because blacks were not allowed to swim there or any other beach in Greater Miami. Three months later, the county opened the first black bathing beach on Virginia Key. At the time, its only access was by ferry.

∞ Wartime Changes Miami

Miami was on its way out of the Depression when the Japanese bombed Pearl Harbor on December 7, 1941. Local leaders went to Washington to convince federal authorities that Miami was a natural area for training military personnel. As a result of this effort, federal dollars poured into the area for the training and recreation of hundreds of thousands of military personnel and their families. This influx filled the economic void left by absent tourists. The Miami area was closer to the war than most American cities. German submarines torpedoed more than 25 tankers off the Florida coast in 1942 alone, one in full view of Miami residents. In response to this threat to American shores, the Navy's Gulf Sea Frontier made Miami its headquarters that same year and took over several floors of the DuPont Building that was dubbed the "U.S.S. Neversink." Soon, most of Miami's hotels were filled with Navy personnel and Naval officers and enlisted men were a common sight marching down Biscayne Boulevard. P. T. boats rested at former pleasure boat docks at Bayfront Park. The Navy housed blimps at Richmond Field, now the site of Metro Zoo. They were used as the first line of defense against the German submarine menace.

By 1943, more than 188 hotels and 109 apartment houses on Miami Beach had been taken over by the Army Air Force. Before the war ended, over 1/3 of all the U.S. Army Air Force pilots, as well as a group of foreign ones, trained on Miami Beach. Matinee idol, Clark Gable, was one of the officers who trained there.

South Florida also became a popular location for recreation and rehabilitation. Over 235,000 white servicemen were entertained by local women at the Miami Beach Servicemen's Pier and the citizens of Overtown ran a club for black soldiers. Full military hospitals operated out of the Biltmore and Nautilus Hotels that had been taken over by Uncle Sam soon after the war began.

Local citizens also joined in the war effort. Successful local war bond drives were aided by appeals from national celebrities. School children participated in stamp programs and tin can drives. Groceries and consumer goods, especially gasoline, were strictly rationed and citizens were encouraged to have "meatless" Tuesdays and plant Victory Gardens in their backyards. Similar to the experience of World War I, however, not everyone was a good citizen. Price gouging and an active black market in goods circumvented price controls and elicited widespread anger by both patriotic residents and tourists. Several national publications featured negative articles about what they perceived as Miami's pre-occupation with making a profit from the war.

The years of the Great Depression and World War II were very difficult years. Despite the hardships, people developed a kindred spirit and common purpose as they fought clear, common enemies called depression and war.

A Close Call

Estelle Caldwell Overstreet
Miami's Day of Infamy, 1933

The Caldwell family moved to Coconut Grove in 1914. Estelle graduated from Coconut Grove High School in 1925, the only graduating class the school ever had. After graduation, she went to work for the first mayor of Coconut Grove, Irving J. Thomas—a job that lasted 37 years. For many years, her husband, J. D. Overstreet, had a popular bicycle shop in Coconut Grove. The following reminiscence was written in honor of her brother and only sibling, Russell L. Caldwell, who was shot between the eyes by Guiseppe Zangara during his attempt to assassinate President-Elect Franklin Delano Roosevelt in Bayfront Park on February 15, 1933. Caldwell survived the attack and died in 1985 at age 75. Estelle Overstreet still lives in Coconut Grove.

Sixty-three years ago today, my brother Russell received his "15 minutes of fame"—but in a nightmarish and violent situation. He was 22 years old, and employed as a chauffeur by a wealthy Coconut Grove widow.

The Miami papers and radios had repeatedly told about the appearance of President-Elect Franklin Delano Roosevelt at the bandshell in downtown Miami. He was returning from a holiday cruise aboard the yacht of his friend, Mr. Vincent Astor, and had promised to make a short speech at the bandshell.

Russell's employer decided she wanted to see the President, so she and Russell went very early so as to get the best seats possible up close—not knowing a would-be assassin sat in a row ahead of them a few feet to their left.

President Roosevelt was confined to a wheelchair, because of polio he had as a young man. He could stand only by support and a cane. One of his sons usually stood by him. On this night he sat on top of the back seat in his open car.

My husband, my mother and I were at home, listening to the radio; we had no televisions in 1933. We were happy that Russell could be a part of such a big occasion and see the man who would become President of the U.S. in 17 days. We heard the glowing welcoming speeches by the mayor and others; and the address by President Roosevelt.

Suddenly, there was pandemonium. The monotonous voice of the announcer became sharp and excited as he realized what was happening when the gunfire started. His new tone of voice and descriptions terrified us at home. It was much later before someone called to tell us Russell was one of the victims and in Jackson Memorial Hospital. They assured us he would be all right.

What a shock! The next morning my husband and I went to the hospital with our 18 month old son Jimmy. My mother was too upset and not feeling well. While we were there, President Roosevelt came to visit Russell. He was in his old-fashioned wheelchair, flanked by his son and bodyguards. He was most cordial and sympathetic. He shook hands with all of us, patted little Jimmy on the head, thanked Russell for helping save his life, but sorry in such a manner. He sent a beautiful flower arrangement with a personal note. Later, he sent an invitation to his inauguration in Washington D.C., as well as a personal letter.

Russell basked in his so-called "fame." He felt he was a hero in his young mind.

He told us he was standing on his bench trying to see the President, who was sitting in his car, when he felt a hard blow to his forehead. He thought someone had thrown a rock. When he put his hand to his forehead, it was covered with blood. A policeman took him to a car and said: "Here's one shot between the eyes."

That was when Russell realized he had been hit with a bullet, and in his mind he was going to die.

The now subdued brick layer, Giuseppe Zangara, was thrown over the trunk rack of the same car that took Russell to the hospital—and sat on by

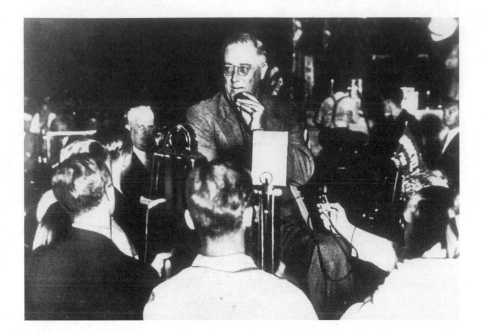

On February 15, 1933, President-Elect Franklin D. Roosevelt addressed 18,000 Miamians at Bayfront Park. Minutes after this photograph was taken, Guiseppe Zangara stood up in the crowd and fired five shots. Five bystanders were hit, but Roosevelt miraculously escaped injury.

policemen. There wasn't enough room in the car. Before reaching the hospital one of the policemen dropped his gun; the car had to stop for that. All the while, blood was dripping in Russell's face and he did think he was dying, he said.

An operation was performed the next morning and several stitches taken. They gave him the bullet. It was flat, indicating it hit something else first, probably a car or the band shell. They said he was probably hit first. The doctor told him the bullet had lodged against a small, delicate bone and had bent it; that if it had broken, it would have killed him instantly. . . .

I kept a scrapbook for Russell. It was full of newspaper clippings, letters he received from friends and strangers, the bullet itself, the letter and Inaugural invitation from President Roosevelt, etc. Years later, he gave it to the Historical Association of Southern Florida in Miami.

Source: Estelle Caldwell Overstreet, "A Sister Remembers" (unpublished manuscript, Miami, Florida, 1996).

Miamians Face the Depression

Star and Mallory Horton Recalling Hard Times

Star Horton and his brother Mallory grew up in Miami during the 1930s. Each worked his way through college and law school and ultimately enjoyed thriving practices in their hometown. They share these recollections of odd jobs they acquired to survive the Depression. The following documents are from an interview and unpublished manuscript by Bud Altmayer, a friend of the Hortons.

Star: From 1931 on, we struggled because after that Dad was never permanently employed. In 1931, the banks closed and my mother and father lost the $300 they had on deposit in the Bank of Bay Biscayne. Mother went to work for Green's Dress Shop downtown on the corner of Miami Avenue and First Street. She worked fifty-four hours a week and they paid her eight dollars a week. That supported the household; it was the only income we had. My father did the housework and Mallory and I helped him. Our sister got married in 1930, so there were just us two kids. We had to go out and hustle to make a living. I sold newspapers; I sold flowers and I sold fresh yard eggs. My father bought cold storage eggs; I put them in a bucket and went house to house selling them as fresh.

Mallory: At one time, I was a bag boy at the Tip Top Grocery. A quart of milk cost ten cents and a loaf of bread was a nickel; a dozen eggs were fifteen cents. You couldn't sell chickens because most everybody was raising them in their backyard.

Star: I worked for O'Neil and Orr Construction Company when I was a freshman at the University of Miami. They were building the Alamack and the Evans Hotels on opposite corners of Thirteenth Street and Collins Avenue on the beach. They hired some of the kids from the University to wheel concrete in wheelbarrows. We called them Georgia buggies. At first, they paid us sixteen cents an hour; I worked my way up to thirty two cents an hour. I made about fifteen dollars a week and glad to get it. We never heard of a minimum wage. We were just glad to be working. They would work us sometimes until seven at night. I remember one week because of the overtime, they paid me $20; that was a tremendous sum. For three or four dollars, I could buy all the groceries I could carry. . . . I recall a woman coming to my mother and telling her there wasn't enough food to feed her eight children. That family had come from Georgia as so many families did at that time. They came from Georgia like the Okies went to California. Mother gave her a can of spaghetti. The woman took the can and tried to split it up between eight kids.

Source: Bud Altmayer and Carin Litman Hanan, "As I Recall . . . Miami in the 30s" (unpublished manuscript, Miami, Florida, 1990), pp. 4, 5, 11, 12.

Rules of the Marathon Dance, 1931

One of the enduring images of the Great Depression was the exhausted figures of marathon dancers. Marathon dance contests became both entertainment and spectator sport, reflecting both desperation and the new attraction to fads. The contest was simple—the couple who could dance the longest won the prize. Marathon dance mania swept Miami. The major site for the contest was at the Cinderella Ballroom that once stood at 25 N.W. 2nd Street. The document that follows is a printed sheet of rules for the contest.

RULES OF MARATHON DANCE CONTEST

No. 1—Contestants will dance 40 minutes and then rest 15 minutes out of each hour, allowing the remaining 5 minutes for the contestants to be awakened, brought out of the training quarters and on the dance floor at the first signal.

No. 2—All male contestants must be clean shaven at all times.

No. 3—Contesting couples must have their feet moving while competing and keep at least 3 feet from other dancing couples. All contesting couples must have at least one hand on each other at all times.

No. 4—Any contestant that shall leave the floor without permission from the judges is automatically disqualified.

No. 5—All contestants are forbidden to receive candy, gum, cigarettes, food or anything to be placed in the contestant's mouth from any other than regular authorized sources and at designated times. Any contestant violating this rule may be disqualified and ruled from the floor.

No. 6—Should a person become ill or injured the person remaining in the contest may dance alone, until such time as he shall be eliminated or disqualified or shall acquire a new partner from the remaining contestants, using the number of the male contestants remaining in the contest.

No. 7—The management reserves the right to disqualify any contestant who is not in good physical health at any time on the advice of a competent physician.

No. 8—Floor rules will be interpreted by the floor judges on duty and no appeal may be had from their ruling

No. 9—Dancers falling to floor through sleepiness or other reasons will have 10 seconds to regain feet.

Source: Brochure: "Rules of the Marathon Dance Contest," (Miami: Ross Amusement Company, January 15, 1931).

Miamians Welcome Cubans, 1933

During the Depression, Miami became a haven for Cuban exiles. General Mario Menocal, a veteran of Cuba's war for independence, was elected President of Cuba in 1912 and re-elected in 1916. In 1931, after leaving office, the openly rebellious Menocal was captured by then Cuban President Gerardo Machado. Menocal left Cuba and chose exile in Miami. The Menocals lived in a mansion on Miami Beach that was the center of exile activism. In August 1933, President Machado was overthrown by popular revolt and Menocal and his fellow exiles left Miami to return home to Cuba. In this prophetic editorial, written as the exiles were leaving Miami, The Miami Herald celebrated the city's acceptance of the Cubans and promised that Miami would always welcome them back.

MIAMI'S LOSS

For some time the population of Metropolitan Miami has included several hundred Cubans, mostly exiles from their country because of their opposition to the rule of General Gerardo Machado. The colony was headed by General Mario C. Menocal, former president of Cuba.

With the sudden retirement of Machado and the rise of a new regime, Miami has begun to lose her Cuban residents, who are looking back to the homeland where they will be welcome and secure once more. Many have already returned, eager to see their island and participate in the joys of victory. Others will follow, depleting our population.

Miami was glad to extend her hospitality to the exiles and will be sorry to lose them, but appreciates their desire to bask again in Cuban sunshine and breezes, to stroll Havana's avenues, to sip the sparkling wines in the cafes, to breathe the air of freedom beneath the palms, as the grim Morro Castle looks down on the city tossed in the storms of patriotism. Not even the glories of Miami can replace the lure of the dear homeland, for which one has longed, fought and suffered.

Miami's gates will ever remain open to Cubans, as well as to men and women from every country and clime and state. Order is being quickly restored in Cuba, and the old charm and new of Havana remains, the flavor of the foreign atmosphere which so appeals to American visitors, the distinctive architecture, the narrow streets, the ancient churches, the Latin characteristics. Going to Cuba is like a trip abroad for resident of the United States. And Cuba is only two hours distant from Miami by airplane, a daylight trip by train and ship. Our mutual interests will continue to grow.

Miami bids farewell to her Cuban friends and wishes them well.

Source: "Miami's Loss," *Miami Herald*, August 17, 1933, p. 6.

The CCC, "Uncle Sam's Constructive Army"

When Franklin Delano Roosevelt created the Civilian Conservation Corps in 1933, thousands of young men (18-25) went to work for Uncle Sam. In Dade County, the CCC created some of the area's most beautiful parks—Greynolds Park, Matheson Hammock and Fairchild Tropical Garden—and helped launch the Dade County Parks system. The CCC, under landscape architect William Lyman Phillips, designed the parks from the greenery to the concession stands. The young men lived in a military atmosphere with strict regimen

and discipline. Their principal camp was across from today's Dadeland. This article, written on the sixth anniversary of the corps' presence in South Florida, describes the lifestyle of the CCC worker.

Dade County's contingent of Uncle Sam's constructive army, the Civilian Conservation Corps—the army that is constructing parks, planting forests, fighting soil erosion and beautifying city and rural districts throughout the nation—will welcome the public today to an "open house" from 2:00 to 4:00 pm at its camp near Kendall.

The occasion will mark six years of endeavor of the corps in Dade county, during which it has cooperated with county forces in creating two outstanding parks in Florida, Matheson Hammock park, south of Coconut Grove, and Greynolds park, near Ojus, and also has aided materially in other outstanding park and beautification work.

Guides will show the visitors around the little city of buildings, most of them long, brown one-story structures in which the youths of the CCC sleep, eat, play and study during their off-duty hours.

An average of 160 men are quartered at the camp according to Lieut. Joel C. Robertson of the 24th Infantry, who is in command of Camp Florida, SP-9, the headquarters of Company 1421 of the CCC.

The average age of corps members now is 19. The average was formerly around 21. Most of the men now employed at the camp come from the Tampa and Deland districts.

In some ways, the day's routine of the corps is as rigorous as that of the army, Lieutenant Robertson explained. Reveille is sounded at 5:30 a.m., and this is followed by calisthenics. Breakfast is served at 6 a.m. and afterward the men clean up their quarters and make up their bunks. They leave for the field at 7 a.m. and return to quarters at 3 p.m. Retreat is held at 5 p.m. The men work but five days a week, having Saturdays and Sundays free.

Much of the time of the men is spent in study. Some enrolled have been found to be lacking in even a grammar school education, Lieutenant Robertson said, and are unable even to write their names. All of the men are required to participate in the educational work offered, however, and a special building is used for instruction and study.

Ample recreation facilities are provided for the men, checkers, ping-pong and bingo being among the most popular.

Religious services are not neglected. Sunday school is help every Sunday morning, and on Tuesday night services are held, a different pastor being sought for each service.

The pay of the men is $30 a month, $8 of which is given him for his own use and $22 as his allotment for home. He is also supplied with all food and clothing without cost. The clothing is a neatly fitted khaki-colored uniform.

There are leaders and assistant leaders who get more pay. A leader draws $15 a month extra and the assistant leader is paid $6 a month extra.

Source: "Dade CCC Camp Observes Sixth Birthday Today," *Miami Daily News*, April 9, 1939.

The "Wide Open" City

Jack Kofoed
Gambling Takes Over, 1929

Jack Kofoed spent 67 years as a newspaperman, 57 of those years as a daily columnist. His writing career began in Philadelphia in 1911 and in 1938, he came to Miami to work for The Miami Daily News. *After serving in World War II, he returned to Miami as a columnist for* The Miami Herald *where he remained until his death in 1979. He left a legacy of 13 books, more than 1,200 magazine pieces and 17,000 columns. The following document from* The North American Review *was written by Kofoed in 1929 when Miami, already deep in depression, allowed gambling and other illicit activities to flourish.*

In the days before the Great Boom, Miami's dream of fame as a winter resort did not include the revelry and wickedness of the Riviera. Drowsing under the winter sun, the small but growing city looking over Biscayne Bay to the sandy waste land that the magic of Carl Fisher later transformed into Miami Beach, took thought principally to sound and careful citizens. The business men of the rural Middle West, with his Rotary, Kiwanis and Board of Trade affiliations, was the type that Miami hoped would build her skyline and increase her bank deposits.

This hope was deepened by the mob of tin-can tourists, rainbow chasers and easy money boys who surged down here in 1925 to grab what they could and leave Miami flat on her protesting back. Floridians wanted stability in a day when nothing had a really solid foundation. . . .

But, in fact, and pretense aside, the Magic City has torn itself away from the staid old dream. Small town business men and retired school ma'ams may still find harbor there, but the real atmosphere has been tinted by the Tex Guinans, Jack Dempseys, Scarface Capones and by a motley crew from Broadway and the race-track. The average visitor is much more likely to ask the location of a famous gambling joint, popularly supposed to have been backed by the late Tex Rickard, than of the First Methodist Church.

I like Miami. It is an absolutely perfect place for a vacation. The sky is bluer and the sunshine brighter than anywhere else in America. Of the more innocent pleasures—golf, bathing, polo, tennis, speed boating, airplaning—there is no end. Of the more sophisticated joys, such as drinking, gambling and eating pompano at Little Joe's, there is equal abundance.

Miami admits these assets privately, but denies them publicly. Hypocrisy is increasing on the shores of Biscayne Bay. Get the dollars, but deny the reasons for them. The city is touchy in the extreme about any fling at her standing. . . .

In a city like this the opportunities for graft by policemen have been enormous. The guardians of public safety became bolder and bolder, and rougher, until Grand Jury indicted the lot. Alexander Orr, Jr., a prominent businessman, who was foreman of the jury, and V. Vernon Hawthorn, State's Attorney, issued the following statement:

"Approximately 300 witnesses have appeared before the Grand Jury, more than ninety per cent of whom gave testimony regarding police conditions, in consequence of which we became convinced that there existed within the Police Department a well constructed organization of unknown strength, slowly but surely destroying the freedom of our citizens, mean-

Police Chief H. Leslie Quigg breaks up illegal slot machines during one of the Miami Police Department's periodic "get tough" campaigns to stamp out illegal gambling. (HASF)

ingless and cruel, practicing habits destitute of moral or civil motives and serving only to gratify a malignant passion.

We feel that the lack of morals and their alliance with gamblers, bootleggers, houses of ill fame and the underworld in general have contributed largely to the amazing growth of open violations of the law in the territory served by them."...

Miami is a charming place for a frolic. So, in a different way, is New York. The under-cover conditions are probably much the same in both places—but New York does not pretend morality.

Source: Jack Kofoed, "Miami," *North American Review* CCXXVIII (December, 1929), pp. 670-73.

Oswald Garrison Villard
"Florida Flamboyant," 1935

Although South Florida showed signs of economic recovery by the mid-1930s, clearly ahead of most of the rest of the nation, all was not well in "The Magic City." The so-called economic recovery left many people behind. Crime was rampant and political corruption was probably worse than in any other period of Miami's history. The following article from The Nation was written by the grandson of the famous abolitionist William Lloyd Garrison. Villard was a nationally known pacifist and crusader for racial equality and women's suffrage, who fought against political corruption.

If one were to judge Florida by the appearance of Miami one would have to say that the depression is over in this state. The streets are thronged with the tourists the city must have in order to live, since it has no other trade; the hotels are jammed; the night clubs flourish; there is building everywhere, with lots beginning to go fast; the newspapers are carrying more advertising by one quarter than a year ago; the FERA [Federal Emergency Relief Administration] reports only 4,000 cases (individuals with or without families) on the relief roll, of whom 1,300 are Negroes and 900 single or widowed women, as against a peak of 16,000 in 1932 and 10,500 in November, 1933. The visitors are spending money freely—before half the horse-racing season was over they had bet $8,000,000 on the "ponies," and there are three dog-racing tracks. True, some of the stores report smaller expenditures per capita than a year ago. But there can be no doubt whatever of the revival of building. Here in Miami Beach homes worth $400,000 and lots valued at $176,000 have changed hands in the past two weeks. The total expenditure for building in the Miami district in 1934 ran well over $8,000,000.

So much on the surface. But all is not so well underneath. Crime is rampant; two days ago men were robbed on the golf links and two caddies were found on the streets of Miami with their skulls fractured. Politics controls the police, so the police testify, as everywhere else, with the result that the men—95 percent of excellent character, a most competent authority assures me—cannot do their duty; if they were allowed to, my informant says, they could clean up both cities at once. There has been a general disposition to run a "wide-open town" to lure the tourists and there was open gambling until a few weeks ago, when the evil began to repel the visitors. In consequence, a judge, the chief of police, a state senator, and other high officials have been indicted, but the senator has already been acquitted and there is not much likelihood of other convictions; anybody who wants to can still gamble with impunity. Beside those aided by the FERA, which can only help bona fide residents, there are a number of destitute or near destitute. The transient camp contains an average of 450 men, and every day some fifteen hobos and wanderers are taken to the county line and "shoved over."

Every worker in Miami must report to the police and be finger-printed, and in many occupations must have a police license before he can work. Wages are low and hours long. One woman writes me that she worked for four days in a laundry ironing nine hours a day and was paid $1 a day. It is charged that in the restaurants men and women work twelve hours seven days a week, and *The Miami Herald* carries advertisements for men and boys to work for board and lodging and $1 a week! "There is more slavery in Florida today," writes an old reader of *The Nation*, "than when Lincoln at the instigation of your ancestors freed the slaves." As for Miami, he writes bitterly: "It is the harlot of American cities and, like many harlots, it is unusually favored by nature."

Source: Oswald Garrison Villard, "Issues and Men: Florida Flamboyant," *The Nation*, March 13, 1935, p. 295.

Living History

Hialeah Park Racetrack
2200 East Fourth Avenue
Hialeah

When the Miami Jockey Club at Hialeah opened in 1925, track betting was illegal, but officials paid little attention to the law. The track owners sold "stock" on the horses and paid "dividends" to the winner all within the law—or so they said.

In 1929, Philadelphia millionaire Joseph Widener took over the track and spent two years completely re-doing the facility. By 1931, the Florida Legislature had approved a bill legalizing pari-mutuel betting at horse and dog tracks. With this act, Widener and his new track were poised to capitalize on the opportunity.

On January 14, 1932, the beautiful new Hialeah Race Track opened in grand style. Its focal point was hundreds of live flamingoes, brought in from Cuba, in the center of the track as well as its beautifully landscaped grounds. (The first attempt at exporting flamingoes failed when the whole flock flew back home to Cuba.)

For many years, opening day at Hialeah was a major social event and many of America's first families attended. In 1963, Helen Rich, of *The Miami News*, described the scene. "I associate opening day at Hialeah only with beauty—beautiful weather, beautiful people in beautiful clothes at the most beautiful racetrack in the world."

Hialeah continues as a major national racetrack and is listed on the National Register of Historic Places.

Miamians Speak Out for German Jews

In May/June 1939, prior to the outbreak of war in Europe, a German passenger vessel carrying more than 900 German Jews fleeing Nazi Germany was refused entry at Havana. While the captain of the St. Louis pondered the dilemma of returning the passengers to Nazi Germany, he sailed up and down the coast of Florida for several days. Fearful that the Jews would wind up in Nazi hands, concerned Americans voiced hope that the United States would absorb the refugees. Among those were a group of Christian ministers and Jewish rabbis in Miami who organized a rally in Bayfront Park in an attempt to convince the Roosevelt administration to accept the Jews. Spurned, the ship eventually returned to Europe but not before countries such as France, England, Belgium and the Netherlands took in hundreds of the refugees. When World War II broke out later that year, many of those Jews, living in soon-to-be conquered countries, once again fell into the hands of the Nazis. Most died during the Holocaust in Hitler's gas chambers. Dr. Glenn James was the popular and dynamic minister of the White Temple Methodist Church in downtown Miami.

AID REFUGEES, MIAMI PLEADS

Fear, sympathy, shame and condemnation were intermingled in a series of talks Wednesday night heard by 1,500 persons gathered in Bayfront Park protesting treatment accorded 907 Jewish refugees aboard the Hamburg-America Line steamer St. Louis bound for Germany.

Fear that "we Americans will lose our own right to life, liberty and the pursuit of happiness" unless we alter our immigration laws depriving others of the same rights, was presented by R. W. Harrison, retired scientist.

"This is the first time in my life I have been ashamed of the human race," Harrison added.

Mrs. Harrison expressed deep sympathy for the unwanted refugees blaming the cause of their plight upon "the worship of the almighty dollar."

Coming to the stand after the close of the regular talks, Rabbi Jacob H. Kaplan of Temple Israel told the group he has six first cousins on the wandering streamer.

"I just want to thank all you people for coming to this meeting," he added as he made a plea for greater tolerance in religion.

Dr. Glenn James, pastor of the White Temple Church said he had received several scoldings during the day for taking part in the meeting. He made a plea for a return to our teachings of Jesus Christ.

Rev. Stanley Lowell, pastor of the Tamiami Temple Methodist Church, offered his own solution with: "Let America now assume her historic role as a refuge for the oppressed."

Admitting there is little that can be done for the refugees now, H. Bodd Bliss, *Miami Herald* columnist, said let this example "contribute its tiny share in the moral awakening and rearmament of mankind."

A touching plea "as men and women, to please do something for these humans" was sounded by Mrs. Horine Wallace, a member of the City Woman's Club.

Rev. Lee Gaines, pastor of the First Nazarene Church, told the group, "I want to treat my fellow man as I want him to treat me."

Rev. C.A. Vincent, chairman of the meeting, assured the group "that whatever is right will win" and closed the meeting by having all stand and sing, "Blessed Be the Tie that Binds."

Source: "Aid Refugees, Miami Pleads," *Miami Herald*, June 8, 1939, p.1.

James G. Collie
My Life with Pride

During the May 1939 Democratic primary, when most people in Dade County were registered Democrats, large numbers of African Americans organized to vote for the first time. On the evening before the primary day, certain white citizens sought to terrorize African Americans to keep them from voting. They carried signs using the epithet "nigger"—a derisive name from the "Jim Crow" era. This time, the Klan did not succeed in its mission. More than 1,000 African Americans voted and the reform candidates were elected to the city council. The vote was so unprecedented that the results were reported in Time *on May 15, 1939. James Collie, who came to Miami from Hard Hill, Acklins Island, Bahamas was one of the people who voted in this historic election. The following document is from an interview done by his son James Collie, who is head of the Drama Department at Howard University.*

I had always been community-minded, therefore, it came as no surprise to my family and friends alike that I would, at some point, put my life on the line for the principles I believed in and the faith I had in the United States Constitution Bill of Rights, and Declaration of Independence. . . .

Only a handful of blacks were allowed to register and vote in local, state and national elections: ministers, doctors, educators. I was proud to have been able to cast my ballot for Franklin D. Roosevelt for President in 1932. On the night prior to the first attempt by blacks to vote in a local election the Ku Klux Klan, dressed in white robes with hoods, rode white horses through the black neighborhood—a tactic designed to intimidate the black citizens from exercising their right of franchise at the polls. But even more disgusting, frightening and devastating was a large truck which bore a tree on its flatbed. From this tree, a black man was hung in effigy, with a sign that read: THIS NIGGER WENT TO THE POLLS. . . .

Sam B. Solomon, a black weekly newspaper editor, rallied a large group of blacks on the corner of Northwest 14th Street and Third Avenue the next morning. He asked those among us who wished to risk their lives to march with him across the dividing line (the railroad tracks) of the black and white communities. We received instructions and proceeded to march east on 14th Street. I am proud to say that I was the number two in line of march. When we reached the polling place, located in a fire station on Miami Avenue at 14th Street, Police Chief Quigg and his officers were waiting patiently for us to provide some reason for our arrest. However, we had a mission of mercy. We wanted to pave the way for blacks; and we did just that.

Later that day, having cast my ballot in the election, I returned home to my wife and children and said: "Today, Daddy risked his life in order that your lives will be made better." Even though they were young, I believe my son and daughter understood all too well the meaning of my words.

Source: James G. Collie, "My Life: With Pride" (Interview, Black Archives and Research Foundation, Inc.), pp. 10-12.

L. E. Thomas
Professional Pride, 1942

Community life and professional organizations in Miami's Colored Town thrived despite legal segregation and "Jim Crow" laws. For decades, professionals and ministers served residents and anchored the area's business life. In this article, attorney L. E. Thomas describes the community's professional leaders. Thomas, who came to Miami in 1935, rose to prominence in 1950 when he oversaw the "Negro Court"—a court
established for the area's black residents and presided over by a black judge. He was featured in a Reader's Digest article, as the first black judge in the South since Reconstruction. His unique court was the first of its kind in the nation. He died in 1989 at the age of 91.

We consider ourselves confined here to the allied medical professions and the practice of law. Both fields are of long representation here. The practice of professions began when this was a veritable wilderness and the men who first came were in every sense pioneers. There were no paved streets, scant street lighting, no sewers, no hospitals, and the opinion of Mr. Justice Taney in the Dred Scott decision was the prevailing attitude, if not the law, when Dr. James Butler and Dr. Culp hung out shingles as the first Negro physicians in Miami. This was prior to 1904 when Dr. S. M. Frazier now dean of the professions entered practice here.

In succession came Dr. W. B. Sawyer, Chief of Staff of Christian Hospital, Dr. A. P. Holly, Dr. H. H. Green, Dr. W. A. Chapman (deceased), Dr. N. R. Benjamin (deceased) and Dr. T. L. Lowrie. Except for a few who came and left after short periods these men composed our medical force up to 1920. Then came Dr. F. D. Mazon, assistant city physician, and Dr. R. B. Ford (both deceased). The number has increased un-

This historic picture was taken of those who created Miami's unique black police force, including L.E. Thomas (rear center), Police Chief Walter Headley, Mayor William Wolfarth and other black leaders (L-R) Dr. Ira P. Davis, Annie M. Coleman and Father John Culmer. (CM)

til we have ten active practicing physicians and surgeons. They are: Doctors A. B. Benson, S. M. Frazier, H. H. Green (on leave), A. P. Holly, S. H. Johnson, T. L. Lowrie, R. H. Portier, W. B. Sawyer, C. M. Smith and J. H. Smith. Trained in the best colleges in America they are mostly general practitioners. Doctors Sawyer, C. M. Smith and Benson practice surgery. Dr. Portier is an accomplished anesthetist. Dr. Johnson is a roentgenologist. He studied radiology in Cook County Hospital and served one year as senior assistant roentgenologist at Provident Hospital in Chicago. He is a member of the American Board of Radiology. He has the most extensive Xray equipment of any private Negro practitioner in the United States. It is the equal of any in private practice in Miami. Dr. Green is a tubercular specialist. He spent two years study of the disease in Chicago hospitals, and two years as resident physician in the Florida State Tuberculosis Sanitarium at Orlando. He and Dr. A. J. Kershaw (deceased) were the only Negro specialists in this disease in this area. Dr. S. M. Frazier and Dr. T. L. Lowrie whose combined years of practice total more than sixty years go away each year to take special summer courses to keep abreast of their profession.

In dentistry Dr. J. R. Scott was the pioneer. He was followed by Dr. J. E. Emanuel. Upon their deaths Dr. A. W. Goodwin became the dean of that profession. Other practitioners in point of service are: Doctors W. M. Murrell, G. W. Hawkins, I. P. Davis and A. A. Farmer. Dr. I. P. Davis and Dr. G. W. Hawkins provide Xray equipment for the group. The dentists of Miami offer the same type of service with the same modern equipment and methods to be found in any large city. Miami has had one or more Negro dentists since 1910.

Dr. G. P. Lewis, owner and operator of the People's Drug Store, is dean of pharmacists. He operates a complete drug business employing five persons. On the prescription counter, he is assisted by Dr. Phillip Dartignier. Dr. E. A Ward is owner and operator of the Economy Drug Store which we believe is the largest drug store owned by a Negro in Florida. The store employs eight or more persons. He is assisted in pharmacy by Dr. Henrietta Jones. The completeness of the stores run by Dr. Lewis and Dr. Ward make it entirely unnecessary for us to leave our own section to purchase anything sold in drug stores. People's Drug, the older store, has filed more than 40,000 prescriptions since 1925. The stores have the unified support of the doctors and together, it is safe to say, fill more prescriptions in proportion to population than any Negro druggists in the South.

R. E. S. Toomey Esquire, First Lieutenant U. S. Army, Spanish American War Veteran, graduate of Lincoln University of Pennsylvania, began the practice of law in Miami in 1913. He is still here, and in his retiring years can boast of a varied and unique experience at the bar. Too much cannot be said for the courage and foresight of Attorney Toomey in pioneering this field in the practice of law when racial prejudice and bigotry was at its worst. The writer came in 1935 and has been most happy in law practice to this time.

Source: L.E. Thomas, "The Professions in Miami," *The Crisis*, March, 1942, p. 85.

Mercedes H. Byron
"Mi-ami" 1942

In 1942, The Crisis, a publication of the National Association for the Advancement of Colored People, edited by W. E. B. Du Bois, devoted much of its March issue to Miami. The in-depth articles covered all aspects of life in "Colored Miami" including business, entertainment, education, religious and social life. They provide valuable historical information about what is now known as Overtown and Liberty City. The following document, written by a thoughtful young Miamian, offers a timeless theme.

Miami—whose growth in the last few years has been phenomenal and rapid enough to be called the "Magic City": Miami—whose very name bespeaks the intrigue and wonder of the "World's Playground": Mi-ami—whose location plays a vital part in its beauty: Miami—a grand city, ideally located, marvelously planned, and miraculously developed. . . .

I am a Miamian—young, free, intelligent, personable—but BLACK. And so for me there are two of them—("Amis" I mean)—Mi-ami and *Their*-ami. *Their*-ami is the "ami" that I and hundreds, yes thousands of other boys and girls whose faces, too, are black may see in news reels and colorful advertisements, or as maids, chauffeurs or other servants of men and women who represent any race except Negro Americans—Germans, Japs, Jews, Chinese, Dutchmen, Cubans, Indians, Spaniards—but definitely no American Negro.

Their-ami is the "ami" that the vacationist dreams about—miles and miles of beautiful Atlantic Beach with a background of towering coconut and royal palms, majestic hotels and apartments, attractively furnished and finished. For *Their*-

Amians, there is beautiful Biscayne Bay, ideal for yachting, fishing sailing, beautiful moonlight rides. It is the "ami" of wide thoroughfares and avenues, of the renown Orange Bowl Stadium. Yes, *Their*-ami is the "ami" I can only imagine and dream of.

For *Their*-ami, there are numerous hospitals, sanitariums, and agencies which make it possible for "them" to recuperate without clustered or overcrowded conditions. In *Mi*-ami's hospitals, patients are, (figuratively speaking) packed like sardines in a can. It is hardly the Miami that tourists look for.

LOOKING FORWARD

Mi-ami, because my face is black is the Miami I see. I look at it too, only through my mind's eye; for I am young, free, intelligent, and as a Negro, I shall be a vital part of our new nation, now engaged in a great war for Democracy's sake—the nation, my brothers and friends will give their lives for. That Miami is a part of that great nation which will enlarge the pattern for the Miami I see. Devoid of Negro slums, housed in the very heart of this great Mecca of American tourists, provided with sidewalks, paved and well-lighted streets, completed school buildings, sufficient playgrounds, parks and Civic Centers for our many boys and girls who have from necessity formed habits of prowling and walking the streets night and day in hopes of finding entertainments, the Miami that I see is the Miami tomorrow!

I have hope, because there is youth—Negro youth. Youth fresh from the various fields of education; youth from fields of music and medicine; youth facing the reality of conflict and disturbances about them, of wars and threats of war, of oppressed nations, races and religious faiths. Here, there is youth—youth who is strong enough to make for himself the privileges of education and the blessed security of work, youth seeking to find a solution to the perplexing problems, seeking inspirations and guidance to build a better *Mi*-ami in which to live.

Truly the symbol of true Negro Miamian Unity—is existence between the two railroad [the F.E.C. and Seaboard tracks]—shall, we hope, limit undesirable conditions in a not far distant future, when the democracy for which we are today making sacrifices will have proved its worth.

Source: Mercedes H. Byron, "Negro Youth Looks at Miami," *The Crisis*, March 1942, p. 84.

Miami Goes to War

The Shock of War
December 7, 1941

When the Japanese bombed the U.S. Pearl Harbor Navy Base in Hawaii on December 7, 1941, it was early Sunday afternoon in Miami. In an era before television, word came first by radio. Within a short period of time, newsboys raced into downtown and neighborhood streets screaming "Japanese Bomb Pearl Harbor" as they quickly sold out their "Extra" editions. The following article from The Miami Herald *records the shock of war.*

There was surprise among those on downtown streets as Herald newsboys screamed the headlines—"WAR—Japan Bombs U.S. Outposts."

At the four corners of Miami Ave. and Flagler St. under the Christmas decorations, groups formed as rapidly as football huddles—and resembling them—to scan the headlines while the newsies frantically dispensed their papers.

"My God," exclaimed a middle aged woman, "they actually bombed us.". . .

To a man, those persons echoed the middle-aged woman's exclamation but each added: "How could they have done it? Where was our navy? Where were our army planes? How could they have gotten that close to our Hawaiian bases?"

In restaurants, drug stores, bus stations and along the sidewalks people gathered in groups and discussed the situation. Their comments were pretty much the same after wondering how the navy and army had let the Japs get to Hawaiian waters.

"Well, it's happened. Now we know where we stand. Maybe this will be the end of this indecision. We oughta lick hell out of 'em now.". . .

There was a grimness about the expressions of the men and women in the street. Their paces seemed quickened. The cars seemed to be traveling faster. The traffic officers seemed pre-occupied. It was hard to get waited on in some stores because of the conversational huddles.

Source: "Man in Street Sees U.S. Indecision Ended," *Miami Herald*, December 8, 1941, p. B1.

Miami Promotes Wartime Tourism, 1942

The war brought a special set of worries to South Floridians who were dependent on tourism for economic survival. Coming at a time when South Florida was just emerging from the Great Depression, this attitude was somewhat understandable, although to many, including some locals, it seemed very unpatriotic. The following document, an advertisement by the City of Miami that appeared in Time *less than a month after Pearl Harbor, is an example of the type of promotion that set the city up for criticism.*

MIAMI'S PLEDGE to AMERICA AT WAR

Above all others, Miami knows how to do one job surprisingly well —to take our God-given warmth and sea and sunshine, and to convert it into rest and recreation and healthful living for the benefit of thousands of visitors

As war's strain and worry grow, there'll be an ever greater need for a warm, wholesome place where those who have earned a brief respite can come to relax, to renew their physical and mental reserves, to fit themselves to do an even better job on the work that's still ahead.

So Miami pledges itself to carry on at the job we really know how to do. We think it's important to keep on supplying the best vacations

in the world to those who need and deserve them—and who can work more efficiently for having had them.

And we pledge that our part in "keeping 'em flying" will be to do our best to "keep 'em smiling", too!

THE CITY OF MIAMI

Source: *Time,* January 5, 1942, p. 34.

Life *visits Miami Beach, 1942*

Soon after Pearl Harbor, fear of enemy attacks, patriotism and empty hotels spurred Miamians into action. It was widely felt that if the government would make Miami and Miami Beach major training centers, South Florida could be saved from another depression. By April, soldiers began to replace tourists in 70,000 Miami Beach hotel rooms. By the end of 1942, 147 hotels had become barracks. Before the war ended, 1/3 of the Army Air Force officers and 1/5 of the enlisted men had been trained at Miami Beach. The following document comes from the December 28, 1942 issue of Life.

America's winter playground, the home of the press agent and bathing beauty, has gone to war. The long, sandy spit of pleasure, crowded with lavish hotels and swarming with tourists, is now a dim peacetime memory. Eternally, Miami Beach still looks pretty much the same. The sun still shines softly on the palm trees, the slow waves lap the warm sand, the wealthy shops still line smart Lincoln Road. But instead of tourists in gay sports clothes, young men of the U.S. Army Air Forces, dressed in drab khaki, march up and down the streets, drill on the green golf courses and live in the hotels. For now Miami Beach is a vast Army training center.

Moving in slowly, the Army has by now taken over almost all of the 332 resort hotels. . . . All of these marching thousands are giving Miami Beach a new vitality and purpose, even more exciting than in the old hectic, pre-war days.

One of the Army's reasons for taking over Miami Beach is its excellent year-round climate. . . . The enlisted men, officer candidates and officers are put through a round of exercise as comprehensive as their course of study. They drill, attend super-

During the war, thousands of young men came to Miami Beach for military training. The Bayshore Municipal Golf Course became a military training field. Recruits went through their calisthenics amidst the sand traps and fairways. (MN)

vised calisthenics, hurdle the perils of an obstacle course in a city park and swim at the long, smooth beach.

When a man first arrives at Miami Beach, he is bewildered by its magnificence and apparent disorder. Men in uniform are everywhere. They fill the lobbies of hotels, dot the seashore and flood the streets with a riot of khaki. In a few days, the new arrival finds that life in the holiday lushness is as rigid and ordered as that in the bleakest of Army training camps. As his pallor disappears, he finds his place in the system. He lives in a room, once fabulously priced, whose floor he has to sweep and whose bed he has to make just like soldiers in wooden barracks. He may study his lessons in temporary classrooms, thrown up on the greens and fairways of a famous golf

course. He eats Army food in cafeteria-serviced mess halls where dinner once cost $5 a plate. His muscles become hard as he exercises in the sun.

Everywhere he goes in Miami Beach, he marches. And everywhere he marches, he sings. The streets rock with the *Army Air Corps* song, *I've Been Working On The Railroad*, or this favorite modernized version of *The Old Gray Mare*:

"The Stars and Stripes will fly over Tokyo
Fly over Tokyo, fly over Tokyo,
The Stars and Stripes will fly over Tokyo,
When Squadron X gets there."

Source: "Miami Beach: It Goes to War," *Life*, December 28, 1942, pp. 65-66.

Kathryn C. Harwood
The Servicemen's Pier, 1941-1945

South Florida was justly criticized for some of its prac-
tices that appeared to be more profit driven than patriotic.
Many, however, worked very hard to help the war effort.
and supported the many soldiers and sailors who were
stationed in the area. One of the most impressive
projects was the Servicemen's Pier started by a group of
local women under the leadership of Kay Pancoast. The
following document was distributed by the Pier Associa-
tion that served more than 4 million personnel before the
war ended.

SO THIS IS TROPICAL LANGUOR

As nearly as possible a civilian atmosphere is
the aim of Pier and Branches, offering the uniformed
man a temporary release from military regimentation.
Officers are excluded except as guests on special occasions that men may not eternally be snapping to attention. Although a college register is kept for their
convenience men are not required to register for ad-
mittance. Volunteers, on the other hand, from president down, sign in and out thus keeping track of hours
and facilitating the receiving of messages. Civilian
visitors are admitted only from ten to noon daily and
to the Pier on Wednesday nights (passes secured from
Army Intelligence) to watch the weekly soldier broadcast, CONTACT, over WKAT. An MP on duty at an
inside gate is the eye of the needle through which every Pier visitor is threaded. . . .

Long skilled at entertaining people away
from home, the Pier women did not make the mistake of setting an arbitrary program of recreation.
It developed through requests of servicemen themselves until it grew into a many branched plan of
activities. No one thought up something that was
"good" for the men and attempted to foist it on them
willy-nilly. By placing a suggestion box where they
could anonymously drop in their written likes and
dislikes they were encouraged to propose their own
entertainment. Oddly enough the resulting program
was of a more serious nature than the women expected. Aside from wadded paper pellets rattling in
the box like popcorn and which, unrolled, read:
"Girls, more girls," there were requests for symphonic
victrola records, drawing materials, Spanish conversation, current events groups, stories of Seminoles,
alligators and early boom days, and one forlorn wish
for some "good Greek home cooking."

"I'd like to learn chess" turned up so often in
the suggestion box that two experts were given sway
in a small room at the Pier. Here Harvard and Yale
move their pawns against Brooklyn and Texas. Bridge,
Parchesi and Gin-Rummy have their devotees in all
the centers. Jig-saw puzzles not finished one night are
left on the tables to be worked on the next. The plick-
plock of table-tennis seems never to cease, while Cow-
Cow Boogie on innumerable pianos attracts iron-
lunged soldiers like bees around a honey pot. It takes
an armor-plated upright to withstand the boogie-
woogie onslaughts, but some of the centers have been
loaned concert grands which magnetically draw musicians from the crowds of soldiers and sailors. Concert
artists formerly of the Metropolitan have sat for hours
at these ivories. Volunteers pause quietly to listen.
Servicemen look up from their letter writing, or put
down their reading to stare into space, dreaming. . . .

Junior hostesses, girls eighteen or over, add
verve and gaiety to all activities. In bright dresses,
gardenias tucked in their pompadours, they chatter
together as clusters of them arrive during the early
evening hours. Many fill regular jobs all day but they
dance just the same, coming back night after night.
Hopelessly outnumbered by servicemen, their dancing evening, which ends with the eleven P.M. closing
hour, is nothing short of an athletic workout. The
men elect a "Miss Keep 'Em Flying" once a month,
and the three girls with the month's highest attendance
record receive engraved silver anklets. . . .

Does the City of Miami Beach feel the Association fills a practical need in the community? Actions speak louder than words. The City has never
failed to lend a helping hand whenever it saw the
chance. . . .

Source: Kathryn C. Harwood, "So This is Tropical Languor," *SP*
(Miami Beach: Recreation Pier Association, September, 1943).

Philip Wylie
"The Battle of Florida," 1944

Philip Wylie was a well known writer who lived in Miami.
He wrote books and magazine articles and was one of the
areas celebrity residents. Mr. Wylie attended Princeton,
worked on The New Yorker *for two years and then turned*
to writing magazine articles, fiction, film scripts and
novels. The following document from Collier's, *was*
written in 1944 after the government lifted the censor-
ship ban on information concerning German submarine
activity off the coast of Florida. Miamians who witnessed
burning ships near their shores were well aware of enemy

activity frighteningly close by. It was not until the censorship was lifted, however, that they realized they were closer to enemy fire than any other part of the continent and there really had been a "Battle of Florida."

After Germany declared war on the United States, Hitler said, "Now we will see what our submarines can do." Only weeks later, the gates of America were embattled. Along the Eastern coast a reluctant citizenry was dimming its lights. By night there were sudden pillars of fire at sea and by day, clouds of smoke. Into every port were carried the charred victims of the U-boats. Oil and debris sullied a thousand miles of beaches, and by March a man with an ordinary rifle could have entered the war against the Nazis by firing his shots from the Florida coast.

The boldness of the submarines in that area was fantastic. Ships headed south in Florida coastal water routinely keep inside the Gulf Stream in order to avoid its north-running current. At some points, the distance between the Stream and land is less than two miles. Ships were sometimes hit by torpedoes which came from submarines lying on bottom very near shore and aiming seaward. . . .

Tankers in tens and then in scores exploded, burned, heeled over and sank. Bursting torpedoes and whistling shells woke people in their houses at night. Ships were hit so close inshore that they might have been reached by rowboats. Quiet old ladies, knitting on their front porches, became battle observers and phoned their reports to military headquarters.

For months, it was as one-sided a fight as any in history. The casualties ran to hundreds, perhaps thousands, and they were nearly all American and Allied. Of the 600-odd merchant ships reported sunk by enemy action to date, it may be that a quarter went down in sight of America. Fishermen for generations to come will count the wrecks lying in clear water on the reefs bordering the Gulf Stream, and standing, at some points, above the surface. The oil supply for the Eastern states was sent up in smoke, and with it, fleets of oil carriers. The dim-out was the first result of this vast holocaust; gasoline rationing followed shortly thereafter.

The watching multitudes ashore wondered with helpless rage where its own Navy was—the subchasers, destroyers and bombers. Their perplexity could not be answered then; it was kept secret out of need. The public, if it had used its memory, could have answered its own furious questions. The Navy—all the Navy a peace-minded public had permitted—was employed elsewhere on even more desperate and es-

sential duties. The Jap was spreading in the Pacific like a disease, and the Navy was there, checking him. England and Russia, both beleaguered, were dependent upon the long and bloodstained supply line to America—and the Navy was there, protecting it. . . .

Our high command made the grim choice of stopping the Jap and of saving the artery to our Allies. Nothing was left for the defense of coastal shipping. The Nazis bled it white. Meanwhile, desk officers, the often-slurred brass hats, were slaving to design a defense, build it, train the men for it and pit it against the enemy. Research, construction, training and actual antisubmarine warfare went on simultaneously. In a period measured by mere months an armada of scientific sub hunters was sent to sea. And by the beginning of a new year ships ceased to burst and burn off Florida. Today, even the dim-out has been lifted. . . .

The first torpedoings off Florida were released to newspapers, and by them to the public, through Navy public-relations officers. "The U.S.S. So-and-So," they would say, "a tanker, was torpedoed off Fowey Rock Light yesterday. She burned and sank, with a loss of seventeen of her crew." One such report came every few days in February and March, 1942, then every day, then several a day. Presently, the name of the ship was censored, and soon thereafter the location of the torpedoing.

Rumors grew where there was ignorance. Rumors of oil on Florida beaches, of barbed-wire fences built on the sand to check invasion, of captured submarines on board which were found bottles of fresh milk from Florida dairies and the ticket stubs of Florida movie theaters. But of the statements, only the one which concerned oil on the beaches was simple truth—the beaches were drenched with oil and littered with flotsam.

Still, the official silence was unbroken. What ships were being sunk, and where, could not be told. There were many vital reasons. Next of kin had to be notified before the rest of the world, when there were casualties. In the case of foreign ships, the government involved had to be told before the public. Every documented announcement gave the enemy a "positive" score in its records. And finally, salvage operations were being conducted on scores of the damaged and sunken ships; to identify them or their location would have been to invite a new attack on valuable and helpless salvage craft. The silences in 1942 bred alarmist armchair rumors, it is true, but a hundred times over they helped to fox Hitler—although the struggle went against us for many bitter months. . . .

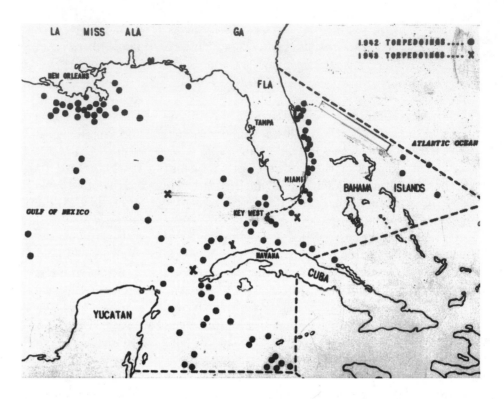

In 1942 and 1943, German U-boats prowled the waters off the coast of Florida torpedoing countless Allied submarines. This map traces the sunken submarines that were so close to South Florida shores that Miamians could see the smoke and flames. (MN)

Victory in the battle of Florida was won by the professionals. It was won in three places—in the planning offices in Washington, in the roaring ship-yards, and, not unappropriately, in the night clubs and tourist hotels of Miami. Many of these were taken over by the Navy early in the war as barracks and lecture rooms. To Miami were sent the SC's—subchasers—PC's—patrol chasers—and DE's—destroyer escorts—as fast as they came off the most re-markable ship-production line in history. To Miami, also, were sent the pick of the men and officers for antisubmarine service. Schooling for them began on a passenger-line pier under the command of Lt. Comdr., now Comdr. E.F. McDaniel, a naval officer who, in the words of his own sailors, "has been at general quarters ever since Pearl Harbor.". . .

The men from the Miami Submarine Chaser Training Center, together with their specialized ships, are primarily responsible for the fact that Florida waters are no longer safe for subs. They police the convoys. They work now in cooperation with an intricate system of patrols and observers. Navy bombers and Coast Guard planes, the watching blimps from a near-by base, crash boats and elaborate communications furnish the balance of an efficient modern combination that protects the seaboard. Its precise nature is secret. But it works.

The war has been swept from America's doorstep. But we Americans should not forget that it was once there—close, menacing and real. Had England fallen in the air blitz, had Russia buckled at Stalingrad, the tide of blood and death that swept our own Eastern coast would surely have moved inland. Only when peace comes will the average seaboard-dwelling citizen realized the vulnerability of his community in the early months of the war and the debt he owes to what was actually a magnificent bluff—a bluff made by the armed services and carried out in part by civilians—but one that fooled the undersea professionals of Hitler's Reich.

Source: Philip Wylie and Laurence Schwab, "The Battle of Florida," *Saturday Evening Post*, March 11, 1944, p. 14, 15, 58.

Bill Moore
Miami During the War, 1941-1945

Everyone was affected by the war and even those who were young children have vivid memories of the war years. Bill Moore was eight years old when the Japanese bombed Pearl Harbor. He lived on S.W. 3rd Street in the Riverside (now Little Havana) section of Miami. Moore graduated from Miami High School and later became a lawyer in Miami and Tallahassee. His reminiscences of the years between 1941-1945 give a picture of what life in Miami was like through the eyes of a child.

When I went to the old Miami Country Club with my father to play golf that beautiful Sunday morning, little did I know that an event was about to take place half a world away that would affect the lives of all Americans for many years to come. Although I was only eight at the time (my father started me on golf at an early age), I remember the shock expressed in the clubhouse when the news came in about the bombing of Pearl Harbor. I had never heard of Pearl Harbor before that day. . . .

The possibility of attack caused a system to be set up in neighborhoods throughout the country whereby "blackouts" were ordered periodically, at night, while air raid drills were conducted. During such a drill all households were expected to turn off all lights and draw the blind or curtains. No matches could be lit, no flashlights or candles used, and even things that might reflect light from the moon had to be covered. "Wardens" for designated areas were appointed—usually for a city block. They would cover their territory on foot during the drill to enforce compliance with the "blackout." Drivers of automobiles and trucks were required to stop and turn off their lights, even though the top half of the light glasses had to be painted opaque black on all vehicles. . . .

It was known that German submarines, called U-boats, cruised the Atlantic coast of the U.S. throughout the war. They sometimes sank ships right off our shores. It was not uncommon to see burning ships off the beach and for debris from those sunken ships to float ashore at Miami Beach and all along the eastern seaboard. . . .

I recall an incident when my father and I were traveling by car on the overseas highway to Key West. The Atlantic Ocean is on one side of the road and the Gulf of Mexico on the other. In broad daylight we saw a German submarine surface and shoot down a U.S. Navy observation blimp. Blimps were used for spotting subs because of their slow speed and maneuverability. Unfortunately that slow speed and the size of the blimps made them easy targets.

Americans were urged to buy war bonds to support the war effort. One popular bond sold for $18.75 and was redeemable at maturity for $25.00. As school children, we saved dimes and quarters, which we placed in slotted cardboard holders. When the collection totaled $18.75, we bought a bond.

"Victory Gardens" were grown in many neighborhoods. The idea was to grow as many vegetables as you could, so that the farm-grown food could be saved to support the armed forces at home and abroad. We grew such a garden in our side yard and ate the vegetables we grew there. . . .

The war also brought about the rationing of many things. Gasoline for cars and trucks was one of the first things to be rationed. Our car had an "A" sticker on the windshield, designating the classification applicable to our car. Coupon books were issued containing coupons or gas stamps that were needed to purchase the rationed gasoline. If you didn't have those stamps, you didn't get gas.

Sugar and rubber products of all kinds (including golf balls, which were made in part from rubber) were rationed or in short supply. Anything made of metal was hard to come by. I used to take a little red wagon (pre-war) throughout the neighborhood and collect old tires and scrap metal to sell to salvage companies that recycled the items into war material. I was willing to clean out garages just for the salvage I could obtain. Copper wiring was a particularly valuable item as were iron, steel and rubber. . . .

Newspaper ads sought women who had long straight hair that had never been subjected to a permanent or harsh chemicals, to sell locks of the hair for use in airplane bomb sights. Dark hair was particularly in demand, providing it met the requisite criteria. . . .

School children too were affected by the war. Erasers disappeared from pencils, because they were made of rubber. Bubble gum disappeared from stores because a main ingredient, which came from Central and South America, was needed in the production of war materials. . . .

There was no television until after the war, but almost every home had a radio or two. My father used to "catch the war news" daily and then hold discussions at the dinner table concerning the news on the various war fronts. Even when we went to the Saturday matinee at the neighborhood Tower Theater, we saw "newsreels" of current war events. These were shown between featured films, most of which had war themes. . . .

Soon after the atomic bombs were dropped over Hiroshima and Nagasaki, the Japanese surrendered. When the war ended in late 1945, there was much celebration in the streets of downtown Miami. My father and I joined the crowds at the intersection of Flagler Street and Miami Avenue. The streets were blocked off so no vehicles could pass and the people could celebrate to their hearts content.

Source: William T. Moore, "Remembering The War" (unpublished manuscript, Crawfordville, Florida, 1996).

On August 14, 1945, enthusiastic Miamians, like the rest of the nation, celebrated the end of World War II. Over 30,000 citizens descended on Flagler street to revel in the moment. (MN)

SPREADING OUT
1945-1960

chapter five
5

"The real shift . . . is the way in which our lives are now centered inside the house, rather than on the neighborhood or the community. With increased use of automobiles, the life of the sidewalk and the front yard has largely disappeared, and the social intercourse that used to be the main characteristic of urban life has vanished. Residential neighborhoods have become a mass of small, private islands; with the back yard functioning as a wholesome, family-oriented, and reclusive place. There are few places as desolate and lonely as a suburban street on a hot afternoon."

Kenneth Jackson
Crabgrass Frontier:
The Suburbanization of the United States,
1985

Following World War II, most of Miami's growth was in the suburbs. Downtown changed little except for a new riverfront hotel—the Dupont Plaza—and the First National Bank building. Both were built on the former Royal Palm Hotel grounds.

On August 14, 1945, thousands of Miamians gathered on Flagler Street to celebrate the end of four years of world war. They basked in the glory of victory—a victory for which Americans and their allies sacrificed and earned. Now, the large number of GI's and their families who had put their lives on hold to fight a war were ready to make up for lost time and get on with their future. Government programs designed to help veterans re-adjust—to get an education and purchase homes—would revolutionize the way Americans lived and worked. These benefits created ripples that touched every aspect of American life.

Business and industry, that produced goods to win the war, re-tooled to produce consumer products like cars and appliances—including the new modern marvel, the Television. Americans, suddenly released from four years of rationing and doing without, went on a national spending spree that helped create a period of economic prosperity.

African Americans fought with great distinction during the war and many returned unwilling to resume second class citizenship. In Miami, as well as in other parts of the South, pressure built to end the strict legal segregation that had been practiced since the city's founding. German persecution of the Jews also caused many Americans to question anti-Semitism at home.

Much has been written about the optimism and conformity of the post-war years that many consider halcyon days. Yet beneath the surface of Betty Crocker and "Father Knows Best" lay racial tensions, the real or perceived threat of world communism, nuclear proliferation and the drift into what was soon dubbed the "Cold War." In some instances, the Cold War turned decidedly hot as in the case of Korea, and once again, many Miamians fought and died for their country.

In this era, Greater Miami burst its pre-war boundaries and spread out in all directions. Before the 1950s ended, the first expressways were under construction and its first suburban shopping malls opened.

∽ The Postwar Boom

In the postwar era, Greater Miami became part of what has recently been labeled the Sunbelt, an area in the south and west that experienced unprecedented growth and development. Many different kinds of people came to live in Miami— ex-servicemen who once trained in the city, tourists attracted to the sun, retirees and people of diverse religious and ethnic backgrounds. As a result, Dade County was one of the fastest growing counties in the nation, its population growing from a little over a quarter of a million in 1940 to nearly a million by 1960.

The role of government remained critical to the nation's economic prosperity. In 1944, President Franklin Roosevelt signed the Servicemen's Readjustment Act into law. Dubbed the GI Bill, this bi-partisan measure honored the sacrifices of servicemen and women and assisted in their economic readjustment to civilian life. The law provided vast government funding for higher education and housing; two engines that fueled the postwar economic boom. It also had a major impact on work and life-style as thousands of GI's became the first members of their family to ever attend college and own their own homes.

∽ "Fun in the Sun"

Other factors also stimulated the growth of Greater Miami in the postwar period. Technological innovation made it a more attractive place to live. Air conditioning became popular in the 50s, creating a more livable year-round environment. Mosquito control, begun during the war, also improved the quality of life in the sub-tropics.

South Floridians, like most other Americans, wanted new or updated consumer goods such as cars, appliances and television sets. This spurred a generation of merchants and entrepreneurs who took advantage of these new opportunities. Adding to the emerging consumer market was a population explosion, known as the "baby boom." New parents spent vast sums of money on toys, baby furniture and other needs.

The new, outlying suburbs and a population increase in older suburban municipalities, far from the core city, produced a different kind of development called shopping malls. Ultimately, these malls

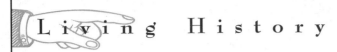

Living History

The Fontainebleau
4441 Collins Avenue
Miami Beach

Miami Beach's largest and grandest hotel, the Fontainebleau, opened for business in December 1954. Built on 44th street and the ocean, the site was once the estate of tire magnate Harvey Firestone. The hotel culminated the dreams of developer Ben Novack who hired architect Morris Lapidus, a then little known designer from New York, to plan the over 500 room hotel. Lapidus' design broke the conventional mold of straight lines and 90 degree angles. Instead, his Fontainebleau Hotel was a sweeping curve, a shape that prompted some of the traditionalists to criticize the building.

Novack named the hotel the Fontainebleau after traveling to the Fontainebleau Palace in France. He so enjoyed the setting that he took the name for his hotel and wanted the interior to reflect the French Provincial design that was popular in America at the time. Lapidus preferred something more modern, and so the architect updated the interior—creating a Modern French Provincial hotel. With its oval columns, marble trim, marble fireplace and rods of gold metal, the Fontainebleau was a palace of contemporary luxury.

Guests could enjoy the solarium, Russian and Turkish baths, gymnasium, pool, cabanas, tennis courts and putting green. When the $15 million hotel opened, stars such as Frank Sinatra, Dean Martin, Jerry Lewis and Liberace performed at the hotels famous LaRonde Room. The Fontainebleau became the focal point of Miami Beach's tourism during its heydays in the 1950s and 1960s.

In 1977, developer Steve Muss and the Hilton Hotels took over the Fontainebleau. Today, it serves Miami Beach's again prospering tourist economy.

hurt the downtown area as more and more shoppers did their purchasing closer to home and with the convenience of abundant free parking.

Fast food restaurants came on the scene and launched a whole new industry and style of convenience and mass production. In 1954, Miamians James McLamore and David Edgerton founded Burger King in an office building on Brickell Avenue where their famous "whopper" could be purchased for 39 cents. From this small beginning, Burger King became a national phenomena and spread around the globe becoming the world's second largest restaurant chain.

The 50s brought television to almost every home and changed the way Americans spent their evenings. Providing in-door entertainment and advertisements for the "good life," television came to Miami in 1949 when Wometco Enterprises began WTVJ, Channel 4, the first television station in Florida. In 1952, the coaxial cable linked WTVJ to national programs, and by the end of the 1950s, television dramatically impacted local news, politics and consumer behavior. TV shows such as "Father Knows Best" and "Leave it to Beaver," reinforced rigid gender roles and images of the "perfect" American family.

Arthur Godfrey, one of the most popular programs on television, gave Miami national exposure by broadcasting his syndicated TV and radio shows from Bal Harbour's Kennilworth Hotel. This weekly program reinforced Miami and Miami Beach's carefully orchestrated image as the headquarters for bathing beauties and "Fun in the Sun."

In the National Spotlight

After the war, South Florida re-emerged as the nation's premier year-round resort. The wide use of air-conditioning, the expansion of the cruise ship business, the development of Miami International Airport and the growth of Eastern and National Airlines brought thousands of new visitors to the region and provided employment for local residents. Packaged vacations to the winter sun, known as the "American Plan," included food and nightlife. These plans became increasingly popular with tourists and led to the construction of a host of new hotels and the expansion of a more recent venue—the motel.

In 1954, architect Morris Lapidus designed the Fontainebleau Hotel, a huge structure on Miami Beach with great curves and modern visual appeal. Lapidus wrote that the hotel was to be "no place like home." Other Lapidus hotels like the Eden Roc

and the Americana created luxury resorts that accommodated large conventions and thousands of pleasure seekers. Lavish nightclubs and hotels with entertainers like Frank Sinatra, Dean Martin, Connie Francis and Johnny Mathis added to the glamour and excitement. After Rock and Roll came on the scene in the 1950s, its "king," Elvis Presley, came to the Olympia Theater where he was greeted by thousands of screaming fans.

Miami also received national attention when leaders like President Harry S. Truman and J. Edgar Hoover, director of the FBI, spoke at major conventions held in Miami and Miami Beach. President Truman frequently passed through Miami on the way to his "Little White House" in Key West. Popular columnist and radio commentator Walter Winchell spent each winter at the Roney Plaza Hotel and often broadcast his regular Sunday evening show from Miami Beach. Well-known television interviewer and host Larry King began his career interviewing celebrities on Miami radio.

New Arrivals, New Communities

Much of the story of Dade County's postwar growth was a tale of expansion beyond the city limits. In 1940, only 36 percent of Dade County residents lived outside the City of Miami. By 1960, the number had increased to 69%. The area we today call Kendall was filled with undeveloped land and vegetable, fruit and horse farms but development was inching closer and closer. Other areas showed phenomenal growth. Hialeah grew from around 20,000 in 1940 to more than 100,000 in 1960. Coral Gables, Homestead, South and North Miami all doubled in population during this era. The late 1940s and early 1950s also witnessed the incorporation of new cities and towns and the development of housing subdivisions in southwestern areas like Westwood Lakes, Flagami and Richmond Heights—one of the nation's first planned middle-class suburbs for blacks.

South Florida also attracted Jews who settled primarily on Miami Beach and in a new suburban area called Westchester. After New York, Greater Miami had the second largest percentage of Jews of any American city. The Jewish population grew from under 10,000 in 1940 to more than 140,000 by 1960. In 1949, a group of prominent doctors and businessmen opened Mount Sinai Hospital on Miami Beach because Jewish doctors were discriminated against in other area hospitals. It became a major hospital serving people of all races and religions. Ironically, it started in Carl

Father Theodore Gibson, leader of the 1956 bus boycott, sits in the front of the bus after the Miami Transit Company ended the requirement that blacks sit in the rear. (MN)

Fisher's old Nautilus hotel that at one time refused Jews as guests.

⊗ Problems in Paradise

Yet suburbanization and consumerism did not prove to be the golden keys to the "good life" that many had expected. Population pressures and expansion created sharp disputes over the use of land. In 1945, the Florida Federation of Women's clubs, which had earlier established Royal Palm Park, gave the land to the state for a planned national park. Through the efforts of leaders like Earnest Coe, and John Pennekamp, the editor of *The Miami Herald*, a 1947 law established the Everglades National Park. That same year another major hurricane devastated South Florida and resulted in a flood control plan by the Army Corps of Engineers. The plan dried up much of the wetlands damaging the fragile flow of what Marjory Stoneman Douglas called the "River of Grass."

Prosperity and tourism also lead to the continued growth of gambling syndicates and organized crime. In 1948, a group of influential citizens created the Crime Commission of Greater Miami to try to clean up the wide-open city. In July 1950, it brought U.S. Senator Estes Kefauver's Senate Committee to Miami to investigate. The Crime Commission and Kefauver's televised hearings had an affect on Miami's burgeoning crime scene. Indictments followed and the public outcry for change was so passionate that most of Miami's illegal gambling establishments folded and for the first time in modern memory, the doors on the formerly wide-open city, closed. (Most of the gambling equipment was packed up and taken to Havana.) In the 1952 mayoral election, Abe Aronovitz became the first Jewish mayor of Miami. His reputation for honesty was rewarded with an overwhelming vote by a city looking for change following the revelations of the Kefauver committee.

⊗ A Segregated City

While many in South Florida enjoyed the postwar boom, blacks continued to struggle for equality. Some change, however, did occur. In 1952, Marian Anderson refused to sing to a segregated audience at the new Dade County Auditorium and it was quietly integrated. Two years later, the Supreme Court of the United States reversed the Plessy v. Ferguson "separate but equal" doctrine thus undermining the legal basis for segregated schools. Change, however, came slowly. In 1959, Dade County's Orchard Villa and

Homestead Air Force Base Elementary Schools became the first integrated public schools in Florida. Following such victories and other national events like the Montgomery's bus boycott in the mid 1950s, opponents of segregation became increasingly assertive. Led by CORE (Congress of Racial Equality) and the NAACP (National Association for the Advancement of Colored People), legal suits and direct action such as sit-ins became increasingly common tactics in confronting legal segregation.

Within this segregated world, however, Miami's African American community maintained a rich social, cultural and business life that centered around the thriving downtown area of Overtown. Famous entertainers such as Nat King Cole, Count Basie and Billie Holiday who performed for whites on Miami Beach and had to stay in Overtown, often entertained there as well. Clubs such as the Knight Beat at the Sir John Hotel and the Zebra Lounge at the Mary Elizabeth Hotel were popular with both black and white audiences.

∞ "Better Dead Than Red"

With the growing power of communist China and the Soviet Union following World War II, Cold War tensions heightened and the idea of fighting communism took center stage. Yet in the anti-communist hysteria, many—especially Jews, labor leaders and advocates of civil rights for blacks—were unfairly labeled as communists. They found themselves harassed by local police and by numerous informers. Liberals, such as Senator Claude Pepper, were widely berated for being "soft" on communism. In the 1950 senatorial campaign, George Smathers defeated the incumbent Pepper after one of the most emotionally charged races in Florida history.

Violence and intimidation often accompanied the growing intolerance. In 1951, terrorists bombed Carver Village, a black apartment complex in a formerly all-white area. Those sympathetic, or believed-to-be sympathetic to blacks, were also threatened. At the same time as the Carver bombing, synagogues were also bombed and the Ku Klux Klan burned a cross on the lawn of the Miami Shores Community Church because a black preacher had spoken there.

By January 1955, *The Nation* published a cover article entitled "The Miami Formula" that detailed attempts by local anti-communist zealots to intimidate and jail those associated with promoting the voting rights of African Americans or others organizing labor unions. Prosecutors and the local press were caught up in the hysteria of alleged communist plots to take over the Miami area. *The Miami Daily News* headlined stories day after day, named names and showed pictures of those suspected of communist leanings.

By the late 1950s, locally, as in the rest of the nation, the Red Scare lessened as noted jurists and television commentators criticized the loss of constitutional protections and civil liberties. The Johns Committee (1957-1965) of the Florida Legislature, however, continued to investigate a variety of groups promoting civil rights and associated them with communism and homosexuality. It sought to force such noted black leaders as Rev. Edward T. Graham and Rev. Theodore Gibson to reveal the membership list of the NAACP in an attempt to intimidate its members. Gibson refused to hand over the lists and was convicted of contempt, fined and sentenced to jail. In an important 1963 decision, the Supreme Court overturned the conviction and upheld Gibson's right to keep the NAACP list private.

∞ Metro is Born

As the suburbs expanded and Greater Miami grew and spread out, it became increasingly clear to many that without adequate planning and centralized control of services, development would be haphazard and deteriorating government services would overlap. *The Miami Herald's* John Pennekamp and lawyer Dan Paul led the call for a powerful county government that would take over selected services from the municipalities and eclipse some municipal power. Several elections were held and a much diluted form of metropolitan government finally passed by a narrow margin. It was the first metropolitan-style government in America.

∞ The End of an Era

As the 1950s ended, Miamians faced a national recession, a slump in tourism and lingering unease about the impact of the Civil Rights movement. Finally, although Miami had long been the destination of Cuban exiles, the late 1950s found the area the staging ground for one of the most dramatic revolutions and subsequent middle and upper class exoduses in modern history. No one at the time realized that the Cuban revolution would change Miami as much as it would Cuba. Another new Miami would emerge from the traumatic years that lay ahead.

Arriving

Tourists Flock to the Area, 1947

By 1947, Americans had put most of the trauma of war behind them and had embraced prosperity and post-war values that promoted family, getting ahead and the benefits of the "good life." Life, one of the most popular magazines in America, described Miami as a vacation utopia, despite the area's tendency to ignore social and environmental problems. To winter-weary northerners, Miami, indeed was a make-believe paradise of pleasure— a respite from work—where the cares of the world were quickly forgotten.

To winterbound northerners Miami is more than a specific municipality—it is a sprawling, tropical Eldorado whose boundaries, fixed more by emotion than geography, range from Coral Gables on the south to Hialeah on the north.

Despite its profligacy, ostentation and venality—perhaps because of them— Miami each year manages to make some two million visitors feel so carefree that the extraction of $220 million from their pockets for the experience is practically painless. . . .

Either by day or by night Miami and its environs present a fairy-land appearance of pastel colors, glittering modernity, jewel-box homes and light-hearted gaiety. This is no accident. From its inception 50 years ago, Miami was promoted and designed to attract outsiders, preferably those with money, and it has since hewn to this line with unswerving devotion. Miami has perennially played host to a wide variety of celebrities ranging from Winston Churchill, who went there to renew his health, to Al Capone, who went there to die. Each winter it becomes the mecca for stage stars, songwriters, playboys, playgirls, labor leaders, big-money executives and big-money gamblers. These it offers an impressive menu of *divertissement*: horse racing, dog racing, swimming, deep-sea fishing, shopping, sunbathing, gambling, nightclubing, astrology, speedboating (sailing, being more strenuous, is not so popular), many, many pretty girls and a climate which insures "359 warm, sunny days out of 365." Busy selling these wares by means of press agents and bathing beauties, it is a small wonder that up to now Miami has had little time for slum clearance (one-sixth of the population lives in a fetid one half square mile of the 16-square mile city), sewage disposal (raw sewage has thoroughly polluted Biscayne Bay), adequate food inspection or hospital facilities.

This outward show and inner spuriousness is epitomized in the case of Miss Miami Beach of 1947. She actually came from Boston. . . .

Miami Beach residents breakfast, lunch, and sometimes dine on the terraces edging their pools. They read there, doze there and sun-bathe there. They play gin rummy, drink *aperitifs* and gossip alongside their pools. Sometimes they even swim in them.

This nonaquatic trend is even more noticeable around the Miami Beach hotels. The distaff side of hotel life, with typical Miamian regard for appearance, tends to make itself up with enormous care; a single dive could ruin hours of work before the dressing table and many dollars' worth of facials. Still another reason is that in Miami Beach the bathing suit is worn to cocktail parties, lunches, dances, teas and on the street, and has been sublimated accordingly. It may be some little thing of pure silk costing only $45, but it may also be a creation of gold-trimmed velvet or sequins and ermine at $145. In any case it must not get wet.

Nonetheless the presence of so many pools, and of so many scantily attired people, all pursuing the common goal of pleasure, is a major factor in giving Miami Beach its atmosphere, unique in the U.S., of uninhibited paganism.

Source: "Babylon, U.S.A. Gets set for its Hectic Hundred Days," *Life*, December 29, 1947, pp. 31-42.

Cuban Tourists Are Welcome Guests, 1949

A post-war increase in Jewish and Cuban tourists also spurred Miami's economy. While thousands of Jews came in the winter, Cubans and other Latin American tourists came primarily in the summer and helped the area become a year-round tourist destination. Many of the Cuban refugees, who fled to Miami a decade later, had spent time in Miami in this era. This excerpt from Newsweek describes the early Latinization of Miami.

Once upon a time the beginning of summer meant the end of the Florida season. Not any more. The flow of extrasection trains filled with frost-bitten New Yorkers still dries up in spring. But people from all over the United States are turning to Florida as a summer resort. And in summer planes from Havana wing in, bringing Cubans by the thousands: rich Cubans, poor Cubans, clerks, professional men, skilled workers, even domestic servants. To Miami, summer is now the "Cuban tourist season."

The Cuban Customs Service estimates that Cubans spent more than $70,000,000 in Florida in

1948. A survey by the City of Miami showed that more than 40,000 persons came there from Cuba between May 1 and Aug. 15, 1948, and a large number went to other cities. The average Cuban stays about four days and spends an estimated $100.

The chief reason for this migration is that a vacation in Florida is much cheaper than at Varadero Beach or any of the small Cuban resorts in the interior. A 30-day round-trip fare by air costs only $34.50. In addition, a Florida vacation means a complete change of scenery, different food, and the opportunity to swim along miles of beach without charge instead of paying the high rates at the few sandy stretches near Havana. . . .

The Cubans are leaving their mark on Florida. Last summer it sounded as if as much Spanish as English was being spoken on Miami streets. Shops hired Spanish-speaking clerks and the city broke out with a rash of signs reading "*Se habla espanol*" (Spanish spoken). Even movie theaters put the word *hoy* (today) over their announcements. A recent Havana cartoon showed a Cuban asking a Miami policeman: "Can you tell me where I can find an American? I want to practice my English."

Source: "Florida Ho!" *Newsweek*, July 4, 1949, p. 36.

Isaac Bashevis Singer
Loving Miami Beach

Isaac Bashevis Singer, the descendent of Hassidic rabbis, came to the United States from his native Poland in 1935. He started working for the Yiddish newspaper Jewish Daily Forward and became a U.S. citizen in 1943. He went on to become a world famous writer and winner of a Nobel Prize for literature. He took his first vacation to Miami Beach in 1948 and lived there part-time until his death in Surfside in 1991. Singer was part of a large migration of northern Jews who came to the Miami area after World War II.

When I first came to this country in 1935, I found that the winters in New York were terribly cold, like the winters in Poland. The winter of 1948 was particularly cold. People used to say it's warm in Miami Beach in the winter, but I couldn't believe it. . . . I also heard about Miami Beach all kinds of stories that the place is vulgar, that the people are funny there. They said all kinds of things about Miami Beach, but if people are vulgar or crazy, I like to know about it. . . .

After we arrived at the train station in Miami, we took a taxi over the causeway to Miami Beach. As

we rode over the causeway, I could hardly believe my eyes. It was almost unimaginable that in Miami Beach it was 80 degrees while in New York it was 20. Everything—the buildings, the water, the pavement—had an indescribable glow to it. . . .

Alma [Singer's wife] would take me into the hotels, just to see the lobby. You could go any day into the lobby of a hotel and just sit down. And I saw all kinds of people; I'd hear all kinds of Yiddish dialects. And by recognizing the Yiddish dialect, I could tell where they came from. And I saw them playing cards and making jokes that I had already heard many times before. . . .

It was remarkable: Jewishness had survived every atrocity of Hitler and his Nazis against the Jews. Here the sound of the Old World was as alive as ever. What I learned is that many people from the *shtetlach*, which I knew so well, came here, and some of them continued their love affairs. . . .

For me, a vacation in Miami Beach was a chance to be among my own people. In those days Miami Beach was a magnet for Jewish people—a place where they flocked like geese to rest and warm themselves in the sun. In the 1940s and 50s, Miami Beach was in its so-called heyday.

Source: I.B. Singer, *My Love Affair with Miami Beach* (New York, Simon & Schuster, 1991), pp. v-viii.

Howard Kleinberg
Miami Becomes Home, 1949

Some who came to Miami after the war were neither tourists nor war veterans. With its climate and apparent prosperity, Miami was a place of opportunity—a place to build a new life. In this piece, a father and mother bring their young son and only child to Miami in search of a better life. The young boy is Howard Kleinberg who later became the last editor of The Miami News. Kleinberg still resides in Miami and today is a contributor to The Miami Herald, a syndicated national columnist and published author.

He was a small black man, and he was walking between the criss-crossing railroad tracks. A railroad worker, he was the first person I ever saw in Florida.

It had just dawned February 22, 1949 and our train was at rest in the rail yards outside Titusville. Florida East Coast Railway's "Champion," which left New York's Pennsylvania Station the day before chugged through the Carolinas and Georgia during the night.

In the early 1950s, Miami's downtown was still a popular community gathering place. Locals as well as tourists went downtown to shop, to visit the family doctor or dentist and go to the one of the many movie theaters. (CM)

Now we were in Florida.

I remember seeing the man spit tobacco juice onto the tracks as our train sat momentarily at a siding. Then I looked up and saw the tops of tall palm trees. I had never seen one before, at least not in the raw.

It all was interesting but not yet pleasing. I was being whisked to Florida by my mother and father against my wishes. I did not want to leave New York.

Sixteen at the time, I was an aimless, mixed-up kid who had soured on school, and gotten in with some less than distinguished company. A change was needed and my father, who had returned from his first-ever visit to Florida just a few weeks earlier, decided that change would take place in Miami. . . .

Well, the train chugged south from Titusville and I hated every mile of it. Somewhere later that morning, I snuck to the train's vestibule to have a cigarette. Only 16 years old, I hid this from my parents but when I became a parent myself years later, it be-

came obvious that kids who thought their parents didn't know were fools. You reek of the stuff! . . .

It must have been sometime around 3 p.m. when we reached the environs of Miami. I had expected to see ocean, sand, coconut trees—the whole post card works—as we rolled in. But that wasn't to be.

The neighborhoods we passed through looked awful and when we finally pulled into the Florida East Coast Railway depot in downtown Miami, I was beside myself with uncertainty.

What a horrible looking place, that train station at Northwest First Avenue and Second Street. Especially coming from Pennsylvania Station. And the part of town around it was pretty rundown as well.

This was my first impression of Miami on February 22, 1949: a shanty town. . . .

With no place yet to live and with my father having no idea of where he would get a job, we came to Miami with literally the shirts on our backs and a nearly-empty bank account.

How vividly I recall that first morning after arrival. I was sleeping on a cot in the Florida room of a family friend's house when I realized my father was shaking me awake. "C'mon," he was saying, "get out of bed. I'm taking you to school.". . .

Oh so reluctantly, I dressed. My father used his friend's car to drive me to Miami High School, on West Flagler Street and 24th Avenue.

The place certainly looked different than the schools I had attended—and left—in New York City. No tall fences, no barbed wire. Trees. Lots of trees; Royal Palms and coconuts. The building looked inviting.

After going through the paperwork, I was escorted by someone—I forget who—to a home room on the west side of the school. As I entered the classroom, my guide introduced me to the teacher and the class.

A girl stood up. Her name was Barbara. She had a sunburned face and she smiled at me: "Welcome to Miami High," she said. And she meant it.

It was then that I realized I was home.

Source: Howard Kleinberg, "South '49" (unpublished manuscript, Miami, Florida, 1995).

Wifredo (Willy) Gort
An Early Refugee

Willy Gort could be called a "pioneer" Cuban refugee because he came to Miami with his family following the Batista takeover in 1954. He attended Ada Merritt and Shenandoah Junior Highs and graduated from Miami High School, Miami Dade Community College and Florida International University. Following graduation from college, he took over as president of his family's photo studio and later was the Executive Director of the Little Havana Development Authority and the Downtown Miami Business Association. He helped found one of the first Hispanic-owned investment banking firms in the United States. Elected to the City of Miami Commission in 1993, he continues to serve in that capacity. The following document is from an interview recalling his arrival and early days in Miami.

My family and I would travel to Miami on weekends during the late 1940s to do some shopping. We believed that Miami ended at the railroad tracks. We would stay at a hotel called the Leamington, which was owned by a friend of my dad's, go to Walgreens and all the special places in downtown Miami. There were hardly any Spanish-speaking people in Miami. Probably the Hispanic—the Cuban population was around 20,000-25,000.

We moved to Miami permanently in 1954. My dad had to leave Cuba for political reasons, so we moved here along with others who were in exile from the Prio regime. When we settled in our first home at 861 S. W. 12th Court—right in the heart of today's Little Havana—we were the only Cubans on the block. There were a lot of different ethnic groups_Greeks, Jewish among others. The first school I attended was Ada Merritt Junior High School. Unfortunately, I did not do too well there and they transfered me to Shenandoah Junior High where I became a better student. There were maybe five or six Hispanics at Shenandoah and I had a hard time trying to learn English. I got a lot of help from the teachers.

At first, we thought we were going to go right back to Cuba so we lived like a tourist for an entire year. When going back didn't look that favorable, my dad opened his business and started Gort Photographic Studio at 1602 S. W. 8th Street. We were the only Hispanic business in the immediate area. Other Hispanic businesses, however, were open down by 8th Avenue and S.W. 8th Street.

I went on to Miami Senior High School and while I was there in 1959, a lot of the Cuban refugees running away from the communists started coming here. Before long, I was the only guy on the block who spoke English, so automatically, my father volunteered me to do all the translation. In the early 60s, there were not that many people who spoke English. There was no bilingual education and no bilingual departments. If you wanted to do anything with the government, you had to take a translator, so I became the translator for everyone, and that got me interested in social service agencies and volunteer work. That's why I became so involved with Miami and why I love it so much; because I've had the opportunity to know many different ethnic groups and I had the opportunity to work with a lot of them.

Source: Wifredo Gort, "Coming to Miami" (taped interview, Miami, Florida 1996).

"The Good Life"

Television Arrives, 1949

On March 21, 1949, television debuted in Miami. After almost two years of negotiations and preparations, Mitchell Wolfson, as owner of Wometco Enterprises, launched Miami into the modern age. He founded WTVJ, then Channel 4, which became the state's first television station. In its initial stages, television was entertainment for only the very rich. Few could afford it and most people saw it in hotels, bars or lined up, rows deep, outside store windows. What they saw were fuzzy pictures, a lot of test patterns and only a few hours of actual programming. In the following document, a journalist describes how an awed yet skeptical public viewed television for the first time.

Last night's television debut over WTVJ was fair to middling as a first night performance, but it will have to improve to keep folks in other people's living rooms during telecast time.

Most of the debut program was on film, jerky film, which was fuzzy and blurred too much of the time. Twice, the four hour program jumped the tracks and the audience was left looking at a card which promised the station would soon be back on the video beam.

The audience was estimated at between 30,000 and 35,000 based on the number of home sets installed and the receivers set up in bars and hotels, the latter two businesses hoping to beat the drop in trade through the television medium.

If TV proved anything last night in Miami, it proved a commercial can be entertaining. The one-hour Admiral radio "Broadway Revue," a variety show, came forth with some sparking commercials, which were, in many ways, much better than the revue itself. . . .

First nighters usually are featured nightmares in the television business, and so, WTVJ didn't fare too badly from this point of view. But the fact remains, the curious will remain curious just so long—and then they will demand a smooth, uninterrupted program which didn't have to be available last night.

It was learned that the station's owners don't expect any profits from their costly venture for a year or two. And even then, they don't know. No one has made even pocket money from TV yet.

In all, it might be said that last night's television held a promise of becoming better, and this is not because it couldn't become much worse, because it could. But the program indicated that real entertainment can be had over the TV medium and station officials said a little time would iron out the technical bugs which will make WTVJ television much more pleasant to watch than it was last night.

Source: William C. Baggs, "Television's Bow in Miami is Somewhat Blurred," *Miami Daily News*, March 22, 1949, p. 2A.

Air Conditioning Transforms Miami

The popular availability of air conditioning brought dramatic change to South Florida. Establishments that once catered to a winter tourist season and closed down in April now welcomed a summer crowd as well. Residents also enjoyed the benefit of cool air during Miami's humid days and nights In the letter that follows, the owner of Miami Beach's Raleigh Hotel commented on the benefits of air conditioning.

April 7, 1952
Hill York Corporation
1225 S.W. 8th Street
Miami, Florida
Attention: Mr. Scott Hoehn

Dear Mr. Hoehn:

Three years ago we purchased two York 1606 Central System Air Conditioners with 2-60HP- 50 tons compressors. . . .

The return on this investment has proven to be quite phenomenal. After we advertised the fact that we had installed the latest in proper air conditioning equipment, we immediately started noticing a very decided amount of new faces in our hotel. It made us feel very happy to hear all the many fine comments our guests gave us for making the hotel so comfortable.

Our summer trade has increased considerably, and we attribute this solely to the fact that our modern air conditioning system has been silently magnetizing the many people who patronize our hotel. . . .

Sincerely Yours,

RALEIGH HOTEL
HARRY W. ANGEL, Owner

Source: Letter, Harry W. Angel to Scott Hoehm, Hill York Corporation, April 7, 1952.

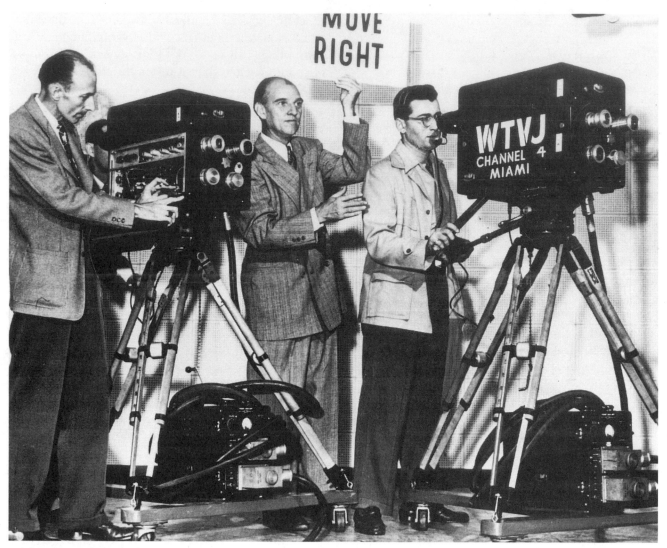

Florida's first television station, Miami's WTVJ, began televising in March 1949. Despite a limited schedule and technical problems, watching television quickly became a favorite pastime. (HASF)

Growing Up With Miami

Adele Khoury Graham
Miami Shores Was Home

Adele Khoury, daughter of a Lebanese immigrant, grew up in Miami Shores in the 1940s-1950s. After graduating from Miami Edison Senior High she attended the University of Florida. She married Bob Graham in 1959 and finished her senior year in college at Boston University. Following her graduation, she taught 7th grade social studies and English. After Bob Graham became governor of Florida in 1978, Adele Graham became a very active "First Lady." She registered as a lobbyist and worked tirelessly for the elderly and for volunteerism *in public schools. Today, she divides her time between Miami and Washington D.C., where her husband serves in the United States Senate.*

I was born at Miami's Victoria Hospital and went home to the Roads section off Coral Way. My father, Gabriel Khoury was born in Beirut, Syria (now Lebanon) and immigrated with his family to the United States when he was very young. The Khoury's were merchants in Eastman, Georgia, where my father grew up. My mother, Mildred Moore, grew up in Richwood, Ohio where her father was a carpenter.

Both my father and my mother moved to Miami during the Boom of the 1920s and met while both were working in downtown Miami.

My mother was a legal secretary for Judge Jefferson B. Brown, who distinguished himself not only as a jurist, but also as an historian. After they were married in 1935, she became a full-time wife and mother and my father became a claims adjuster for Prudential Insurance.

When I was four years old, we moved to Miami Shores which was considered a "far-out" northern suburb. Our house, which they bought completely furnished down to the dish towels, was located within eyeshot of Miami Shores' main street—N.E. 2nd Avenue. Living in Miami Shores was like living in a small town. The Shores movie theater was one block away and the Food Palace grocery store was on the corner.

I started first grade at Miami Shores Elementary School and went on to Horace Mann Junior High that was only about two years old at the time. Miami Shores had what was called the Community House that had a lot of activities for kids. My parents were involved in the school—my father founded the "Daddy's Club" and my mother was president of the PTA. They both worked to get a library built in Miami Shores. We also had the Miami Shores Country Club that was owned by the city and open to all Miami Shores residents. After they built a pool there, it became a popular gathering spot for kids. We often rode our bikes to the pool after school and on weekends.

Teenage years in the 50s seem so simple now—years filled with happy recreation and healthy fun. There were many friends—all mostly alike with families an active part of daily endeavors. Of course, there were some who had more than others but this didn't seem to matter. We shared the adventure of growing up with the first years of T.V., an occasional room air-conditioner and freedom to roam across our growing city (usually by bus) not the least bit concerned about our safety.

I would walk to the corner of my block in Miami Shores and board the bus to downtown Miami. There we would gather on Saturday to visit Burdines and go by a "Five and Dime" like Kress' or McCrory's to purchase a favorite 25 cent tube of lipstick. Royal Castle hamburgers (15 cents each), tiny and delicious, along with their famous birch beer was our favorite lunch.

On special occasions, when we were properly dressed (often with hats and gloves), or after a good report card, my mother would take me to lunch at Burdines Tea Room. Dessert was their elegant ice cream fantasy, the "Snow Princess." It was a small china doll half-figure resting on top of her "skirt" which was mounds of ice cream covered with whipped cream and silver balls. I also remember Burdines' neon Santa, and carnival type rides on top of the building in downtown Miami. (I also met my future husband in a downtown men's store one Saturday afternoon when I was a teenager.)

In high school, our social life centered around our clubs (we joined as many as possible and wore each and every pin) and the telephone. During the week we would plan for the weekends. Movies, school dances, football games and sock hops kept us always in motion. We carried small "45" record players around from house to house with our own pile of prize rock and roll 45 rpm records that cost about 79 cents each. The first 3-D movies were a hit and I can remember the eye strain and the large cardboard glasses we wore. A bunch of us rode the bus to the Sheridan Theater on Miami Beach's 41st Street to see the first one ever— "Bwana Devil."

We were completely loyal to our high schools and our devotion to football went beyond imagination. The most significant event was the Miami Edison vs. Miami High game held on Thanksgiving Day. It was not unusual for 30,000-40,000 Miamians to come to the game. The goal post for the first year we beat them (1952) stood proudly in the Edison center patio. To this day, we still celebrate the few victories Edison had over Miami High.

After the football games we gathered at Pickin' Chicken drive-in which had the most amazing contraption to deliver the best lime freezes in town. On occasion, to celebrate a victory or a birthday, we put liquid soap in their ornate waterfall which led to many suds and bubbles blowing around the cars.

These were wonderful days. How fortunate I was to be born and raised in this wonderful city. We grew up and matured with Miami and watched it change from a small city to an international metropolis.

Source: Adele Khoury Graham, "Growing up in Miami Shores" (unpublished manuscript, Miami, Florida, 1996).

Enid Curtis Pinkney
Overtown Was My Town

Enid Pinkney is a native Miamian who graduated from Booker T. Washington High School in 1949. She worked for the Dade County Public School System for 36 years before retiring as Assistant Principal at South Miami Middle School. Involved in community activities such as the Black Archives and Dade Heritage Trust, she truly has made a difference in the community. Here, Pinkney remembers growing up in her "Miami."

Living History

The Miami Times
900 N.W. 54th Street

Rachael and Garth Reeves. (MH)

The Miami Times is Miami's premiere African American owned newspaper. Its history is the history of the pioneer Reeves family. The first issue of the *Times* was published on September 1, 1923 by Henry E. Sigismund Reeves, a Bahamian printer who moved to Miami in 1919. He originally planned to move to New York, but friends persuaded him to stay in Miami. It was a decision he never regretted.

He and three of his friends, Rev. S.A. Sampson, Dr. Alonzo P. Holly and Mr. M.C. Bodie, started the Magic Printing Company, which launched *The Miami Sun* on January 3, 1920. This paper only lasted five months because of a shortage of newsprint. Refusing to be discouraged, Reeves bought out his partners and launched the *Miami Times* that has continued in the Reeves family ever since. His son Garth followed his father as editor and publisher. Garth Reeves has been deeply involved in the community especially as a strong voice for civil rights and against racial injustices. Today, Rachel J. Reeves, Garth's daughter, continues the Reeves' leadership at *The Miami Times*.

In 1979, *The Miami Times* moved into a strikingly modern new home at 900 N.W. 54th Street. The poured concrete structure was designed in 1959 by renowned Miami architect, Alfred Browning Parker for General Capital Corporation. The building won local, regional and national awards. Parker attended Miami schools and graduated with a degree in architecture from the University of Florida. He has practiced architecture in Miami since 1946 and has designed many Miami landmarks including what is now the home of the Hard Rock Cafe at Bayside. Widely honored, he was named a Fellow of the American Institution of Architects.

Renowned architect Alfred Browning Parker designed The Miami Times *building in 1959.* (Stoller © Esto)

I was born at 1827 N.W. 5th Court, Miami (Overtown) Florida. My father, Henry Curtis, came to Miami from the Bahamas in 1910. He made his living doing gardening on Miami Beach and attained the position of Bishop in the Church of God of Prophecy. My mother, Lenora Clark Curtis was also born in the Bahamas. She came to Miami in the early 1920s and worked as a maid. My parents were a loving couple and shared that love with my brothers, Samuel, Henry, Isreal, my grandmother, Melvina Clark, my aunt Beulah Clark Ferguson and me. My grandmother and aunt moved to our house because my parents lived on the premises of the people for whom they worked at 4609 Pine Tree Drive, Miami Beach. My brother, Isreal was born at that address, but the people at the Bureau of Vital Statistics refused to put Miami Beach on his birth certificate. The place of birth on his birth certificate is Miami.

I went to Dunbar Elementary School as did all the other children in our neighborhood. We were made to feel that Dunbar was the best school in Miami. We were given a good background in the academics by teachers who cared about us. If we misbehaved, the teacher would come to our house and report our misbehavior to our parents. They did this even though they had to walk to our house, because many of them did not have cars.

There were various activities that we shared in. We helped to raise money for the school by participating in the "Miss Dunbar" contest. The person raising the largest amount of money became "Miss Dunbar." The winner also had to have good grades and conduct. We had a graduation play to celebrate our promotion from Dunbar Elementary School to seventh grade at Booker T. Washington Junior-Senior High School.

High school at Booker T. Washington was educational, inspirational and exciting. Teachers were concerned that we learn our lessons; become good citizens and learn social graces in an atmosphere that enhanced our culture and heritage. The school was the citadel of the community. It was the place where I met famous people who spoke to the students or to the community at vesper services on Sunday afternoon. It was the place where I saw and met Joe Louis, the heavy weight champion of the world and had an opportunity to have a picture taken with him as president of the Student Council. I met Mary McLeod Bethune, founder of Bethune-Cookman College, Freida DeKnight, food editor of *Ebony Magazine*, Dr. Benjamin Mays, president of Morehouse College, Dr. Joseph

Boyd, political scientist of Atlanta University and other famous people of the day.

It was to represent Booker T. Washington that I attended many integrated meetings in Miami such as the Florida Chain of Missions which was held at the Miami Women's Club. This was before any civil rights laws were passed. The Florida Chain of Missions was an all day meeting. We could not eat lunch at the Miami Women's Club. We walked from the Miami Women's Club to Booker T. Washington High School, had lunch and walked back to the Miami Women's Club and were there for the afternoon session. Ms. Marie Roberts and Mrs. Mayme E. Williams took every opportunity that was available to take us to integrated gatherings.

Booker T. Washington High School was not only an institution of learning, it was an institution of culture and heritage. It was an institution of joy. It was the place of joy for our Senior Prom. The theme of our Senior Prom was "Bon Voyage." The day prior to our Senior Prom we wore "Bon Voyage" clothing such as sailor hats, dresses with sailor collars, sailor pants, uniforms and other apparels relating to sailing. Mr. Albert F. Crosby, shop teacher, and his students built a huge beautiful ship decorated in blue and white, which were our class colors. The ship was placed at the entrance of the artistically decorated cafeteria through which all of us had to pass in order to get to the dance floor. The decorations carried out our class theme. Our class play was "Don't Take My Penny," directed by Sarah Scott Martin.

One of the activities that I remember fondly was "Fellowship Day." It was the day that the three African American schools—George Washington Carver, D.A. Dorsey and Booker T. Washington—met together in fellowship. We wore our caps and robes and participated in a parade in the City of Miami as well as an assembly. Our "Class Day" assembly was the time that we read our last will and testament and discussed our class history. Our "Senior Breakfast" was held at St. Francis Xavier Catholic Church with the church as our host. I believe that this was arranged by Mrs. Mayme E. Williams who was a member of the church and wife of principal, Charles L. Williams. Our "Class Outing" was at Key West, Florida. We went on a chartered bus. It was my first time in Key West and to see the seven mile bridge. We also had a "Class Tea" and "Memorial Service."

It was safe to walk in Overtown at night. We kept our doors unlocked and windows opened. Even though my parents worked, the neighbors kept an eye on us and would tell our parents if we did something that they knew our parents would not approve.

Although my parents became United States citizens, they continued to consider themselves Bahamians. We lived according to Bahamian traditions. We ate pigeon peas and rice, boiled fish and grits with avocado pear, commonly called Nassau Butter, conch fitters, conch and okra soup, fried fish, guava duff, coconut tarts, crab and rice and other Bahamian dishes. Some of our fruits were papaya, sapodilla, sugar apples, Spanish limes and tamarinds. My aunt also learned to cook American dishes such as collard greens, cornbread, black-eyed peas, sweet potato pie and other dishes. If we were sick with a cold, we boiled a bush called Sarasee. If our stomach was upset, we steeped aloe and drank the water,

My social life centered around the church and school. I could only listen to my friends talk about the movies they had seen at the Modern Theatre on Third Avenue, the Ritz Theatre on Second Avenue or the Harlem Theatre on 14th Street. We were not allowed to go to the movies because of my parents' religious beliefs. Nor was I allowed to attend dances at the Community Center or St. Agnes Episcopal Church's Parish Hall. Nevertheless, I enjoyed the events that I was allowed to attend. That is why "Miami is my Beloved."

Source: Enid Curtis Pinkney, "Growing up in Overtown" (unpublished manuscript, Miami, Florida, 1996).

Helen Muir
Remembering Miami Beach

Helen Muir came to Miami in 1934 from the New York Journal *to direct publicity for Miami Beach's Roney Plaza Hotel. She has been writing about South Florida ever since. An author of several books and a columnist/contributor to both* The Miami Herald *and* The Miami News *as well as many national magazines, Muir has also been widely honored for her work in support of libraries. The following document is excerpted from her popular 1953 book,* Miami U.S.A. *which has been updated and is still in print. Muir's description of Miami Beach refutes those who say that in this era, Greater Miami was a "sleepy Southern village."*

The spit of swamp and mangrove between the ocean and the bay has turned into a shining city. There is no other place like Miami Beach in the world. Forget Smith's and Hardie's Casino with its high-flying flags; forget Fisher's Miami Beach which was, for all its grandeur, small intimate. Now visualize miles of modern shining hotels, every shade and shape of hotel, block after block of colored monuments to tourism, rimming the broad Atlantic, curving as the land curves, each a contained little world designed for fancy living. . . .

Miami Beach, all seven square miles of it, is a play city, highly organized to offer every type of entertainment man craves. Industries are outlawed, there is no black settlement and therefore no white-created slum area. . . .

Necessarily not all hotels can sit on the ocean's edge but a good many have access to it and all hotels, great and small, have swimming pools. The swimming pool shares honors with the bathing beauty as the area's symbol of youth, beauty, and carefree outdoor existence.

There is no cemetery but one of several funeral parlors sits next to a large night club. . . .

Even during the season's height because of the recent introduction of motels north of Miami Beach, it is possible to stay close to the ocean for as little as ten dollars a day. . . . The growth of motels may be judged by the fact that in the Sunny Isles neighborhood where they flourish owners estimate their worth to be about thirty million dollars. . . .

On Lincoln Road double sidewalks, separated by cool green planting, permit window shoppers to dawdle without impeding those on business bent. Rows of royal palms tower above the walks, and here under the shaded awnings visitors peer at displays by Hattie Carnegie, Peck and Peck, De Pinna's Saks Fifth Avenue, *et al*. . . .

Women dress to the teeth when they go nightclubbing. Furs and formal gowns, sparkling jewels and orchids are in evidence at such top show spots as Ciro's or the Latin Quarter. Rated fourth in the U.S.A. in the field of night club entertainment by the American Guild of Variety Artists, Miami Beach emphasizes single headliners like Sophie Tucker, Joe E. Lewis, Edith Piaf, Jimmy Durante, and Lena Horne, and omits name bands. . . .

In Greater Miami there are sixty licensed night clubs and nearly three thousand restaurants: Armenian, Spanish, Italian, French, Swedish, Greek. Choose your cuisine. . . .

Last winter the toy manufacturers came up with a replica of a lady tourist—a doll complete with mink coat and sunglasses. This typical Gold Coast baby sold for two hundred and ninety-five dollars. . . .

By the mid-1950s, Collins Avenue's hotel row was in its heyday. Many new hotels, including the famous Fontainebleau, were built in this era and spurred the growth of packaged vacations and new air travel. (MN)

A visit to Miami Beach is tied up with the Miami moon, the Atlantic Ocean, swayng palms aglow with indirect swaying rhumba dancers, gallons of sun-tan oil, martinis. Gallons of Chanel Number Five. Gallons of everything.

Source: Helen Muir, *Miami U.S.A.* (Coconut Grove: Hurricane House Publishers, Inc., 1953), pp. 270-83.

John Underwood
Nothing Like Winning, 1952

Long before any Miamians had heard of the Miami Dolphins and the University of Miami was not known for its winning teams, the Thanksgiving night game between the Edison Red Raiders and the Miami High Stingarees was the best game in town. It was not unusual for more than 40,000 fans to watch these cross-town rivals. The article that follows was written by former "Red Raider" John Underwood when Edison, after 28 years, finally defeated Miami High. Underwood captured the mood of the game and the enthusiasm that carried over to a post-game parade down Flagler Street and a rally in Edison Center. Subsequently, Underwood wrote for Sports Illustrated *and authored several books.*

Screams of a vengeance, finally attained after 28 long and bitter years, echoed across the north side of the Orange Bowl last night as a dynasty died. Down below in the little dressing room where so many Edison football teams had borne the Thanksgiving failures against Miami High, a lanky coach took a physical beating and enjoyed it.

Ed (Pop) Parnell and his Edison Red Raiders, denied the privileges of the victor in 30 games, let loose and Edison Center was still ringing this morning. They roared approval last night and Parnell, exhausted and bruised from well-wishers, was the happiest of them all. The Edison rooters were too much for the goal posts; they came down in a hurry and as Parnell was being half-lifted, dragged and back slapped into the center of the field to meet [Miami High coach] Charlie Tate, he ran into goal post traffic as all four bars were being transported into the Edison student section. They were last seen in Edison Center, atop a school hangout.

Tate was waiting and it was hard for him. But he pumped Pop's hand hard and long. "I'm happy for you," but his choked-up voice tried to overcome the bedlam. . . ."I'm happy for you, Pop."

"Charlie . . . it's been a long spell." Parnell practically had to scream to be heard and had to tear away from Edison supporters. This was his Thanksgiving day. A day he'd dreamed of from 1932 to 1942 and again from '50.

He finally made it back to the boys and got the planned shower ducking for such an occasion. So did the other members of the coaching staff. But water didn't bother him, he even tried to drink some of it and laughed all through the deluge.

The win must have possessed Parnell. He talked like he'd never talked before. Newspapermen used to prying things out of the veteran coach, flipped notebook pages furiously as Parnell rattled on. . . .

Finally Pop let his boys out into the milling throng of half-crazed supporters and they were headed last toward a giant bonfire, squarely in the center of the 62nd Street, Second Avenue intersection.

They congregated and congested there until the wee hours of the morning while helpless cops muttered on parked vehicles and waiting fire engines, their attempts to put out the blaze completely thwarted, stood motionless.

Source: John Underwood, "Parnell Enjoys Bumps, Dousing," *Miami Daily News*, November 28, 1952, p. 2B.

President Harry S Truman
Everglades National Park, 1947

On December 6, 1947, President Harry S Truman dedicated Everglades National Park. It was a day of victory for a dedicated group of citizens who had tried for 30 years to preserve the natural environment. Among the dignitaries on the stage were Seminole leaders, Ernest Coe, early leader of the effort, and John Pennekamp, editor of The Miami Herald *who was a driving force in its success. The following document is excerpted from President Truman's dedication speech.*

Not often in these demanding days are we able to lay aside the problems of the times and turn to a project whose great value lies in the enrichment of the human spirit. Today we marked the achievement of another great conservation victory. We have permanently safeguarded an irreplaceable primitive area. We have assembled to dedicate to the use of all the people for all time, the Everglades National Park. . . .

The battle for conservation cannot be limited to the winning of new conquests. Like liberty itself, conservation must be fought for unceasingly to protect earlier victories.

Public lands and parks, our forests and our mineral reserves, are subject to many destructive influences. We have to remain constantly vigilant to prevent raids by those who would selfishly exploit our common heritage for their private gain. Such raids on our natural resources are not examples of enterprise and initiative. They are attempts to take from all the people for the benefit of a few. . . .

Source: "Truman Speech," Miami Daily News, December 7, 1947.

Marjory Stoneman Douglas
The Cost of Development, 1947

Marjory Stoneman Douglas, the daughter of Miami Herald *founder and editor Frank Stoneman, was a reporter for* The Miami Herald *beginning in 1915. She later wrote articles and fiction for national publications. In 1947, she wrote* River of Grass—*a beautiful book about the Everglades that provides both a historical and poetic account of the area's unique environment. In the 1970s, she founded "Friends of the Everglades" and launched yet another crusade to save her beloved "River of Grass." The following document is excerpted from her classic work.*

Miami rejoiced, after the Depression, in its increasing growth. It grew as great cities seem to grow, as if there were places and times in which human activity becomes a whirlpool which gathers force, not only from man's courage and ambitions but from the very tides of disaster and human foolishness that otherwise disperse them. It grew almost in spite of the mistakes of its people, by some power which puts to work good and bad, fineness and cheapness, everything, so long as it has fiber and force and the aliveness that makes more life. Miami grew with the tough thrust and vigor of a tropical organism. Its strength was that nothing human was foreign to it.

It had a hundred thousand regular inhabitants and more, twice that in the area, double that again as the winter crowds filled stores and narrow streets and the elaborate race tracks and the night clubs; all year round, a steady growth of working residents, children crowding the schools, houses and trailer camps and apartments going far beyond the city limits. High buildings crowded downtown streets. Traffic conditions were impossible. The old Royal Palm Hotel was torn down, its gardens gone, in anticipation of some enormous citified structures. Where there had been trees were bare ugly parking lots. But in the outlying districts gardens grew deep and green and life went on quietly under the same sun. . . .

If all these cities were growing too fast for any but sporadic improvements, their streets still too narrow, their utilities inadequate, the problem of their colored slums still unsolved, with no adequate future planning, they were hardly aware of it yet. Nobody then thought much about the Everglades.

From Homestead north along the railroads the increasing vegetable fields stretched out to the drying Glades. Packing houses hummed in the season as the trucks came in from the fields with loads of potatoes and beans and tomatoes. Dark green groves of avocadoes and mangoes reached out around the Redlands. Everybody made money again in the years between light frosts. Broward County extended its vegetable fields enormously along the South New River Canal. Palm Beach County, west of Lake Worth, sent out thousands of trainloads of winter vegetables. . . .

Everything was worked out with scientific exactitude, as directed by the Experiment Station or the laboratories of the sugar company, where soils are tested by light rays that cast a spectrum on a screen. The huge fields are set with dikes and irrigation ditches from which pumps bringing up the water level to a required height every twenty-four hours. A tractor drags a cylinder six inches under the surface to make a covered drain like a long mole hole. Fertilizers and chemicals are added, plants dusted against insects. Wise growers are bringing in cattle to be fattened through the winter on half of their fields planted to grass, and with which the crops are rotated.

The result is that more and more saw grass is burned and cleared for greater holdings, more ditches are dug, more water pumped from the lowered main canals. More vegetables are shipped. Cane is raised to the capacity of the mill and the government allotments.

The landscape everywhere about this country, which never sees the far levee-hidden surface of the great Lake Okeechobee, is crammed with the bustle and energy of people making money in a hurry: trucks on the roads, the far glitter of green things growing under the sun. At night, in the first vegetable boom days, the lights of juke joints blazed across the dark, crammed with excited white men and women. Men worked hard. Crops came fast. Money was big.

There is still the curious fever of a mining town that has struck pay dirt. It is like mining vegetables. The quick, fierce crops take from the soil, as miners do, what the work of centuries put there. When the season here is over, many of the carrot men go north to plant more carrots, the celery men plant more celery. Next year they will be back, many living in hotel rooms, without their families, detached from any interest in local problems, thinking only of profits. They have little or no feeling for the strange flat brillant country.

Source: Marjory Stoneman Douglas, *The Everglades: River of Grass* (Coconut Grove: Hurricane House Publishing, 1947), pp. 350-56.

Suburban Frontiers

Nixon Smiley
Pioneering in South Dade, 1951

Nixon Smiley was a well known reporter for The Miami Herald, *a local historian and environmentalist. He worked at the paper from 1940 until retirement in 1973. He also served as director of Fairchild Tropical Garden. An accomplished author, Smiley wrote nine books including* Knights of the Fourth Estate—*a history of* The Miami Herald. *Smiley died in 1990. Here, he remembered his early days in the then wilderness of South Dade.*

But in 1951 Miami was still in her innocent years. In many ways it was still a small town with small-town ways. The great building boom of the 1950's—the prosperous Eisenhower years—was not yet underway. Most of Dade County's half-million residents lived north of Flagler Street. Much of South Dade was rural—pine woods, groves, vegetable farms. Except for the small communities that had grown up along U.S. Highway 1 and the Florida East Coast Railway, you drove through pine woods much of the way between South Miami and Homestead. Then, taking a zigzagging road from Florida City to the newly dedicated Everglades National Park, you drove through a solid forest of pines, palmettos and slender silver palms. The air was abuzz with the rasping of cicadas, and in the spring thousands of zebra butterflies drifted above the frequently burned-over forest understory. So large was this unique forest you discounted any possibility that one day it would be gone. Perhaps in 100 or 200 years, you might have said. Yet, within 20 years it was to disappear before the bulldozers of land developers, and even where the pines were left on the lots of green belt subdivision, the understory palmettos and other native plants were cleared for replacement with grass and exotic ornamentals.

When we moved to Montgomery Drive it was a narrow, roughly paved street on which you seldom saw a vehicle. Our friends had trouble finding our house, partly concealed among the pines and palmettos a hundreds yards north of the street. A bulldozed road, little wider than an automobile, wound through the woods from Montgomery Drive to our house. Although a new development, Town and Ranch Estates was going up on the south side of Montgomery Drive from us, fewer than a dozen houses had been built. Many of the owners wondered if they had made a bad decision in buying so far out in the country, three miles from the nearest grocery, drugstore or gasoline station. On weekends people drove out from the city to look at Town and Ranch's newest houses on display—houses designed by a coming architect, Alfred Browning Parker. Despite the attractiveness of the houses there was a reluctance to buy. The area was remote, and Parker had not yet become famous. A short distance away was a five-acre piece of pine woods for sale at

$500 an acre. I passed the word to a fellow reporter who was planning to build a house as soon as he and his wife could decide on a site. After looking at the property he said to me: "What are you trying to do, get us out in the sticks?" They built on a city lot where financing was easier to get and where utilities were no problem.

You needed a pioneering spirit to build on five acres in South Dade's countryside in 1951. Rattlesnakes lurked in the palmettos; and, in the fall, hunters shot quail and doves so close to our house that shotgun pellets showered upon our white gravel roof. When we complained, the hunters laughed. They had not sympathy for anybody crazy enough to build a house "in the sticks."

Source: Nixon Smiley, "Pioneering in Suburbia," *Tequesta* L (1990), pp. 6-8.

Bob Graham
Growing up in Pennsuco and Hialeah

Bob Graham, who was born in 1932, grew up on his family's Pennsuco dairy farm, eight miles northwest of Hialeah on Okeechobee Road. His father, Ernest R Graham, came to the area after World War I to manage the Pennsylvania Sugar Company's Everglades operation. When the sugar cane growing experiment failed, Graham purchased the company's land and later opened a dairy there. Beginning in the 1960s, his family developed the planned community of Miami Lakes from their former cow pastures. At about the same time, Bob Graham was elected to the Florida Legislature. In 1978, he became Governor of Florida and served for eight years. In 1986, he was elected to the U. S. Senate.

From its beginning, Hialeah was a frontier town. The name itself, which is of Seminole-Creek origin: *halyakpo*, "prairie," and hill, "pretty," describes the original settlement. Early Seminole Indian encampments consisted of palmetto-thatched homes suspended on poles above the frequently inundated ground. The Seminole population dominated Hialeah well into this century. The school that I attended for nine years, the combined Hialeah Elementary and Junior High School (now South Hialeah Elementary School), was built in 1924 as a school for Seminole children. . . .

My father, Ernest R Graham, had opened his dairy in Pennsuco in 1932. His few delivery drivers, with glass bottles of milk and other dairy products, refrigerated by blocks of ice, were frequently stopped by

Young Bob Graham stands in front of his family's farmhouse on Okeechobee Road in Pennsuco, near Hialeah. He went on to become Governor of Florida (1978-86). In 1986, he was elected to the United States Senate. (Bob Graham)

the Hialeah Police. The truck was parked in an especially hot area of the police department's parking lot to assure that the ice would melt and the milk would go sour while the driver was being fined and awaiting bail. My father vowed to do something about this.

That something took the form of the first of two significant decisions that he and my mother made in February of 1936. Dad announced his candidacy for the Florida State Senate with one of his principal campaign pledges being to clean up Hialeah. . . . The second decision made in February of 1936 was to have a baby. . . .

Hialeah entered World War II still a quite small city. Its population in 1940 was less than four thousand. During the war, South Florida became a significant part of America's arsenal that included the construction of small Navy vessels. It was also the prime location for training thousands of military aviators. Hialeah was the home town for many of the people engaged in this military effort. After the war, as South Florida went through another period of growth, Hialeah exploded as Miami's working man's town. This growth was punctuated by occasional natural disasters. . . .

In late September and early October 1947, two hurricanes hit within thirty days of each other. While the wind storm damage was not excessive, they left behind a flooded South Florida. On the day after the hurricane—which happened to be Columbus Day 1947—we looked out of the second story window of our coral rock Pennsuco home and saw nothing but water. One adult remarked with ironic humor that if Columbus had come to South Florida in 1947 rather than the Bahamas in 1492, he would have turned his boats around and gone back to Spain.

My family left our home in a pre-war Dodge hitched by a chain to a high-wheeled tractor. One of my most vivid memories as a ten-year old is holding on to the back of the driver's seat of that tractor and looking down through two to three feet of water to make sure we were staying over the yellow line that ran down the middle of Okeechobee Road. Drifting off the edge of the road would have been disastrous.

Like many other families, we sought temporary shelter in Hialeah as the town demonstrated another one of its characteristics, neighborliness—particularly, in time of need. My parents and I were out of our Pennsuco home for fifteen months as the waters receded and the reconstruction began.

My lifetime support for public education is largely influenced by my own experience at Hialeah Elementary and Junior High Schools. I do not know where you could have gotten a better education in life or teachers more dedicated to stimulating your mind than in that handsome two-story atrium, which in the 1940s and 1950s still educated a few of the Seminole children it was built to serve. . . .

Hialeah Elementary and Junior High had a mixed student body. Many of the students were very poor. I took a yellow school bus from Pennsuco to Hialeah every school day for nine years. On the way to school, the bus would pick up children from small farm houses. One red-headed boy, who had been crippled by polio, lived with his parents in the fuselage of a former Navy sea plane moored to a dock in the Miami River. Ours was truly a classless community and we all learned from one another.

As I graduated from Hialeah Junior High School in June of 1952, the graduation ceremonies were held in the then new Essex Theater in the Flamingo Shopping Center. It was a happy day and time. We had all been challenged by the unique experience of this frontier town. Excited, we were ready to move on to the senior high school stage of our own lives and the town—now the City of Hialeah—was awaiting its next frontier experience.

Source: Senator Bob Graham, "Hialeah Memories" (unpublished manuscript, Washington, D.C., 1996).

Attacking Gambling and Corruption

The Grand Jury Reports, 1950

The Dade County Grand Jury that served from May to November 1950 addressed the serious problem of gambling and corruption. Nicknamed the "racket-busting" jury, it issued a record number of indictments against gamblers and public officials charged with allowing illegal gambling to flourish. The Miami News reprinted the entire summarizing report in the hopes that its would heighten Miami's awareness of the serious problem of illegal gambling. The following document is an excerpt from that report.

We are in no sense a "blue-ribbon" jury. We had no more than average awareness of civic problems. We represent all classes of economic groups and all geographical sections of the county. We are of varied racial origin, religious background and political sympathies. . . .

As a group of representative citizens of Dade County we were all aware that gambling existed in this county, and quite realistically we assumed that it could not exist on a widespread scale without protection flowing from the corruption of public officials, but when we entered upon this task we little realized the extent of the evil and the great necessity for dealing with it. . . .

[We returned] indictments against several dozen persons and corporations whom we found to be the key figures in the operation of the "rackets" in Dade County.

By the term "rackets" we mean that combination of organized, professional gambling with official greed, stupidity, incompetence and willful disregard of the oaths of public office which serves annually to mulct millions of dollars at unfair odds from careless

Organized crime came under harsh scrutiny in the late 1940s and early 1950s through the actions of the Greater Miami Crime Commission. In July 1950, U.S. Senator Estes Kefauver of Tennessee (left) held televised hearings on organized crime in Miami. (HASF)

or unwary citizens and visitors; which enriches and elevates to positions of power and prominence those who willfully disregard the majority laws and codes of ethics; which parisitically feeds upon the labors of our citizens and the abundancce of our natural resources; which creepingly corrupts a widening circle of our citizenry and officials; and which is steadily destroying public faith in elected officials and hence destroying faith in representative govenment.

GENERAL OBSERVATIONS

For many years there has been virtually no law enforcement worthy of the name against professional gamblers and organized racketeers in Dade County. Chieftains of gambling rackets have thus been permitted to become prosperous, and even influential, able to contribute substantial sums directly and indirectly to the campaign funds of favored candidates for artificial positions in the intended system of law enforcement. . . .

The gambling fraternity and their fellow travellers urge that South Florida owes its prosperity and much of its population to the relative unobstructed opportunity to gamble. This specious reasoning disregards fundamental truths. It discounts entirely the value of our climate, unbathed beaches and natural resources of land and sea. It overlooks the myriad installations, facilities and attractions, untainted by gambling or racketeers, which are available to and [in] daily use by tourists and permanent residents who have no desire to gamble. . . .

WITNESSES

We have examined a total of 79 witnesses on matters concerning gambling rackets and related neglect of duty, inefficiency and corruption in public office. Several of these witnesses cheerfully came from banks, institutions and public offices. Their function was to provide or identify documentary and other corroborative evidence. Several were from the Sheriff's office. We felt that some opportunity should be afforded to the deputies themselves to assist us in discerning the prevailing state of affairs in that office. With the exception of those not then currently employed as deputies, their memories were short and vague when approaching potentially embarrassing subjects, their reluctance profound. . . .

POLICIES FOLLOWED

We have evidence before us identifying more than two hundred locations where professional gambling was conducted in this county in 1949 and 1950. From other evidence before us we estimate that additional locations existed on a permanent or semi-permanent basis during 1948, 1949 and early 1950 so that the total of gambling locations requiring space, furnishings, one or more telephones, and a staff of employees dependent on volume would be at least three hundred in Dade County.

These locations are not momentary sidewalk pitches of street gamins, or little backroom crap-games. They are places of business where operators pay rent, take leases, install telephones, and sometimes even air-conditioning. In addition to its basic equipment a "horse-room" betrays itself in other ways. Customers easily find it. Diligent investigators can certainly do as well.

Casinos, or gambling clubs, are not easily concealed. They operate at night and until early morning, when signs of activity are noticeable. In the confident mood achieved by the better-entrenched casino operators in Dade County these outward signs of activity were unmistakable. Bright lights, parked cars, tuxedoed "heavies" or guards at the doors, taxicabs arriving with guests whose fare would be paid by the management. . . .

Under all the foregoing circumstances no law enforcement officer can honestly claim lack of knowledge that widespread gambling existed.

Source: "We, the Jury, Report," *Miami Sunday News Magazine,*
December 10, 1950, pp. 16-22.

Managing Growth

Frank Lloyd Wright
Critiquing Miami, 1955

Frank Lloyd Wright was a world renowned architect celebrated for his designs that incorporated the natural environment into man-made structures. On November 3, 1955, just four years before his death, Wright made his first and only visit to Miami. Speaking to an organization called the Fashion Group of Miami, Wright commented on Miami's architecture and its deteriorating natural environment. In this speech, uncovered from an old reel of tape and published in The Miami Herald, *Wright spoke with great foresight, explored the city's aesthetic roots and urged Miamians to create their own unique architectural heritage.*

We were coming in on the plane looking over this great, marvelous and very beautiful plateau and what do we see? Little tiny subdivisions of squares, little pigeonholes, little lots, everything divided up into little lots, little boxes on little lots, little tacky things.

And you come downtown and what's happening? Plenty of skyscrapers. You call them hotels. You can't tell whether they're hotels or office buildings or something in a cemetery. They have no feeling, no richness, no sense of this region.

And that, I think is happening to the country. It's not alone your misfortune.

But you, where you have all these exquisite, lovely, beautiful things with such charm, why don't you learn from them? Why don't you do something down here that belongs?

You have nothing in Miami that belongs to Miami, practically. It has a character. It has charm. It has these beautiful coral reefs, this white sand, these palms, these flowers, this beautiful growth on so slender a soil, these things that grow in salt water—trees. Think of it!

You have all these marvelous natural resources, and did you go to school to learn what to do with them? You didn't. And why didn't you? There's no such school to go to.

Why are we so ignorant that we live in little boxes and Realtors can sell us something that a pig would be ashamed to live in, really, if a pig could talk and protest?

And you don't protest. You buy. You're perfectly satisfied, apparently. They'll give you anything you'll take. And they'll degrade you to the level of the pig if you don't look out. And you should look out. . . .

Nature must be ashamed of these hotels that you're building down here. Nature must be ashamed of the way this place has been laid out, and patterned after a checkerboard and parceled out in little parcels where you stand on each other's toes, face the sidewalk, your elbows in the next neighbor's ribs.

And the whole thing, demoralization; there is no inspiration there. There is no quality there, nothing for a free people in a free nation. Nor are we free. . . .

It seems to me that there is no conscience in our architecture. There is no conscience in this thing that is planted on Miami. Where did it come from? What is it? Have you ever analyzed it? Have you ever really looked it in the face? For what it is? Is that the best human beings can imagine? The best they can do for humanity—pile them up in these great aggregations of boxes, these things that look like a diagram on the ground turned up edgewise for you to look at? . . .

We're going to have an architecture of our own. That is the basis of culture. You must understand that a civilization is nothing more than a way of life. The Indians had it before we got here and a better one than we seem to be able to produce in some ways.

What is a culture? Culture is the way of making that way of life a beautiful way of life.

What have we done about it in Miami? What have we done about it anywhere? Miami is no worse than any other part of the country except that your opportunities were greater. Except that you've had distinctive character of your own, except that things that grew here for you had a beauty and a character, too, you'd say, of their own.

All that's the matter with Miami are the Miamians, they're you people. . . . Nobody's done this thing to you; you've done it to yourself. You've allowed it to happen to you, haven't you? Of course you have.

How do you get out of it? Why don't you turn about? Go up the other way. Refuse to register in any of these hotels. Refuse to live in any of these boxes they offer you at a cheap price. As a matter of fact, they want at least three times what they're worth. Why pay it? . . .

Who knows now when we're looking at a building what it's for? You don't know whether it's an office building or a hotel, and I'm willing to go further and say a church or anything else, a night club, a restaurant, a motel. There seems to be no sense of proportion, no sense of the appropriate. It's been lost somewhere down the line. Now where is it?

Well, let's bring it back. What's to hinder [you]? You. Only you. You folks are in the way. You folks are Miami and that's the tragedy of it. We can't do anything with Miami until you change. . . .

If a civilization can't get something of beauty, something of concordant harmony, something admirable born, why should it ever have been?

And when a thing goes wrong for the spirit, when the human element in it suffers degradation or denial as it does [in] these buildings you're building, what are you going to do? Put up with it? No. . . .

But I do think you ought to take it to heart because it's an old-timer, an old campaigner talking to you, and for 62 years now I have some 647 buildings built. And every one of them has been a tribute to the spirit of man. They haven't been throwaways and they haven't been expedient.

So believe what I've said to you in the spirit in which I've said it. I do know something about what I'm talking about. And never have I stood up on a platform to talk to people about anything except what I myself experienced . . . but I know a bit about the thing I've done, and I'm passing it on to you for what it's worth. Goodbye.

Source: "Frank Lloyd Wright: Straight Talk about Miami Architecture," *Miami Herald*, April 1, 1984, p. E1

In September 1958, Baptist Hospital was dedicated on land that had recently been a horse ranch and riding stable. Kendall Drive, still a rural road, is in the foreground. The area was so undeveloped that when Kendall Drive was widened in 1964, it was called "The Road to Nowhere." (Baptist Hospital)

Villa Vizcaya
3521 South Miami Avenue
Miami

When Dade County purchased Vizcaya in 1952 for $1,000,000, part of the original 180 acre estate had already been sold off. Mercy hospital sat in the midst of part of the former gardens and Bay Heights took up part of the old farm.

When Vizcaya first opened to the public, people were astounded by its grandeur and amazed that something this magnificent had slumbered for years behind its protective bouganvilla draped walls. James Deering, heir to the International Harvester fortune, purchased part of the Brickell family's impenetrable forest in 1912 and began construction of his magnificent home in 1914. Two years later, on Christmas Day, Deering moved in. It remained his winter home until his death in 1925.

Vizcaya was far and away the most magnificent residence ever built in Miami—a claim that, arguably, still stands. The estate included a seventy room villa, a pool, formal gardens, undisturbed hammock forests, farm and farm buildings.

F. Burrall Hoffman, Jr. was the principal architect with Paul Chalfin as his associate. Hoffman, although only 28, also designed Henry Flagler's luxurious Ponce de Leon Hotel in St. Augustine. Diego Suarez was the landscape architect. He was educated in Florence, Italy and specialized in the great Renaissance-style gardens that he recreated on the shores of Biscayne Bay.

Great Italian villas inspired the design. The building, created out of South Florida's native rock, forms a square with each corner of the

(John Gillan)

square—punctuating the skyline and providing an endless view of the bay. The villa is complete with detailed ornamentation, balconies and terraces. It also has what were considered very "modern" conveniences—a bowling alley, smoking room, swimming pool and elevators. The furnishings, that Deering and his architects and designers collected from all over Europe, were given to Dade County by the family when the county purchased the house.

Today, the villa and gardens are South Florida's premiere attraction and the location of many memorable events.

Dan Paul
The Birth of Metro Government, 1957

Dan Paul is a Harvard educated local attorney who has been extremely active in environmental and governmental affairs. Few, if any, have had a greater impact on local quality of life issues. As an advocate for civic improvements, Paul has defended the Everglades, worked to

preserve parks and helped create Dade County Art in Public Places. He has championed referenda that have controlled bayfront set-backs and use of public lands. In the following document, he writes about the creation of the Dade County Metropolitan Charter and the Citizens' Bill of Rights. Paul served as draftsman for the documents which remain today as the primary outline for Dade County government.

By the end of the Second World War in 1945 there were 27 cities in Dade County and an increasingly large population in the unincorporated areas of the County without municipal services. However, all grants of governmental power had to come from a rurally controlled Legislature in Tallahassee.

It was rapidly becoming apparent from the citizen's demands that a new governmental structure was required. The cities and the County needed the power to deal locally with these new urban problems.

In 1956 the Dade County Home Rule Constitutional Amendment was adopted by the voters statewide which authorized Dade County to create a County-wide metropolitan government with home rule powers to pass local laws without having to ask the Legislature in Tallahassee. The first steps had already been taken when the School Districts were consolidated into a County-wide system and the County Health Department was created to serve the whole area.

As a result of this Home Rule Constitutional Amendment Dade County voters adopted the Metro Charter in 1957 creating the first metropolitan government in the United States. This new government which quickly acquired the nickname "Metro" was to deal primarily with the area-wide problems created by the large population growth. It was to be run by a Manager and the Board of County Commissioners. . . .

Among the first things this new government did was to adopt a number of measures of County-wide application (e.g. a standardized building code for all the cities and the County and a County-wide traffic code). The cities at first were not happy with this powerful new government which had the power to override city ordinances. They fought this new government and sponsored several unsuccessful referendums to restrict its powers. Although Metro won every election this continuing political turmoil delayed moving ahead on a number of County-wide problems like a County-wide water supply system and solid waste disposal.

As the years passed the cities finally came to realize they could not solve these problems alone and that they needed Metro's help. Most of the cities then began to work with Metro instead of fighting it.

As a result, the true promise of Metro began to be realized. A County-wide land use plan was adopted, a County-wide water supply system was created, and Metro was able to provide police, fire, and other municipal services to the people who lived outside of the cities and to those cities that opted to use Metro's services. Metro built a major airport and seaport to serve the whole area, took over the operation of Jackson Memorial Hospital, and began to build a rapid transit system.

Metro is almost 40 years old and is going into a new governmental phase. All the County Commissioners are now elected from districts. Two new cities have been created and several more are in the planning stage. The voters have decided they want a strong Mayor to head this government and to move forward with more leadership. The first strong Mayor will be elected in the fall of 1996.

There are still many area-wide problems to be solved. All local governments are squeezed financially and there are still big governmental jobs ahead. An area-wide public transport system is still not a reality. Parks are deteriorating or being commercialized and many citizens are dissatisfied with the performance and cost of their local governments.

The new Mayor will have a big job ahead of him. The Metro Charter gives him [or her] the power to deal with these challenges. But in the final analysis it will be the citizens who will determine how fast he [or she] will be able to move forward.

Source: Dan Paul, "Metropolitan Government Comes to Dade County" (unpublished manuscript, Miami, Florida, March 1996).

An Intolerant Time

The Pepper-Smathers Election, 1950

The 1950 fight for the U.S. Senate nomination in Florida was one of the the most divisive in American history. It pitted the veteran New Deal incumbent Claude Pepper against Representative George Smathers of Miami. The campaign made anti-communism an election tool. Smathers, later a close friend John F. Kennedy, won the election and served in the U.S. Senate until his retirement in 1968. Pepper served the Miami area as a Congressman from 1963 until his death in 1989, emerging as the preeminent champion of the elderly. In recognition of his public service, President George Bush awarded Pepper The Medal of Freedom. The following article examines the political tides of the time and prophetically predicts Claude Pepper's future.

Mr. Smathers said that he was no "classmate of Alger Hiss," and Mr. Pepper said that *he* had not been born in Atlantic City. Mr. Smathers said that he did not wear the "red tie of Harvard," and Mr. Pepper said that *he* was no tool of corporations. Ex-marine Smathers said that Pepper was a fellow-traveler, and Mr. Pepper insisted that he was more southern than Margaret Mitchell. Mr. Smathers made it clear that he was a white man's candidate, and Mr. Pepper told the people, 'see the federal highways I have brought to you.'

After fourteen years to the left and slightly to the south of the Democratic Party, Claude Pepper has found that even in politics, death (as *Time* has observed) comes to all men.

In this case, resurrection is not impossible, Pepper has a lot of political capital left. But just now the brow is definitely clammy.

Mr. Smathers had it figured pretty well. First he repudiated the CIO [Congress of Industrial Organizations] support he had enjoyed in 1936. Then he chose his issues: FEPC, [Fair Employment Practices Commission] Communism and "creeping socialism." His selections demonstrated an admirable sense of fitness, Florida being reasonably wealthy but non-industrial, a Southern state (its Yankee immigrants usually find racial attitudes as easy to acquire as a tan), backward in some inland areas, and as generally conservative as any agricultural state is expected to be.

Mr. Smathers made the most of these issues in a rather nasty way. Mr. Pepper, on the defensive all the way, replied in kind, hitting Smathers as a reactionary and tool of big money. Smathers, with his opposition to the Fair Deal, his anti-Communism (McCarthy-type), and covert racial appeal, won the primary with the biggest majority a Florida senatorial candidate has won in years.

Pepper was vulnerable. He had a deadly record of friendliness towards the Soviet Union during the immediate post-war months. He had open, strong labor support, but labor itself is not influential enough in Florida to counter the anti-labor feeling that can be aroused against it. Pepper was sympathetic towards Negroes and won almost solid support from them, but again their support (Florida is only 10% Negro) was not enough to balance off the effect of white supremacy propaganda.

A liberal candidate in the South is most vulnerable to a ruthless opponent on the very issues that make his candidacy worthwhile. Even a mild "separate but equal" stand on the racial question lays the Southern politician open to vicious undercover attack. . . . The cry of the demagogue is shrill and deafening, but, blessing in disguise, nobody's nerves can stand it forever.

Source: "Mr. Smathers and Mr. Pepper," *Commonweal*, May 19, 1950, pp. 141-42.

Thelma Anderson Gibson
Feeling Descrimination

Growing up in Coconut Grove during the 1930s, Thelma Anderson Gibson aspired to be a nurse. Unable to attend Jackson Memorial Nursing School because of her color, she went to nursing school in North Carolina, joined the Nurses Cadet Corps and finally returned to Miami in 1947 as a registered nurse. She went to work in the "Colored Ward" at Jackson and was not allowed to work with whites. She ended her full-time nursing career as Head Nurse and Supervisor of the Out-Patient Nursing at Mt. Sinai Hospital. Between 1984-1990 she was a member of the prestigious Public Health Trust that oversees Jackson Memorial Hospital. Thirty-seven years earlier, that same hospital kept both patients and professionals segregated. She was re-appointed to that board in 1995. In 1967, she married the Reverend Theodore Gibson and continues as a prominent community leader. In a recent interview, Gibson recalled her training.

I was in the Cadet Corp when I went into nurses training in 1944. When we finished in January 1947, many of us went to a different place for additional training. Because I was interested in operating technique, I was sent to Meharry [Hospital and Medical School] along with three of my classmates.

When I wrote to Jackson [Hospital] for a job, I asked for a job in the operating room and they hired me. When I got here and they discovered I was colored they said they would not have any colored nurses in the operating room and I could work on the surgical floor. [They told me that] as soon as they got to a point that they could put colored nurses in the operating room they would transfer me there. After three years of being there and them not transferring me, I left and went down to R.E.J. Hall's clinic. Then I went to Washington for a year and came back to Jackson and they still were not ready to put colored nurses in their operating room.

[I was] disappointed, really disappointed, but I had to work and I went to a three year program because I felt the need to help my family. I took the job hoping that in a year or two I would go to the operating room and the frustration was such that I just left after two years.

[It was] a frustrating time and you knew it was because of the color of your skin that you could not get [the hospital] positions. But if you had to work, you worked and I guess all of us did a lot of things with tongue in cheek to make money.

Source: Thelma Anderson Gibson, (taped interview with Christine Ardalan, Miami Florida, March 3, 1995).

Stetson Kennedy
Terrorists Strike at Home, 1951

In 1951, racism exploded in Miami. Terrorists repeatedly bombed Carver Village, a black housing project in a formerly all white neighborhood. They also targeted several synagogues in retaliation for Jewish sympathy and support for the black community. Journalist Stetson Kennedy wrote about the situation for The Nation. *Earlier, he had infiltrated the Ku Klux Klan in Georgia and had exposed it to a national audience. A former resident and frequent visitor to Miami, Kennedy also wrote the widely read* Southern Exposure.

The terror that engulfed this resort city since the succession of dynamite blasts designed to drive Negro residents from their homes and Jews from their places of worship is at least as intense as that caused by the Nazis' first forays from the beer cellars of Munich. Anti-Negro and anti-Jewish violence in Miami is not new. The local Klaverns have long used terror to keep Negroes inside the ghettoes assigned to them, and their program for exploiting any minority has included anti-Semitism. At a "klavalkade" at Live Oak, Florida, the Miami Klan distributed anti-Semitic leaflets printed by Gerald L. K. Smith and kept shouting: "You folks are lucky; we're from Miami where we have both niggers and kikes to contend with!" But the racial violence now rife is worse than anything Miami has known in the past. More than a quarter-million dollars damage has been done to Negro and Jewish buildings by the last half-dozen blasts alone, and the absence of human casualties is largely due to chance.

The campaign began on September 22 when two bundles of dynamite weighing 100 pounds each made a total loss of an unoccupied sixteen-unit building at the Carver Village housing project for Negroes. Walls were cracked and windows shatterd for fifty blocks around. One bundle of dynamite, eighty sticks,

failed to explode, but no fingerprints could be found. Instead of questioning Klansmen, Police Chief Walter Headley released a statement charging that investigation of the bombing "pointed strongly to the conclusion that it was part of a Communist plot to incite racial hatred." Pressed for further facts, Chief Headley explained: "We cannot go into details at this time." The local press ran scare headlines: "New Carver Village Explosion Linked to Reds."

Several months earlier Carver Village, containing 216 dwelling units, had been set aside for Negro occupation from the extensive Knight Manor project previously occupied by whites only. Though Carver Village fronts on a "Negro neighborhood," white opposition to its use by Negroes mounted. Traditionally, such opposition in Miami has been expressed by "property owners' associations" and other civic organizatons, including the KKK, through protest meetings and demands upon city officials for remedial action. In the agitation over the Pinewood project a few years ago, the Klan burned several dwellings, touched off fiery crosses on the project boundaries, and proclaimed through loudspeakers: "When the law fails you, call on us!"

In the case of Carver Village, the city commission had voted, four to one, a week before the big blast of September 22, to "condemn" the property "for municipal use other than public housing." An injunction was filed to prevent the city from taking such action and a hearing scheduled for December 17. . . . Not content with the city's solution, fifty white citizens led by Ira D. Hawthorne immediately banded together as the Dade County Property Owners' Association, and obtained a charter from the state of Florida as a "benevolent," non-profit (tax-exempt) organization. The association, which in the weeks before the blast claimed an increase of 200 members, took the position that the city should invoke "emergency police powers" to evict all Negroes from Carver Village, without waiting for a court ruling on the condemnation proceedings.

At a meeting of the group the day after the blast, Hawthorne said, "We didn't want what has happened to happen, and we don't want it to happen any more. . . . The city commission doesn't realize how high the tension is out here. I'm afraid there is going to be bloodshed both ways if this thing keeps up."

Source: Stetson Kennedy, "Miami: Anteroom to Fascisim," *The Nation,* December 22, 1951, pp. 546-47.

Rabbi Leon Kronish
Fighting Prejudice and Bigotry

After World War II, Miami Beach became the center of American Jewish life during the "winter season" and by the 1960s, an overwhelming majority of Beach residents were Jewish. Rabbi Kronish came to Miami in 1944 from New York and founded Temple Beth Sholom, helping to build one of the most prominent Jewish congregations in the United States. A strong Zionist, he worked tirelessly to support the state of Israel that was founded in 1948. He also was well known for his support of the arts through the Temple Beth Sholom Concert Series under the leadership of Judy Drucker. A man of inexhaustible energy and passionate commitment to human rights, Kronish was not afraid to take on unpopular causes. A sermon delivered at Temple Beth Sholom on May 10, 1957 illustrates his commitment to integration.

The story of segregation is a sordid and sinful one. Who is there among us who, in the tangled troubled realm of race relations is so righteous that he doeth good always and sinneth not through his own prejudices and bigotry, his own acts of exclusion and segregation? WE may self-righteously squirm at the spectacle of segregated buses in the South but we are not averse to joining in keeping 'lily-white' the very neighborhoods from which we as Jews were until recently banned. If this problem has no relevance to Judaism; if we refuse, no matter how many statements we have previously made, to continue to 'cry aloud and spare not,' if we fail to take such action as may be without our power to end every vestige of discrimination, then Judaism really has no meaning or relevance to life itself."

Source: Leon Kronish, quoted in, Henry Green, *Gesher Vakesher, Bridges and Bonds: The Life of Leon Kronish* (Atlanta: Scholars Press, 1994), p. 109.

Rabbi Leon Kronish of Temple Beth Sholom is pictured with Rabbi Max Shapiro of Beth David on a trip to Israel in 1949. (Temple Beth Sholom)

Small Victories

Helen Muir
Working Together

In 1925, the late Elizabeth Virrick and her architect-husband Vladimir came to Miami on their honeymoon and decided to stay. She became an activist in 1948 when she organized the Coconut Grove Citizens Committee for Slum Clearance with Father Theodore Gibson. In the 1960s, she organized Coconut Grove Cares to give ghetto kids a chance and to help ex-convicts rebuild their lives. A park, pool, public housing and gym bear her name. The following excerpt is from Helen Muir's book, Miami U.S.A. *Muir, a long time resident of Coconut Grove and close observer of the scene, was a friend of Virrick and a Citizen's Committee for Slum Clearance volunteer.*

Coconut Grove was as guilty as the rest of Miami in ignoring its slum conditions, in refusing to allow the Negroes to expand, in closing its eyes to the shocking lack of sanitation. It was as though the poinciana trees and the mangoes, all the dooryard planting that made art studies out of shacks, covered up the awful truth. Occasionally a white woman would get exercised about the living conditions of her laundress or maid and quarrel with a white landlord, but twenty-seven percent of these Negroes owned their own homes.

They had few toilets. Outside privies were the norm. They were still using wells, long since polluted, for drinking water. Their garbage was not picked up because seldom was it put out in proper containers and there was a city law about requiring uniform containers. . . .

It is likely that nothing dramatic in the way of reform would have occurred if it hadn't been for one woman—tiny, blue-eyed Mrs. Vladimir Virrick, Kentucky-born wife of a leading Miami architect. In 1948 she led a crusade to clean up the slums. It started when she went to a meeting and heard a Negro Episcopal minister, the Reverend Theodore Gibson, say expressively, "My people are living seven deep." All night the words reverberated in her mind and next morning she presented herself at Father Gibson's home.

"What can I do to help?" she asked. Her only daughter was away at college and she was prepared to plunge into the task ahead.

This is what happened, and at once: A group of twenty-four whites and Negroes met at Mrs. Virrick's home. There were ministers, a Negro policeman, a lawyer, a welfare worker, a writer, a housewife among the group. They made plans. They sent out posters calling for "an old-fashioned town meeting to form the Coconut Grove Citizen's Committee for Slum Clearance." It was summertime—August. Two hundred Grove-ites attended the meeting.

The campaign began with Negro block leaders, women, inspecting garbage pails. There were forms to fill out. One block leader classified twelve garbage pails as rejected, nine fair, and six good. The committee bought pails and offered them at wholesale prices. They set about checking screening, sponsored a rat-killing campaign. . . .

In November they began on the plumbing. At night, when it was too dark to disturb the eyes, the city was in the habit of sending men around to remove excrement. This work cost the city ten thousand a year. The Citizen's Committee worked vigorously to persuade the Miami city commission to pass a law ordering the people of the slum area to connect with the city's water mains and to install flush toilets, sinks, and septic tanks. White landlords fought this move undercover. But the city commission passed it. . . .

Source: Helen Muir, *Miami U.S.A.* (Coconut Grove: Hurricane House, 1953), pp. 265-67.

LeRoy Collins
The Courage to Change, 1960

LeRoy Collins is considered one of the greatest governors in Florida history. He became governor in 1955 and served until 1960. He is remembered for his leadership on many issues, but his most enduring legacy is in the area of civil rights. In 1956, after observing racial unrest in Tallahassee, Collins, who at first condemned black activism, began to change his views. From that point forward, Collins spoke out for moral leadership on the race question, refusing to take hard-line stands like many other Southern governors. Instead, he spoke out for justice and equality. The following document is excerpted from a state-wide radio and television address he made during this time of racial turmoil.

Well, I want to talk to you about race relations. Frankly, I had a group of my friends come over to see me yesterday and they said very frankly, "Governor, we don't think you should make this broadcast you are talking about tomorrow afternoon." I asked why and they said, "Well, you have less than a year now to serve in this office and certainly you know that

Florida's Governor Leroy Collins, seen here with President Dwight D. Eisenhower, gave Florida a strong moral voice for change. (Jane Collins Aurell)

whatever you say is going to make some people mad, and we just don't see the reason why you should stick your neck out or become involved in a discussion of that very explosive issue."

Well, frankly, I don't follow that sort of logic. I believe this is a very grave and serious matter facing the people of this state, affecting all of us, and I think the people of this state expect their governor to have convictions, and I think the people of this state when their governor has convictions about a matter expect him to express those convictions directly to them. . . .

Now let me say this, I believe very deeply that I represent every man, woman and child in this state as their governor, whether that person is black or white, whether that person is rich or poor, or whether that person is influential or not influential. . . .

Now let me review briefly something of the history of this racial strife that we are contending with. It was on last February 1 that four Negro college students from a North Carolina college went into a Woolworth store in Greensboro, N.C. They bought some tooth paste and other minor items at one of the counters, then turned over to the lunch counter and ordered a cup of coffee. The waitress there said, "I'm sorry, we do not serve colored people here." One of the students said, "Why I have just been served here.

I bought a tube of tooth paste over there." She said, "Well, we serve you over there, but we do not serve you here."

That was the first of these demonstrations. Many followed there in Greensboro involving hundreds of people. . . .

And we have had many throughout our state and, unlike some people assume, not all of these demonstrations were sponsored by students; in fact, only a minority have been sponsored by students. . . .

But what is the legal situation about these so-called demonstrations?

First, I want to say this to everyone of you: that we are going to have law and order in this state.

I don't care who the citizen is, he is going to be protected in pursuing his legal rights in Florida.

And that goes for every place in Florida.

Now under our free enterprise system and under our laws a merchant has the legal right to select the patrons he serves. And certainly he is going to be protected in that legal right.

The customer, of course, has the legal right to trade or not to trade with any man he wants to—and, of course, there is the right to demonstrate and the people should be protected in that right, too. . . .

But actually, friends, we are foolish if we just think about resolving this thing on a legal basis. In the first place, our merchants have much involved so far as their business prosperity—not to have racial tensions of this order.

Boycotts can be extremely damaging and will be extremely damaging to their businesses. And, of course, any racial tension brings about depression in business and depresses generally the business spirit of any community. . . .

And so far as I am personally concerned, I don't mind saying that I think that if a man has a department store and he invites the public generally to come into his department store and trade, I think then it is unfair and morally wrong for him to single out one department though and say he does not want or will not allow Negroes to patronize that one department.

Now he has a legal right to do that, but I still don't think that he can square that right with moral, simple justice.

Now you may not agree with that. Strange things develop in respect to these relations. . . .

Source: LeRoy Collins, "Talk to the People of Florida on Race Relations" (speech presented on statewide television and radio, Jacksonville, Florida, March 20, 1960).

OPENING DOORS
1960 · 1980

chapter
6
six

"I am cognizant of the interrelatedness of all communities and states. I cannot sit idly by in Atlanta and not be concerned about what happens in Birmingham. Injustice anywhere is a threat to justice everywhere. We are caught in an inescapable network of mutuality, tied in a single garment of destiny. Whatever affects one directly, affects all indirectly."

> Martin Luther King,
> "Letter from Birmingham Jail," 1963

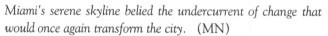

Miami's serene skyline belied the undercurrent of change that would once again transform the city. (MN)

By 1959, Miami's version of the so called "good life"—that early television portrayed and thrust into the American consciousness—attracted large numbers of new residents. Growth, with the inevitable change it causes, continued into the 1960s as Miami opened its doors to hundreds of thousands of Cuban refugees. By 1980, Dade County's population reached more than one and one half million people. The suburbs burst their boundaries and formerly outlying areas of the county changed from farmland and Everglades wetland into instant—and distant— subdivisions.

Change, however, was about more than just numbers and geography. The rising movement against segregation and racism coincided with the arrival of the Cuban refugees. This happenstance of history, combined with other volatile issues that were sweeping the nation—civil and women's rights, environmental reform, the distrust of governmental authority, the Vietnam War—created a time of challenge to the old order and the old networks that maintained it. Before the 1980s began, new cultural and political forces emerged.

Few cities had ever been faced with as much sudden change as Miami experienced in the 1960s and 70s. More than 400,000 Cuban refugees transformed a growing city into a vibrant international metropolis. Although racism continued, legal segregation ended. Blacks slowly gained status and held major elective and appointive positions. Women moved into places they had never before trod. The economy survived two recessions and an equal number of booms. Environmentalists raised the consciousness of a generation, became a powerful political force and, for the first time, successfully challenged rampant, unfettered growth. Most of all, due to an accident of history—the Cuban Revolution—the city actually lived up to one of its old slogans, and became the "Gateway of the Americas."

∞ Exiled to Miami

On January 1, 1959, Americans and Cubans who had been exiled since the Batista coup of 1952, greeted the triumph of Fidel Castro and the Cuban Revolution with enthusiasm. This euphoria was shortlived. When Castro embraced Soviet communism, an ever-increasing number of Cubans fled the island and sought refuge in Miami. Some of the early refugees were able to leave the island with part of their wealth intact, but many more were forced to leave everything behind and start over again from scratch.

The emotional difficulty of leaving a country that was so close—with so many relatives located within several hundred miles—and yet so distant, caused much human suffering. The revolution and subsequent exile broke up Cuban families and orphaned children had to be cared for. New homes needed to be found. Language was a barrier and professional careers could not easily be resumed. Discrimination had to be endured.

At first, Miamians paid little attention to the Cuban refugees. Exiles had come in and out of Miami many times before. The Catholic church, the local Cuban community and various charitable organizations stepped in to help the refugees. As time passed and the situation in Cuba deteriorated, more and more refugees streamed into Miami. Late in 1960, Miami leaders convinced the U.S. Government to supply federal financial support to what up to that point had been a local concern. The federal refugee program gave each qualified head of household food stamps and $100 a month. The federal government also gave the refugees surplus food. Many refugees recall receiving cheese and peanut butter. Cheese was a welcome commodity, but many Cubans, unlike their American counterparts, did not know what to do with the peanut butter.

After 1962, the old *Miami News* tower became the symbol of American liberty for Cuban exiles. Used as a processing center, it was subsequently renamed the Freedom Tower. Before it was closed in 1974, more than half a million Cubans had passed through its doors.

A young Irish priest named Bryan Walsh, who was head of the Catholic Welfare Bureau, initiated one of the most meaningful refugee programs when he realized that many unaccompanied children were being sent out of Cuba. He founded what was later dubbed Operation Pedro Pan. It ultimately helped find temporary housing and, if needed, foster families for more

Today, the building known as the Freedom Tower stands as Miami's own Statue of Liberty to hundreds of thousand Cuban refugees who passed though its doors to be processed as new residents. Built in 1925, the Freedom Tower was originally known as the Miami News Tower, home of *The Miami Daily News* which began in 1896 as *The Miami Metropolis*. The building, reminiscent of the Giralda Tower in Spain, was designed by the prestigious firm of Schultze and Weaver that also designed New York's Grand Central Terminal and Waldorf-Astoria as well as Miami Beach's Roney Plaza and Coral Gables' Biltmore.

The Miami News moved out in 1957 and it remained vacant until 1962, when the U.S. Government rented the building and turned it into the Cuban Refugee Processing Center. From 1962 until 1974 its halls were filled with Cuban refugees who came to sign up for the federal assistance program and received surplus food. When the refugee center closed in 1974, the building again became vacant.

Zaminco International bought the building and began a major restoration in 1987. It reopened in December 1988 with a grand gala benefiting Dade Heritage Trust, the county's largest

(Walter Marx)

historic preservation organization. Unfortunately, its new use as a catering hall was not successful and the building closed once again and was put on the market amidst tangled legal problems. As Miami celebrated its Centennial, the building was lit up in all its splendor. The final fate of what has been described as Miami's favorite building, however, remains in doubt.

---

than 14,000 unaccompanied minors whose parents sent them out of Cuba for safe keeping.

As the exile community grew, Riverside, an older part of town, became the center of Cuban life and Miami's own "Little Havana." The neighborhood sprouted a host of stores, churches, parks, and professional offices where most business was transacted in Spanish. Many who had been professionals in Cuba worked as waiters or janitors in one of Little Havana's restaurants or in local hotels. Through economic and social networks, Cubans helped each other with bank or "character loans," job referrals and housing. Many Cuban-American women had to take low paying jobs as maids and in Miami's garment industry to help support their families. This often caused conflict within

the family structure. Yet overall, their startling economic achievements were later labeled the "Cuban Miracle."

∽ On the Brink of War

The first wave of Cuban refugees, "The Golden Exiles," believed they would soon return home. The feeling increased after the CIA organized a brigade of exiles into an invasion force to free Cuba. Early in 1961, the brigade left from Miami's Opa-Locka airport en route to Guatemala for further training. (After Carlos "Carlay" Rodriguez Santana, member number 2506 of the brigade was killed in a training accident, the group of freedom fighters called themselves "Bri-

In the 1960s, Miami's Tamiami Trail became know as Calle Ocho after Cuban refugees moved into the old Riverside/ Shenandoah neighborhood and transformed it into their own "Little Havana." (HASF)

gade 2506.") The brigade was made up of professional soldiers, mercenaries, former politicians and many idealistic young men, some still teenagers. They were fused by one common bond—hatred for Castro and a belief that the full power of the United States was behind them.

On April 17, 1961, members of Brigade 2506 landed on the south coast of Cuba near the Bay of Pigs. The Brigade never received the groundswell of support they expected in Cuba, and the United States called off critical air support for the mission. In the end, 80 members of the Brigade died in the fighting, another 37 drowned and 1,180 others were taken prisoner. Miami's refugee community felt devastated and betrayed.

The situation in Cuba only grew worse. In the fall of 1962, after aerial photographs showed that Soviet missile launch sites were under construction in Cuba, Miami became an armed camp. Troop trains rumbled through town, tent cities appeared in South Dade to house military personnel and missile installations sprouted in Homestead tomato fields. The situation grew extremely tense. War was avoided after the U. S. blockaded Cuba and gave assurances that it would not invade the island, as long as the missile sites were dismantled. Relations between the two countries, however, remained sour. Castro suspended all air flights to the U.S. causing terrible hardships for those with families already in Miami. Desperate, many Cubans set out by sea in small boats and even inner tubes if that was all that was available. In 1965, Castro and the U.S. government negotiated a "Memorandum of Understanding" and thus began the so called "Freedom Flights," that brought 230,000 additional Cubans to the United States by 1973 when they ended.

With the failure of the Bay of Pigs and America's agreement not to invade Cuba after the Cuban Missile Crisis, it was painfully clear to the Cuban refugees that Miami would no longer be a temporary home. If Castro remained in power, they would not be able to return to their island home for a long time—if ever. As the Cubans struggled to build new lives in South Florida, Miami, like the rest of the nation, also experienced other dramatic political and social changes that characterized the 1960s all across America.

∽ Struggles for Equality

Throughout the 1950s, the struggle for racial equality in Miami gained momentum under the leadership of Rev. Edward T. Graham and Father Theodore Gibson, two presidents of the NAACP. By the end of the decade blacks were no longer forced to sit at the back of the bus and some public facilities had been integrated. Then in April 1959, CORE, led by Dr. John O. Brown, began sit-ins at downtown Miami chain stores in an effort to end discrimination at the lunch counters. Martin Luther King visited the city on several occasions to lend his support.

Miami Mayor Robert King High provided moral leadership in this difficult time. Popular and moderate in his approach to racial issues, he ran for Governor of Florida in 1964 and became the first Miamian to ever achieve a slot in the Democratic Party run-off. (In this era, victory in the Democratic Primary assured election.) He died a short time after loosing the run-off to Haydon Burns. Steve Clark replaced him as Mayor of Miami. (Clark would later hold the record for the longest tenured political leader serving as mayor of both Metro and Miami.)

African Americans made significant, albeit limited, economic and political progress during the 1960s. Although racial segregation in schools had been deemed unconstitutional by the 1954 Brown decision, it persisted in practice. Following successful passage of the Civil Rights Act of 1964, integration had stronger legal protection in the courts. Although two Dade County schools had been integrated in the Fall of 1959, few other schools were integrated until the early 60s. Dade County Junior College (now Miami Dade Community College), opened in 1960 with two campuses—one for blacks and one for whites. It was integrated in 1962—the first integrated college or university in Florida. Integration went a step further in 1970 when Federal Judge C. Clyde Atkins ruled that all staff, teachers and administrators in Dade County Schools must be integrated. The following year, he paired a group of formerly white schools with a group of formerly black schools. Many other schools, however, remained single race institutions.

Although gains toward equality were made in public education, thanks to the federal courts, new federally funded highways like I-95 sliced right through the heart of downtown Overtown, virtually destroying it. It displaced twenty-four thousand people and left the formerly vibrant neighborhood in ruins. Athalie Range, who became the first black on the City of Miami Commission in 1966, and Father Theodore Gibson, who served for nine years, left a lasting legacy. They led their fellow white commissioners and the public on the way to addressing racial discrimination in Miami and fought for the rights of both black and white people. On the state legal, Joe Lang Kershaw

was elected to the Florida Legislature in 1968 followed by Gwen Cherry in 1970.

Pride in being of African descent was on the rise across the nation by the mid-1960s, through "black power" movements. Adding to the sense of racial pride was the rise of Cassius Clay, who trained at Miami Beach's Fifth Street Gym and defeated Sonny Liston at Miami Beach for the national championship. A short time later, he became a Black Muslim and changed his name to Mohammed Ali.

In the mid-70s, Americans of all races watched the TV series "Roots" which sympathetically traced the identity of author Alex Haley's family back to its African heritage. Locally, the tireless work of historian Dorothy Jenkins Fields helped uncover many long-overlooked documents and a new picture emerged of the history of African Americans in South Florida. Her efforts led to the creation of the Black Archives, History and Research Foundation of South Florida, Inc., located at the Joseph Caleb Neighborhood Center.

Miami was also the focus of an important battle defining the separation of church and state. What was known as the Chamberlain Case grew out of the long standing opposition to the widespread use of Christian rituals in the Dade County Schools. The Supreme Court of the United States reversed the Florida courts in 1964, effectively outlawing certain religious practices in the public schools.

M. Athalie Range (center), the first African American on the Miami City Commission, joined Mayor Steve Clark (left) and the other members of the city commission to dedicate the under expressway mini-park named in her honor. (CM)

In the Limelight

Greater Miami came into increased national prominence by the mid 1960s through the efforts of advertisers, public relations experts and the ever more powerful medium of television. National news expanded to a half hour in 1963; color television programs began the next year and local news stations expanded their operations. Due in part to the sensitivity heightened by TV news, Miamians marched in sympathy for the young children killed in a bomb blast in Birmingham, Alabama in 1963. The power of television was also underscored when publicist Hank Meyer negotiated a deal to broadcast the popular Jackie Gleason show from Miami Beach every week. Like "Miami Vice" two decades later, this exposure thrust South Florida into the national consciousness and spurred tourism. In 1964, one week after the Clay-Liston fight, local promoters were estatic when the Beatles made their first American television appearance on the Ed Sullivan Show, broadcast from Miami Beach. Hundreds of teenagers skipped school to greet the shaggy-haired foursome at the Miami Airport. As the Beatles' influence grew, schools passed rules against Beatle-like haircuts and local police departments banned sideburns on their officers.

Protesting Conventions

Disenchanted by Kennedy's assassination in 1963, racial divisions and the growing conflict in Vietnam, young people became increasingly angry and disillusioned. Many reacted in the words of Timothy Leary by "turning on, tuning in and dropping out" and embracing "hippie" lifestyles—symbolized by long hair, love beads, peace marches, drug use and protests against social injustices and the war in Vietnam. In Coconut Grove, Miami's hippie haven, rebels filled Peacock Park and spilled over onto the sidewalks of the business community.

Nineteen sixty-eight was a tumultuous year. In the wake of the Martin Luther King and Robert Kennedy assassinations and the escalation of the Vietnam War, American cities were in turmoil. Discontent erupted in Miami during the Republican Convention held on Miami Beach in 1968. Just as Richard Nixon was accepting the Republican nomination for president, angry African Americans, a scant six miles away, rioted against decades of perceived police brutality, unemployment and poverty. Critics held up challenges to the social order as proof that Miami, like the rest of the nation, had sunk into chaos and anarchy.

The mood of protest extended to other areas of society as well. The elderly, joined the Gray Panthers, to assert and defend their rights. Miami Beach became a Gray Panthers "capital" as an increasingly elderly population moved in. This migration was spurred by a new venture—the condominium which was first introduced into Florida in the 1960s. Many older hotels on Miami Beach were converted into small condos that attracted the elderly. These senior citizens gained a strong supporter when former Senator Claude Pepper was elected to the House of Representatives in 1962. He became an outspoken advocate for the elderly and disadvantaged and rose to become Chairman of the House Select Committee on Aging.

Even the Miccosukee Indians declared their independence from the Seminoles and demanded recognition as a separate tribe. The federal government acknowledged their independent status in 1962.

Labor associations existed in Dade County since the early 1900s but unions remained weak until World War II. Union power increased with the rise of Miami International Airport and the building boom of the 1950s and 1960s. In the context of hostile state laws, however, organized labor never became as powerful in South Florida as it was in northern industrial areas even though national labor unions held their winter meetings at Bal Harbour. In 1968, one of the more dramatic strikes in Dade County history involved the teachers who demanded higher salaries and better working conditions. A large group of Dade County teachers stayed out of the classrooms for three weeks. In response, many former school teachers and parents stepped in to keep the schools open. Despite attempts to break the union's power, it made great strides as the bargaining agent for the teachers. From that time forward, unions became an integral part of all future teacher-school board negotiations.

When Miami Beach hosted both political conventions in 1972, civic leaders braced for the worst. The anti-war movement was at its height and many radical activists camped out in Miami Beach hoping to disrupt the meetings. The Democratic Convention passed fairly peacefully. A few weeks later, the Republican Convention drew angry protesters from a variety of social groups. The demonstrations escalated into confrontations and by end of the convention over 1,000 people had been arrested and some 2,000 lawmen were called into action.

That June, four Miami Cubans and the former CIA operative E. Howard Hunt had been arrested breaking into the Washington D.C. Democratic Party headquarters in a building named Watergate. No one at the time realized the impact this event would have on the nation's history. Before the investigation was over, Watergate became a household word and President Nixon, who had his vacation White House on Key Biscayne, was forced to resign.

∽ Optimism and Activism

Along with the various forces promoting greater equality, business and educational leaders sought to stimulate economic growth, refocus interest on the downtown area and broaden opportunities for cultural enrichment. Despite the uncertainties of the times, in the early 70s, the economy experienced its greatest boom since the 1920s. New skyscrapers rose in downtown Miami and along Brickell Avenue. In 1972, the Dolphins had a perfect season winning an incredible 17 straight games and a Super Bowl title. When the Freedom Flights ended in 1973, Miamians prided themselves on how well they had absorbed 500,000 newcomers who were now busy building new lives for themselves in Miami. The city had a new, young Hispanic mayor, Maurice Ferre, who had great visions for the future. In a spirit of togetherness, the county declared itself bi-lingual in 1973—a status that would later be rescinded in a divisive 1980 referendum.

A new state college, Florida International University, opened its doors in 1972 illustrating the broadening educational needs of the area. Voters approved a $553.5 million Decade of Progress bond issue, the largest such bond issue in the United States that year. Originally proposed by County Manager Ray Goode and his staff, the funds were matched with federal and state money and used for many county projects. They included: Metrozoo, Metrorail, MetroMover, Tropical Park, Coral Reef Park and part of Jackson Memorial Hospital.

Spurred by anger toward private developers who seemed to ignore environmental concerns, citizen groups organized and became more politically conscious during the 1960s and 70s. A ground swell of public opposition led to the abandonment of a number of development projects in South Florida like SeaDade and the Everglades JetPort. Miami's indefatigable Marjory Stoneman Douglas, now in her 80s,

came out of retirement to lead the fight to protect the Everglades' fragile ecosystem and stop ever encroaching development on this unique resource. In 1966, *Miami News* editor Bill Baggs led the fight to preserve the Cape Florida Lighthouse and create a state park on land that was about to fall to condominium development.

This unprecedented wave of optimism came to an end with the 1973 Arab oil embargo and a downturn in the local economy. South Florida motorists, like the rest of America, sat in long lines at gas stations and worried about the future. South Florida plunged into a deep recession—the worst since the 1930s. Construction ground to a halt and skeletons of half-finished buildings once again dotted the skyline. By 1975, unemployment rose to a frightening 13.7 percent. Desperate business leaders undertook a series of initiatives to reinvigorate Miami's economy. Alvah Chapman, president of *The Miami Herald*, was instrumental in creating the Chamber of Commerce's Downtown Action Committee. The committee worked with a newly energized Downtown Development Authority, Mayor Maurice Ferre and the public sector to revitalize the downtown area, spur public investment and develop the city as a center of Latin American trade and tourism. Hank Meyer, a well known publicist, coined the phrase "New World Center" for Miami. The committee adopted this name and became the New World Center Action Committee and promoted re-vitalizing Miami as the center of the New World.

The county passed a Comprehensive Development Master Plan for Metropolitan Dade County in 1975 (though never fully implemented), that included broader citizen task forces and the promotion of public access to policy making.

As Miami entered the 1980s, the idea of the New World Center was taking shape. The influx of new residents, the majority Spanish speaking, gave the city an international flavor and a connection with Latin America. New banking laws, aimed at foreign dollars, turned Miami into an international Wall Street. A rapid transit system was under construction and for the first time since the 1920s, the steel skeletons of buildings dominated the skyline. Despite the turmoil, Miamians were proud of how well they had handled the incredible events of the past 20 years. Few cities had ever been faced with as much sudden change. No one, however, ever dreamed that the 80s would make Miami over once again and change it for all times.

Miami's Cuban refugees wait at Miami International Airport to greet friends and family fleeing Cuba. By the late 1960s, a new Cuban refugee arrived in Miami every seven minutes. (MN)

The Exiles

The Impact of Cubans on Miami, 1960

When the Cuban refugees arrived in Miami beginning in 1959, their presence strained the social and economic resources of the city. The newcomers flooded the job and housing market and strained educational and social welfare budgets. This 1960 article from the national magazine Business Week *examines the impact of the refugees on Miami and how the city responded to their needs.*

While thousands of sun-seeking tourists from the wintry North pour onto the beaches of Florida's Gold Coast, the city of Miami and surrounding Dade County struggle with another, less favorable tide— bringing with it the grim problem of how to help 45,000 penniless Cubans who have fled Castro.

The refugees arrive in Miami at a rate of 1,600 a week. Most of them trudge the city's streets looking for work, sleep in slums, live on charitable contributions. Few jobs are available for them. Two former Cuban supreme court justices, for example, are counted lucky to be holding jobs as dishwashers in beachfront hotels. A university professor sweeps floors in a school. Doctors work in hospitals as orderlies.

What started as a trickle in the early days of Castro is now a flood that threatens to turn into a deluge. The Cuban foreign ministry has disclosed that in the first 10 months of 1960 it issued nearly 65,000 new Cuban passports. Many holders of these passports are still in Cuba; in Santiago and Havana at least 30,000 are trying to get tourist visas to the U.S.

Why They Come—Why is the number of refugees mounting so fast? Some come merely from caution, to be out of reach of trouble. But many are moved by an unconcealed, boiling hatred for Castro. "I'd rather live like a dog in the U.S. than be under the thumb of Castro's militia," says one professional man. Another, voicing the fear many feel, says pro-Castro Cubans are settling grudges by filing false charges against people they don't like.

It wasn't until six months ago that Miami's refugee problem started to become acute. Until then the city's Cuban population of 50,000 was caring for its own, and local relief agencies were adequate. Some earlier exiles managed to bring along cash or jewelry; others had relatives or friends here.

But when Castro earlier this year turned on the managerial middle class, then began seizing U.S. property, a mass exodus began.

Double Trouble—Miami's own mounting unemployment problem compounded the difficulty. Right now 5.3% of its work force, excluding the refugees, is unemployed. Counting in the estimated 10,000 Cuban refugees out of work, Miami officials put unemployment at more than 6%.

Says Miami Mayor Robert K. High: "We've simply run out of jobs, even the most menial." Local relief committees are overburdened, too. Centro Hispano Catolico, a relief center opened by the Dominican Order, had been handling 100 cases a month. Now it gets 100 to 150 a day.

New Homes—One solution is relocation. Many of the Cubans, however, do not want to be relocated; most believe they can hang on in Florida until Castro can be overthrown.

Tracy S. Voorhees, who was handed the task of resettling the Cubans by President Eisehower, is trying to make them understand that Castro will be in Cuba longer than they think. "As more go hungry," Voorhees says, "we find more willingness to strike out for other cities where work is available. . . .

Government Help—Until November efforts to aid the refugees were limited to these private organizations, and small civic groups in Florida. But their funds were rapidly being drained away, and Miami civic leaders began to appeal for state and federal help. Florida's Governor LeRoy Collins responded with $35,000 for an employment office.

Early in November, Collins and Miami businessmen got word to President Eisenhower that federal aid was needed. The President called in Voorhees—who had resettled thousands of Hungarian refugees in 1955—and later allocated $1 million from Mutual Security Agency funds. Voorhees is using the money for relocation efforts.

Matching the Need—Job offers elsewhere are few, however. And though the majority of the refugees are educated, experienced professional men, the language barrier bars employment for many.

The immediate task of keeping Cubans from starving is still being carried on by churches and private relief agencies, with financial aid from some businesses. One company, Texaco, Inc. has contributed $100,000. Cardinal Spellman, the Rockefeller Foundation and a Baptist church group each gave $10,000.

The gathering consensus, though, is that this is "not enough." Some officials are calling for massive federal aid. Among these is Thomas E. Wintersteen, director of Dade County's Welfare Planning Council. "The problem is too big for private groups," says Wintersteen. "The load gets bigger each day." Others calling for direct federal aid, say Cubans are starving while the government tries to relocate them.

Source: "Resettling Cuban Refugees," *Business Week*, December 31, 1960, p. 80.

The U.S. Senate
Hearings on Cuban Refugees, 1961

In December 1961, the United States Senate held a series of hearings to examine the problems connected with Cuban refugees and their impact on Miami. Community activists, academic officials and religious leaders went before the group to give testimony about the Cubans and their adjustment to Miami. In the excerpts that follow, three different leaders give their testimony to the Senate Committee. Included in their presentation was a film produced by WTVJ that highlighted the exiles' plight and Miamians' reaction to their presence.

Statement of Ralph Renick, News Director, WTVJ, Miami, Fla. Accompanied by Manolo Reyes, Newscaster, WTVJ.

MR. RENICK: The Miami skyline, constantly expanding, reflects the tempo of life in the bustling city below, a city with a distinctly Latin flavor. Always a favorite tourist and business center for Latin Americans, Miami is now a place of residence for probably 100,000 Cuban refugees. They have their own newspapers, their own shops and bars, churches and signposts, and their own, largely Cuban districts. But, with this apparent self-sufficiency, the refugees also have to contend with a growing resentment from the old-time residents of Miami. Here is how the man on the street feels about his Cuban neighbors. . . .

VOICE FROM THE FILM: I like the Cuban people personally but I think they are wasting their time because they are taking away a lot of jobs from poor people and I think they should distribute them around the country and every city should take away a thousand or two thousand Cubans.

VOICE FROM THE FILM: I am not prejudiced toward anybody but in my estimation we should take care of our own people first before we give any help outside to anybody else.

VOICE FROM THE FILM: It's not a matter of liking or disliking the Cuban people. The fact is that they are here and we have a responsibility to take care of them. I believe the Federal Government should do something toward relocating them and seeing that they are employed and are able to sustain themselves.

MR. RENICK: The Dade County school system is straining its resources to provide special classes for Cuban children and for the adults who want to learn English. These adult night classes are intensive, geared to fit the newcomer into our English-speaking society. There's also a local educational program to teach English-speaking people Spanish. So far the list is 175 names long and growing fast, people who meet Cubans in daily business, neighbors of the refugees, welfare workers, and parents whose children bring the Cuban children home to meet them. . . .

MR. RENICK: Refugee and resident mix together in the hectic pre-Christmas shopping scramble in downtown Miami, often unaware that one does not speak the other's language. The Cuban has helped ease the economic recession on his Miami neighbor by giving whatever money he has to the local economy. The refugee has been responsible for an extra $100 million yearly flow into Miami business, money which critics say has come out of the pockets of American taxpayers. Relief checks are given to some 15,000 refugee families at an average of $75 per month. This is more, the critics say, than many American families can get for their own needs. The issues are clear enough in the minds of many, more unemployment, a boost in the economy, some public misbehavior, but largely a law-abiding people who pay their bills on time.

My colleague, Manolo Reyes, who is the Latin news editor, himself is a Cuban refugee and he would like to make a comment on his viewpoint on the Cuban impact on Miami.

MR. REYES: One of the grave problems that confronts them in this delicate matter is that within 50 minutes of flight time the Cuban arrives to start a new kind of life, to encounter a series of customs that he does not know, and that are carried out in a language that he does not speak. His first step is to go to Immigration, then to the refugee center, and afterwards to await the arrival of a check in order to have some money with which to begin his new life.

When Cubans leave their homeland, they come under the most terrible mental pressure you can imagine. All of them arrive here frightened, believing that they are going to be denounced, looking around with suspicion and fear, and with their hearts broken because sometimes they have had to leave beloved relatives, all the places dear to their hearts, the fruits of years of work and sacrifice, properties—everything. They have made a complete sacrifice in order to begin anew. Some have the impetuosity and youth for it. Others are in the decline of their lives.

But the Cuban does not have any way to learn the customs of Miami; he can only acquire them through practice. As is natural, this brings about friction with the Miamians when they see the Cubans crossing in the middle of the block; when the Cubans greet each other warmly with an embrace on the sidewalks, Latin style, without realizing that they are blocking the way; when they talk loudly, and so forth. . . .

I believe also that if a good campaign is launched to sell the Cubans the idea of relocating themselves within American territory, it would be well received. It must be remembered that when the Cuban arrives in Miami he finds in that city democracy, liberty, aid, and above all, the familiar faces that he used to see in Havana, in all parts of Cuba; he hears his own language spoken; there are places in south Florida that are similar to certain Cuban places, especially the streets of Havana; and finally, the tropical climate is practically the same in Miami as it is in Ha-

vana. All these details and even more, make the Cuban feel at home, as though he were in the home that he lost because of Communist betrayal. For that reason, his relocation in other parts of the United States is made more difficult.

If he leaves Miami, he will not hear again the profusion of Spanish; he will not see the familiar faces; and he will be exposed to the most intense cold that he has ever known. . . .

Cubans don't want to leave Miami, because they feel they will be abandoning all hopes of freeing their homeland of the Communist yoke. . . .

The Cuban exodus from communism has created a unique situation in Miami. This city, the gateway to the Americas, has become a vast laboratory of democracy.

STATEMENT OF REV. BRYAN O. WALSH

My name is Father Bryan O. Walsh. I am the executive director of the Catholic Welfare Bureau of Miami, a multifunction child and family welfare agency. I am also a member of the standing committee of the directors of the National Conference of Catholic Charities, a national coordinating agent for the 315 Catholic social welfare agencies throughout the country. On November 30, 1961, 54 agencies in 47 dioceses in 30 States were active in the Cuban refugee program. It is my privilege today to

Father Bryan Walsh assists some of his young charges with their school work. Operation Pedro Pan helped more than 14,000 unaccompanied Cuban minors find new homes in the United States. (UM)

testify on the problems of the Cuban refugees as a representative of the National Conference of Catholic Charities. I have been closely associated with the Miami Cuban refugee problem from the very begining. . . .

When the Cuban refugee found himself in Miami without resources, he turned to the one institution that was familiar to him for help—the Catholic Church. Thus, it was that the health, welfare, and educational agencies of the diocese of Miami were the first to feel the impact of his presence. A word of tribute is due to the tremendous role played by Miami's permanent Cuban colony in welcoming their friends and relatives into their homes. It was only when the resources of this section of the community were exhausted that the rest of Miami even became aware of the problem. . . . We are faced with the fact that to expect a family, a mother and father and four, five or six children to even survive on $100 a month when they have to pay about $65 a month, perhaps for an apartment to live in, and they have $35, maybe, in cash left for all services, everything they need—the surplus food, of course, is a big help, but little more than a dollar a day is very little to get by the month on. It is a real hardship to these people.

Now, I know it is a real hardship to a great deal of our own unemployed and the rest in Miami, too, who do not get help and they need it. We have a tremendous—the voluntary agencies in Miami and our welfare programs, have tremendous problems in that regard. But the individual hardship is very, very great.

I know from my own experience among Cuban families and how they get their kids to schools—it is remarkable—on this little more than a dollar a day that they have. This is what leads to so many other problems in regard to overcrowding apartments or houses—19 persons living in a one-family residence, which I know of myself. They combine together because they cannot afford the rent.

Source: U.S. Congress, Senate, Committee on the Judiciary, *Problems Connected with Refugees and Escapees,* before a subcommittee of the Committee on the Judiciary, Senate, 87th Congress, 1st session, 1961, pp. 136-45, 224-30.

Beginning Again

Gustavo Pérez Firmat
The 1.5 Generation

In 1960, when the Pérez Firmat family came to Miami from Cuba to wait out the Revolution, Gustavo Pérez Firmat was 11 years old. He later became a poet, fiction writer, scholar and professor of Spanish at Duke University. He describes his generation of Cuban Americans as the 1.5 generation—born in Cuban and raised in Miami. His books, including Life-On-The-Hyphen: The Cuban American Way *and his beautifully written autobiography,* Next Year in Cuba *illuminate this theme. In the following excerpt, he comments on the impact of exile and the central role of Calle Ocho in the Cuban American imagination.*

Exiles live by substitution. If you can't have it in Havana, make it in Miami. The Cuban-American poet Ricardo Pau-Llosa wrote, "The exile knows his place, and that place is the imagination." Life in exile: memory enhanced by imagination. Like Don Quijote, every exile is an apostle of the imagination, someone who invents a world more amenable to his ambitions and dreams. It's no accident that for over twenty years the most popular eatery in Little Havana has been the Versailles restaurant, which is all cigar smoke and mirrors. Surrounded by reflections, the exile cannot always tell the genuine article from the hoax, the oasis from the mirage. Exile is a hall of mirrors, a house of spirits. . . .

During the 1960s and 1970s Calle Ocho, or Eighth Street, was a busy bustling one-way throroughfare lined with restaurants, supermarkets, gas stations, bakeries, florists, fruit stands, barbershops, car dealerships, furniture showrooms, appliance stores, botanicas (stores for religious artifacts used in Afro-Cuban rituals), funeral parlors, and schools. Anything one needed could be found on Calle Ocho, which was located in the heart of Little Havana. As sociologists put it, the community that sprang up around this street was institutionally complete. An individual who lived there could be delivered by a Cuban obstetrician, buried by a Cuban undertaker, and in between birth and death lead a perfectly satisfactory life without needing extramural contacts. Little Havana was a golden cage, an artificial paradise, the neighborhood of dreams. . . .

Source: Gustavo Pérez Firmat, *Next Year in Cuba* (New York: Doubleday, 1995), pp. 82-4.

Operation Pedro Pan, 1960

Operation Pedro Pan was organized in 1960 by Father Bryan Walsh of the Catholic Charities to aid Cuban children who were sent to the United States by their parents to avoid military conscription and communist indoctrination. Between 1960-1962 over 14,000 unaccompanied Cuban children came to the United States. The children, mostly teenage boys, settled in camps in the South Florida area before they were placed in permanent homes all across the United States. Sara Yaballi was a Cuban exile nurse who served as the Head Nurse at South Dade's Matecumbe Camp. Sara was not simply a nurse to these children. She also gave them love, support and was their mother figure. The correspondence that follows is part of her collection that she donated to the Cuban Archives at the University of Miami Library. The letter below is a note of thanks from a mother who is still in Cuba.

Ana E. Lopez
A Note of Gratitude, 1962

Artemisa *July 15, 1962*

Ms. Sara Yaballi

My Dear Lady:

It is my sincere desire that you are well and in the company of your family.

I hope you will forgive me for taking the liberty of writing you even though I don't know you. I am the mother of P. Lucas and Oreste and they have spoken so well about you. They care very much for you and mention you in their letters.

Sarah, you cannot imagine how grateful we are to you for everything you have meant to them. I pray to God to bless you and reward you for everything you have done. I also pray that you are able to continue offering others your kind and gentle services. This is my sincere desire and hope, as a mother who has had to suffer the misfortune of being separated from her beloved children.

Sarah, I wrote you on the 29th of May, but Oreste tells me that you never received my letter. I am very sorry about this as I was looking forward to hearing from the person who has helped my sons so very much in these difficult times. It is in times like these that one most appreciates a helping hand. My

sons had never before been away from us. At least they are happy and getting accustomed to the situation.

In parting, please accept from me a warm embrace. From now on, please count me among your friends.

Greetings,
Ana

My address is: Ana E. Lopez
General Gomez #3615

Source: Letter, Ana E. Lopez to Sara Yaballi, July 15, 1962, Coral Gables, Florida, University of Miami Cuban Collection.

Eduardo Padron
"A Welcomed Burst of Freedom"

Eduardo Padron came to Miami without his parents when he was 15 years old. He graduated from Miami High School, Miami Dade Community College and got his Ph.D. in economics from the University of Florida. He started teaching at the new downtown storefront campus of Miami Dade in 1970 and quickly rose up the ladder. In 1980, he became head of the Wolfson campus, a position he held until 1995 when he was named the District President of the much honored five campus college. Dr. Padron has been widely honored for his key leadership roles both nationally and in the Miami community.

Imagine how leaving one's native homeland would obviously present tremendous mixed emotions for a young person! Particularly one like me who was leaving behind what I will forever cherish as the epitome of ideal parents and familyhood.

Departing Cuba, an island befit by its beautiful natural environment but where opportunities and liberty are next to none, to migrate to a nation known as the land of plenty, became a distinct reality for me at a youthful, adolescent age. . . .

My arrival into the United States of America can duly be described as a welcomed burst of freedom that simultaneously transformed my being from adolescence to adulthood.

In recalling my first practical encounter with freedom it remains very clear to me that this occurred when I visited the downtown Miami Freedom Tower which housed the Cuban Refugee Processing Tower.

Such an awesome building! Marked by elegance and a manifestation of dignity, the intricate architecture of the Freedom Tower was certainly a stunning sight to behold.

I quickly blended into the general hustle and bustle of numerous adults, senior citizens and children. It occurred to me that the massing coupled with the level of chatter and laughter in the place even reminded me somewhat of downtown Havana; but surely this was just an insignificant illusion. For the real issue at hand was that I was now in America and it would only be a matter of moments before my name and personal information would be permanently recorded on official U.S. documents for the purpose of my becoming a legal immigrant. . . .

They and I were all in that striking infrastructure, the Freedom Tower, for the same reason—waiting to be processed!

There was certainly a wonderful feeling of warmth and friendliness that emanated from the great structure in which we stood. This was very comforting to me and I would imagine to my fellow citizens as well.

My turn came and ended with a brief interview, and my being allotted a block of government surplus cheese and a bag of powdered milk. . . . I had been processed!

To this day the Freedom Tower remains one of the most distinctive buildings that I have encountered. My emotions continue to become stirred whenever I reflect upon my encounter with freedom and the Freedom Tower.

Source: Eduardo Padron, "Arriving in Miami" (unpublished manuscript, Miami, Florida, 1996).

Dangerously Close

J. Rafael Montalvo
Fighting for Freedom, 1961

J. Rafael Montalvo was 18 years old when he joined the Bay of Pigs invasion in April 1961. Son of a prominent Havana pediatrician, he was a student at Georgia Tech and had recently graduated from Havana's La Salle del Vedado High School. After his capture, he was imprisoned in a Havana jail for 21 months until his release in December 1962. He returned to Georgia Tech and graduated with a degree in industrial engineering in 1966. He worked for Eastern Airlines until opening his own aviation maintenance service in 1981. His moving account recalls his idealistic fervor for his homeland and the cause and the sense of betrayal he and the others felt after being abandoned and left on their own.

The class of 1960 took Havana with passion that spring. Graduation, the promise of a just society, and the prospect of work or college filled our minds while our souls were turned on by the vibrant city.

By early summer the reality of the new political order began to destroy our lives. The sound of the firing squads, repression, armed mobs, confiscations and plain acts of injustice punctuated our every day.

At summer's end life became hell.

Our concerned parents sent us away by the thousands. My father advised me one day that the next day I would leave for Georgia Tech. The sudden exit and evil left behind burned our insides. Every value we had acquired from our parents, our plans for the future, and the safety of our families that we had left behind were all threatened.

Soon we heard about an operation being organized under the patronage of the United States government. A military exile force was being trained in the Guatemalan mountains. A serious effort, we thought, hand in hand with a good friend! The debate among students on priorities dominated our evenings. Duty to country versus the need to continue on with studies and please our families. In the end, many of us concluded that our first duty was to our families and that the best way to fulfill that duty was to help provide them with a free country. We made peace with God, said our goodbyes and left for the Guatemalan mountains. I remember thinking in the long flight to the training camps that we were heading for sure death and certain victory. Our families, friends, and our countrymen would be free again, forever.

The camps were high in the mountains nested in thick jungle and commanding imposing views of the countryside. The hard training, difficult terrain and discomforts disappeared in the beauty of the environment and the enthusiasm and spirit of the troops. A well-trained winning team, that's what we were. Freedom fighters!

One day we were flown to a port on Nicaragua's Caribbean coast. The ships were there with armaments loaded, bombers were at the airport and war drums were beating.

Spirits soared as we readied for battle and boarded the ships while the paratroopers camped at the airport.

The three day voyage to Cuba was marked by sightings of the U.S. fleet, our friend, and solemn thoughts as death got closer. The voyage drew us together and we became better soldiers and better friends.

The landing was at night, a moonless, dark and confusing night. With adrenaline pumping—the glory of the moment: fear and fury, under constant fire, teeth clenched—determined, we went into battle. We took the beach and captured the eighty man garrison.

Morning changed everything. The sky filled with enemy planes that were not supposed to be there. They sunk two of our ships, one with over 100 men on board, the other with most of our fuel and communications equipment.

We pressed on and met with our paratroopers. We could not go far, however, as we were missing the men on the sunken ship. That day and that night were hell as only war's hell can be. Castro's forces came in by the thousands and with tanks. There was cannon fire and napalm bombs and tracers and white phosphorous and dead everywhere. We died as we had to. We had won the night.

The second morning brought a withdrawal to the main landing area and we sang the national anthem in protest as we retreated—fighting back tears for the terrain that was left behind that had just been free.

Hell continued as 70,000 men pressed on us while we began to run out of ammunition. As the day progressed, the supplies did not arrive, the circle around us tightened and we died some more. Our friends promised: "we are coming in naval, air, and land support." Victory was certain.

The third day we went on the offensive to clear the beaches for the promised help and we fought hard and beat them back. We killed some more and died some more and we held on to a precious piece of free land. We ran out of ammunition and help never came.

"You are on your own now" came the message from the war ships we would see so close. Too late for any organized retreat, too late to escape. We had earlier refused an offer to evacuate.

Without hope, still unable to comprehend the defeat, we headed to the mountains. But the mountains were not there and along the way were thousands of men.

They captured most of us and killed some of us. They took us to the beach where you could see that the warships had sailed away.

We had not won and we had not died. They walked through jeering mobs asking for the firing squad. They loaded us on trucks and paraded us through small towns where all the townsfolk—men, women, and children—those that we were going to liberate, shouted slogans at us and asked for the firing squad. They loaded some of us into air-tight trucks and we died some more.

Imprisoned in Havana, how differently the city looked from that hill than it had looked last spring. We were tried. In reality, our friend [the U.S.] was tried for fostering the invasion. We were requested, as only communists can request, to cooperate. But you must understand, we had not won yet, our friend was still our friend and we had not died yet. We refused to cooperate and were sentenced to thirty years of enforced labor.

Twenty one months and one missile crisis after we were captured our friend exchanged medicines for our freedom.

The return to Miami on Christmas Eve of 1962 was painful. Freedom was painful. The families of our dead were painful and listening to our friend President Kennedy promising to return our flag to a free Cuba was painful.

We went on, many to continue to fight all over the world, side-by-side with our friend, others, to become good citizens and raise families in a free land.

And we still go on, you see. We have not died and we have not won yet.

Next time you happen to see some somber looking older men—still passionate and intense—around April 17, perhaps you will understand.

Source: J. Rafael Montalvo, "Fighting for Freedom" (unpublished manuscript, Miami, Florida, 1996).

The Military in our Midst, 1962

The world came perilously close to nuclear war in October 1962 during the Cuban Missile Crisis. After the Kennedy Administration instituted a blockade of Cuba, the Russians finally agreed to withdraw their missiles from the island. President Kennedy, in turn, agreed not to invade the island or allow others to. Cubans in Miami were furious with what they saw to be Kennedy's betrayal. Yet there was another dimension to the crisis. Americans, racked with fear over the possibility of nuclear war, prepared for disaster. For Miamians, the Cuban Missile Crisis hit especially close to home. This excerpt, from

The South Dade News Leader, *describes the terror and preparation in Homestead and South Dade—the part of South Florida where most of the troops were housed. The News Leader is a weekly newspaper that is now in its 84th year of publishing.*

South Dade is the center of a major military buildup which, according to Congressman Dante Fascell and County Manager Irving McNayr, will increase in size and power until the Cuban crisis is ended.

No official information on our military buildup from military sources is available. The information officer of the HAFB [Homestead Air Force Base] states, that "all inquiries of this sort are referred to the Defense Department in Washington."

But troops are moving into the area in ever increasing numbers in troop trains of 45 and 50 cars. A passenger agent of the Florida East Coast Railroad stated that 2,000 troops with equipment arrived in South Dade on Tuesday night alone. These trains have been coming in at the rate of three a day.

On one train seen by *News Leader* reporters, there were five passenger cars for troops and 40 flat cars loaded with Jeeps, trucks and other military transportation. . . .

Many of the troops coming into Homestead are immediately dispatched to the Keys in motor transports. A *News Leader* reporter watched such a convoy, and on each troop truck a guard armed with a carbine was "on watch." These convoys were escorted by Metro motorcycle officiers who, according to Metro Captain Charles Fisher, merely escort the troops to the Monroe County line. . . .

Tuesday afternoon the Strategic Air Command "cancelled all leaves and recalled all personnel," according to an official of the Homestead base, which is one of the principal SAC bases.

This Homestead base is the hub of the present military buildup in South Florida, according to Congressman Fascell, and its importance in this operation will increase.

Homestead residents notice the increase in takeoff and landings by planes from the base.

Source: "Man, Equipment Awaiting Action," *South Dade News Leader*, October 25, 1962, p. 1.

Preparing for the Worst, 1962

South Dade residents were advised to stock up on canned foods, water and first aid supplies to see them through a week or more of emergency.

In a statement to people from Perrine to Florida City, Homestead Mayor Richard Conley, head of an emergency survival plan for South Dade, urged residents not to panic, but to gather food and equipment to care for themselves and their families.

Conley said he will designate three types of community facilities—shelters, emergency first aid and casualty stations, and food storage and supply warehouses.

Most likely to be called into use will be the Homestead Armory, the big field house at T.J. Harris Field, the gymnasiums of area schools, and other large buildings, such as community centers and shopping centers, he said.

STORE WATER

If the survival plan is put into use, instructions to the people of South Dade will be issued by Conley over Radio Station WSDB, 1430 on the dial, he said. The station plans to operate 24 hours a day in the event of a crisis.

Conley recommended that canned foods, such as meats, fish, fruits, beans, peas, soups, cereals, tinned baked goods, jellies, dried or canned heat or propane, a fire extinguisher, a battery radio and extra batteries,

Jubilant families embrace returning Bay of Pigs prisoners on Christmas Eve 1962. The U. S. obtained their freedom by giving the Cuban people $62 million in food and medical supplies. (MN)

bedding, can opener, pocket knife, eating utensils, paper plates and cups and tightly-covered large cans or pails for garbage were recommended.

SHELTER SPOTS

Conley quashed the widespread notion that people who survive a nuclear blast must spend the next two weeks living in a closet. Even if the explosion is nearby, those who live through it will have a few minutes in which to gather their families, pick-up last minute articles before radio-active dust begins to reach them, he said.

An innermost room, especially if it is window-less or if its windows are protected by stacks of books, mattresses, etc., is a good makeshift shelter, Conley said.

A hot water tank, which usually holds from 20 to 50 gallons of water, is an auxiliary supply, the mayor said. And food, if covered, is safe to use, because any radioactive beams pass through it without harm. Any fruit which can be peeled is safe to eat, he said.

Source: "Stock Pantry, Conley Advises," *South Dade News Leader*, October 25, 1962, p. 1.

The Struggle for Equality

Dr. John O. Brown
The Civil Rights Movement in Miami

Dr. John O. Brown, a Miami ophthalmologist, was a project director of the Congress of Racial Equality in Miami (CORE) during the 1950s and 1960s. He helped organize civil rights demonstrations and protests in Miami. He met with Martin Luther King, Jr. several times during the 1960s. On the occasion of the first national observance of Martin Luther King's birthday, Dr. Brown remembered the struggle in an article he wrote for The Miami News.

The simple dictum, "Miami—No! No! Your-ami! Yes! Yes!" very subtly describes black Miami in 1955, prior to the civil rights movement.

It meant 100 percent segregated schools, lavatories and drinking fountains, and no service in restaurants. Blacks clustered in strictly outlined areas, such as Overtown, Coconut Grove, Liberty City, Brownsville, Opa-locka and in true ghettoes, such as Overtown's "Goodbread Alley." Plymouth Congregational Church in Coconut Grove rejected my family's membership application in 1956. That was the norm for white churches here.

Yes, this was definitely not "My-ami" at the time of my arrival here. The glitter of Miami Beach was not shared across Biscayne Bay. (Some of the Miami Beach hotels at least allowed blacks to attend the shows and let black entertainers stay in the hotels.) Apparently the only thing to draw blacks was the beautiful subtropical climate.

Blacks found their main income sources in teaching and in working as domestics and in construction. Most hotels on Miami and Miami Beach were not serviced by blacks, as many people have been led to believe. Very, very few black professionals lived in this community—five lawyers, 15 medics, five dentists, three pharmacists, and no more than 20 registered nurses, as well as I could count. Here was a perfect target for civil rights activity. The local NAACP began the legal battle with its own school desegregation suit in 1956. Suits against segregation on buses and golf courses quickly followed.

There seemed to be little activity for mass participation until the Congress of Racial Equality (CORE) entered with sit-ins at lunch counters in McCrory and W.T. Grant variety stores. Protests followed against Royal Castle hamburger chain, the movie theaters on Flagler Street, Shell City Supermarket's lunch counter and limited boycotts of several department stores.

Miami also had several marches down Flagler Street and numerous public meetings featuring speakers that included Dr. Martin Luther King, Jr.; Thurgood Marshall, who [was later] a U.S. Supreme Court justice, NAACP leader Roy Wilkins and James Farmer, a CORE founder.

Probably most motivating was the National CORE meeting and its picketing of Shell City Supermarket. There were also the Crandon Park "invasion" and integration of municipal pools.

But the initial thrust here was in public accommodations and schools. After this was accomplished, housing and jobs became targets.

The Great Society programs provided artificial jobs and development of many sub par areas. Model Cities and low-income housing programs, family health centers and regional clinics abounded, as well as minimal training programs for jobs. Many professionals came here as a result of governmental job opportunities, increased educational facilities and affirmative action programs.

Undoubtedly, there has been progress in this community, but very much needs to be done. With the influx of people from the Caribbean, Central and South America, the competition for the inadequate number of jobs has increased. Crime is on a rampage, fueled by the illegal drugs and the widening gap between "haves" and "have-nots."

A national administration, appearing insensitive to the poor and the aged and being negative toward affirmative action, has not helped.

An educational system geared to the needs of the underprivileged students and increased vocational training would be most desired.

We are working toward the day when we can proudly say "Miami," but there are still shadows of "Your-ami" lurking in the background. The dream of Dr. Martin Luther King Jr. has not been fulfilled, but the nightmare of "Your-ami" has almost disappeared.

Source: John O. Brown, "Martin Luther King's Legacy," *Miami News*, January 20, 1986, p. 7A.

Father Theodore Gibson
Refusing to Yield, 1961

Theodore Gibson was one of the most prominent black leaders in Miami's history. A pastor at Christ Episcopal Church in Coconut Grove, he fought for civil rights and equality. He led the bus integration fight in 1956. He also worked for the desegregation of public schools and the integration of public facilities. Beginning in 1959, he battled the Florida Legislature when their investigative committee, led by Senator Charley Johns, subpoenaed the list of NAACP members. The committee, working in the height of Cold War paranoia, wanted the list to search for alleged communists. Gibson refused to turn it over, was indicted for contempt of court and sentenced to six months in jail. The Supreme Court overthrew the conviction with a narrow five-four ruling. The NAACP list remained a protected document under the rights of "free and private association." Gibson later became a City Commissioner serving from 1972 to 1981. He died in 1982. Here, The Miami Times examined the controversy over the NAACP list.

Leaders of the Florida Legislature are sharpening the ax for sit-in demonstrators and others working for integration and civil rights in this state.

When the Legislature meets in April, one item on the agenda will be a threat to jail the Rev. A. Leon Lowry of Tampa, state president of the NAACP and a Baptist leader. . . .

Recently the Florida Supreme Court upheld a 6-month jail sentence given the Rev. Theodore Gibson, head of the Miami NAACP branch, for his defiance of the same committee. Father Gibson, who is rector of Christ Episcopal Church, is appealing to the U.S. Supreme Court.

The Florida high court overturned a similar sentence given the Rev. Edward T. Graham of Miami, who even refused to say if he was a member of the NAACP. Mr. Graham is former president of the Miami NAACP.

The three ministers are among 47 persons in the United States who have defied such legislative committees on the ground that the purpose of these committees is to block integration and other social progress. These 47 take their stand under the First Amendment to the U.S. Constitution, guarenteeing freedom of speech, press, religion, association and protest.

Mr. Lowry summed it up when he said: "It is quite apparent that the committee's action is an attempt to intimidate and label an organization and to weaken it. We have been pressing for our rights in almost every area and that is why they are after us."

Mr. Graham and Father Gibson were sentenced after the committee cited them for contempt. In Mr. Lowry's case, the committee voted to ask the legislature to jail the minister when it meets. The assembly can keep him in jail during its whole session if he still refuses to cooperate. . . .

Father Gibson said recently: "I shudder to think what would happen if the segregationists could get their hands on the membership lists of an organization like the NAACP. I don't look at this as a personal matter at all, but rather as something which concerns all posterity.". . .

NAACP leaders and the Florida Civil Liberties Union are among groups fighting efforts to punish ministers, professors, students and other working for civil rights and integration.

Source: "Legislative Committee Plans to Jail NAACP Leader," *Miami Times*, January 21, 1961, p. 2.

Gala Brown
A Student Leader Fights for Equality

Gala Brown, daughter of civil rights leader Dr. John O. Brown, was a pioneer in her own right. At Gladeview Elementary, she was one of only a few blacks in ithe school. As a high-school student, she led a protest at the predominantly white Miami Edison High School demanding black representation on the cheerleading and majorette squads. In her extraordinary story, Gala remembers those days when teenagers made history.

All my life—all 10 years of it at the time, I had attended "colored" schools for my primary education. I remember being quite happy and contented going to those schools, and wasn't even cognizant of the fact that all of the children who went to school with me were only colored children. I didn't think this at all unusual and it suited me just fine. I was also not aware that a better quality of education could be offered me at a "white" elementary school. The fact

that I was not aware of these things did not mean that my parents weren't aware. And so in 1961, when Dade County schools first desegregated, my parents moved me from all-black Floral Heights Elementary to Gladeview Elementary, an all-white school, where I was most definitely in the minority. Never before had I felt so different and out of place. Though thrust into an entirely new learning environment, I performed well in my school work and I was even given the opportunity to be a school patrol officer. Yet, I still did not feel good about being one of only a few colored students in the entire school.

In 1962, I entered seventh grade at Miami Edison Junior High School, where I learned even further the meaning and feeling of being a "token." I was the only Negro girl in the entire school that year, with only two Negro boys—one of whom withdrew after a brief stint. If I had felt uneasy at Gladeview, those feelings were greatly multiplied by my experiences at Edison. I recall vividly being called "nigger" by children who really didn't even know me. How could they

Dr. John O. Brown talks to students at Miami Edison Senior High during the 1968 sit-in led by his daughter, Gala, seen sitting next to principal William Duncan. (MH)

judge me as a person just by the color of my skin? However, I've always been one to not let a situation get the best of me—which was instilled in me by my parents, particularly my father, Dr. John O. Brown, who was a civil rights pioneer in Miami—and did my best to persevere and put my mind to the tasks of getting a good education. Again, I did well in my school work and became active in school sports. In ninth grade, I became the school's first Negro cheerleader, a major feat personally and racially. I "overcame" by the process of "assimilation." I had gone from feeling tolerated in grade 7, to feeling accepted by grade 9. By this time also, more Negro children had been admitted to the school, and I was glad for the company. Some of these new students became my new friends, many of whom are still close friends of mine 30 years later. The irony of becoming friends with the Negro students however, was that my white friends now felt betrayed by me and friendship ceased, post haste. It was hard to understand how and why girls I had known well for years, who had come over to swim in our pool and had slept overnight in our home, could pass me in the hallways at school and act as if we never knew each other. I didn't know friendship had colors, and that I had to make a choice.

In 1965, I entered Miami Edison Senior High School, which was a continuation of earlier learning experiences in racial tolerance. By this time, the school was well populated with black students—though still disproportionately. Because I performed well academically, I was enrolled in several honors courses. Again I was only one of a few, if not in some instances, the only Negro in the class. It hurt me to enter the hallways of the school and find the first classroom on the main floor, the one nearest to the exit door, "crowded" with Negro students, who were placed in this remedial class—almost automatically upon entry into Edison, so it seemed. It seemed unfair, and though I might have felt "privileged," I felt again as a "token."

It hurt even more to know that at Miami Edison Senior High, 50% of the football players and 80% of the track team at that time were Negroes, yet there were no black cheerleaders or majorettes, though several had trained and auditioned. Not to mention that with a population of over 450 black students, Negroes on the faculty, counseling, teaching and coaching staff were highly disproportionate. As a result of this inequality—which was discrimination through and through—the black students felt it incumbent to let it be known that we were not willing to accept this situation or allow it to continue. An appeal was made to the principal, in the form of a closed meeting with selected student representatives (Jaquetta Bland, Leroy Lang, and Patricia Culpepper), in which a list of concerns were submitted and requested to be addressed at once. Either due to our youth or our color, I'm not sure whether it was either or both, the concerns were not taken seriously and not addressed at that time.

Let me share with you from a human relations perspective, when people are discontent due to practices that are unfair (as well as unnecessary)—especially when it is obvious only certain groups of people are being treated that way—"dismissing" their concerns is like adding "fuel to the fire." Since attention could not be received from this approach, a civil protest in the form of a "Sit-in," emanated. It was only through this forum that the seriousness of our concerns could be demonstrated and as a result, the administration gave us its full attention. The success of this effort was that the school appointed Diane Dyes as the first black cheerleader and Shirlyn Rawls and Shirlyn Kirkland as the first black majorettes. These changes were implemented immediately, however, they were not well received by the white students. It was a challenging year for the cheerleader and majorettes who bore the burden of being "firsts" due to a school mandate. People had been forced to accept the change, but it didn't mean they had to accept the persons who brought about the change. Nor was it easy for some teachers to accept that I, Gala Brown, having been accepted by Miami Edison since grade seven, could be unhappy with the way things were and to the extent of leading this demonstration. I recall my honors English teacher being appalled by this event, and making her displeasure with my participation in it known by stating that "I was not like the rest of those Negroes." Yes, I may have been fair-skinned and of above-average intelligence, but I was, and always will be one of them. I guess because I was "one of them" explains why in the yearbook for the year I graduated, 1968, my photograph and existence in the school is conspicuously absent—and its cover, which had always been red, was brilliantly white that year.

In all fairness, I must admit that through those struggles, I have become a more enlightened person. My school experiences encouraged me to pursue my higher education at an all-black institution—which I did by attending Fisk University. It also emblazoned deeply into my memory the prophetic words of Dr. Martin Luther King who stated, ". . . I have a dream that my four little children will one day live in a nation where they will not be judged by the color of their skin, but by the content of their character." Twenty-eight years later, I still have this hope for my two children.

Racism, I know, is not an inherited trait, it is learned behavior. Teach our children well—teach them to love.

Source: Gala Brown Munnings, "My Childhood Experiences with School Desegregation in Miami, Floirida in the 1960's" (unpublished manuscript, Miami, Florida, 1996).

Championship Seasons

"And Away We Go"

Hank Meyer, a public relations executive, worked out a deal with local TV owner Mitchell Wolfson to have the Jackie Gleason Show broadcast to a national TV audience from Miami Beach. This put South Florida in a weekly media spotlight and extended its aura as a place to live the "good life." When the show ended in 1970, Gleason continued to live in South Florida. After his death in 1987, the Miami Beach City Commission renamed the auditorium from which his shows were broadcast the Jackie Gleason Theater of the Performing Arts.

If there is anything new readily apparent in the flatlands of Florida it is the considerable protuberance of M. Jacques Gleason, who now arrives seasonally in the Southland, rather like the horses at Hialeah, except sooner, to take up residence, gainful employment, and sport. M. Gleason, whose golf stance now figures in full-page advertisements for the State of Florida, whose likeness graces hotel flyers, and whose name shines from marquees all over town, traces his presence in the city to an item that appeared in the column prepared by Earl Wilson. One day over a year ago, in the course of dispensing world news to the uninformed, Mr. Wilson ran a line announcing that Jackie Gleason, then resident in a huge armory in Peekskill, New York, would like to play golf 365 days a year, a trick possible in Peekskill only with the aid of snow sweepers, ice cutters, anti-freeze, and flannel underwear. The line was espied by a zealot named Hank Meyer, who labors on behalf of Miami Beach. Meyer was soon in touch with Gleason, inviting him to do his shows within the confines of the sunlit fiefdom he represents, where by happy coincidence, golf is played 365 days a year. The cost of sending the show back to New York by cable would be too expensive, but it would be possible on tape. In an epic phrase rivaling the immortal catchwords uttered at Bastogne and by Perry on Lake Erie, Gleason said, "Pal, it's beautiful. Let's do it."

After ten weeks of negotiations among Gleason, Miami Beach, and CBS, it was all set. Gleason would come south in September and begin a series of telecasts until the show went off for the summer. He would sell his house in New York and he would play golf in Florida 365 days a year. And then it happened. The cameras available in Miami Beach were inadequate. The deal was off. Bulletins from Gleason headquarters described him as "feeling awful." Meyer, however, was not ready to let go. "How much would it take to buy the equipment you need?" he asked. Back came the awesome answer: between $500,000 and $600,000. Said Meyer, "I want twenty-four hours to raise the money." He went to Mitchel Wolfson, a Floridian born in Key West and now living in Miami Beach. Wolfson heads Wometco Enterprises, Inc., a giant combine listed on the New York Stock Exchange, which deals exclusively in leisure-time businesses: theaters, television and radio stations, soft-drink bottling companies, vending machines. They also own the Seaquarium, a local porpoise playground and aquarium, and Flipper, the television porpoise. . . .

When Gleason came south for his second season there was the usual sendoff party by Toots Shor in New York. Miami papers printed special editions, which were distributed in Manhattan. The fourteen-car train pulled out of New York with 100-odd musicians, technical and management staff, the June Taylor dancers, assorted columnists, and professional imbibers. With a rasp of its whistle, which had been tuned to sound like "Away We Go!" it rumbled south, stopping for mayors, bands, and committees. The temperature was in the 90s the August day it chugged into Miami, but there were 4,000 people on hand, three bands, and a waiting motorcade of vintage cars. Thousands more lined the curbs. . . . Gleason's name gleamed from movie and hotel marquees the length of the beach. Next to bagels, he was the biggest thing in town. The show landed in the top ten last year for the first time, and Miami Beach, whether because of Gleason or some less obvious reason, had the greatest winter and the greatest summer season in its history. . . .

Meyer sees a direct ratio between Gleason's promotional push and business on the Beach. In his dressing room after the show recently some of his staff were huddled over a Kiplinger letter that described in broad detail the amazing summer just experienced in what has always been a hard-to-sell season along the Beach. The Kiplinger pundits looked for reasons, came up with such possibilities as more money to spend, more vacation time, more flights, and summer package tours, etc. Jack Philbin, Gleason's manager read it all. "How do you like that?" he said. "Not a mention."

Source: Horace Sutton, "One Man's Miami," *Saturday Review*, October 9, 1965, pp. 36-40.

The One and Only Perfect Season, 1972

On Sunday January 25, 1973, Don Shula and the Miami Dolphins made sports history. By beating the Washington Redskins in Superbowl VII, not only did the Dolphins win the Super Bowl, they completed a perfect season— 17-0. Miamians were ecstatic and showed more community togetherness than anytime in recent memory. This Miami News editorial commented not just on the team, but on its impact on South Florida. Don Shula coached the Dolphins through the 1995 season and became the winningest coach in history.

A BETTER IMAGE, AND FUN TOO

Well, for Miami this is next year. Thanks to the marvelous victory of the Dolphins in Super Bowl VII, 25 other American cities can wait 'till next year while Miami savors the national championship starting yesterday.

Much has been written in these columns and elsewhere about the cohesive effect of this special football team on the community. It has provided a rallying point for a people whose roots are new and thin and whose allegiance tends to remain "back home."

We think the Dolphins have also improved the community's appearance to the rest of the nation. Because of our bathing suit image—not entirely undeserved—the country at large has a difficult time taking any of our institutions seriously . . . our solidly based businesses, excellent universities, fine symphony, growing medical center and so on.

At the risk of attaching too much importance to a football team, we suggest that the image of the Dolphins as a professional organization of championship caliber has rubbed off on the rest of the town, and that people across the country speak of Miami with new respect.

For that, but mostly for week after week of absorbing, nail biting, exciting entertainment, our thanks to Joe Robbie, Don Shula and all the Dolphins, and our congratulations for a superb, never to be forgotten championship season.

Source: "A Better Image, and Fun, Too," *Miami News*, January 15, 1973, p. 12-A.

Don Shula led the Miami Dolphins to its perfect 17 game victory streak in 1972, providing Miamians with a strong dose of optimism and togetherness. (Don Shula)

Widening Opportunities

Robert H. McCabe
Education for Everyone

Robert McCabe came to South Florida in 1949 as a college student and never left. He started his career at Redlands School and also taught and coached at South Dade and Coral Gables Senior High. After he received his Ph. D. from the University of Texas in 1963, he began his career at Miami Dade Community College. He opened the South Campus, now Kendall Campus, in 1968 and was named District President in 1980. During his tenure, Miami Dade was named the number one community college in America. Dr. McCabe has received many honors including a MacArthur Fellowship in 1992. He retired from Miami Dade in 1995.

I arrived at Dade County Junior College as Assistant to the President on August 20, 1963—the day the furniture was being moved into Scott Hall, the College's first permanent building. It was an exciting time. Students were registering for the impending fall term, and there was great anticipation about occupying the new building.

The College had opened in 1960 on the site of the closed agriculture school adjacent to Central High. Classes began in any space that could be found, including wooden buildings that had been used by the agriculture school. Some of the staff still laugh about holding classes in ex-chicken coops labeled "Laying House No. 1" and "Laying House No. 2." In addition, a small center operated at Northwestern High School. In 1962, the College moved to the current North Campus site, and occupied the converted World War II barracks.

I had just come from a program at the University of Texas to prepare community college administrators. The University and nine other centers in America were working in this field to keep pace with the community college movement which was sweeping America. There was great optimism in America. Institutions like Miami Dade believed in providing opportunity for everyone were right in keeping with the times.

I was impressed that in 1962, the newly appointed President Peter Masiko Jr. closed the all black Northwestern Center to integrate the college. It was the first integrated college or university in Florida. It provided African Americans the first opportunity to attend college south of Daytona Beach. This had been accomplished with little fanfare, and no incidents. That action demonstrated the commitment to be the college for all people. It has been the theme of Miami-Dade from its beginning until today. It is what all of us who have been involved with the College continue to be most proud of.

In 1965, I was the chief administrator who opened the new South Campus, which we called the Palmetto Center. We opened with approximately 1,000 students, operating in three portable buildings adjacent to Palmetto High School and in the high school after three o'clock. Faculty offices were spread among several churches in the vicinity. We planned to move the following year to the new South Campus. As it turned out, come Fall 1966, the buildings were not ready. Three thousand students enrolled, and we had to scramble to find make-do places to accommodate them. The Suniland Theater was two blocks away, and we taught general education in the theater with as many as 900 students in a class. Most remarkable was the use of the auxiliary auditorium at Congregation Beth Shira directly adjacent to Palmetto High School. In the morning, the facility was used as a pre-school. At noon, after the pre-schoolers left, their furniture was removed and tables and chairs placed throughout the facility so it could be used for faculty office hours. At 2:30, that furniture was removed and different furniture moved in to accommodate the performing arts groups of the fledgling campus. This cycle went on each day for a full semester.

By the Winter term, we moved to the beautiful South Campus (now Kendall) at 104th Street. Interestingly, when that site was selected, it was criticized by one of the local newspapers for being in the "middle of nowhere," 104th Street did not extend that far west, Kendall Drive was a two-lane road, unpaved from 107th Avenue west. The people planning the facilities actually rode horseback to get to the site. Now, that campus is the largest community college east of the Mississippi River.

The college began with a plan to eventually have 3,000 students. By the time I retired in 1995, enrollment exceeded 50,000, over one million persons had taken courses, and over 200,000 had completed degrees or certificates. The college had more black and more Hispanic students than any American college or university. Miami Dade Community College had been named the best of the 1,100 community colleges in America, and had also been selected as the institution that was doing more to improve teaching and learning than any college or university.

From its founding until today, Miami-Dade Community College has been the place of opportunity for all the people of Dade County.

Source: Robert McCabe, "Can You Imagine Miami Without Miami-Dade Community College?" (unpublished manuscript, Miami, Florida, 1996).

Bill Baggs
Teachers Walk Out, 1968

In February and March 1968, thousands of Dade County teachers joined others from across the state in a mass resignation action to pressure the governor and legislature to provide more resources for teacher salary and educational budgets. Union leaders Pat Tornillo and Janet Dean held a widely publicized debate on the issue with Governor Claude Kirk at Miami's Marine Stadium. The following article was written by Bill Baggs, a popular Miami News *editor and columnist, who was sometimes called the conscience of Miami. He, along with Ralph McGill of the* Atlanta Constitution *were considered the two strong Southern liberal voices of the era.*

The meaning of what has happened in Florida these last few days is that school teachers in our state no longer can be taken for granted.

They have composed themselves into what amounts to a union, and events of the present hint strongly that the teachers are going to be organized even better in the coming year.

Many persons around here are bitter about this new reality.

"They have a contract and they ought to honor it," said a prominent accountant.

A lawyer observed: "Say a teacher makes $6,000 a year. That's not bad pay for 180 days of work."

And yet another lawyer: "Teachers don't belong to unions."

These gentlemen might be surprised to learn that the humans closest to the teachers, that is the students, express much sympathy for the teachers. They realize something that many parents do not.

The school teacher today is given the most sensitive work in society. The teacher becomes the custodian of the young minds, and in many instances, a kind of part-time parent who tries to build moral character in the young. . . .

The argument that the teachers should honor the contracts they have with the state is difficult, if not impossible, to refute. The teachers would be strik-

ing on better moral ground if they walked away from the blackboard after their contract expires. . . .

However, the primary fact in all this is that the politicians can no longer tame the school teachers in Florida with promises or threats. A new day has come. You may like it, or you may not like it. But it is a new reality. . . .

Here in atomic America, in an age of the jet, in the backstretch of the 20th century, we were regarding the school teacher in Victorian terms. Somehow the teacher was beyond the reach of the economic turbulence which involves plumbers, steel-workers and railway men. The teacher was something special. The teacher was good. The teacher was interested only in teaching.

Some of this is true enough. But the teachers must eat, and prices are up, and the teacher wants a little of the affluence which distinguishes our society."

Source: Bill Baggs, "A New Day," *Miami News*, January 19, 1968, pp. 1, 6.

Roxcy Bolton
Standing Up for Women

Feminism, a movement for women's rights, developed new power in the late 1960s and 1970s. Lead by Betty Friedan, women organized to demand the end of discrimination on the basis of sex. The National Organization for Women (NOW) was formed in 1966 and women fought for the adoption of the Equal Rights Amendment. (The ERA amendment was not ratified by enough states, including Florida.) In Miami, the face of feminism was Roxcy Bolton. Motivated by a desire to make the world a better place, Bolton helped to change the status of women in South Florida. This profile of Bolton was written in honor of her recognition for the Spirit of Excellence award given annually by The Miami Herald *to those who distinguished themselves through community service.*

Even now, few people idle in neutral at the mention of Roxcy Bolton's name.

In the past 20 years, Florida's pioneer feminist has been called a crank, a scold, a stateswoman, a damned fool and a heroine. For the causes that wrench her heart— equal rights, rape, the abused, the homeless—she has led sit-ins and marches, flung open the doors of staid old-boy inner sanctums and turned stereotypes upside down. Born in the cotton-and-corn belt of Mississippi, she is a genteel Southern woman

In 1971, Roxcy Bolton, Miami's pioneer feminist, lead a demonstration against the insensitive treatment given rape victims. As a result of these protests, Jackson Hospital opened a Rape Treatment Center that became a model for America. (HASF)

who long ago learned that white gloves are not nearly so effective as boxing gloves.

"I'm an old-fashioned country woman, and I believe the simple, direct approach is what works," she says. "You have to dare to be bold. Women sometimes will talk about a problem, agonize about it too much. You've got to go out and, like the Marines, hit the beaches. You can't just hang around. You've got to move."

A master of effective confrontation who thinks quickly on her feet, Bolton argued against the men-only grills at two leading downtown department stores with the withering barb, "But men and women sleep together. Why can't they eat together?" When one TV station owner claimed women were too delicate to carry cameras on location, Bolton countered she could carry two of her three children upstairs at the

same time and was none the worse for it. When the men in charge of the hurricane center balked at Bolton's plea that they stop always naming tropical storms after women, she suggested honoring U.S. senators (as in Goldwater annihilates Arizona) instead, and the point was made.

"I'm gonna have to get rambunctious as all get-out," she will say from time to time about some injustice ("No justice. Just us.") that has come to her attention. With one ear glued to the telephone ("Tell him Roxcy Bolton's calling. It's an *emergency*.") in the kitchen "command post" of her Coral Gables home, she has summoned a steady parade of weary, wary public officials and corporate bigwigs from conferences, meetings and, in at least one case, from the shower to plead for everything from the Equal Rights Amendment and women's admission to the country's service academies to the right of Miami mothers to nurse their babies in public.

Now 62 ("It's been a good old journey, but I'm getting impatient. So many things I feel ought to be done by sundown, and time is running out."), Bolton was an early local and national leader of the National Organization for Women and pushed to establish Dade's Commission on the Status of Women. She is proudest, however, of her roles as founder of Jackson Memorial Hospital's Rape Treatment Center, Crime Watch and Women in Distress, the first rescue shelter of its kind in Florida.

Less trumpeted are her countless solo struggles: for the woman about to be replaced in her job by someone younger and better-connected; for the woman who wants to play the tuba in the Army band; for the man who is demoted from his city job because he cannot read to fill out newly instituted reports; for the prostitute working to earn her high school equivalency diploma; for the woman who sleeps and eventually dies on the steps of a downtown church. It is no wonder any letter addressed simply Roxcy (or in one case, The Great Roxcy), Coral Gables, Fla., arrives in due course at Bolton's home.

As time has passed and philosophies have mellowed, Bolton has come to be treated with a deference that often eluded her early on. "It's a different ball game," she says.

"Most people at least realize women have a right to be in the parlor and not always in the kitchen and the bedroom."

Source: Margaria Fichtner, "Roxcy Bolton: A Pioneer for Women's Opportunities," *Miami Herald*, October 18, 1988, p. 1C.

Buffalo Tiger
"We Want to Teach You," 1974

The development of native tribes in South Florida came to major turning points following the Indian Reorganization Act of 1934. In 1957, the Seminoles were recognized as a separate tribe and five years later, the Miccosukee people (who lived along the Tamiami Trail) separated from the Seminoles. In the following document, Miccosukee Chief Buffalo Tiger speaks about the Miccosukee's need to educate people, maintain their identity and build pride.

I'm not trying to antagonize you, but my speech has to try to make you understand that I have to divide the Indian and white-man Indian.

The real Indian, my people, were forced back in the glades of swamp and sawgrass after the war. They've been peaceful. For a hundred years they saw the white man in other areas take the Indian's land, and bind his land, and use his land. The food they had, the farming they had, the lake we once so loved is shrinking, and they begin to realize it. So in the 1950s we began to look and try to find ways to live Indian life, Indian way, so we talked to white man's government in Washington. That continues. At the same time we have continued to try to secure food and land and rights for the Indians. So we finally have come to make agreements with the United States. We wanted to keep our language and we wanted to keep our traditional beliefs and live the way we wanted to live.

We are learning white man's way. It's education I'm talking about. We are living our lives and walking with you. In 1962 we adopted by-laws and began to work with the United States. That does not mean we signed a treaty. We only agreed to work with the United States, and the state also. We developed a tribal government and schools. There we teach the English and the Indian, as agreed. Now we have started to develop our own history books and our own language books. They are supposed to be taught in our own school. We want to teach you some of the language we speak, some of the things we know about ourselves. We don't want whites to tell us what we are, but for us to tell ourselves what we are, how we feel. . . .

Teachers should recognize what Indians really are. We were just kidding each other a while ago. You find young people today on reservations saying, "Well, it's going to be cowboys and Indians." Indian kid doesn't want to play Indian. He wants to play winning side; he has to be cowboy. To be Indian you are just a loser. That's the attitude the young Indians are being taught through television. This type of attitude is giving us problems like suicide, depression, and loss of confidence. I don't mean just here in Florida. To really have good Indians we must train Indians, and make sure they really know how to be proud of what they are before they go into white man's society. . . .

I think the public should realize that to the Indians it's survival. I don't think we can make Indians into white men, and I don't think we can make white men into Indians, but we can understand, live together, work together, and we can get along.

Source: Buffalo Tiger, quoted in John K. Mahon, ed., *Indians of the Lower South: Past and Present* (Pensacola: Gulf Coast History and Humanities Conference, 1975) pp. 28-30.

Protestors and Warriors

Theodore White
New Voices, 1972

Much of the ferment of the 1960s and 1970s came from the anti-war movement as well as the increased participation in the political process by African Americans, women, gays and Hispanics. Nationally renowned political writer Theodore White came to Miami in 1972 to report on activities at both major party conventions. While the Republican National Convention nominated Richard Nixon for a second term, the Democratic National Convention, which nominated anti-war advocate George McGovern, broke many traditions by giving various dissidents a forum to present their views before a national television audience. It was part of the movement for greater "participatory democracy" that was the hallmark of the period. Yet as White's account illustrates, these new voices were seen by some to illustrate a disturbing trend in which arbitrary formulas represented diversity.

What was moving across camera was a family discussion within the dominant left wing concerning the platform, program and purpose on which it would bend the old Democratic Party. On most major matters, McGovern control could hold firm. . . . But by the very philosophy of "participatory democracy" that had recruited its marchers, it could not impose discipline without first allowing debate. And open debate exposed for millions of Americans thoughts, ideas, proposals which had for decades been swept into the dark rooms of their culture and there locked up. . . . [On] each side of every issue, the politics of the convention imposed a new pattern of speakers—each trio of advocates must include a man and a woman, a black and a white. Constantly, one knew, the McGovern command wagon was in control—its whips raking up votes, commanding majorities on the "safe" side of such cultural issues as might alarm the traditional Democrats beyond the hall. But it was the parade itself that was important, the puncture of the past by new images. No matter how few or many people were tuned in at the wee hours of the morning to hear the endless talk, no matter how loyal were the Democrats who stayed watching to the end, the convention gave the sense of a movement rushing through and beyond the political and cultural limits all politicians had up to now accepted. . . . Open politics is exhausting, for open passions tire the spirit; the executive mind avoids open politics, for executive decision requires another kind of energy. . . .

Theodore White, *The Making of the President, 1972* (New York: Bantam Books, 1973), pp. 239-40.

Charles Whited
"Are There No Heroes?"

Charles Whited was an award winning writer for The Miami Herald. *He joined the newspaper as a reporter in 1962 and became a columnist in 1966. When he died of cancer in 1991, the community lost one of its most eloquent spokesmen. In this selection, Whited looks back at the anti-war demonstrations during the 1972 Republican Convention. His description recalled not just the images of protest, but also the struggle with law and order. For Whited, this echoed his own personal struggle. Did he fit in with those inside the Convention Hall—the politicians and business types? Did he belong outside with the youth culture and anti-war demonstrators?*

Well, Elvis is dead, too. John Wayne is dead. The Lone Ranger is unmasked. Are there no heroes left?

We meld into the '80s. There is a great pondering about where we've been, where we're going, what it all means. Maybe this is why I look back so intently at that hot fragment of 1972 in Miami Beach. It must have meant something.

The old chaos was winding down, after all; the old wrathful coming-together of the '60s, the old collision between Radicals and Establishment, between youth and everybody over 30, between Right and Left, hawks and doves, was having a last big public surge. People thought they knew who the bad guys were in 1972. It happened there in Flamingo Park, there on Washington Avenue, there on Meridian Avenue, in a place called Miami Beach.

"Hell no, we won't go! Hell no, we won't go! Hell no, we won't go! Hell no, we won't. . . ."

I remember it, sweet Jesus, like yesterday. I remember that climactic night around the Convention Hall when it came together. The steel fence gleamed in searchlights. Phalanxes of state troopers formed ranks in the streets, in the lurid glare of floodlights and TV lights. The troopers were armed with clubs, facemasks, shields. The troopers reminded me of Roman centurions. The troopers pushed against the shouting, shaggy hordes who wanted to storm the fence; pushed back against the shaggy, angry, hyped-up, bombed-out mob.

There were soft plops of tear-gas canisters. Gas gushed.

There were roars from the crowd.

In the closed-up apartment houses nearby, battened as if against a hurricane, old Jews peeped fearfully between their blinds and thought of other sorrows. . . .

And inside the Convention Hall, in the great cavern of blue smoke, Richard Nixon, in a suit of banker's blue, upthrust his two arms and waggled his fingers in twin Vs and spoke piously of a new national destiny. I watched him and heard him from the press gallery and was dubious, knowing not why. I remember thinking that as mad as the scene was in the streets, I felt more at home there. But this country had a raging hunger to believe, and I felt that, too. We were weary of violence, weary of revolt, weary of war, desperate for leadership. We wanted to believe. So in the next election, we gave Richard Nixon the most lopsided mandate of votes in this country's history, and I was among those Nixon voters. The mandate, I hasten to add, came from those citizens who bothered to vote at all. Fifty-three percent did not. And this, too, spoke volumes and would become part of the crazy patchwork of the '70s: non-participation by a turned off constituency.

"Hell no, we won't go! Hell no, we won't go! Hell no, we won't go!"

Source: Charles Whited, "Ten Years Out of My Life," *Miami Herald*, December 30, 1979, *Tropic Magazine*, p. 13-14.

Ted Bridis
Victory of the Spirit

The Vietnam War affected the generation growing into maturity in the 1960s—especially its young men. All were affected by the war—some more than others. Ted Bridis, a native Miamian, born in 1945. He graduated from Miami Senior High School in 1963 and played defensive end on the 1962 National Championship Stingaree football team and was selected to The Miami Herald *All- City Team. Bridis attended The Citadel, a military college in South Carolina on a football scholarship. In 1969, he went to Vietnam as a combat engineer platoon leader. In February 1970, he lost both legs above the knee and his right arm below the elbow from enemy mortar fire. Today, Bridis works in Miami as an engineer at the U.S. Coast Guard Civil Engineering Unit. In the following document, Bridis tells the story of how the war changed his life.*

September 1969 found me as a second lieutenant in the U.S. Army Corps of Engineers. My current two year assignment as post engineer at Two Rock Ranch Station, an Army Security Agency station in northern California, should have finished my active duty obligation without a tour in Vietnam. However the attrition of the war resulted in a notice to all engineer officers that each would spend a tour in Vietnam. Mine was to begin in November.

I had married my Miami High School sweetheart, Sallie Fox, while attending *The Citadel*. We now had a one year old son, Ted Jr. Television had brought the Vietnam War, the My Lai massacre and the war protests to us as background noise. Even on active duty the war had not touched us yet. Now we had to deal with it. . . .

I flew to Saigon and spent a week in Saigon for in-country orientation, then received my assignment as a combat engineer platoon leader with A Company of the 26th Engineer Battalion. . . .

The defensive perimeter was well established and they were building living bunkers by the time I arrived. . . . Work was hard and long. We usually worked 14 hour days all week with half a day off on Sunday. Twice rockets were fired at our compound but nothing was hit. They came from long range in the mountains, were not very accurate and were mostly a nuisance. . . .

As construction wound down at LZ Hawk Hill we began getting field missions; sweep a road for mines, clear a landing zone for helicopters, blow booby traps, etc. Then we got a one company size mission that would change my life. It was to clear a forward fire base called LZ Mary Ann. I was part of the reconnaissance that selected it. . . .

On the third morning, February 22nd, I arose with the mountain chill and went to get water to fill canteens to make hot chocolate. On the way back to my foxhole I walked across the top of the hill silhouetting myself in the rising sun. I made a perfect first target for a mortar barge. I heard the round whistle through the air and turned to see it go into the ground six feet behind me. I heard a ringing bang and saw the shrapnel and earth rise up to meet me. Everything went into slow motion as if I was billowed up on a cloud. Real time came back as I hit the ground. I lifted my right hand and saw a jumbled mass of bloody fingers at odd angles. My feet were laying flat on the ground in different directions attached to me by ragged bloody pants. I fell near the command bunker and was pulled in immediately. At that time tear gas erupted. We had intelligence of nerve gas which now gave us alarm. I was angry that they would not put on my gas mask which they could not due to the extent of my injuries. I was carried out to the medivac helicopter three times before there was room to take me. The artillery unit had come in late the night before without time to dig in. They took enormous casualties.

Once airborne in the medivac I felt cold and then saw a bright light through the fog. It must have been the sun. But I remember asking if I was going to be okay. The coldness left me and the light seemed to answer that Sallie needed me and I would make it for her sake. I was never concerned with my survival from then on.

In fifteen minutes I was in triage at the surgical hospital in Chu Lai. After being prepped for surgery I awoke once to be told there were several head injuries to be treated before me. The next time I awoke I was in recovery. I lifted my arm to see my hand gone but I had to ask the nurse about my legs. She told me they had to be amputated also. My calm reaction surprised me. I knew a boy in high school that lost part of a finger and I was traumatized thinking about losing a body part. Now my only thought was what's next, now that I get to go home early.

I was not recovering well from the surgery. I was hallucinating and running a high fever. My surgeon was baffled. His middle of the night call to an internal medicine specialist saved my life. I had suffered a traumatic kidney failure. I was rushed to Saigon where I underwent dialysis treatments for three months. Since the only way I could pass fluid was by sweating my fluid intake was limited to one liter a day. I was constantly thirsty. I looked forward to dialysis because you leave about 12 ounces of fluid in the machine. That was enough to allow me a can of Seven Up. I would make the Vietnamese orderlies who pushed me to stop at water fountains. I was disciplined for drinking therapeutic whirlpool bath water. Near the end of April my kidneys began functioning and I was allowed to celebrate with my first beer.

On April 24th after a one day stop in Tachikawa, Japan, I finally went home at least as far as Walter Reed Hospital in Washington D.C. I was assigned to a ward for amputees in the basement nicknamed the snake pit. It was a great morale booster. Spirits were high. If someone got down, someone in worst physical condition threw a water balloon or stole his sheets. There was a wheelchair dance line and trips into town for contraband through the fire exit. All the trash cans held beer. Then my greatest boost came when I saw my wife for the first time. I had dropped from 200 to 120 pounds and looked like hell. Our nervousness was dissolved by the long goofy smiles we gave each other. . . .

Finally the real trip home to Miami arrived. Sallie accompanied me on a medivac jet. We spent the first night at Andrews Air Force Base in preparation for the next day's flight. There were no accommodations for her, so for the first time in eight months we slept together in the same bed. You would think a jet could whisk you home in hours. Well it took three days to reach Miami. . . . Finally we landed at Homestead Air Force Base on May 5th. Unlike most Vietnam veterans there was a brass band to greet me and a key to Dade County was presented by the vice mayor.

From Homestead I was taken by ambulance to the VA Hospital in Miami. My recovery was swift from there on. . . . I was an in-patient for only two months while a final skin graft was made and I was fitted for prosthesis. . . .

I had a multitude of visitors from family to close friends to mere acquaintances who just wanted to know they were concerned. But there was one important visitor that hospital regulations would not allow in my room, my two year old son, Ted Jr. The director of the hospital, Tom Doherty, arranged a private meeting in his office. . . . It still amazes me how much young children comprehend. The meeting was wonderful. He did not hesitate to jump in my lap to play. His main concern was that I could not make the wheelchair ride fast enough. . . .

I left the hospital in early July in time to celebrate Independence Day with my family. I continued as an out-patient for another year taking rehabilitation. I learned to walk on prosthesis, type one handed and generally get into shape. Sallie made my rehabilitation an exciting new beginning, always pointing forward to the next challenge. We took my return to family life as a series of victories over small challenges: gaining enough strength to sit up without getting dizzy, transferring from bed to wheelchair, using the toilet, controlling a one-arm drive wheelchair, driving a car, and becoming fully independent. Sallie made up a rule that I could not use my disability in the domestic arguments that were sure to come up. I always thought that was a very insightful way of making me deal with reality. Unbeknownst to me, in order to foster my independence, she fought off attempts by family and friends to coddle me. There was no time to look back at the loss. For years I was proud of my single-handed victory over my disability. Now I realize there was another pair of hands holding me up while I learned first to crawl and then to walk.

That was 26 years ago. In that time I completed my masters degree at the University of Miami and continued my practice of civil engineering. I now work for the U.S. Coast Guard as an engineering supervisor. I have also pursued my love of the South Florida outdoors. I fish, dive and canoe the Everglades wilderness waterway. I am certified as a rescue SCUBA diver. Recently I took up wheelchair racing and I am invited to Atlanta for the Paralympic time trials in five track events. Sallie and I had a daughter, Tracy, a year after my return from Vietnam. She earned a degree in Orthotics and Prosthetics from Florida International University and now practices in Fort Lauderdale. She repairs my prosthetic arm. Ted Jr. is a correspondent with Associated Press in Evansville, Indiana. He credits the newspaper stories about my return from Vietnam for his interest in journalism. Both are happily married. Ted Jr. and his wife will present us with a grandson in July.

Source: Ted Bridis, "A Miami Native Returns from Vietnam" (unpublished manuscript, Miami, Florida, 1996).

New Environments

Dante Fascell
Biscayne National Park

Dante Fascell represented Miami in Congress from 1954-1992, eventually serving as Chairman of the House Foreign Affairs Committee, one of the most prestigious positions in Congress. He enjoyed broad popular support, and his work in Congress helped secure the creation of Biscayne National Monument in 1968. His sponsorship of other pieces of environmental legislation reflected his concern over the regional impact of the "Big Sugar" industry on the ecological balance of the Everglades. In 1994, he returned to his alma mater for an interview with University of Miami students, excerpts of which are printed below.

Big sugar never bothered me one way or the other, but local objectioners did. They supported my opponent, my Republican opponent before, after, and during five different campaigns. . . . Understand, they didn't retaliate—they were just protecting their position. There was some Republican opposition which supported my opponent in two general election campaigns in which the main issue was Biscayne National Park. So it was a major political fight because I was strongly in support of establishing the park and I felt strongly about it of course.

But the principle decision had already been made, by the people themselves in Dade County regardless of the opposition from my Republican opponent, and others. The earlier fight was brought on by a decision by the County Commission with regard to the proposal made by an investor—a very

Dante Fascell greets supporters during his successful crusade to create Biscayne National Monument in the Florida Keys. It became Biscayne National Park in 1980. (MH)

wealthy investor—out of Canada and Brazil named Daniel Ludwig. He was going to spend all kinds of money to put a major oil port [Sea Dade] in South Dade County. . . .

So I can't take a lot of credit. I was just, basically, riding the wave of popular opinion. But I also personally didn't want the port. I grew up fishing those waters, sailing those waters and swimming in Biscayne Bay and south of Biscayne Bay. It just seemed a shame to me to build an oil port in the middle of that area and convert the thirty-three islands that make up Biscayne National

Living History

Cape Florida Lighthouse
Key Biscayne

The Cape Florida Lighthouse on Key Biscayne is Dade County's oldest and most enduring structure. It was saved from destruction by the dedicated effort of the late Bill Baggs, editor of *The Miami News*. Through Baggs' unrelenting campaign, the State of Florida purchased 406 acres on the tip of Key Biscayne and the lighthouse in 1966. It was later re-named the Bill Baggs State Recreation Area in his memory.

Built in 1825, as one of the first projects commissioned by Congress after Florida's territorial annexation, the Lighthouse survived hurricanes, Indian attacks and the weathering of time.

What we see today is a rebuilt structure. In 1836, during the Second Seminole War, Indians attacked the lighthouse and killed assistant lighthouse keeper Aaron Carter while lightkeeper John Thompson narrowly escaped death. The lighthouse was not rebuilt until 1846. During the restoration process, workers discovered that the original builder of the tower, Noah Humphreys, used hollow walls in its construction to increase profits by 50%. By 1855, the Lighthouse, complete with solid walls, operated again—providing comfort and strength to the sea weary traveler. Within a few years, however, the lighthouse was darkened again by Confederate guerillas. Rebuilt after the Civil War, the lighthouse was decommissioned when the Fowey Rocks Light was completed in 1878.

(John Gillan)

The State partially restored the lighthouse in the early 1970s and rebuilt the keepers quarters. By the 1990s, however, the old tower needed extensive repairs. Restoration under the leadership of Dade Heritage Trust and with the help of State of Florida Historic Preservation Grants, the lighthouse has been restored and was re-lit and re-dedicated as part of Miami's 100th Birthday celebration.

Park and turn it into another major city like Miami Beach.

We have something so unique, it doesn't exist anywhere else in the world. The same can be said about the coral reefs off our shores. They should be protected. They are the last remaining reefs on the mainland of the United States. A national preserve for that purpose, I thought, was a major objective that should be achieved. I was very fortunate because in the latter days of my career, some events occurred that got popular attention through newspaper and television. Two

ships ran aground on the reef. Preserving the reef from ships running aground is really not the issue in establishing the sanctuary. But that event enabled me to get the bill passed for a maritime preserve.

This was not an original concept because the first maritime park was brought about through the efforts of John Pennekamp. But Biscayne was a good follow up. Now we have the state park and then right next to it we have the federal preserve, which goes all the way down beyond Dry Tortugas, which I was able—also at the last minute—to get changed. Both Key

Biscayne and Dry Tortugas [were changed] from monument status to park status. I never did like the idea of calling those parks monuments. There's not a hell of a lot of difference but everybody understands when its a park, not everybody understands when you say monument. Immediately you have a picture of the Statue of Liberty or George Washington or something. . . .

The whole question of preserving the Everglades is not that simple. Its not just the farmers and the sugar-cane growers against everybody else. In 1947 we had a big storm. I got in a boat at Flagler Street and 12th Avenue by the big Firestone Station that was there. We rode in that motor boat all the way out Flagler Street, crossed over and went into Hialeah. We met with U.S. Senator Bob Graham's father who had a diary out there. We're standing in the middle of Hialeah in hip-waders. We talked about this flood, and its effect on drinking water, and on residential area. We talked about the people who had perished and agreed that something had to be done to prevent or mitigate this massive disaster should it strike again.

So a big plan was put in motion—the Central and Southern Florida Flood Control District—it involved twenty-seven counties. It's the world's largest man-made effort to deal with the flow and conservation of water in the history of man. So that's a pretty big project. And the idea was to contain the water, preserve it, control the flow so that you wouldn't have floods that wiped out farms, killed people, and drowned homes. You would still have drinking water, you had to maintain the pressure and the flow in the aquifer, and then of course you would need a flow that would take care of the Everglades.

A nice concept, done by engineers and scientists. The only trouble is it didn't work the way we thought it would. However, the state and federal government started spending money on it. Today we're still learning that all of the things that the best brains could give us at the time just didn't work as planned. For example, we're just going to have to deliver more water on a regular basis to Everglades National Park or there won't be anything there, everything will be dead and the same way with Florida Bay. So arose the idea of channeling the water, in other words making the canals deeper, wider, straighter. The project was able to deliver more water, but it was also delivering more pollutants. So a change was made. . . .

They tried to maintain a head in the water conservation and storage areas. Dikes were built to improve and control the flow of fresh water. One of the problems is that there is now so much population

that the water is being consumed faster than it can be replenished. The water impoundment areas didn't work too well because, a simple thing, no matter how deep the dikes, the water went deeper. So it just wouldn't stay in one place long enough to be impounded in sufficient quantities. In other places, millions of gallons of fresh water was being released into the Atlantic and the Gulf of Mexico. Diagonal dikes were conceived to help hold the water but the water just kept flowing under them.

Source: Dante Fascell (taped interview, Coral Gables, Florida, Institute for Public History, University of Miami, March 2, 1995).

The New World Center, 1976

In 1976, a group of Miami's top business leaders met on the empty 38th floor of the bankrupt One Biscayne Tower to focus on the future of downtown Miami. Miami was in the midst of deep economic recession. From this meeting came the New World Center Action Committee through the Greater Miami Chamber of Commerce . They launched a concerted civic effort to revitalize the area. Under the leadership of Alvah Chapman, then President of The Miami Herald, *the group recruited public and private investment and oversaw the extraordinary re-building of downtown Miami. Today, Chapman is the retired Chairman and CEO of Knight-Ridder,* The Miami Herald's *parent company, and remains active in countless community organizations. His endeavors include chairing "We Will Rebuild" after Hurricane Andrew and the Community Partnership for Homeless, Inc. This excerpt, written in 1976 by legendary publicist Hank Meyer, described the New World Center, a name he created.*

Today, public and private initiative has galvanized some $1.5 billion worth of projects that are completely transforming the heart of Miami—where Henry Flagler's massive wooden Royal Palm Hotel started it all 80 years ago—into a sophisticated center of business and finance, culture and education.

And a highly significant fact about this vast outpouring of investment is that it is comprised almost equally of public funds and private investment, about 60 percent public and 40 percent private, to be more exact.

The roster of New World Center projects in being, under construction, or now coming off the drawing boards reads like an instant megalopolis.

There's a $315 million government center of federal, state and local office buildings replacing a

Highways and shopping centers were seen as emblems of progress during the 1950s and 1960s. I-95 sliced through downtown Miami largely destroying Overtown while the 25 miles of Palmetto Expressway, seen here, linked Kendall with Golden Glades. (M N)

former rundown section of midtown, a $225 million private investment that will transform an island at Miami's front door into a complex of residential and office buildings, a $50 million convention center, a newly-opened $76 million megastructure that brought downtown Miami its first new hotel in 11 years, an $87 million residential complex and marina now taking shape on downtown Biscayne Bay, several midtown city blocks mushrooming as the New World Center campus of Miami Dade Community College and Florida International University, a $795 million rapid transit project and people mover system to bring people downtown from the suburbs and move them conveniently around the area when they get there, millions of dollars worth of new downtown parks, river walkways and general beautification.

Obviously, a concept of this magnitude and scope didn't, like Topsy, "just grow."

It represents the fruits of dedicated civic effort on the part of some of the best brains and finest talents in Miami—brains, and talents and decision-making ability that money couldn't buy.

The genesis undoubtedly occurred four years ago when Alvah H. Chapman, Jr., president of the *Miami Herald* and the Knight-Ridder Newspaper group, was named chairman of a new, action-oriented committee of the Greater Miami Chamber of Commerce, the New World Center Action Committee.

Chapman had put his vision for Miami in a nutshell:

"I have a simple philosophy: Of all the cities in America, one has to be the best. One has to make the most progress. One city has to show the way. Some city has to write the book on civic progress. Why could not that be this Greater Miami community?"

Source: Hank Meyer and Associates, "The New World Center" (press release, Miami, Florida, October. 1978).

Al Burt
Living on the "Urban Frontier"

Al Burt graduated from the University of Florida and worked in Atlanta and Jacksonville before beginning his long and distinguished career with The Miami Herald *in 1955. He served as city editor and Latin American editor and became a roving Florida columnist in 1973. Widely honored, Burt retired in 1996. In the following article, Burt sees the vitality of Miami.*

Miami reminds me of youth breaking away from home. The old folk are unhappy about it, but the young give up certainties as though they were shackles. They are too raw and confident to worry, eager to test themselves in the survival contest.

But there is a peculiar difference here: home is the one breaking away, changing, leaving the settled folks to move to new things. The trauma is greater than usual. This time it is the older folk who are being pried loose from certainties and it is not easy for them.

Miami appears to have grown young again, casting aside old dreams and startling ways, racing toward a new kind of life it does not yet understand, gambling on discovery. Rather than nodding off with the old folk, Miami goes roaring into the 80s dependent on a reckless vitality to roll over mistakes and make new paths. . . .

Who gets the chance to be young again? Miami has, and the experience appears to alternate between being both more painful and more euphoric than the first adolescence, the Roaring 20s. . . .

Miami bubbles and boils, making history faster than even South Florida ever saw before. This is an urban frontier, full of the risk and turbulence and opportunity that all true frontiers offer. . . .

To me, Miami does not look much like a place where the gentry take their ease now, not any more. She appears young and wild again and she has left the old home. For some, this may seem cruel, but she has gone and nothing will change it. If we older folk cry and complain, it will not matter. If we cheer the best strains emerging, it might. On the frontier, nostalgia is a waste of time. Good things could wait for those lusty enough to find it exciting rather than scary.

Source: Al Burt, "Miami Today: The Best of Times?" *The Miami Herald Tropic Magazine*, September 28, 1980, p. 30.

THE HEMISPHERIC CITY
1980 - 1996

chapter
seven
7

"Future cities won't be national. They are becoming regional hubs and some of them are becoming global cities. Global cities belong politically to the nation in which they are embedded, but in terms of everything else, they belong to the world. As such, they are the crucible of a new culture being born."

Wally N'Dow
New Perspectives Quarterly, 1996

In only 100 years, the place where the river met the bay had been transformed from an isolated tropical outpost into a great "Hemispheric City" alive with future possibilities. (DDA)

Miami's image changed forever in 1980 when, in the course of a few months, it was struck with a series of disasters that would have permanently crippled a less resilient place. For an area that traditionally sought publicity, Miami was not prepared for the type of headlines—riots, refugees, drowning boat people, crime, drugs, anger—that it garnered in 1980. Was Miami a Paradise Lost?—a question Time Magazine *had boldly asked on its cover?*

Miami's problems were real—racial and ethnic conflicts, yawning gaps between rich and poor and rampant big city crime and violence. Many wondered if people from different cultural backgrounds could learn to live together with dignity and mutual respect. Much of the rest of the nation wrote Miami off.

As it had displayed in earlier crises, however, Miami exuded its legendary "gritty resourcefulness" and ability to rebound from the worst kind of situations. The tragedies of the early 80s became rallying points for those committed to bringing Miami back from the brink of disaster.

By the late 1980s, Miami emerged as what author T. D. Allman called a "City of the Future"—a laboratory of 21st Century America when America itself will experience what Miami is experiencing now. As Greater Miami begins its second hundred years, its proven ability to absorb a variety of people and adapt to change will determine its future as the nation's first truly "Hemispheric City."

∞ Not the Best of Times

As the new decade dawned, an undercurrent of tension lay just beneath the surface of Miami's sunny image. The economy was booming again yet many were not benefiting from this new prosperity. This disparity bred a sense of futility and anger among many local residents. Closely related to these problems was the scourge of drugs and crime that struck Miami in epidemic proportions by the late 1970s. South Florida's inviting coastline made Miami a major depot for illicit drugs just as it had for illicit liquor during Prohibition. Billions of dollars of drug money corrupted law enforcement, undermined families and caused an unparalleled wave of violence and crime.

In February 1980, Johnny Jones, the popular superintendent of schools, was indicted for attempted theft of school property. Jones was the highest ranking black official and one of the most respected black leaders in Miami. To the black community, his indictment seemed unfair, symbolizing years of discrimination and mistrust.

Another trauma came by sea. In April, Castro allowed more than 125,000 people to leave Cuba through the port of Mariel. Thousands of boats from South Florida—the so-called "Freedom Flotilla"—brought back the refugees that included some hard core criminals and individuals suffering from mental disorders whom Castro had discharged from Cuban institutions. Although the national news media created powerful negative stereotypes of the "Marielitos," the majority of the newcomers were legitimate refugees who fit easily into the area. The federal government, however, failed to spread the financial strain of the immigrants more evenly into the national budget and South Florida was left with most of the financial burden.

In the midst of the Cuban refugee crisis, an all-white Tampa jury acquitted four white Metro-Dade policemen of the December 1979 beating death of black Miami insurance agent Arthur McDuffie. The verdict inflamed Miami's black community resulting in the worst rioting in local history—and the nation's most frightening riot since 1968. Eighteen people lost their lives, more than 3,000 lost their jobs and property damage exceeded $80 million. For three very long days, the violence swirled in predominantly black neighborhoods with the worst of the conflict occurring in Brownsville and Liberty City. Smoke filled clouds, loomed above the riot stricken areas—symbolic of the anger and despair of Miami's black community.

Other groups of refugees also came to Miami including more than 50,000 Haitians and about 75,000 Nicaraguans. Most of the Haitians were escaping the repression of the island's long-time Duvalier family regime. Unlike Cubans, Haitians were considered economic and not political refugees and were detained in the Krome Refugee Center for long periods of time and often deported. This situation caused deep resentment within the Haitian community. The majority of Nicaraguan refugees were opponents of the Marxist oriented Sandinista government and by 1990 they made up the second largest Hispanic group in the county.

∞ Rebounding in Prime Time

While critics condemned television and the image industry for its endless hype, Miami's experience showed that it had both positive and negative results. On the one hand, beginning in the 1970s, national news consultants promoted "happy talk" local TV formats that focused more on sensational aspects of the news, such as sex, violence and personal tragedies. Ralph Renick, the dean of Miami television newscasters, decried the new trend of commercialism and em-

barked on a national crusade to return television news to its journalistic roots. *The Miami Report on the Civil Disturbance* pointed a finger at television for sometimes inadvertently enlarging the riot by on-the-spot coverage that attracted outsiders. The conflict between maintaining civil order and the unfettered gathering and transmission of the news was difficult to resolve. On the other hand, television helped bring Miami back into the national spotlight through the popularity of "Miami Vice" that ran for five seasons beginning in 1984. In response to the show and the buildings it highlighted, pastel colors became enormously popular throughout the region. Still, the show featured one violent shoot-out after another. Its world of drug smug-

In the spring of 1980, a South Florida "Freedom Flotilla" set out for Mariel to rescue more than 100,000 Cubans who wanted to leave the island. (MN)

The futuresque MetroMover, completed in 1986, zipped by the CenTrust Tower on its way around downtown Miami. (Walter Marx)

gling, corruption and crime underscored both the violence, beauty and high fashion trendiness of the Miami area. Miami had become a city of beautiful colors and stark contrasts.

Life imitated art as Miami's skyline changed dramatically reflecting its increasing prominence and creativity. Startlingly original buildings with open spaces and innovative features that sometimes reflected the older Art Deco style, broke the more conventional modes of box-like functional architecture. Bayside Marketplace, designed by the Rouse Corporation, also provided downtown with a new waterfront gathering place for the first time since the 1920s, when Elser's Pier was torn down to make way for Bayfront Park.

The completion of Metrorail and MetroMover by the mid 1980s, inspired many. Others remained critical that it disproportionately served the interests of a few.

For most of its history, Miami had been so busy pandering to tourist's interests that it failed to fully develop its own cultural institutions except for a few like the Greater Miami Opera that started in 1941. By the late 1980s, however, Miami had a new cultural center designed by renowned architect Philip Johnson that included the Historical Museum of Southern

Florida, the new Metro Dade Main Library and the Center for the Fine Arts. The CFA joined an art scene that included major museums like the University of Miami's Lowe Art Museum, Miami Beach's Bass Museum of Art, North Miami's Center of Contemporary Art as well as numerous private galleries. South Florida also established several annual Film Festivals, the New World Symphony, Miami City Ballet and a New World School of the Arts, with its internationally recognized program for talented high school and college students. Finally, in 1995, Caesar Pelli was selected as the architect for the new Performing Arts Center to be built on Biscayne Boulevard.

Art took on a new dimension in the 1980s. In 1983, Christo Javacheff, a Bulgarian artist, created "Surrounded Islands" in Biscayne Bay. Christo worked—against increasing disapproval—for two years to get permission to wrap the islands with 6.5 million square feet of pink polypropylene. When Christo and his diverse group of volunteers finished, many people, traumatized by the events of 1980, smiled for the first time in three years.

In 1978, Dade County passed the Art in Public Places Ordinance. Brainchild of attorney-activist Dan Paul, Mayor Jack Orr pushed for its passage. It required that one and one-half percent of all public construction costs be devoted to art. Metrorail stations, government buildings, public housing, even a garbage dump were enriched with a variety of art forms. Miami also developed a new sound—reflective of its diverse population. Gloria Estefan, Jon Secada, and Arturo Sandoval won Grammy Awards and topped the record charts. Movie studios, attracted by the warm climate and unique architecture, filmed popular offerings like "The Specialist," "True Lies" and "Miami Rhapsody." Fashion models and movie stars such as Sylvester Stallone, Madonna, Sophia Loren and Cher became part-time residents, giving the area a high profile.

By the 1980s, more and more people from all cultural backgrounds developed a new sensitivity to the value of historical memory. Ruth Shack led the fight for a county preservation ordinance that, for the first time, made historic preservation a part of public policy throughout the county. It required municipalities to either create their own preservation boards or come under the county board's jurisdiction. Miami Beach's Art Deco District, the child of Barbara Capitman, brought Miami Beach back into the national limelight. The Black Archives, History and Research Foundation of South Florida spearheaded the

Dade County's Art in Public Places ordinance brought Miami wonderful public art like the Claes Oldenberg and Coosie van Bruggen's "Dropped Bowl of Oranges in Slices and Peels." (Walter Marx)

restoration of several significant Overtown landmarks as part of the Overtown Folklife Village.

The Sanford L. Ziff Jewish Museum of Florida, the Wolfsonian Museum of Decorative and Propaganda Arts and a moving memorial to the victims of the Holocaust brought a new cultural perspective to Miami Beach.

A melange of schools of higher education dotted the landscape from predominantly Catholic Barry and St. Thomas Universities to the historically black Florida Memorial College. Miami Dade Community College with its open-door policy and five campuses became acclaimed as the leading community college in the nation. Miami's major research universities—the University of Miami and Florida International University—gained national prominence.

In sports, Miami teams rivaled the nation's best. The Miami Hurricanes captured the college foot-

ball national championship in 1983, 1987 and 1989 and were deemed the team of the decade. In 1992, they made sports history when they became champions for the fourth time in 10 years. Although the Miami Dolphins celebrated their silver anniversary in 1990 with a mediocre record, Coach Don Shula, who became the winningest coach in history, remained, even after his retirement in 1995, a sports and Miami hero.

The Miami Heat joined the NBA in 1987, the Florida Marlins threw the first pitch in the 1993 baseball season and the Florida Panthers skated onto the hockey scene in 1993. Topping off Greater Miami's sports offering was the Miami Grand Prix that moved from Bicentennial Park and the streets of downtown Miami to the new Homestead/Dade Motorsports Complex in 1996. That same year, however, disputes over public financing for sports facilities found Miami in competition with Broward County for several sports franchises and a new arena. On a brighter note, Miamians celebrated together when the Florida Panthers, South Florida's Cinderella hockey team, surprised the nation by wining their conference and facing Colorado for the Stanley Cup.

∞ A Political Mosaiac

By the end of the decade, Cubans were established community leaders gaining positions on all levels including the Dade County School Board, Dade County Commission and the Miami City Commission. After Claude Pepper died and Dante Fascell and Bill Lehman retired, two Cuban Americans, Lincoln Diaz-Balart and Ileana Ros-Lehtinen, and an African American, Alcee Hastings were elected to the United States House of Representatives in their districts. This change of leadership, marked the beginning of a new era.

African Americans assumed a number of other important leadership roles including city managers, city attorneys, three consecutive police chiefs, the head of Jackson Memorial Hospital and the chair of the Dade County School Board. When Art Teele became Chairman of the Dade County Commission and Alcee Hastings and Carrie Meek were elected to Congress, African Americans rose to high levels of power. This new political clout of African Americans and Hispanics grew with the introduction of single-member districts in county elections and a re-drawing of Congressional districts to better reflect race and ethnicity.

Tensions between Miami's diverse populace sometimes boiled over. In 1990, when South African anti-apartheid leader and Nobel Peace Prize winner Nelson Mandela visited the area, Cuban American city officials snubbed the foreign dignitary because his earlier pro-Castro statement. Miami's African American community, led by attorney H. T. Smith, responded by organizing a national tourism boycott of the area. The boycott stopped more than $12 million in tourist and convention money from coming to Miami—an area that they believed did not respect African American accomplishments. After three years, the boycott was lifted when, among other things, promises were made that included building a major African American owned hotel on Miami Beach.

Many saw the dramatic rise of Cuban political and economic power as a Cubanization of Miami. They often yearned for the "good old days" when one rarely heard any language except English and Miami was a more homogeneous, less exotic place. An increasing number, however, appreciated the rich cultural diversity of the area and its new role as a "Hemispheric City" and bridge to Latin America. Miami became the cruise ship capital of the world and its airport ranked as one of world's largest. Competing for tourists with the Orlando area, the area's uniqueness derived, in part, from its glitz, glamour and spectacle as well as its array of ethnic festivals and folk arts. No longer simply a tourist haven, however, Miami towered as the region's international banking and financial center even following the devastating effect of the savings and loan crisis of the early 1990s.

Miami entered the 90s as a great international city. Loss, however, always accompanies growth and change. Increased crime threatened a sense of security and people rushed to barricade their streets and wall-in their properties. Sprawling suburbs in Dade's vast unincorporated area created a sense of powerlessness and alienation from a distant source of government. As a result, incorporation fever set in as old as well as newly defined neighborhoods sought closer control over their own destinies.

∞ "The Spirit of Miami"

On Monday August 24, 1992, the ultimate loss of control occurred when Andrew, a fierce category 4 hurricane roared into the middle of people's lives and left a trail of ruin in its wake. It had been 28 years since the last major storm had hit South Florida and many people had never been through one. Andrew earned the dubious distinction of being the most destructive storm in American history. It left 15 people dead, 160,000 homeless and property damage in excess of $20 billion. Out of the rubble, however, a new spirit and sense of community developed as people came together to help each other. Community leaders organized a committee called "We Will Rebuild" that raised money and provided manpower to help the most needy.

The aftermath of Andrew proved that Greater Miami's diverse people could work together. Keeping the spirit of community together was more elusive. It was increasingly apparent that only continuing dialogue between people of different races, ethnic groups and walks of life could build a permanent sense of community in a diverse, extended urban region like Greater Miami. Dialogue between people was indelibly associated with Miami when President Reagan met Pope John Paul II in 1987 and even more strikingly in early December 1994, after President Bill Clinton chose the area as the place to hold the "Summit of the Americas."

During their history-making meeting in November 1987, Pope John Paul II and President Ronald Reagan strolled together through the gardens of Vizcaya. (HASF)

As Miami celebrated its Centennial in July 1996, citizens came together to honor the people who created the city and directed its destiny. It was a time to be proud, to reflect on the past, to exult in present accomplishments and to look with hope toward the future.

⬦

"Paradise Lost?"

125,000 Cubans Arrive in Florida, 1980

In April and May of 1980, after Cuban dictator Fidel Castro announced that anyone who wanted to leave the island nation was free to go, thousands of boats left Florida to pick up Cubans who wanted to come to America. This so-called "Freedom Flotilla," pulled off the most impressive sea rescue since World War II's

Dunkirk. Before it ended, 125,000 Marielitos, arrived in the United States, most settling in Florida. The following selection is excerpted from Newsweek *and reflects a national perspective.*

From Key West to the panhandle, the State of Florida seemed to have turned into a gigantic refugee camp. Thousands of people from Castro's Cuba poured in with no place to go, no coherent U.S. policy to deal with them and a growing resentment against their pres-

Exuberant Mariel refugees crossed the Florida Straits looking forward to a new life in the United States. (HASF)

ence. A thousand bedded down on cots hastily set up in the Orange Bowl, while thousands more made do at two former Nike missile bases. At Eglin Air Force Base, construction crews worked around the clock to build a "tent city" that will soon be able to hold 10,000 refugees. But all the effort by volunteers and government officials was simply unable to keep up with the massive influx. "It is out of control," said one harried official in Key West.

By the weekend, the once-manageable stream of Cubans seeking reunion with their families in America had become a deluge of more than 30,000 refugees in helter-skelter flight to the Promised Land. In a single day last week, 4,500 Cubans arrived, surpassing the total in any one month during the peak of the "freedom flights" from Cuba in the mid-1960s and early 70s. The three-week total was also more than double the monthly number of Indochinese "boat

people" admitted during last year's far more orderly refugee-relief effort. Nobody knew just how many more would come; estimates ranged as high as 250,000, a remarkable defection from a country of 10 million. "It's just a constant barrage of people," sighed Dade County official Danny Alvarez. "There's no end to it. Nobody thought it was going to be like this."

The unexpected size and speed of the influx created a dilemma for Washington. President Carter declared that the United States would "continue to provide an open heart and open arms" to the Cubans, and his Administration took several steps last week to cope with the problem. Carter authorized the use of $10 million from the refugee-emergency fund to feed, transport and process the Cubans in Florida. . . . The government has also flown in 500 tons of food and equipment, including a mobile hospital and portable showers.

Much of the necessary assistance has come from volunteer agencies such as the U.S. Catholic Conference, the International Rescue Committee and Church World Services, which have shouldered the task of relocating the refugees. It hasn't been easy. Even those Cubans with relatives in the Miami area often bring outdated addresses or phone numbers, leaving the volunteers to pore through the Miami phone book in search of relatives. As many as half of the Cubans have no one in the States to turn to. In those cases, the volunteer agencies try to line up sponsors, often Cubans and others of Latin background, to take them in. . . .

Most of the Cubans. . . .will have to contend with a rapidly growing backlash in Florida and around the country. Gov. Richard Lamm of Colorado said he didn't want the refugees in his state—and Sen. Donald Stewart of Alabama said he didn't even want them at Talladega Prison. Residents of Ft. Walton Beach, Fla. near Eglin, signed a petition to turn the Cubans out and the Ku Klux Klan threatened an anti-Cuban rally there last weekend.

In Miami, which is already a bilingual city with 500,000 Cubans, many residents feared that new refugees will compete for scarce jobs and housing and further transform the city into a Little Havana. The Dade County school system asked the federal government for $20 million in aid to help cover the cost of educating the Cubans. And when Cuban and Haitian refugees were ruled eligible for Food Stamps, state officials warned that they might have to reduce benefits for 900,000 Floridians already receiving Food Stamps.

Source: Dennis A. Williams, *et al,* "The Cuban Tide is a Flood," *Newsweek,* May 19, 1980, p. 28.

Healing and Coming Back, 1980

Following the double trauma of the McDuffie Riots and the Mariel exodus, Miami lay stunned and bloodied. It was a time of deep despair for the city. Many simply wrote Miami off and moved or stayed away. The document that follows is excerpted from a moving and soul searching full-page editorial in The Miami Herald *that challenged Miamians to fight for Miami's soul because without a soul, Miami had no future.*

It is half-past time that all of us who care about Miami sat down and had an earnest talk about how close we are to destroying it. That's no overstatement. It's true, and every person who has watched and comprehended what has happened to Miami these past six months knows it is true.

Miami is sick—so sick that if it were a person, it would have to be hospitalized. A person exhibiting such profound symptoms of fear, anxiety, hostility, and self-destruction would have to be sedated and kept quiet.

The malaise that has left Miami disoriented, in agony, and in danger of destroying itself was borne by fire and water. The fire of Liberty City and the

In May 1980, after a verdict exonerated four Miami policemen in the death of black insurance agent Arthur McDuffie, thousands of Miamians rioted in protest. For three days, parts of the city burned. (MH)

water of Mariel have left Miami faltering, uncertain and divided, at the most crucial point in its history.

Not faltering physically. There is enough frenetic building going on in Metropolitan Miami that the place, like the hair on a corpse, will keep growing even if we allow the fire and the water to consume its soul.

That's what is in mortal peril: Miami's soul. What a crushing tragedy it will be if we who live here let that happen. What a loss if we let this special place, with all its special promise, collapse inward upon its fears.

It will collapse, it surely will, unless we who earn our livelihoods and rear our children here, unless we who came here for opportunity or retirement or sanctuary from political oppression, unless all of us, singly and together, take hold and prevent it from collapsing.

Can we? Yes, we can. It will take arduous effort, and time, and co-operation toward common purposes such as few cities ever have exhibited, but if we care to, we can do it.

The crucial question is, *Will we?*

Well, now's the time to find out.

Now's the time to find out whether the Miami that once assimilated 600,000 Hispanics—and became an international financial center because it did—will now in its frustration let "Hispanic," and especially "Cuban," become four-letter words.

Now's the time to find out what Cuban Miamians, and through them Miami's 150,000 other Hispanics, are made of. God knows they've got enough problems. They're trying to absorb a new culture and a new language without relinquishing the heart and the tongue of their homelands.

Now's the time to find out whether black Miamians, who have never been more than pawns in the hard-nosed game of prosperity, are going to be permitted to become players instead. The McDuffie Riots did not occur merely because a white jury acquitted white policemen of killing Arthur McDuffie, a black man. The McDuffie Riots happened as well because, in the 12 years since Miami's first black riots in 1968, the fundamental causes of blacks' seething discontent had barely been addressed, much less corrected.

Blacks, English-speaking whites, Hispanics: These three groups make up Miami's biracial, tri-ethnic population. Each group has its own problems, its own priorities, its own prejudices. Somehow, some way, each group must come to realize that

the sickness that afflicts Miami cannot be cured unless all swallow some of the medicine needed to restore community health...

BACKLASH OF FEAR

Miami's chief adversary is fear. It wears a hundred masks, lurks in a thousand corners. Fear of crime. Fear of change. Fear of customs we do not share. Fear of languages we cannot comprehend. Fear that what has happened to us by fire and by water may happen to us again. . . .

Psychologists say and experience proves, that the best way to conquer fear is to confront it head on. The act of confrontation helps to diminish the fear by dragging it out of the mind's irrational shadows into the arc lights of mind's reasons.

If that premise is valid for one individual, it should be valid for a community of 1.6 million individuals. In that belief and hope, let's confront some of the fear.

Source: "Miami: A Time for Healing," *Miami Herald*, November 3, 1980, p. 6-A.

Time Magazine
"Trouble in Paradise," 1981

When Time Magazine *hit the newstand with its infamous cover story on Miami, many Miamians protested loudly and passionately. Many felt that they had been kicked when they were down. The area, already reeling from a series of crises, saw this national focus as a direct threat to its economic future that still depended on tourism. This article served as a catalyst for action. The following document is excerpted from that article.*

South Florida—that postcard corner of the Sunshine State, that lush strip of hibiscus and condominiums stretching roughly from Palm Beach south to Key West—is a region in trouble. An epidemic of violent crime, a plague of illicit drugs and a tidal wave of refugees have slammed into South Florida with the destructive power of a hurricane. Those three forces, and a number of lesser ills, threaten to turn one of the nation's most prosperous, congenial and naturally gorgeous regions into a paradise lost.

Consider what South Florida is up against: When the FBI issued its annual list of the ten most crime-ridden cities in the nation last September, three of them were in South Florida: Miami (pop. 347,000) was in the first place, West Palm Beach (pop. 63,000) was fifth and Fort Lauderdale (pop. 153,000) was eighth. Miami last year had the nation's highest murder rate, 70 per 100,000 residents, and this year's pace has been even higher.

An estimated 70% of all marijuana and cocaine imported into the U.S. passes through South Florida. Drug smuggling could be the region's major industry, worth anywhere from $7 billion to $12 billion a year (vs. $12 billion for real estate and $9 billion for tourism, the area's two biggest legitimate businesses). Miami's Federal Reserve branch has a currency surplus of $5 billion, mostly in drug generated $50 and $100 bills, or more than the nation's twelve Federal Reserve banks combined. Drug money has corrupted banking, real estate, law enforcement and even the fishing industry, whose practitioners are abandoning the pursuit of snapper and grouper for the transport of bales of marijuana ("square grouper," as fisherman call it) from freighters at sea to the mainland. About one-third of the region's murders are drug-related.

Since the spring of 1980, when Cuban President Fidel Castro opened the port of Mariel to those who wanted to leave, about 125,000 "Marielitos" have landed in South Florida. In addition, 25,000 refugees have arrived from Haiti; boatloads of half starved Haitians are washing up on the area's beaches every week. The wave of illegal immigrants has pushed up unemployment, taxed social services, irritated racial tensions and helped send the crime rate to staggering heights. Marielitos are believed to be responsible for half of all violent crime in Miami. . . .

The Latins are gradually turning the region into their own colony. Of the 1.7 million residents of Dade County (Miami and environs), 39% are Hispanic (vs. 44% white and 17% black). It is estimated that by 1985 the Latins will become a majority in Dade, outnumbering non-Latin whites 43% to 42%. . . .

The signs of Cuban influence are everywhere. Miami's Little Havana, the epicenter of the Cuban community that stretches along Eighth Street (or Calle Ocho), is a foreign land. In Antonio Maceo Park (named for a black Cuban patriot), old Cubans pass the time playing dominoes or reading Spanish-language newspapers that carry headlines like THE PLAN TO INVADE CUBA IS READY. *The Miami Herald*, the city's largest newspaper, is printed daily in Spanish as *El Herald*. Its circulation: 421,236 in English; 60,000 in Spanish. Three television stations and seven radio stations in South Florida broadcast Spanish programs. There are six Spanish legitimate theaters, two ballet troupes and a light opera company. Some stores in Little Havana even carry the helpful message: *Habla inglés* .

Yet just beneath that cosmopolitan veneer, ready to erupt, are tensions between the Cubans and their fellow Floridians. Dade County voters last year approved, 3 to 2, an ordinance that forbids the spending of its public funds to promote bilingualism. The bad blood has risen dramatically since the arrival of the Marielitos last year. Whites in particular resent picking up the tab of caring for the newcomers, but the animosity spills over on all Cubans. "I wonder who really upsets whites the most," says Monsignor Bryan Walsh, who ran a resettlement program for Cuban children in the 1960s, "the poor Cuban on welfare or the rich Cuban with three Cadillacs and a Mercedes out buying the country."

The blacks are upset by both kinds of Cubans. Stuck on the bottom rung of South Florida's economic ladder, they have always resented the more prosperous Cuban minority. With the arrival of the Marielitos, blacks feared that they would lose out in the scramble for the few low-skill jobs available in the region. Even in Liberty City, the black enclave in North Miami where 18 people died in last year's riot, the Latin influence is apparent. White store owners who abandoned their businesses are being replaced by Latin landlords. "The only things blacks have in Miami are several hundred churches and funeral homes," says Johnny Jones, a former Dade County school superintendent. "After a generation of being southern slaves, blacks now face a future as Latin slaves.". . .

The shocks of crime, drugs and cultural tensions have already spawned the beginnings of an Anglo exodus from Miami and its environs. Some 95% of the election registrations now being cancelled by citizens leaving the region come from white voters. Says Jeff Laner, 26, a native of Miami who moved this year to work as a stockbroker in Kansas City: "I was going to be damned if I had to learn a foreign language to get a job where I had lived all my life."

One image from the travel brochure that still rings true, an apt metaphor for a region blessed by God and not yet ruined by man, is the sturdy mangrove. It is found nowhere in the U.S. but Florida. With its gnarled roots stretching down into salty water that would kill most other plants, the mangrove traps silt, shelters wildlife and otherwise improves whatever it touches. Through boom and bust, hurricanes and real estate development, the mangrove has stood its ground. South Floridians surely will too.

Source: James Kelly, *et al.*, "Trouble in Paradise," *Time*, November 23, 1981, p. 23-4, 31-32.

Finding the Cause of Unrest, 1982

A bi-partisan commission, appointed by the president, examined racial tension and social conditions in Miami. It concluded that blacks experienced racial isolation on all levels—employment, housing, education and the justice system. Its 350 page report, presented to President Reagan and Congress, was controversial. Some hailed its findings as accurate assessments while others questioned the Commission's research methods and conclusions.

The black community in Miami is characterized chiefly by its isolation from the city as a whole. Blacks are in the city, but in a crucial sense, they are not part of Miami. They are not in the politically and economically powerful sectors that control community resources and make community policies. Their concerns have not been a priority for the city, the county, or for the private sector. Their frustration fed the violence that recently erupted in the wake of what was viewed as yet another in a long line of abuses suffered at the hands of an unresponsive and uncaring officialdom.

The isolation of Miami's black community results from a series of events that have contributed to the deterioration of what was once a vibrant and viable community. What Miami needs is a recognition of the causes for the alienation that has overtaken the black community and a commitment by responsible leaders at all levels in both the public and private sectors to provide the leadership and resources and exert the effort to turn this situation around.

One of the events that precipitated the isolation was the physical destruction of a large portion of the black community by the municipal government. Under the urban renewal program, the city tore down a massive amount of low-cost housing, forcing large numbers of blacks to leave their traditional neighborhoods and move into other areas that could not accommodate them. New units of low-cost housing were never built to replace all that had been demolished.

In a city with a vacancy rate of less than one percent, the remaining low-cost housing has become severely deteriorated and overcrowded. The consequences are isolated and desperate ghettoes. . . .

Blacks are isolated in Miami's economy, as well. Although the local economy continues to grow at a rate higher than that for the Nation as a whole, there are few black entrepreneurs, and the black unemployment rate remains high. Stymied by their own lack of capital and their inability to obtain capital from commercial lenders, would-be black business people fall through the cracks of unimaginative and non-accommodating programs of the state, local and federal government. Blacks with the education and talent to succeed in business often leave Miami for other parts of the country that appear to offer more opportunities for blacks. . . .

Compounding this situation is the fact that justice in Miami is administered in a way that excludes blacks and appears incapable of condemning official violence against them. Black complaints of police violence are common in the city. The incident that took the life of Mr. McDuffie was one of many confrontations between black residents and the system that is supposed to protect all of Miami's inhabitants. . . .

The proportion of the youth in the Miami juvenile justice system who are black is more than three times as great as in the Dade County population. . . . Services for rehabilitating juveniles are grossly inadequate. . . .

As indicated throughout the report, Miami suffers the range of urban problems that seem endemic to all major American cities today. The vast majority of the black community, regardless of economic status, feels powerless and frustrated. It is possible to identify and perhaps to ameliorate some of the sources of tension, but any long-term solution requires a coordinated attack on the underlying causes of racial isolation and exclusion.

Source: A Report of the United States Commission on Civil Rights, *Confronting Racial Isolation in Miami* (Washington, D.C.: U.S. Commission on Civil Rights, 1982), pp. 308-13.

Living History

The Historic Overtown Folklife Village
N.W. Second to N.W. Third Avenues
N.W. Eighth to N.W. 10th Street

Dorothy Fields, the founder of the Black Archives, spearheaded the revival of Overtown including the 1915 Lyric Theater seen here.

Miami's Overtown is rich in cultural history. Its streets hold the memories for some of the areas most prominent citizens. Located adjacent to downtown Miami, west of the railroad tracks, this area was assigned to black workers at the time the City of Miami was incorporated. Despite the obstacles of segregation, this pioneer African American community developed into a thriving business and entertainment/cultural district. From the 1930s to the early 1960s, it was a tourist destination known to residents and visitors as "the Strip," "Little Broadway" and "the Great Black Way." Over the years, Overtown lost its magic.

Today, due to the efforts of Dorothy Fields and the Black Archives History & Research Foundation of South Florida, the area is making a comeback. Three sites—the Chapman House, the Dorsey House and the Lyric Theater—have been restored. In addition, a portion of the Ninth Street Pedestrian Mall is now complete. Future plans include redeveloping two blocks of the original area into an entertainment and cultural district. The Village will again become a tourist destination, focusing on the history and arts of the black Diaspora, particularly the Harlem Renaissance.

Historic Sites Listed on the National Register of Historic Places

The Lyric Theater
819 N.W. Second Avenue
Built in 1913 by Geder Walker, an African American businessman and entrepreneur, the Lyric is Miami's oldest theater.

Greater Bethel A.M.E. Church
245 N.W. Eighth Street
This congregation organized several months before the City of Miami was incorporated in 1896. The present church was built in 1941.

D.A. Dorsey House
150 N.W. Ninth Street
The home of Dana Albert Dorsey, Dade County's first African American millionaire, the house was originally built in 1915. The Black Archives reconstructed the house in the 1990s.

Mt. Zion Baptist Church
301 N.W. Ninth Street
The congregation was organized September 17, 1896, the same year Miami was incorporated. The present structure was built in 1941.

The Cola Nip Building
227 N.W. Ninth Street
Built in 1925 by Osborne Jenkins and William Sampson, this was Colored Town/Overtown's only manufacturing plant—bottling soda water known as "Cola Nip." Later, the first floor became a branch office of the Atlanta Life Insurance Company.

Humoring Ourselves

Dave Barry
Moving to Miami

Dave Barry was born in Armonk, New York in 1947 and "has been steadily growing older ever since without ever actually reaching maturity." In 1982, when Miami really needed a reason to laugh, The Miami Herald *flew Dave in from Philadelphia to make us laugh at ourselves. It worked. Four years later, Barry actually moved to Coral Gables where, he writes ,"all forms of human activity are illegal." In 1988, Barry won the Pulitzer Prize for commentary. He has written 16 books and the CBS television series "Dave's World" is based on two of his books.*

I should explain how we came to move here. For the past three years, I've been a full-time employee of *The Miami Herald*, but my family and I have been living in Glen Mills, Pa., a small town in suburban Philadelphia. This was part of an overall Master Plan under which the entire *Miami Herald*, which desperately needs additional parking space, was going to move to Glen Mills, but this plan had to be abandoned when marketing surveys showed nobody up there wants to read about the Dolphins. So we decided to move down here.

When we told our friends and neighbors about this decision, they never said: "Great!" Or: "How nice for you!" What they said was: "WHY?!!!" They thought we were fools.

This is the famous South Florida Image Problem you have heard so much about. It is definitely real. I mean, these people live next to *Philadelphia,,* the only city in the United States ever to protect a neighborhood from housing violators by dropping a bomb on it, yet they all recoiled at the very name "Miami," as though we had told them we were moving to a condo in Beruit.

"But we like Miami," we would tell them. "We want to move there.". . .

I live in Coral Gables, where all forms of human activity are illegal, including: pickup trucks, polyester clothing, smirking without a permit, bobbing for apples, excessive use of garlic and dancing the "Funky Chicken." Life itself is illegal in Coral Gables. This keeps property values up. . . .

Insect control down here is no job for amateurs. If I were to hit one of these fully mature subtropical cockroaches smack on the forehead with a ball pen hammer, all I'd do is anger it. It might decide to charge, and my only chance then would be to lure it outside, in the hope that the lawn would get it.

Our lawn grows like a venereal disease. The Lawn Man comes around regularly and subdues it, after which there is a period of about two hours when you can walk safely on it, but you had damned well better make sure you are standing on the driveway when it regains consciousness and starts lashing out with violent new growth tendrils. . . .

It is generally assumed that any person you encounter who is not a member of your immediate family is a robbing raping dope-dealing pit-bull owning murderer. And although FBI crime statistics show that the chances of this being the case are actually only about one in three, you can understand, with all the negative publicity, why people tend to be paranoid. The problem is, this makes them seem rude. Some people act so rude down here that you will occasionally hear even former New Yorkers commenting on it, which is pretty comical when you consider that in New York it is considered the height of politeness not to step directly on a prone sidewalk body unless you're certain it's dead.

Maybe it would help if we all tried to be more aware of other people's fears. When we deal with strangers, we could try to put them at ease right out front by means of a reassuring statement such as: "One coffee, please! I'm not going to kill you! (¡Uno cafe, por favor! ¡No voy a matarte!") This could even become the basis for a nationwide promotional campaign:

South Florida. . . .
We don't want to kill you.

I have to admit that we have also become fairly paranoid, just from driving around and looking at our neighbors' houses. Back in Pennsylvania, our neighbors had signs outside that said things like "The Johnsons" and "Holly Oak Farms," whereas down here they say PROPERTY PATROLLED BY ARMED DOG and WARNING: LAND MINES IN LAWN. So of course we had the Lock Man come and install powerful new locks everywhere, and like everybody else down here we have become obsessive about locking up. A person could be deafened listening to the dead bolts being slid into place around our house when we go out to turn on the sprinklers. Eventually, of course, we're going to lock ourselves outside without our keys, and the mosquitoes—they are always watching—will see us on the doorstep, and they'll sound a General Alarm, and we will be dead people. . . .

I guess this is starting to sound kind of whiny. I don't mean it to be. I don't want to sound like those people who voluntarily move down here to get away from the cold weather, then spend all their time bitching about how hot it is. Although now that I mention it, it is pretty darned hot, isn't it? Also humid. To prevent spoilage, we've taken to keeping everything—bread, salt, aspirin, socks—in the refrigera-

tor. But I'm not complaining. As I said we really do like it here, and we hope to make lots of new friends who will come over and stand around our living room. And maybe later, if there's a cool breeze and the mosquitoes are feeling lenient, we can go outside and enjoy the sweet scents and sounds of the subtropical night. Maybe toss some meat to the lawn.

Source: Dave Barry, "Miami. See It Like A Neurotic," *Miami Herald*, September 7, 1986, *Tropic Magazine*, pp. 13, 15, 19-21.

Rebounding in Prime Time

William O. Cullom
The Civic Spirit, 1980

Bill Cullom became President and Chief Executive Officer of the Greater Miami Chamber of Commerce in September 1981. During his tenure, the Chamber grew from 700 member firms to more than 4,000. Hispanic-owned business members now account for 37 percent of the Chamber's membership up from 7 percent in 1982. Cullom has been involved in many areas of the community and has received many honors including the Silver Medallion Humanitarian Award from the National Conference of Christians & Jews and the Leonard L. Abess Human Relations Award of the Anti-Defamation League. In the following document, Cullom recalls the business community's response to the crises of the early 1980s.

Alvah Chapman, retired Chairman and CEO of Knight-Ridder, has provided "the epitome of leadership," according to Bill Cullom, for many projects that have made a real difference in Miami. (Chamber of Commerce)

The civic spirit of Miami in the early 1980s was that we could handle any problem that was or will confront us. There was never a feeling of despair or that any situation was not solvable. Miami leaders, in my opinion, were the very best in the nation, and they were at the right place at the right time.

One of the unique characteristics of the leaders was that most of them had held responsible positions in the service during World War II and were simply prepared to handle major problems.

The epitome of leadership at that time was Alvah Chapman. His military training and military bearing simply made him the right person for some of the problems we faced. Although he was involved in everything, it was in late 1981 that we made a decision to divide up two of our biggest problems facing us.

The two problems were: first, major crimes and the drug situation and second, the aftermath of the race riot in Liberty City. Both of these situations were magnified by the 130,000 Mariel refugees that were adding to the crime problem and taking jobs from segments of the community that were in competition for unskilled labor.

The day before Thanksgiving in 1981, I asked Dr. Bill Stokes to put together everything he knew about crime and to make a presentation to every civic leader I could find. He did a terrific job and everyone felt something had to be done.

The Chamber had decided three months before I joined them in September of 1981, to let someone work on the crime situation. When I arrived, I knew something had to be done and done quickly.

After the meeting Walter Revell and I went to see Alvah Chapman and asked him to be chairman of a then informal group, but later became Miami Citizens Against Crime. He said he would do it if we would do a few specific things. One, we had to take over his responsibility of working in Liberty City on fulfilling some of the promises made to the black community. Charlie Babcock took this responsibility. We also said we would hire a full time executive director, and we hired retired Admiral Van Edsel. We would also give staff support and administration support from the Chamber. In my opinion, Alvah Chapman provided the best leadership and led the best organization ever founded in Miami or any other place in the nation to fight crime and drugs. The organization was immensely successful. Crime went down, drugs were diverted to other cities or stopped. It was such a successful group that after several years it declared victory and went out of business as other groups should do from time to time.

At the exact same time, another group under Charlie Babcock was organizing our response to promises made by government leaders after the 1980 riot. Some of the best leaders and best minds in Dade county were working on this. Mike Cook, now chairman of Deloitt Touche, the late Jim Batten, then a Vice-President of Knight-Ridder, Ray Goode at that time with Charlie Babcock's company, Ron Frazier, architect, the late Hood Bassett from Southeast Bank and Frank Borman from Eastern Airlines.

Alvah Chapman had agreed to help us until we had the funds raised to build a Business Assistance Center in Liberty City. We first had to re-visit the hiring of a company in Minneapolis called City Ventures, that came on board before I joined the Chamber as an outside contractor. We were successful in getting them dismissed in April of 1982 so we could do our own plan. Our plan was to provide one million dollars for a Business Assistance Center, two million dollars for good capital, 2.1 million for Liberty City Industrial Park and $300,000 for a Skills Training Center. We announced in April 1982 that we were going to raise $5.4 million for Liberty City and most of the Dade's civic leaders thought it would be impossible. We would break another promise to the black community.

The Miami business community, under the leadership of Alvah Chapman, Charlie Babcock, Hood Bassett and Frank Borman raised 6.9 million dollars at one lunch on July 2, 1982 at the Omni Hotel. This is the most private money ever raised for the inner city in the history of the USA and it still stands as an event unmatched here or any where else.

From that moment on, Alvah Chapman worked on crime and Charlie Babcock worked in Liberty City. In my opinion, both were immensely successful in doing civic work. They will never be surpassed here or any where else. . . .

The early 1990's took out a lot of our spunk. When we lost Eastern Airlines, Southeast Bank and AmeriFirst, I knew that things were going to be tough for a while. . . . A new generation of leadership was being installed. We moved into long range planning with a focus on international trade, bio-technology, film and entertainment plus other high tech businesses.

In 1996 our economy is very strong and our gross county product has been determined. Dade County has a larger economy than 21 states. Our 1995 gross County Product is estimated at 55 billion dollars. Dade County and Miami is a world class place and is looking forward to a great future.

Source: William O. Cullom, "Miami Leadership" (unpublished manuscript, Miami, Florida, 1996).

T. D. Allman
"The City of the Future," 1983

T. D. Allman is a native Floridian now based in New York. He has written several books and has contributed to many publications among them Harper's, Vanity Fair, The New York Times *and* Esquire. *Here, in an article in* Esquire, *Allman responds to Miami's negative image and captures the area's unique qualities that he believes are the key to its future. Four years later, his book* Miami: City of the Future *was widely acclaimed.*

WHEN IT COMES to understanding the events that have overtaken Miami recently, even those people who have lived there most of their lives are like that alligator. The changes have been so big and have come so rapidly that not even the human brain can comprehend them all.

Is Miami race riots and drowning boat people, the drug and crime capital of the United States, or is Miami the world's newest great city, as the local boosters like to say? Is Miami the crisis of the elderly or some Sun Belt fountain of perpetual youth? The American Dream or the Florida nightmare?

After two visits there I came to one conclusion. Miami is the most fascinating city in America right now, precisely because practically everything everyone says about it, both good and bad, is true. Some of the reasons Miami is such a compelling place to visit:

In one sense the TV newsreels are right. Every major national problem we face has converged on Miami lately, and from Miami Beach to Liberty City you get the sense that Miamians of all kinds have had to look big challenges in the face and do something about them. The travails of recent years have given Miami a lot of pain. But they've also given Miami something else—a kind of character, a gritty resourcefulness and an ability to rebound from the worst kinds of crises, which is one of the city's most attractive qualities.

Not that Miami is all problems. Indeed, it offers pleasures and excitements only a handful of major cities anywhere do. Miami is paella and ballet in Little Havana, the dolce vita of Coconut Grove, the art deco bohemianism of South Miami Beach. It's racing and flamingos at Hialeah, sailing on Biscayne Bay, and landing marlins in the Atlantic Ocean. In the United States only New York and Los Angeles clearly exceed Miami in sheer cosmopolitan, urban excitement. Yet the richest "cultural" experience I had there was one you can't find in any concert hall. At Sunday morning mass in Little Haiti, thousands of worshipers sang "Vini, Jouinn Jézi" ("Come Find Jesus"). As this Creole hymn vibrated out into the surrounding slums, one could sense what people coming to Miami have always believed and, for all the city's problems, still believe today: this is a place where even the most impossible dreams can come true.

Source: T. D. Allman, "The City of the Future," *Esquire*, February 1983, pp. 39-40.

"Miami Vice" Premieres, 1985

When "Miami Vice" premiered in 1985, it permanently altered the city's image of itself. New buildings went up in the "Miami Vice" colors—pink, and turquoise—and old buildings were renovated to fit the "Deco" style. Many criticized its violence and lack of dialogue, but few doubted that it made viewers look at Miami in a new way. The show became a national sensation, and made the cover of Time. *The following excerpt from* Newsweek *described the show's visual feel.*

The rat-a-tat sound of machine gunfire resolves into a pulsing electronic rock beat. Staccato images flashed by. A flock of pink plumed flamingos. Bikini

"Miami Vice" stars, Don Johnson and Philip Michael Thomas, made the cover of Time in 1985. "Miami Vice" changed the way the world saw Miami. (Time)

clad girls on the beach. Race horses bursting from the starting gate. The ocean speeding by under the bow of a boat. And, of course, the familiar art deco logo, glowing in vibrant turquoise and pink.

If viewers are not sufficiently hyped up by the credit sequence of NBC's *Miami Vice*, chances are they will be before the hour is over. The pilots whiz by with a minimum of exposition, the dialogue is tough and spare, the rock music almost nonstop. Characters may be shot in lyrical long shots or bathed in moody lighting or framed against semiabstract pastel backdrops. The local color of South Florida is augmented by the local colors: flamingo pink, lime green, Caribbean blue. *Miami Vice* has been filmed under what may be the strangest production edict in TV history: "No earth tones."

Source: Richard Zoglin, "Cool Cops, Hot Show," *Newsweek*, September 16, 1985, p. 60.

Michael Mann
Architecture as "Backdrop," 1985

Michael Mann brought an architectural vision of Miami to millions each week through his popular television series—Art Deco and Post-Modern buildings in a dreamy, pastel palette. Yet the executive producer of "Miami Vice" expressed amazement that the city changed its image to match the one that he created. The following article is excerpted from The Tampa Tribune.

"About a year into the series, everywhere you went in South Beach had a fresh coat of pastel paint," he said, shaking his head.

Mann spoke to nearly 5,000 architects at the opening ceremonies of the 1987 National Convention of the American Institute of Architects at the Orlando Convention Center recently. His remarks often were accompanied by clips from "Miami Vice," as well as his other work: "Crime Story," "Thief" and "Manhunter."

"Architecture in film has only one function," he said. "That function is to express a feeling, to have effect. The construction does not have to endure. Further, the way it expresses feeling varies radically. It can be dynamic, such as Hitchcock's use of a high Victorian house in 'Psycho.' The architecture there becomes as threatening as the character.

But architecture can also express feeling in a more passive, supporting and general way, such as when it's used as a backdrop," he said. "That's what we do in Miami Vice." We use design to create a backdrop, a terrain. It's Miami, but it's not the *real* Miami. It's a Miami designed only for dramatic purpose. It is artificial terrain for Crockett and Tubbs and our stories to perform upon.

It's sunbaked, hot, the streets are always black and wet at night. It seems to leak fast money, fast cars, fast clothes, fast men and fast women. It's dangerous. And even its industrial wastelands— like the hull of a freighter on the Indian River [Creek] at night—are redolent with the atmosphere of a tropical Casablanca. That's what we set out to do," Mann said.

"The backdrop is used in lieu of the real Miami, which we intentionally ignored, with a couple of decades of brown and tan buildings, French provincial, imitation Tudor and some bizarre types of architecture for which there is no appellation," he added.

Mann admits that in the early days of the show, he relied heavily on suggestions from the Florida South Chapter of the American Institute of Architects for locations to be filmed.

"But at this point, we have vast files on all of the interesting houses in Miami," he said. "Six location managers have scouted the entire city. I mean, we've been doing this for three years. So a lot of location scouting *now* is done out of a file drawer.

Mann said that when he was shooting the pilot and the first couple of episodes, "a few staffers would wake up at 2 or 3 in the morning and go out nightriding—just looking at things in Miami," he recalled with a grin. "They would come up with a great bridge, and this bridge had the most fabulous vantage point of the Indian River [Creek] with these three hulks sticking up and one strip of neon in the background. . . . A lot of dedicated people came up with these places that Miami took for granted."

Mann's file drawer full of locations is divided into two major types. "In the political economy of *our* Miami, there are only two economic classes," he explained: "Low-rent, who live in old buildings that rich people used to live in, in the art deco district, and highrent, who live in mostly modernist and post modernist homes. Now, this is a rather extreme selection. But we create a Miami through this production design that *feels* like Miami."

Source: Renee Garrison, "TV Show Altered Miami's Image," *Tampa Tribune*, June 28, 1987.

Beth Dunlop
View from the MetroMover, 1986

In 1984, after 14 years of debate and delays and $1.3 billion, Miami's Metrorail began operation. Rising above traffic congested streets, the system offered fast and safe transportation from Overtown to Dadeland. By 1989 the system had been extended from Dadeland to a new Tri-Rail Station in Hialeah. In May 1986, a downtown link called the MetroMover (PeopleMover) opened and many believed that Miami's downtown would prosper once again. In this article, marking MetroMover's premiere, award-winning Miami Herald *architectural critic Beth Dunlop saw both the promise and emptiness, the wealth and poverty, and the unity and contradictions of the rapid trainsit system as well as Miami's downtown.*

Ride the Metromover and you can see the vast promise of downtown Miami: the broadness of its avenues, the sweep of its bay front, the fine details of its historic buildings and the bold patterns of its modern architecture.

Pass Central Baptist Church and you will see details that elude you from the sidewalk—carved angels, rosette windows. The elegant profile of the Freedom Tower seems etched against the eastern sky. The sleek bands of Centrust's tower and the seductive geometry of Southeast's black-and-white granite cladding have a commanding presence.

But ride MetroMover, and you will also see the pervasive problems of the downtown: It is an unavoidable confrontation.

Far too many buildings are far too decrepit. Historic structures have been abused and neglected. It is astonishing to see how much of downtown Miami's open space, excepting of course Bayfront Park, is given over to parking lots. There is more squalor than grandeur, and for a great city in the making, that is pretty sad.

The intricacies and subtleties of the city unfold somehow more clearly from 25 feet up; it is a vantage point that offers great insight. On Metromover, you can be eye-to-eye with angels and still see the difficulties that bedevil downtown Miami. . . .

Miami's has never been an inviting or walkable downtown; it is dirty and noisy and even a bit threatening. The sidewalks are narrow and littered. Too many shop windows are crammed full of cheap merchandise, with no understanding that pedestrians might enjoy seeing the goods arrayed. There are few places to stand and chat, fewer to sit and talk.

On the Metromover, it is much easier to understand the depleted stature of Flagler Street, Miami's main street. Flagler Street should be resplendent; it should rivet our attention. Instead it is skimpy and dreary. Try to capture its imagery as the MetroMover glides by it, and you simply can't.

The ride underscores some of our worst architectural and political mistakes—the erection of the old library at the foot of Flagler Street, the building of the bleak towers at the Miami Center. The half-finished projects—Miami Center with its unclad garage wall that was once to have been attached to two apartment towers, Brickell Key with its skeletons of incomplete condominium towers looking as if they were some kind of archaeological ruin—give silent testimony to the fits and starts of the urban economy.

Yet the picture is not all bleak—far from it. Metromover shows off some of the city's transcendent beauty—natural and man-made resources that somehow survive the insensitivity that has dominated downtown development over the years. Biscayne Bay appears brilliant and blue; Biscayne Boulevard looks regal with its rows of royal palms. The Miami River—and there is only a quick glimpse of the river—looks, as it should, like a real city's working waterway, not the synthetic, sterilized rendition of a river some cities have, and it is very evocative. The best buildings of the city—and there are dozens of them, big and small—look quite grand from this vantage point, and that is as it should be.

Metromover's 1.9 mile loop pulls downtown Miami together. It gives it a coherence that the city has always lacked—a sense of boundaries, a way to be connected.

It isn't a substitute for solving the many, many problems Miami still faces, but it's a start.

Source: Beth Dunlop, "MetroMover Reveals Promise of Downtown," *Miami Herald*, April 20, 1986, p. 1K.

Only in America

Luis Botifoll
"The Great Cuban Miracle"

Luis J. Botifoll, a successful lawyer and former editor-in-chief of the major daily Havana newspaper, El Mundo, *left Cuba on August 22, 1960. Botifoll, like so many other Cuban refugees, initially believed that he would soon return to his island home. When this did not happen, he immersed himself in exile causes. He also became involved in the founding of the Republic National Bank and became the bank's chairman. The bank provided what they called "character loans" to Cuban exiles who had little collateral but were good credit risks because of their integrity and sense of responsibility. Today, Botifoll is one of the community's most prominent Cuban Americans and serves as Chairman-Emeritus of the Board of Republic National Bank. He has received many awards including* The Miami Herald *Spirit of Excellence Award. In this piece from his biography, Dr. Botifoll explores the Cubans' influence on the emergence of modern Miami and Miami's influence on the Cubans.*

There lived then [in 1959] in the city some ten thousand Cubans, three thousand of whom were residents. The rest were in the city as a result of the political crisis on the island. Aside from the Cubans, there were some five thousand Hispanics from various other Latin American countries.

In those days when our massive exodus began, Miami was going through an acute crisis. . . . It was not only because of the current national depression but it was due to local problems as well. To begin with, tourism had slowed down. Also, the construction business had fallen into a slump after having enjoyed a bonanza. In consequence, there was widespread unemployment. This was the reality that confronted the first Cubans to arrive in 1959. . . .

The case of us Cubans is totally different. We didn't leave our country in search of more promising economic horizons. We left for political reasons and came in waves from all strata of the population, without regard to social or economic differences. Had not Castroism become a fact, we wouldn't be here. . . .

How much did this influx of Cubans affect the state of Florida? Tremendously. In 1959, we were just 2 percent of the population of Miami; in 1962 the number rose to 10 percent, in 1964 to 14 percent, and in 1984 we are 42 percent. We are an incontrovertible reality.

This population segment represented a great market emerging alongside the existing American market. The large mass of new arrivals led to the sprouting of so many of our businesses. These prospered on the patronage of the new shoppers, totally apart from what was happening in the American sector, which continued with its own set of customers.

One factor to keep in mind is that the Cubans came to a city where much remained to be done; therefore, there was ample opportunity for the enterprising. That would not have been the case if instead of Florida the mass of the arrivals had headed for New York, as some did. But if the miracle had taken place in some other city, one other fact of supreme importance would not have occurred: the attraction that Cuban Miami developed for peoples from Central and South America. . . .

Existing banking regulations were reformed so that international banks could be established; improvements were made at the port and airport; a free trade zone was declared; steps were taken to develop a rapid transit system; and personal contacts were initiated with entrepreneurs from Europe and South America.

All this was part of a leap into the future. Within this new reality it is easy to see that Miami has assimilated more than seven hundred thousand Cubans, who, with their work and their imagination and their creativity, have capably contributed to making a small tourist town into a real financial metropolis. . . .

I cannot possibly conclude this talk without citing an impressive detail: while in 1959 the financial status of Cubans was zero, in 1983 it has reached a level of six billion dollars. . . .

One other detail of utmost significance is that, according to the latest data, American exports to Latin America went up to thirty-three billion dollars; one-third part of those shipments is negotiated through Miami.

I cannot finish this offhand exposition without remarking that Miami's financial projection has not been exclusively toward Latin America. Part of it has been within the United States itself. That explains why so many famous stores have opened branches in this city and also the fact that right now three billion dollars are being invested in constructing new buildings in the downtown area by American and non-Latin investors.

Finally, the cordial reception and the generous understanding extended to us by the most representative and prestigious of the Anglo-Saxon community must be publicly recognized and declared. The few hostile irate voices that have been raised against us do not really count.

Source: Octavio R. Costa, *Luis J. Botifoll : An Exemplary Cuban* (Miami: University of Miami North-South Center, 1992), pp. 118-25.

Ileana Ros-Lehtinen
Living the American Dream

The first Hispanic woman elected to Congress, Ileana Ros-Lehtinen was born in Havana on July 15, 1952, and came to the U.S. when she was 7 years old. She studied at Miami Dade Community College and Florida International University and became a teacher and education administrator. In 1982, Congresswoman Ros-Lehtinen was elected to the Florida House of Representatives, and later, in 1986, the State Senate. In 1989, she was elected to the U.S. House of Representatives in a special election to fill the vacancy caused by the death of Claude Pepper. Today, Ros-Lehtinen continues serving the 18th district which includes Little Havana, South Miami Beach, Coral Gables, Coconut Grove, Key Biscayne and suburban Miami. In this account, Ros-Lehtinen remembers her early years in Miami and discusses the community's influence on her own life.

Like many Miamians, my family and I came to this country as refugees from Communist Cuba. I have discovered, as many who have come to our city from all over the world, that we have much to be thankful for in this land of ours. Based on my personal experience, I have found America, and especially Miami, to be a place where there is opportunity for anyone regardless of their background.

As a seven-year old child, I left Cuba with my family in 1960. We settled in Miami's Little Havana section which became the first home of many refugees from Cuba. Our deep roots in South Florida are revealed by the fact that except for a brief stay in York, Pennsylvania, as part of the Federal Refugee Resettlement Program, my family has always lived in the Miami area.

My education in Miami began at Shenandoah Elementary School and I later attended nearby Riverside and Southside Elementary Schools. Recalling those early years, I wish to credit the excellent bilingual education program which Dade County had for giving many refugee children like myself the ability to communicate in English at an early age. . . .

My political career in many ways follows the evolution of the Cuban-American community from community activism to elected office in the 1980s. The creation of single member legislative districts in 1982 for the first time gave Hispanic-Americans and other minority groups the opportunity to have direct representation in the Florida legislature. Along with three other Cuban-Americans, I was elected that year to one of these newly created districts in Dade County, be-

coming the first Hispanic-American woman in the state legislature. In 1986, I moved further up the political ladder becoming the first Hispanic- American to be elected to the Florida State Senate. . . .

I learned in politics that the open and tolerant nature of our democratic system permits any individual to be judged on their merits regardless of their sex or national origin. I am proud that many individuals of different backgrounds helped me to achieve a number of historic firsts in Florida politics with my election to the Congress in 1989.

After being re-elected twice and running unopposed for the first time in 1994, I recently became the chair of the House International Relations Subcommittee on Africa and the vice chair of the House International Relations Subcommittee on the Western Hemisphere. This was the first time that an Hispanic woman was designated as chair of a House subcommittee.

I have been very grateful for all of the opportunities which this wonderful country has given to me, my family and thousands of refugees. Our community of South Florida has been especially understanding of our strong desire to live in democracy, liberty and freedom. Miami is today a cosmopolitan city with cultures as diverse as anywhere else in the world. Miamians have made all of us feel at home and refugees from every point in the globe are so blessed to have found a safe haven like this. We all face an exciting and challenging future but only if we all work together can we keep this as our Magic City. As a refugee, I have found Miami to be all that I ever dreamed it would be—I remember thinking of this great town on the flight from Havana to Miami over 35 years ago and I have <u>not</u> been disappointed!

Source: Ileana Ros-Lehtinen, "Ileana Ros-Lehtinen and the Cuban-American Experience in Miami" (unpublished manuscript, Miami, Florida, 1996).

Miami's Little Haiti

Between the 1970s and today, well over 100,000 Haitians came to Miami. Desperate, fearful of violent repression by proponents of the Duvalier regime, and often beset by grueling poverty, these exiles found a different fate than the Cubans who were fleeing communism. Many were detained for long periods in the Krome Detention Center. The area along N. E. 2nd Avenue from 36th to 87th Streets became known as Little Haiti and reflected the brightly colored buildings with Creole signage that looked like home. The following account, by Miami Herald Tropic Magazine writer Meg Laughlin, shows the continuity of island traditions in Miami.

Across an ocean, Haiti struggles to heal. Like all exiles, the eyes of Miami's Haitians focus on the struggle in their homeland. They care passionately about their past, and Haiti's future. But while the attention of the world remains on what's happening in Port-au-Prince, something remarkable is happening on Miami's east side, between 36th and 87th Streets, in the neighborhood known as Little Haiti, home to the largest community of Haitians in the United States (with a population of about 60,000). An outsider sees a collection of small storefront businesses featuring hand-painted signs in Creole and small homes in turquoise, yellow, fuchsia—colors strikingly bold against the dusty yards and drab apartment buildings. Here, those who fled Haiti's oppression and poverty go about the uncertain and often painful business of settling in a new, not always hospitable land. They strive, against great odds, to re-create what they treasured about their homeland, and find that they are overwhelmed by the American reality. So they regroup, discover new ideas and new ways to use old ones. They invent, merge, and of necessity create a new culture that is not entirely Haitian nor familiarly American.

This new culture is a work in progress, burdened by poverty and prejudice, but buoyed by hope and ingenuity. Adapting old ways to new circumstances, a community is coming of age. . . .

When Sonia Vallon came here from Port-au-Prince in the late '70s, she set about trying to make Miami her home. She made her house cozy for her husband, her little boy and herself. She got a job in a shoe factory. She became a U.S. citizen. She made friends. She invited her brother to move in with her. She went to Mass.

But no matter what she did, she was still lonely.

In Port-au-Prince, she was used to a different kind of life. Everyone knew everyone else's business. People were always going in and out of her house. Vendors were always hawking their wares

In 1986, Miami's Haitian community filled the streets of Little Haiti to celebrate the fall of "Baby Doc" Duvalier. (MH)

on the street in front, people were always walking past. There was an openness about day-to-day activities, a constant intermingling of lives that Sonia took for granted.

When she moved to Miami, she was struck by how isolated people were from one another. She couldn't believe that people lived alone, going into their houses at night and closing the door. She couldn't understand why neighbors didn't gather on the streets when they got home from work to talk about their day. It depressed her to see all the nursing homes full of people who didn't want to be there, and to know that her child, Charles, couldn't play on the block without her watching his every move.

She missed the open-door life in Haiti. The snooping. The arguing. The in-your-face workings of a crowded community. She missed the comforting lack of privacy.

The closest she could get to what she calls "the give and take of Haiti" was at Notre Dame D'Haiti, the Catholic church in her neighborhood. Any day of the week, Sonia can pull into the parking lot and see the card table with huge aluminum pots that smell of Haitian street cooking: chives, scallions, thyme and garlic cooked in bacon grease. Ragout of calves' hooves. Yellow cornmeal with beans. Rice with coconut milk.

Zette, with her head bound, stirs the pots, and a couple of people are always hanging around talking. About politics. About what they heard on the radio. About what's going on in Haiti. About the next event at the church.

Sonia makes it a point to be at everything at the church: the Masses, the candlelight vigils for Haitians in Haiti, the memorials, the funerals for people who died trying to get to Miami, the prayer meetings.

The Mass at Notre Dame D'Haiti, Sonia was relieved to find, is as Haitian as it is in Haiti. The services are in Creole. There are drums and electric guitars and lots of singing. This is surprising, because the priest, Father Tom Wenski, is Polish American. "But he's more Haitian than a lot of Haitians," Sonia points out. The sermons often center on issues of social justice, causing the congregation to break into spontaneous applause. And most important to Vallon, there is a large charismatic group that enables her to practice the Catholicism she grew up with in Haiti, which emphasizes the physical presence of the Holy Ghost.

Source: Meg Laughlin, "A Brave New World," *Miami Herald,* December 25, 1994, *Tropic Magazine,* pp. 6, 11.

Daudeline Meme
The Awakening

Daudeline Meme, the fourth of six children in a Haitian family, is a senior at Miami Edison Senior High School. She is involved in various clubs and organizations in and out of school. For the second consecutive year, she is the Assistant Editor-in-Chief of Raiders of The Lost Words, *Edison's literary magazine. She is also an active member of the Future Business Leaders of America, and maintains a challenging schedule of Advanced Placement classes. The valedictorian of her class, Daudeline will enter Dartmouth College in the Fall of 1996.*

I have often heard it said that children are the cruelest of all; I have first hand knowledge of this. Eleven years ago, I moved to New York from Haiti. I was six years old—and an outcast, because I didn't speak the language, nor was I aware of the customs. Ironically, I was harassed not only by Black American students, but also by Haitian students. You see, at that time it wasn't cool to be Haitian—it was a curse. I remember one day, while walking home from school, a student threw a rock at me and yelled, "Haiti Kid! Why don't you go back to Haiti? We don't want you here!" His rock missed, but his comment did not. It hurt more than the rock ever could have. I have no recollection of the rest of the walk home. Another time a student, whom I thought was my friend, asked me if I had H.B.O. (I didn't but don't we all want to impress our friend?) So I said, "Yeah, I have H.B.O." Next thing I knew the whole class roared with laughter. I was flabbergasted—what did they find so funny? I turned around and asked the girl in the seat behind mine. She told me, between bouts of laughter, that I'd just admitted to having "Haitian Body Odor." To say that I was hurt is an understatement. I felt as if I was the most inferior being in the whole world. To tell the truth, I don't remember what happened after that, but that incident will stay with me always.

Needless to say, I was not in a nurturing environment. I wasn't encouraged to be myself—so I became someone else. I denounced everything that was ME. I was no longer Daudeline but "Darlene". When asked by some one if I was Haitian I would say (with a thick Haitian accent) "I ain't Haitian, I ain't one of them." I had many friends. But, I'm ashamed to say that I, myself, picked on Haitian students—as I was picked on before I became "Americanized". As they say, in order to be in the crowd you have to do as they do. And I did, but my heart wasn't in it. Sure I wanted to be popular and have friends, but I always felt like a traitor to my people. Of course, most people knew that I was Haitian (with my accent and all). So I came up with a new lie. I no longer denied being Haitian instead I said, "I was born on the plane—closer to America of course." I was proud of my ingenuity, but not of who I was.

Then in 1988 we moved to Miami. It all began again: new school, new friends, new me. I don't recall how, but I became a member of a self-confidence group at school. I didn't want any part in it—I'm not crazy. But as the sessions continued I realized that the group was my life line. It was there that I began to have pride in who I am as well as in what I am. It gave me the confidence that I needed in order to be myself. When I looked in the mirror, I no longer saw a person who wanted to be like every one else but a unique individual with a unique name. A person I wanted to get to know. And there began my reform. I denounced everything that wasn't me, including my adopted name "Darlene." Daudeline was back! Ever since then I've felt that my name symbolizes who and what I am. I've never settled for being called by any other name. To be referred to by another name would mean that I am insecure in who I am and want to be someone else, which of course I don't.

Once again we moved—this time to New Jersey. This time I was ready to face a new school, and make new friends. But I didn't need a new me—I was secure in who I was. The students at my school, in fact, made it easy for me to be myself. I was the only Haitian student in my class, and this made me special. Because I spoke a different language and represented a different culture, I was treated almost like a celebrity. Students would often ask me how to say certain words in Creole. Although these were mostly curse words, I didn't mind! I was popular. And as my self-confidence escalated so did my grades. I was always a good student, but then I became a great student. I graduated third in my class, and had the honor of wearing a golden tassle to signify my achievement. The week before graduation a classmate of mine wrote in my autograph book "Daudeline, you are one of the smartest kids in the class. Maybe next time you'll be number one." That really moved me, and I swore I would do my best to make that come true.

For the fourth time we moved, but back to Miami. When I got to my new school I had a cultural shock—I'd never seen so many Haitians in one place (excluding Haiti of course). And I'd never been so proud to be Haitian. Almost every school has a slogan attached to it and Edison's is "Haiti High". That is very apt name since this school is predominantly Haitian. I remember my first day at Edison, I was sitting in the bleachers during P.E. class when a boy approached me. He introduced himself, and struck up a conversation. During the course of the conversation he said, "If any one asks you if your a 'yank' say no." I wondered what "yank" was so I asked him. He replied that a "yank" is a Black American student who isn't of Caribbean decent. So I told him that I was Haitian. He didn't believe me (I'd traded in my Haitian accent for a New York one), so I said a few words in Creole. He said, "It's a good thing that you are Haitian cause if you weren't they would beat you up." I was flabbergasted, but the irony didn't escape me. It was just like my elementary school days except now it was cool to be Haitian.

At Edison I flourished, and as before so did my school work. I achieved my goal; I am number one in my senior class. And because of the constant contact I spoke my native tongue more fluently. I also became more obsessed with my name (if that's possible, right?). If someone mispronounces my name, I am quick to correct them. I remember back in August of this year, it was the first day of school and my A.P. English teacher mispronounced my name. Every one turned and looked at me, I didn't disappoint them. I said, "I'm sorry but that's 'Door-daleen'." Then they all laughed and made comments like "That's Daudeline for you" or "Don't you ever mispronounce her name, she might have a heart attack!".

Well, I wouldn't have a heart attack, but I would tactfully inform you that you are inadvertently insulting me by calling me by another name. In *Romeo and Juliet*, by William Shakespeare, Juliet asked, "What's in a name?" In my case, I'm in my name; it represents ME. As I said before, I believe that my name symbolizes who and what I am. But even more it is emblematic of all that I've been through, all that I'm going through, and all that I will go through.

Source: Daudeline Meme, "The Awakening" (unpublished manuscript, Miami, Florida, 1996).

A Future for the Past

Barbara Baer Capitman
Why Save Art Deco?

Barbara Baer Capitman "discovered" Miami Beach's famous Art Deco District and led the fight to preserve it. She founded the Miami Design Preservation League in 1979 and spearheaded the effort to make the Art Deco District the first 20th Century district listed on the National Register of Historic Places. Later, she helped launch Art Deco Societies in cities all across America. In this speech, Capitman outlined the goals of the preservation movement and the importance of understanding our architectural heritage. Capitman died in 1990, but her legacy lives on in Miami Beach's Art Deco District.

The creation of the Art Deco District is a splendid story of our time that may continue to be written for decades. In a few brief years this slice of American life has been rescued from destruction and oblivion, raised Cinderella-like from ignominy and obscurity to prominent national consciousness and, yet, perhaps will still fail.

This one square mile hard-to define resort, city neighborhood, tropic, dense, sad, decayed, beautiful, funny place still could be wiped out by uncaring land hustlers and developers. Despite the exhibits, articles, films, lectures, government attention and the dreams of young people who want to recapture the gentler world of their parents and grandparents . . . despite the majesty of the attention of the National Register of Historic Places, that repository of sacred American monuments, Old Miami Beach may still be defeated—its key buildings demolished, its streetscapes spoiled, its generous shore front given over to tasteless condominiums forever barring views of the green Atlantic.

It is the struggle to save this place and its population that captures the imagination, rather than the amazing change in our values and perceptions that has made early 20th century architecture and design, suddenly after a time of neglect, so important. . . .

As a nation, we are rediscovering the 30's in art, literature and popular culture. Benny Goodman, couturier fashions by Chanel, the social realist paintings of Ben Shahn and William Gropper, the range of novels from Michael Arlen to D. H. Lawrence, the poetry of Edna St. Vincent Millay and Stephen Spender—are all being replayed. . . .

As you walk through these streets, remember that the architects and planners who created them had a set of values that were in some ways much like our own, and in other ways perhaps more sensitive, more idealistic, more optimistic. . . .

The District with its rare old-fashioned charm, is at this time the nation's best hope for studying and reliving those vibrant days of the 30's. Our young people are today not well informed about the past that belong to those of us who are older. Our heroes are not theirs. . . .

This barrier island beach, close to the green-blue Gulf Stream, the home port for voyagers to the

Barbara Capitman, seen here at her mother's desk, was the main force behind the creation of Miami Beach's Art Deco District. Her unrelenting promotion, joined with the Miami Design Preservation League that she founded, made Art Deco an international phenomena. (MH)

Caribbean and South America, a world of sports and the outdoors, is a cultural treasure as well as a physical one. Its revival has sparked a new wave of music, art, and literature. . . .

Source: Barbara Baer Capitman, "Saving the District," *The Art Deco District: Time Present, Time Past* (Miami: Miami Design Preservation League, 1980).

Arva Moore Parks
Respect for the Past

Arva Parks is a native Miamian who has been researching and writing about her hometown for more than 25 years. She is the author of many books and films about Miami. But more than an historian, Parks is a leader, participating in many different arenas. She is an indefatigable advocate for historic preservation and many Miami landmarks have been saved through her leadership. She served for nine years as one of the two Floridians on the Board of Advisors of the National Trust for Historic Preservation and was recently appointed by President Bill Clinton to the Federal Advisory Council on Historic Preservation. She was inducted into the Florida Women's Hall of Fame in 1985. The following document was excerpted from the Foreword of the book Places in Time.

Our historic places are history's safety deposit boxes. They store memories and safeguard the lessons of the past. They hold precious pieces of our lives and connect us to each other. When they are lost, they are gone forever.

Until recently, Miamians had little respect for the past. This is understandable considering the age of the city, its constantly changing nature and the fact that most of us came from someplace else. In our lust for what we call progress, we have allowed and even encouraged people to tear down the old and replace it with something new. As a result, we lost our yesterdays: pre-historic middens, sturdy pioneer dwellings, the proud infant-city and grandiose boomtime dreams. Whole communities, entire eras, bulldozed, paved over and obliterated. Sometimes great and exciting new projects, magnificent pieces of architecture and better neighborhoods rose from the rubble. Often, however, expressways, parking lots, strip-shopping centers and banal new buildings spread like a plague across the land squeezing the life out of special places that told the city's story. Sometimes, after it is too late, we mourn the loss.

The late Royal Palm Hotel is a good case in point. Built by Henry Flagler in 1896, the same year Miami was incorporated, the Royal Palm Hotel was the young city's heart and soul and its only reason for being. It was a sprawling five stories tall, painted bright yellow and had more than 750 rooms. Its footprint included most of today's Dupont Plaza parking lot and its surrounding park and garden covered all the property between the river and bay, S.E. 2nd Avenue and S.E. 1st Street. One can only imagine what an attraction the Royal Palm would be today if it still stood in the heart of downtown Miami. Unfortunately, the Royal Palm was torn down more than 60 years ago and the site became a parking lot. Today, people flock to historic hotels even those that are make believe like Disney World's Grand Floridian that are similar in scale and ambiance to the old Royal Palm and other grand hotels of the era.

Although we have lost large chunks of our past, . . . even in ever-changing South Florida, all is not lost. Some treasures, like the Biltmore Hotel, have been rescued and restored. Others, like the Barnacle and the Charles Deering Estate, are now in public ownership and thus belong to all of us. Still others await our attention and care. These special places . . . are not imitations. They are real. . . .

Those eager to search out Miami's elusive, often scattered past, can actually find it. Within the walls and in the gardens and landscapes of our historic places, we can still reach out and touch history and feel the presence of the people who made it.

Today, all of us who live here are creating our own past. Will those that follow appreciate us enough to value what we have created? We will be remembered only if we build well and create a new respect for our visual heritage.

Source: Arva Moore Parks, "Foreword," *Places in Time: Historic Architecture and Landscapes of Miami* (Miami: Florida International University School of Design, 1994), p. ix.

Living History

Historic Art Deco District
Between Fifth Street and 23rd Street
Atlantic Ocean to Lenox Court
Miami Beach

In 1979, Miami Beach's famous Art Deco District, amidst strong opposition, became the first 20th Century area to be listed on the National Register of Historic Places. Art Deco refers to a style of architecture and design that is sometimes called Streamline Moderne or Depression Moderne that was popular on Miami Beach from the late 1920s to the early 1940s. A mile square, more than 400 buildings within the district have been listed as significant for their Tropical Art Deco or Mediterranean Revival (the favored style of the 1920s).

The Art Deco District is largely the brainchild of Barbara Baer Capitman who "discovered" the architectural treasures in the early 1970s and formed the Miami Design Preservation League to support their preservation. She spent the rest of her life trying to get the world to appreciate Art Deco.

By the mid-1980s, her dream came true and South Beach, or SoBe as it is sometimes called, became a major international tourist destination as the Art Deco style and verve became hugely popular. The success of the Art Deco District sparked the renaissance of Miami Beach and gave those who believed in the value of historic preservation a major victory.

Renovated hotels on Ocean Drive and throughout the area have captured national praise and imagination and provide a vivid backdrop to cafe-dining and people watching. Each January, the Miami Design Preservation League hosts Art Deco Weekend that celebrates the architecture, music and timeless jazz of the 1930s—the heyday of the Art Deco movement.

Miami Beach's famous Ocean Drive. (Bob McCabe)

Blown Apart, Brought Together

Dr. Pedro Jose Greer
Helping the Homeless

Dr. Pedro J. Greer is a native Miamian who founded the Camillus Health Concern, a clinic which provides health care to the homeless. As an intern in 1984, Greer treated a homeless man with tuberculosis and became appalled at the lack of available medical treatment for the homeless in Miami. Working within Camillus House, Miami's homeless shelter, Greer set up a folding table and prowled the streets treating the homeless. He then created a formal clinic within the shelter and has been recognized nationally for his tremendous community contributions. When Hurricane Andrew tore through South Dade on August 24, 1992, Greer recognized that Miami's poorest areas needed medical attention. Dr. Greer has received many honors for his work including a MacArthur Fellowship and a Miami Herald Spirit of Excellence Award. In the piece below, Greer recounted his experience after the storm when he traveled to South Dade to help the poor and the homeless.

At 6:30 a.m., the phone rang, with friends checking on us from out of state. They had heard Coral Gables was the worst hit. Those were the earliest reports and they were inaccurate. As we looked out the windows, our situation did not seem bad, except for our oak tree, our mango tree, our ficus, all of which were down. But the rest of the neighborhood looked as if it had been hit by a bomb. Some homes had their tiles ripped off by the wind, but most of the nearby houses were still standing. The trees were a different story. Our neighborhood had been rich with trees, now almost every one was down.

With no electricity for the automatic door opener, I couldn't get my Jeep out of the garage. Finally, Jaime, a neighbor, helped me force the garage door open, and we set out, with Alana [his daughter], to survey the area. No streets were navigable. I drove through people's yards, over tree trunks, through golf courses, over median strips. Later in the day, I finally made it downtown to the Camillus Clinic, where many of the homeless were. Ruth Tyler, R.N., head nurse at the clinic, and I realized that none of the water in the county was drinkable. We got hold of a batch of insulin syringes and cut off the tips so they couldn't be used for injecting narcotics. Into each syringe, we put the equivalent of 12 drops of Clorox, which would purify a gallon of water; Bruce Netter, a social worker

volunteer, and I distributed 400 of them on the streets that first day, Monday.

With no refrigeration at the clinic, which was also flooded, the local TV Channel 4 volunteered to store our drugs and insulin and other supplies in its employee refrigerator. The facility is fairly close to the clinic so we went back and forth whenever we needed supplies. We were able to operate that way until our power and refrigeration came back. Their help made it possible to take care of many people who would otherwise have been medically stranded.

The next day, Tuesday, Camillus Clinic was open and fully functioning. By afternoon, I felt okay about leaving. . . . I can't even remember how long it took us. But the eerie and strange part of the trip was that I didn't know where I was. This is where I was born and raised. I played high school football in a stadium here. I know the area well, I drive the road very often. But all the landmarks were gone. It was impossible to orient myself, and it was terribly disturbing, especially the weird sensation of driving past playgrounds in the midst of destruction and seeing the slim metal frames of children's swings still standing on their four legs.

We went to the most underserved area, an impoverished part of town, where migrant workers were housed. The South Dade Labor Camp on Tallahassee and Campbell Roads was devastated with little left standing. This community housed approximately 2,000 migrant workers. A church and its storage building were completely blown away, but inexplicably, the small building next door, formerly a two-to-three-day-a-week clinic, still stood. With my two [medical] students and eight others who arrived even before we did, I went in and we completely cleaned out the clinic, which was ravaged by the storm and waters, as well as by looters. We restocked it with supplies we carried in my Jeep and opened our clinic on Tuesday afternoon. A palm tree, which had fallen in front of the clinic door, served as the waiting-room bench where people could sit.

Our group split up into teams of two and three and walked the camp. The heat was so intense, it was nauseating. We went from door to door—or rather from wreckage to wreckage—to see what people needed. Incredibly, the migrants we visited extended their hands to help *us*. What little food they had, they offered us; what little water they had boiled, they offered us. If I learned any lesson for this experience, it was about the resilience and the caring of these people and the way they shared what they had.

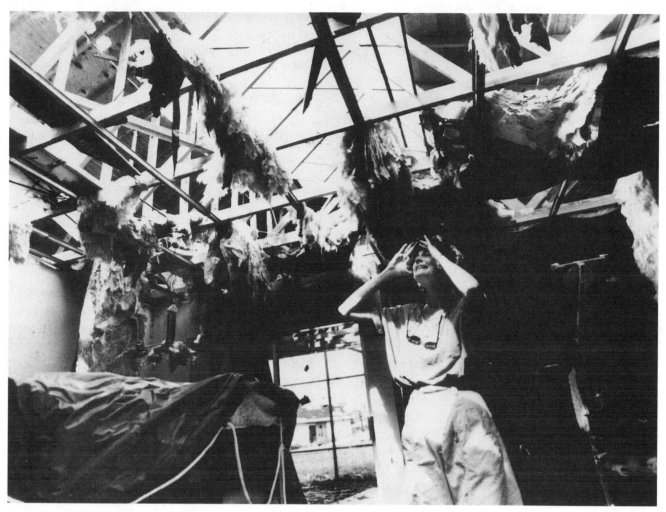

Hurricane Andrew hit South Florida with a fury at dawn on August 24, 1992. Sharon Hench looked up in despair at what was once the roof of her Country Walk home. (MH)

Our first patients were infants and young children with dermatologic diseases and in diarrheal states. And then we began to see adults who had never been treated for hypertension, endocrinopathies, and, particularly, diabetes. With no refrigeration or anywhere to keep medications, it became even more difficult.

We followed the same course at the Everglades Labor Camp, which was completely destroyed. This had been a trailer park, and all the trailers were now twisted masses of metal. Before the storm, 4,000 migrant workers and their families were housed here. Many were undocumented aliens; some were Guatemalan Indians who could not speak Spanish, let alone English. They were often afraid and were accustomed to hiding from anyone they perceived as official. . . . Of course, the situation worsened when the armed services arrived in uniform and with rifles. But the armed forces were very effective, cooperating with us and

other civilians, making every effort to help our work proceed as well as possible. . . .

From the devastation of the hurricane came some positive things. Apart from destroying the community physically, it knocked down walls that divided us. It also blew off the thin veil of bureaucracy that our local and state governments maintained to hide the poverty that was there. The opportunity to help people far, far exceeds anything that had ever been offered to us before. As one medical student told us, "These are the people who put the food on our table every day." I've learned from Hurricane Andrew that as a community and as a country we can work together to make things happen.

As a physician, my responsibility is to my patient, regardless of that person's ability to pay. It is a time-honored lesson that we must all follow and pursue, in the hope that students will learn by example, and the tradition of the physician as healer will continue forever.

Source: Dr. Pedro J. Greer, "A Letter from Homestead, Florida," *Cortlandt Forum*, November 1992, pp. 139-44.

Leonard Pitts, Jr.
Victims Become Victors, 1992

When Hurricane Andrew devastated South Florida, Miamians once again confronted adversity. In a display of community spirit, citizens of all economic levels joined together to rebuild the city. Music superstars Emilio and Gloria Estefan were no different as they organized a hurricane relief concert. Some 50,000 South Floridians came to Joe Robbie Stadium to hear such performers as Whoopi Goldberg, Jon Secada, Jimmy Buffet and Paul Simon. In this article, Herald *columnist Leonard Pitts reviewed the concert and the spirit behind it.*

It was there from the beginning, and it only grew as the shadows lengthened and darkness stole over Joe Robbie Stadium. It was a thing without a name, a thing more sensed than seen.

But it *was* there. There in the thunderous roar, out of all proportion to his fame, that greeted singer Jon Secada when he strolled out onstage. Because it was that kind of crowd. The kind that just plain *needed* to roar. You got the feeling—and intending no disrespect to the talent that played Saturday night's Hurricane Relief concert—that this

crowd would have given a standing ovation to a TV test pattern. . . .

The crowd that came to the benefit concert, headlined by Gloria Estefan, Whoopi Goldberg and others, raised more than a million dollars for hurricane relief. The more than 50,000 concertgoers seemed to need the music less than they needed one another, needed the sense of being together after the storm.

And needed one thing more.

That thing more sensed than seen. Needed release after four weeks of numbing despair. . . .

Oh, you should have been there then. Should have seen the dancing, the toes tapping, the fingers clapping and the hands thrusting toward the sky, their fingers splayed, their cares set free. The roiling stopped. The bubble burst.

Yeah, it was like that. And in that moment, something changed. The crowd turned a corner as one, victims chose to become victors. It was party time. . . . Then the community's sense of release and relief crested and broke like a wave on the shore. It began when Emilio Estefan, an organizer of the concert, came on stage and introduced TV weatherman Bryan Norcross, hero of the storm.

Said Norcross, "For those of you who spent that horrible night with us, it's a night we'll never forget, and I hope we'll never repeat. . . . This storm has unleashed a spirit in South Florida before. Let's all commit ourselves tonight to never, ever let it die."

Source: Leonard Pitts, Jr., "Concert Provides Relief—and Release," *Miami Herald*, September 27, 1992, p. 23A.

The Hemispheric City

Miami, City of the Nineties

The International Edition of Vogue *did a special supplement on Miami in early 1995. A French reporter spent several weeks in Miami interviewing people and trying to capture the spirit of the town for a European audience. She painted a vivid picture of what she described as the nation's first "Hemispherical City." The following is excerpted from this issue.*

Each decade has its city. Naturally, Miami is that city for the United States of the 1990s. It is time to shelve the old image of a colorless city where, between color prints and kitsch bric-a-brac, lazy coco-

nut trees yawn. Miami is pink with glitz and glamour, promise and lavishness. It voluptuously exhales success and, without really believing in itself yet, has exploded in every direction. It is a freshly-invented formula that combines tropical languor and vitality, beach and asphalt, economic boom and leisure, ethnic diversity and communication systems, culture and night life. And much more than trend or a form of vertigo, Miami is already a signature. The Hong Kong of the Americas has scarcely awakened yet people are already flocking to it from everywhere, especially Europe, to have fun and take advantage of this twilight moment upon which a city, watching itself glitter, sets its seal.

Source: "The Hemispherical City," Vogue (Supplement), December 1994/January 1995, p. 5.

President Bill Clinton
"The Spirit of Miami," 1994

Beginning on December 9, 1994, Miami played host to the leaders of the Western Hemisphere who convened for three days of discussions in Vizcaya's sumptuous surroundings. The eyes of the world focused on this historic "Summit of the Americas" and strengthened Miami's claim as the nation's "Hemispheric City." President Clinton labeled the sense of optimism and co-operation that prevailed, the "Spirit of Miami."

In a way, sustainable development is an unfortunate phrase because it has so little poetry about it. But the meaning is very profound. It means to me that we must pursue short-term goals, consistent with our enduring value. It means we must pursue individual opportunity, consistent with our responsibility to our larger communities. It means we must share in the Earth's bounty without breaking our bonds with Mother Nature. It means we must take for ourselves in ways that leave more for our children. It means we must expand the circle of those who are able to live up to their God-given capacities, the women, the indigenous people, the minorities, the poor children of this hemisphere. . . .

The agenda we have embraced is ambitious and worthy. We have actually committed ourselves to 23 separate and specific initiatives and more than 100 action steps protecting the diversity of plant and animal species, phasing out lead in gasoline, reducing infant mortality, improving education and health care. Our goal is to create a whole new architecture for the relationship of the nations and the peoples of the Americas to ensure that *dichos* become *hechos*, that words are turned into deeds.

So we come to the end of this historic Summit of the Americas, as we proclaim the dawn of this

For several days in December 1994, the Miami area was the site of one of the most important gatherings of hemispheric heads of state to ever take place. Many noted a hopeful "Spirit of Miami" signalling the growth of new dialogue and understanding. (DDA)

new partnership, as we say we have done this to put our people first and we have kept our eye on tomorrow, let us remember that the road ahead will be full of challenges and difficulties and that beyond all of the specifics of what we have done, perhaps most enduring is the friendship, the spirit of trust that has been built here. There is truly a spirit of Miami.

And in future years when the difficulties mount up, when it is difficult to sustain the hope about which President Aristide spoke so beautifully, may future leaders remember the spirit of Miami. *O espirito de Miami. L'espirit de Miami. El espiritu de Miami.* The Spirit of Miami.

Source: William Jefferson Clinton, "Remarks at the Final Session of the Summit of the Americas in Miami, December 11, 1994,". quoted in *Public Papers of the President of the U.S.* Volume II (Washington: U.S. Government Printing Office, 1995), p. 2494-2495.

"Under the spell of the warm sun a city grows.
From verdant jungle to shining glass reflecting growth—spontaneous, constant, heightened by the flush.
Only the sky is changeless." Arva Parks

EPILOGUE
MOVING ON IN PLACE

"How hard it is to escape from places. However carefully one goes they hold you—you leave little bits of yourself fluttering on the fences—little rags and shreds of your very life."

Katherine Mansfield
Memories of LM

City of Miami harbor and police boats take kids out in the bay for the annual Baynanza Day sponsored by Metro-Dade Department of Environmental Resources. Each year, since 1982, thousands of South Floridians—from toddlers to senior citizens—come together to clean up Biscayne Bay and improve the quality of life for everyone. (MH)

"Place" roots our existence. It marks our beginning and our end. It gives us identity and shapes our character. It grounds our memories. It reflects where we came from, where we live, where we work, where we meet, where we have been and where we are going. Place brings continuity to human life. It joins past to present, present to future, and us to each other.

Just as place defines us, we define place and give it meaning. We make, change and write place's history. Those of us who live here today, joined by all who have lived here in the past, have created and continue to recreate this piece of earth we call Miami. Our roots may be elsewhere, but most of us are grafted—one way or another and in varying degrees—into Miami's fertile soil.

Miami's future will flower from this hybrid root system. What will it be like? Should we create a broad framework of multiple identities, or an amalgamation that seeks to promote a larger vision? Who are we anyway? Should we merely see ourselves as Americans in a narrow sense, as people of African heritage, as "Anglos," Cubans, Hispanics? Don't we often overlook our common identity as Miamians?

Living in modern Miami prompts us to be busy, to make and spend money, to protect ourselves and our families. Too often, we define our needs in very personal terms either as individuals or as part of a group. We seem to have lost sight of the larger picture—of ourselves as Miamians, as civic beings interacting with the variety of people who live here with us. We have lost most of the public places that once acted as focal points of community life and have failed to develop new ones.

Thus, Miami continues the struggle to define itself and build a lasting identity. It is easy to see why this has been a daunting task. Most of us, now and in the past, came from someplace else. We often leave our sense of place back home or try to transplant "back home" here. We have destroyed most of our visible past as the wrecking ball of economics beat against continuity. We have allowed others to constantly reinvent us—one trendy, glittery, unreal image after the next.

We have seen community spirits soar when teams like the Dolphins, Hurricanes and Panthers have championship seasons. We come together in a meaningful way when faced with a tragedy like Hurricane Andrew but the bonding doesn't last.

Will we ever be more than the shifting sands of our beaches, the glow of our brilliant sun and the uncertainty of our raging storms? If we can come together and recognize the fact that we are creating a city unique in American history, we will have built something of lasting value.

As editors, we have become increasingly aware that the process of linking time, people and place cannot find easy closure. Many who know Miami best often say "stay tuned" because they know Miami seems to change almost daily. Writing this book has helped us appreciate the challenge of change and how the richness of our diverse people can reawaken a sense of our place within a larger community. Our final pieces call for Miamians to move on in place.

Will this book be more than just another book on Miami—another stone thrown into the Miami River—the steady stream that has witnessed all that has gone before us? We hope that it will create ripples that carry each of our voices into a broader circle of community expression.

The following comments made by leading Miamians can help us see our way on the longer journey toward building a sense of history and place and ultimately community. As we celebrate Miami's Centennial, may we come together in place and move on to our shared future.

GREGORY W. BUSH   ARVA MOORE PARKS

Hialeah High graduate Pedro Zamora spoke about AIDS to local schools and churches. He gained national recognition as a member of MTV's "The Real World." (MH)

Taking Responsibility

Pedro Zamora
Spokesman for "The Real World"

Pedro Zamora came to Miami during the Mariel boatlift and settled in Hialeah with his family. At the age of 17, Zamora learned he was HIV+ and became an AIDS educator and activist. He visited schools, churches and Congress, answering questions about the illness and preaching the importance of safe sex. As one of the few young people speaking out about the disease, Zamora was a powerful and sought-after AIDS activists. In 1994, Zamora became part of the MTV show "The Real World." The show put eight strangers, all young adults, in a house together in San Francisco and filmed their lives and interactions. With his presence on the show, Zamora, his cause and illness, gained a wide audience. Millions followed his health weekly on television. On November 10, 1994, just days after the season's last episode of "The Real World" aired, Zamora died. This excerpt is from the cover letter of Zamora's application to "The Real World."

Hi! My name is Pedro "Peter" Zamora. I am a 21 yr. old, gay, Cuban American living with HIV/AIDS. I came to Miami in 1980 along with 125,000 other Cuban refugees. I found out I was HIV+ during a high school blood drive. I was 17 yrs. old and a Junior in high school at the time. During the past 3 yrs. I have visited countless schools, educating my peers not only about the facts surrounding HIV/AIDS but also sharing how it feels to live with it.

So why should I be on The Real World? Because in the real world there are people living productive lives who just happen to be HIV+. I think it is important for people my age to see a young person who looks and feels healthy, can party and have fun but at the same time has to take 5 pills daily to stay healthy.

On one of your episodes this season you had an HIV+ guy come in and talk about HIV/AIDS with the group. He was there for a few hours and left. I wonder what kind of issues would have come up if that HIV+ guy would be living with the group. Sharing the bathroom, the refrigerator, the bedroom, eating together. Everyday for six months. . . .

Even though I am HIV+ and it is a big part of my life, it is <u>not</u> all that I am. Coming from a large Hispanic family (which is extremely supportive of me and my work) I am used to sharing both my living space and my life with others. . . .

I know that being on the "Real World" would mean exposing the most intimate details of my life on national television. How comfortable am I with that?

Well, I do that through my job every day. If I can answer the questions of an auditorium full of 5th graders with inquiring minds, I am sure I could do it on national television.

Source: Pedro Zamora, Letter to "The Real World," as quoted in Hillary Johnson and Nancy Rommelmann, *The Real Real World*. (New York: MTV Books/Pocket Books/Melcher Media, 1995), p.158.

Building Community

Jeb Bush
The Spirit of Community

Jeb Bush is the son of former President George Bush. Arriving in South Florida with his Mexican-born wife, young Bush went into real estate with Cuban-born developer Armando Codina. He became Secretary of Commerce under former Governor Bob Martinez, and was the Republican candidate for Governor of Florida in1994. Inspired by the work of former Secretary of Education William Bennett, Bush wrote Profiles in Character *(co-authored with Brian Yablonski) from which this piece is excerpted.*

Writing about the New England township, a long standing pillar of the community in America, Tocqueville said, "The strength of free people resides in the local community. Local institutions are to liberty what primary schools are to science; they put it within the people's reach, they teach the people how to appreciate its peaceful enjoyment and accustom them to make use of it."

In Florida, we do not have the strong history of the New England township. Our history has been one of growth and movement. It does no good to romanticize the small-town way of life in the 1800s for it tended to foster a separate and distinct set of advantages and disadvantages that would be difficult to replicate in this day and age.

Nor can we ask our urban populations and suburban middle class to become small towns. We must accept Florida's development and urbanization. Nine out of ten of our residents live in an urban area. Small towns are a dying breed in many parts of the state. We must accept the fact that urbanization and development mean that most of our communities tend to blend into each other. Main streets give way to strip malls.

As I drive to work each morning, I pass through three separate communities—Kendall, South Miami and Coral Gables. Unless I note the subtle changes of the street signs, I would have no idea that I was driving through separate communities.

While we should avoid getting into the business of small-town worship, we can still draw from the small town its better qualities and apply them to our own communities around the state. Foremost, it is the civic mindedness and participation often associated with the small-town way of life that is needed the most in our neighborhoods. We need to capture the small-town spirit of community and attachment. Recent studies suggest that the more engaged a community is in its civic affairs, the more likely it will experience successful outcomes in areas such as education, urban poverty, unemployment, the control of crime and drug abuse and health.

Source: Jeb Bush and Brian Yablonski, *Profiles in Character* (Miami: Foundation for Florida's Future, 1995), pp. 145-146.

Janet Reno
Building Character

Janet Reno was born in Miami in 1938 to Miami Herald and Miami News reporters Henry Reno and Jane Wood. She graduated from Coral Gables High School, attended Cornell University and then Harvard Law School. In 1971, she became staff director for the Judiciary Committee of the Florida House of Representatives and later came back to Dade County to serve as a prosecutor for the state attorney. When State Attorney Richard Gerstein retired in 1978, Reno was appointed as his replacement. She strongly addressed such issues as domestic violence, dead-beat fathers and juvenile crime. South Floridians appreciated their serious yet idealistic state attorney, re-electing her to five consecutive terms. In 1993, President Clinton selected Reno to be the United States Attorney General. She joined Secretary of

Treasury Robert Rubin and Environmental Protection Agency Chief Carol Browner as one of the top-ranking South Floridians working with President Clinton in Washington. In this speech, given as the commencement address at the University of Miami, Reno traces her values and independent spirit to the lessons she learned from both her mother and the South Florida community.

Think of this community that surrounds this great University. In 1896 it published its first newspaper, which editorialized that the community of 1,500 people should incorporate. Now look at what Miami is today in less than a century.

In 1926 this University opened its doors one month late because of a disastrous hurricane. It survived the hurricane, it survived the depression, it survived the war, and look what it is today.

As a child I would take a buggy down the Dixie Highway because we had run out of gas rationing tickets and didn't have enough for gas. I would look over at what is now this building and see a concrete steel skeleton against the sky, a skeleton that was never finished because of the depression and then the war. Just look now at what the people who have come before you have built.

But it was more than just brick and mortar. In 1929 there was a rather precocious 15-year old child who came to this University. She decided to run away from home in the process. There was a great headline, "Three UM Girls Missing, Foul Play Feared."

Well, she just ran away for the heck of it, for a great adventure.

She came back and the University threatened suspension. She went in to see Dr. Ashe and Dr. Ashe gave her another chance. She was my mother, who for the rest of her life would quote from Molly Column, who gave a guest lecture series here, a lady who would talk about physics that she'd majored in, a lady who learned how to build a house because of what she learned in that physics course. A lady who one day told me that she was going to build a house. We said, "What do you know about building a house?" She said, "I'm gonna learn" and she talked to brick masons and to electricians and plumbers and she learned how to build a house. Out in what is now Kendall she dug the foundation with her own hands, with a pick and shovel, she laid the block, she put in the wiring and the plumbing and my father helped her with the heavy work at night.

She and I lived in that house until she died, just before I came to Washington. When I was state's attorney, every time I drove down the driveway with a difficult problem and came around through the woods and saw that house standing there, it was a symbol to me that you can do anything that you really want to, if it's the right thing to do and you put your mind to it.

That house taught me another lesson . . . [When] Hurricane Andrew hit, at 3 o'clock in the morning, she got up, old and frail and dying, and she sat down in her chair and she folded her hands. As the winds began to howl, she sat there totally unafraid because she knew how she had built that house. As we went out that gray dawn into that disaster, it looked like a World War I battlefield. But the house had lost only one shingle and some screens. It was a symbol that if you build it the right way, if you don't cut corners, if you put in good materials, you make a difference. . . .

I remember in the afternoons after school, when she wasn't building the house, my mother taught us to play baseball, to appreciate Beethoven's symphonies, and taught us to play fair. She spanked us, she loved us with all her heart, and there is no child care in the world that will ever be a substitute for that lady in our life. Surely, if we can send a man to the moon we can develop work place technology that will give us—your generation—the chance to spend quality time with your children.

But we have an extraordinary challenge. As I come to Washington, I see a world that has become global in nature, a global economy, global migration, crime, health care, and environmental problems. We are faced with an opportunity. We have technology that can do so much, that can bring us together in seconds but that technology is also an instrument of disaster. Even as we have such opportunity and challenge, we also face so many people around this world reaching back in time, looking for their roots, looking for whence they came, taking pride in their tribal and ethnic traditions. But as they reach back, they see too often see the hatred and bigotry that divide the tribes and ethnic groups.

If we are to live in this world, we have got to understand that we all are one and . . . that it be our mission to bring understanding and peace to all people, whether it be in the neighborhood, the community, the nation or the world.

Source: Janet Reno, "Commencement Address" (speech presented at the University of Miami, Coral Gables, Fla., May 13, 1994).

Andres Duany and Elizabeth Plater-Zyberk have become internationally known architects by promoting renewed attention to neighborhoods, town planning and the need for a more human scale in the built environment. (DPZ)

Elizabeth Plater-Zyberk
Building Neighborhoods

Elizabeth Plater-Zyberk and Andres Duany are an internationally known husband-and-wife architectural and planning team. Together, they are pioneers of what has become known as the new urbanism movement— making comfortable, safe and amenable neighborhoods. They have designed nearly 100 projects including the award winning Florida Panhandle community of Seaside. In addition to their own work, Duany is an adjunct professor at the University of Miami School of Architecture and Plater-Zyberk became the school's dean in late 1995. Here, in this interview, from Miami Today *Ms. Plater-Zyberk discusses the philosophy and importance of new urbanism.*

Q: The architect's role in the community is important?

A: I'm always surprised when I read headlines in a row that are about the physical environment in a way that we see the issues to be united but probably other people don't notice. Articles about traffic, school congestion, a homeless shelter or some sort of community need may seem unrelated but we architects and town planners understand they're very much related to the distribution of the physical en-

vironment and that's something that can be better controlled.

We've already been making that kind of contribution in the community and we look forward to continuing to do so.

Also, we have a role as educators to inform our community about the importance of good design, not as a cosmetic issue but that it can add immeasurably to the quality of life, then make the discussion about the design accessible to this community. Architecture shouldn't be a mystery. . . .

Q: What is your definition of new urbanism?

A: It's a school of thought that promotes regional neighborhoods and the design of urban spaces according to certain principles as the best way to build and grow human settlements.

Q: As contrasting with urban sprawl, malls sprouting out in the suburbs?

A: The new urbanism promotes a series of principles for metropolitan organization at the regional scale— five principles of good neighborhood design. Then it also has something to say about how you put streets and blocks together to detail out these neighborhoods.

There's a kind of diagram you can imagine of how a metropolitan area can be made of three elements—neighborhoods, corridors and districts—then what makes up each of these elements. Corridors can be roadways, railroads, green belts.

Q: What are those five principles of good neighborhood design?

A: It has a center and an edge, which promotes social identity.

It has a limited size: a quarter-mile radius, a five-minute walk from center to edge, which promotes walking and interaction among residents and whoever else is there —workers, visitors, etc.

It has a mixing of uses and housing types so that you might walk to some services and have, hopefully, a mix of the residence types so it's not a homogeneous, exclusive setting. Being able to walk to transit and children to school becomes part of the picture as well.

The fourth principle is an interconnected network of streets with a fairly small block size, so that walking is pleasant, safe and interesting, where one can choose different routes. This also keeps the local traffic off regional streets, because if you need to drive somewhere you can do it internally, you don't need to take the one road out to go to your store for a bottle of milk.

There is the principle of appropriate sites for public and civic buildings—a meeting hall or a place of worship is not along the highway like a shopping center, but becomes one of those monument buildings which contributes to the identity of the place as well as to participation in civic life.

The detailing of public spaces is very important. This may be the crux of the principles of the new urbanism, what makes it different from the way we have been building cities and suburbs in the last 40 years, because here we're promoting the importance of the space first, that buildings make public space— streets, plazas, boulevards—rather than making themselves objects.

Dixie Highway could in fact be a boulevard of some beauty, if there is some recognition of how all the buildings along it should add up.

Q: Looking at the community, what do you see as an outstanding issue?
A: Growth in South Florida I think is something of great concern to many of us teaching at the university. It seems to be a great part of the political picture—so much of the county commission's time is taken up dealing with issues of growth.

This is not unique to Dade County or South Florida, of course; it's an issue I've encountered in my work all over the country, especially the coastal and Sunbelt areas, and what seems like probably an impossible picture of social, economic and environmental issues. I really think that those are the three topics by which you can outline the concerns.

Here in South Florida we really could work on an organization of that picture by which to guide our future. I think if we all come from different places and different pasts, then perhaps our future is our best common ground and we should somehow be addressing that directly as a community. We have to figure out a way holistically to head on, so that the kind of piecemeal crises that are always coming up have some principal framework within which to have decisions made.

Miami's economic future is largely dependent on how it's going to manage its physical environment— and that's something I think cities and metropolitan areas around the country are coming to terms with,

understanding that economic competition is now metropolitan rather than national.

It's about city states. There are many metropolitan regions that are addressing this head on. They understand that in order to compete and to serve their residents' economic future the best, they're competing on an urban scale, that companies make decisions about where to locate based on issues of education, quality of life and physical amenity, whether things work or not, whether traffic is overwhelming. Those are problems, thus translated to economic problems.

Source: "New U of Miami Architectural Dean, Elizabeth Plater-Zyberk," *Miami Today*, September 14, 1995, p. 4.

Leslie Pantin, Jr.
Serving the Community

Leslie Pantin, Jr. was born in Havana, Cuba and has lived in Miami for 37 years. He graduated from Christopher Columbus High School and Florida State University. Few Cuban Americans have been involved in or contributed more to the total community. He was a founder of the Kiwanis of Little Havana that created the Calle Ocho Open House that has grown into a ten-day festival called Carnaval Miami. As president-elect of the Orange Bowl Committee, he is the first Cuban American to hold that position. He is also co-chairperson of the Miami Centennial Committee and serves on numerous other community boards. In 1993, The Miami Herald identified him as one of the 100 people who had shaped the history of South Florida. In the following account, he recalls the beginning of a unique concept for bringing the community together.

Since its formation in 1975, the Kiwanis Club of Little Havana has had a goal in mind, to serve the Miami community. The first group of members that chartered the Club were friends that graduated from college a few years earlier, all of them Cuban American in their 20's. The tradition of volunteering and civic involvement was new to them.

The Kiwanis of Little Havana's best known project is Calle Ocho Open House. It started in 1978 as a 15-block party. The idea: To follow the American tradition (the open house) of asking your new neighbor to your home so that you can get to know each other better. In the first year, the Kiwanis Club of Little Havana invited the entire community and expected only a few thousand and were delighted when 100,000 turned up!

Calle Ocho Open House is Miami's favorite block party. Hundreds of thousands of Miamians come together to celebrate and experience Miami's vibrant Latin beat. (MH)

By 1985, the attendance grew to well over one million people and the festival expanded eight more blocks. The largest conga line was recorded in the *Guinness Book of World Records* in 1988 when over 119,000 people danced to the super hit "Conga" led by Gloria Estefan. Calle Ocho now features 23 blocks of excitement with musical stages, dance groups, folkloric troupes, sampling sites, youth sites, and over 500 vendors offering a variety of dishes. . . .

Since the start, Calle Ocho has had the purpose of bringing our community closer together. In fact, its original name was "Open House Eight an invitation to Southwest 8 Street." The intention being that it was friendly and inviting. Ironically, it was the guests, mainly the non-Hispanics, who gave it its now famous name of Calle Ocho.

Over the years, Calle Ocho has served as a vehicle for all the community to learn about Cuban popular culture, its music and food. Recently it has also helped to showcase other Latin cultures.

Mainly funded by surpluses of Calle Ocho, the Kiwanis Club of Little Havana strives to reach the community with other projects. The building of large playgrounds in public parks started in 1989, designed by the area kids and built by Kiwanis volunteers with enthusiastic help from the surrounding community. The first of such playgrounds was built at Douglas Park, bordered by three different ethnic communities. The second playground has a special group of kids in mind, the physically challenged. Situated at A.D. Barnes Park, it was specially designed and built for the handicapped. . . .This park is the only one of its kind in South Florida.

Although "Little Havana" is our last name and Calle Ocho is our best known project, we are proud that not only do we strive to bring the community closer together, but we help all kids in our hometown.

Source: Leslie Pantin, "Kiwanis Club of Little Havana: Organizers of Calle Ocho Open House," (unpublished manuscript, Miami, Florida, 1996).

Carrie Meek
Building Community

Congresswoman Carrie P. Meek, the first African American elected to Congress from Florida since Reconstruction, has had successful careers as a public servant, college administrator and educator. She served for 13 years in the Florida House of Representatives and the Florida Senate. Elected to the U.S. House of Representatives in 1991, she has earned a national reputation as a skilled legislator and an effective leader. In this inspirational message, Meek addresses the University of Miami graduating class and urges the graduates to make a difference in their community.

I want you to look at me, and I want you to listen to me—granddaughter of a slave, daughter of a share cropper, daughter of a mother who washed and ironed to send me to school so I could be here today, so that I could receive this honorary doctorate degree and be able to address you in this great sunshine of Florida, in the morning of your lives. This is a great privilege for me.

The knowledge that you graduates have gained from this great university gives you power. My message to you this morning is to know how to use that power—not to abuse it, but to use it for the betterment of the lives of others. . . .

Those of us in public service yearn for basic, simple wisdom, the fruit of decades of generational struggle. The yearning for opportunity for all. For we must be mindful that past generations of our fellow Americans from every race, color, gender and creed have had to struggle. And they found that the task of building our nation into a nation of great opportunities was not an easy struggle. . . .

Two things I want to do here today: Number one is to inspire you. No matter what your background is, no matter what you did before you came here, it doesn't matter today. <u>Now</u> is the time when you show your true worth. <u>Now</u> is the time when you get your second wind, to go forward and push forward into life and to do your very best. . . .

The second thing I want to do here today is to stress to you the importance of political astuteness and the need to know what is going on in the world around you.

Do not take off your mortar board and gown and throw them in the closet. Don't put your degree on the shelf and forget about it. Remember, your education is a springboard to help you go farther in life. . . .

I have witnessed the signing of the peace accords with President Rabin and Yassar Arafat. I shook hands with President Nelson Mandela in South Africa. I was there when President Clinton reached out to President Aristide in Haiti, and I was present when King Hussein of Jordan addressed the Congress. I have seen all of the great kings and queens and leaders of the world who have come to Washington.

But what I cherish most of all is the feeling I get from being here today with you. You graduates are important, and so are your parents and families, the faculty, the trustees—these are the real important people in the world, not the kings and queens who come to Congress, but you—you are the ones who truly inspire all of us.

I don't need to spend a lot of time describing to you the kind of world you face. It would be superfluous to do that. You understand the world you are in. You understand globalization. It's going to bring new problems and new conflicts. The jobs don't seem to be there. Nothing seems to be secure. . . . There is a lot of hate in this world; there's a lot of suffering. And all we hear is more and more about cutbacks and downsizing. . . . The long-term prospects may look dim. It looks like the world of work that we have known is disappearing. But it is not.

Remember that my first reason for being here today is to inspire you. The second reason is to try to improve your political astuteness. On top of all of this, I want to urge you to "keep your hand on the plow." Keep your hand on the plow—hold on. Be sure that the knowledge you receive here at the University of Miami becomes a useful tool that you use to help you achieve. . . . America is a great country. Dade County is a wonderful county. Miami is a beautiful city. You are a part of all this. Exercise your reciprocity—share with others. Do not put your diploma on the shelf; do not forget to help other people.

Finally, here is some advice that has served me well over the years, which is my graduation gift to you. First, develop a strong sense of community. Second, find ways to serve your community. Third, keep involved in the community in the coming years. And fourth, keep the flag of idealism flying, so that you can continue to help others.

I'm going to end with these words from The Rock, a poem by T. S. Eliot:

"Though you have shelters and institutions,
Precarious lodgings while the rent is paid,
Subsiding basements where the rat breeds
or sanitary dwellings with numbered doors
or a house a little better than your neighbors;
When the Stranger says, 'What is the meaning of this city?
Do you huddle close together because you love each other?'
What will you answer? 'We all dwell together
To make money from each other'? or 'This is a community'?
. . . .And the stranger will depart and return to the desert.
Oh my soul, be prepared—each of you—for the coming of the Stranger,
Be prepared for him who knows how to ask questions."
I thank you.

Source: Carrie P. Meek, "Commencement Address" (speech presented at the University of Miami, Coral Gables, Fla., May 12, 1995).

Moving on in Place

Howard Kleinberg
The Challenge of Diversity

Howard Kleinberg moved to Miami in 1949 from New York and graduated from Miami High School where he fell under the tutelage of legendary journalism teacher Barbara Garfunkel. He began as a student reporter for The Miami News *while still at Miami High. He rose from sports reporter to Editor-in-Chief, a position he held from 1976 until the paper folded in 1988. He has been involved in many community endeavors including membership in the Orange Bowl Committee and as a leader in Congregation Bet Breira. Kleinberg's love affair with Miami is long and deep and his weekly columns in* The Miami Herald *show his strong sense of community. The following article was one of his national columns for Cox News Service that is distributed by* The New York Times *News Service.*

Trying to put her best face forward, this city likes to boast that she is an international city.

What that translates to, however, is that Miami is so awash in ethnic and racial diversity that it works at cross purposes. Instead of the cultural melting pot associated with earlier American history, this ethnic and racial diversity is constructed as a series of highly defended city-states, flags held high, daring the other guy to cross a line or utter a single word that can be seen as an insult—knock-the-chip-off-my shoulder stuff. . . .

In Miami, you often are known more by your heritage than you are by your name or deeds. During political campaigns, candidates are more identified by their nationality than by their party; when juries are seated, the issue is not the competence of the jurors but their race and nationality; criminal acts seemingly are greeted with relief if it is learned that the suspect was of the same background as the victim.

So segregated is this town that there are Chambers of Commerce for all. There is a Greater Miami Chamber of Commerce but there is also a Latin Chamber of Commerce. There is another Chamber of Commerce for blacks as well as one for women. There is one for Colombians and there is one for Argentineans. There are others; I lose track.

It is rare that you see a local car without a bumper strip boasting of some nationality, or a small national flag hanging from the rearview mirror. Thus, cutoffs and near-car accidents are reacted to by referring to "those damned (choose your nationality)." Then fingers get pointed, fists waved and, sometimes, pistols fired.

All of this adds up to carrying diversity too far.

Historically, this separation can be traced to the white power structure but in Miami, there are two power structures: the traditional downtown white structure and the growing Cuban American power structure. All of those out of power point the finger of blame to those in power.

There is no doubt that similar conditions exist in every other urban center of America. But Miami is a city of overreaction.

It is a city whose heart flutters whenever an unfounded rumor is spread of Fidel Castro's mortality, or an impending attack on Israel.

It causes a boycott call by local blacks when a proclamation of welcome for visiting Nelson Mandela is withdrawn by the city commission because Mandela spoke favorably about Castro, Gadafi and Arafat; both actions being overreactions.

It bleeds over politics in Nicaragua, El Salvador, Jamaica and Panama, among others.

The only time I can recall anyone saying the whole town was together on any one subject was when the Miami Dolphins won back-to-back Super Bowls a decade-and-a half ago. There needs to be a better criterion—or a better team.

Source: Howard Kleinberg, "Melting Pot Boils Over in Ethnic Miami," *New York Times News Service*, December 13, 1990.

Katy Sorenson
"Let's Cut Each Other Some Slack," 1996

In February 1996, a number of Dade County Commissioners walked out or pointedly failed to attend a ceremony honoring former US Ambassador to the UN Andrew Young, allegedly because of his earlier comments regarding Fidel Castro. The incident seemed reminiscent of the snub of Nelson Mandela by the City of Miami Commission a few years earlier. The Mandela incident prompted the three year black boycott of conventions in Miami and Miami Beach. This time, the Community Relations Board helped call a special commission meeting to discuss the Andrew Young incident. At this meeting, real dialogue occurred between the commissioners that went beyond much of the earlier posturing. Perhaps the most moving statement of this extraordinarily honest exchange was provided by Commissioner Katy Sorenson. Commissioner Sorenson, who was elected in 1994, was a highly honored community activist before her election—especially in the area of public education.

Following the dedication ceremonies in May 1996, Commissioner Katy Sorenson stands in front of the county's newest Art in Public Places sculpture—"the M"—created by Roberto M. Behar and Rosario Marquardt. (Arjelio Hernandez)

I don't really think this is about just Andrew Young even though he was the lightening rod of the day. I think it's really more about feelings than it is about facts and its a lot about pain. There's a lot of pain here. And there's so much pain from so many people who are represented here. Now I am the fifth generation on my Irish mother's side and I am the fourth generation on [my] Swedish-Norwegian father's side. So I don't carry the pain personally of what the English did to the Irish because it's too many generations removed from me, you know, so it's not something I carry with me.

But all of you have much fresher wounds and you're all in a way much younger because of those fresh wounds. And the African American experience of slavery—that wasn't so long ago. It was only a hundred and thirty years ago. It wasn't that long ago. And the pain that African Americans feel about not just Andrew Young but about Overtown and about a lot of other issues - I understand that.

And I understand the pain of the Cubans too. To lose a country is something so serious; it's like losing a parent, only more so because its collective. And I have in-laws who left Latvia and . . . my father-in-law was pursued by the Nazis and the Soviets and so my in-laws were in displaced persons camps for four and a half years and they lost their country before they came here. So I have some association with their pain.

But that's what this is really about. It's trying to get over that pain and the only way we can get over it is by being compassionate to one another. We have to cut each other some slack. We have to understand that there's a lot of pain to go around for everyone.

But we're the role models. We're the ones who people look up to. And everything we do is magnified a hundred fold. Everything that we say as individuals is just blown up and we all know the effect that we have when we make public statements and so every action we take is just so serious and so critical.

In addition to Andrew Young we've had the Cuban Brothers [to the Rescue], we've had the murdered Israelis, we've had today the Overtown issue. And in addition, it's Women's History Month. Now, for women, there's a lot of pain too. We've only had the vote in this country for seventy-six years. So there was a whole lot of discrimination and pain for being women and there still is: there's domestic violence and there are so many other issues that relate to women. And in this very county, the number of women who have achieved positions of power compared to the number of men—we haven't caught up yet.

So we're still evolving everybody. We haven't gotten there yet. We are not perfect yet and to expect us to be perfect is really too much. It's too much for the press. It's too much to expect of each other. We just have to forgive each other a little bit and realize that we're trying the best that we can. And in our own way and everyone in his or her own way is trying to move us forward. And sometimes we make mistakes. And, you know, there's another day and there's always a new redemption every new day. And something that was very meaningful to me that happened on Tuesday. I received some compassion from someone that I didn't expect it from and that was my colleague Natasha Millan. It moved me deeply because it was something I didn't expect but it was very meaningful to me. So, let's cut each other some slack. Let's try and understand each other a little more. Let's not try and always ascribe negative motives to each other. Let's think that maybe each one of us is trying to move an agenda forward that's positive for the whole community and then let's do it together. Thank you Mr. Chairman.

Source: Katy Sorenson, (comments presented at the Dade County Commission Meeting, Miami, Fl., March 7, 1996).

Tere Zubizarreta
A Future Together, 1996

Tere Zubizarreta has been in the forefront of bringing Miami's Latin and Anglo communities together. She arrived in Miami from Cuba in 1960 and remembers getting her first coat from Goodwill Industries and borrowing an outfit from a friend to go on a job interview. Today, she is CEO of one of the top Hispanic advertising agencies in the country. She has been a leader in many community agencies from "We Will Rebuild" to F.A.C.E. (Facts About Cuban Exiles). She has been an active United Way volunteer for over 20 years and was one of the first two Hispanic women on the Orange Bowl Committee. She has not forgotten her roots. In 1995 she was a founder of G.R.A.S.P. (Guantanamo Refugee Assistance Project) that provided help for Cubans held at Guantanamo awaiting processing.

As I drive over the Rickenbacker Bridge and look at the Miami skyline. I cannot help but whisper to myself "How Beautiful My Miami Is." And then I look back to October 7, 1960, when I arrived from Cuba with my husband and four month old son to a very different Miami. For starters, the city was only a temporary haven to us Cuban refugees who were leaving our homeland in search of freedom. Temporary, because we firmly believed that the United States would never allow a Communist base 90-miles from its shores. So we came by the hundreds, with just the clothes we were wearing, penniless or with very little money, to wait out Castro's final hour.

I remember the tallest buildings were the Courthouse (nicknamed by Cubans as "Cielito Lindo"), and the then empty *Miami News* building which soon became Freedom Tower, "La Torre de la Libertad" or "el Refugio," as we called it. Much of Hialeah and Westchester were pasture land, and downtown Coconut Grove consisted of a marina, a park, and one circular office building on an empty, somewhat elevated lot. It was on this lot that a little wooden house became the central recruiting place for volunteers to join the CIA trained invasion forces later known as "Brigade 2506." On a rainy morning in early January 1961, I drove my husband to that site and bid him good-bye as he boarded a bus that would take him to Opa-Locka airfield and the military plane that would take him to the training grounds in the mountains of Guatemala.

All of our hopes were placed on the success of that small group of young Cubans who were ready to restore democracy to our beloved homeland and ensure a safe return to all that we had hastily left behind.

On the morning of April 17, 1961, the invasion forces—all 1,200 of them—landed in the southern part of Cuba named "Bay of Pigs." Three days later, the invasion had failed, our dreams were shattered, and we came to the realization that Miami would be our only place to live—our adopted homeland.

I often say that Cuba is my motherland and the United States is my fatherland. But for the past 36 years Miami is my adopted HOMELAND. And while I do not forget my roots—the land where I was born, spent my childhood and grew up bathed by ocean breezes; smelling the sweet scents of the tropics, admiring the tall royal palms flirt with the morning sun, waking up to the chants of the street vendors; and listening to the roaring waves under the deep-blue night sky—I have transplanted all those feelings and re-live them every day of my life under the freedom skies of "My Miami."

As a proud Cuban-Miamian, I strive to help achieve unity among all people of Miami. For Miami is a city that encompasses the best of many parts of the world. The city's residents come from as near as Kentucky to as far as the Patagonia—from the nearby Caribbean islands to the frozen fields of Russia—from the proud land of the Aztecs and the Mayans to the industrious Orient—from the luscious African plains to the arid desserts of the Middle East. A beautiful bouquet of cultures and colors and rhythms that make Miami worthy of its name: "The Magic City."

This Magic City needs an infusion of UNITY. Most importantly, it needs a spirit of trust in one another and a return to the feeling of camaraderie that seems to be eroding out of control. But how can we achieve unity? What must we do to get the unity ball rolling? One prescription is a strong dose of COMMUNICATION—of sharing our life experiences, our

In August 1995, the United Way brought many diverse Miamians together for their "Twenty-four Hour Countdown for Kids." Working around the clock, volunteers completely painted and landscaped historic Southside School. Their united effort not only beautified the school and brightened the hearts of its mostly immigrant student body, it also demonstrated what people can accomplish when they work together. (United Way)

likes and dislikes with one another with honesty and with a strong desire to build permanent bridges among all segments of our total community.

When I started volunteering for the United Way some 20 years ago, I began to experience that wonderful feeling of unity. I was able to share my ideas with people from different backgrounds—to help and touch the lives of my fellow Miamians from all parts of the county, no matter what the color of their hair, eyes or skin; no matter what their accent or their age, or their political beliefs, or their status. Together, we learned to search for inner beauty instead of judging people from their external facade.

I have always had one goal in mind: to help make Miami—my homeland—become a community where all can live in a true spirit of brotherhood and to maintain this current of friendship and unity continuously flowing every day of our lives.

We did it in 1992 when we were faced with the worst natural disaster in our history. Let's not wait for another blow from mother nature to show the true colors of the spirit of Miamians. Let's begin practicing this new feeling of togetherness as we move into our second century—opening the doors of our hearts and our homes to a fellow Miamian who looks and acts differently from us.

Source: Tere Zubizaretta, "A Future Together," (unpublished manuscript, Miami. Fl., 1996).

Ms. Rome's second grade class at Coconut Grove Elementary School represents Miami's future and its hope for tomorrow. (Martin Berman)

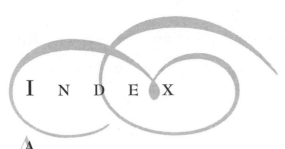

INDEX

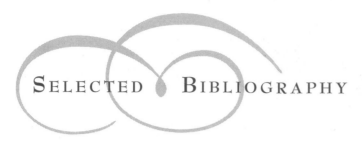

SELECTED BIBLIOGRAPHY

The following bibliography is limited to books that are available in South Florida libraries. Most of the research material for *Miami: The American Crossroad* came from primary sources—manuscript collections, diaries, government documents and reports found in the following research libraries:

Black Archives, Joseph Caleb Center, Miami, Florida

Cuban Exile History Archives, Florida International University, Miami, Florida

Florida Collection, Miami-Dade Public Library, Miami, Florida

Charlton W. Tebeau Library of Florida History, Historical Association of Southern Florida, Miami, Florida

Special Collection, Richter Library, University of Miami, Coral Gables, Florida

Louis Wolfson II Media History Center, Miami-Dade Public Library, Miami, Florida

The most valuable printed sources on the history of Miami are *Tequesta* and *South Florida History Magazine* publications of the Historical Association of Southern Florida. Other valuable articles are found in the *Florida Historical Quarterly*, the *Florida Anthropologist* and *Broward Legacy*. Newspaper sources include *The Miami News*—formerly *The Miami Metropolis*— (1896-1988), *The Miami Herald* (1910-1996), *The Miami Times* (1923-1996) and *The Tropical Sun*. An invaluable new source for understanding Miami is *Miami Today* (1983-1996).

Books

Akin, Edward. *Flagler: Rockefeller Partner and Florida Baron*. Kent, Ohio: Kent State University Press, 1988.

Allman, T.D. *Miami: City of the Future*. New York: Atlantic Monthly Press, 1987.

Ammidown, Margot and Ivan Rodriguez. *Wilderness to Metropolis*. Miami, Florida: Metropolitan Dade County, 1982.

Anderson, Edward C. *Florida Territory in 1844*. Edited by W. Stanley Hoole. Alabama: University of Alabama Press, 1977.

Anderson, Marie. *Julia's Daughters: Women in Dade History*. Miami, Florida: Herstory of Florida, Inc., 1980.

Arend, Geoffrey. *Great Airports: Miami*. New York: Air Cargo News, Inc., 1986.

Armbrister, Ann. *The Life and Times of Miami Beach*. New York: Alfred A. Knopf, 1995.

Ballinger, Kenneth. *Miami Millions*. Miami, Florida: Franklin Press, 1936.

Barrientos, Bartolome. *Pedro Menendez de Aviles*. (1567). Trans. by Anthony Kerrigan. Gainesville, Florida: University of Florida Press, 1956.

Blackman, E. V. *Miami and Dade County, Florida*. Miami, Florida: Victor Rainbolt, 1921.

Blake, Nelson M. *Land into Water—Water into Land*. Gainesville, Florida: University Presses of Florida, 1980.

Born, Donna. *The Road to Somewhere*. Miami, Florida: Arva Parks & Co., 1990.

Boswell, Thomas D, ed. *South Florida: The Winds of Change*. Miami, Florida, Annual Conference of the Association of American Geographers, April 1991.

Bramson, Seth H. *Speedway to Sunshine*. Erin, Ontario: The Boston Mills Press, 1984.

Blight, James G, et al. *Cuba on the Brink: Castro, The Missile Crisis, and the Soviet Collapse*. New York: Pantheon, 1993.

Brookfield, Charles M. and Oliver Griswold. *They All Called it Tropical*. Miami, Florida: Banyan Books, 1977.

Bucuvalas, Tina, Peggy A. Bulger and Stetson Kennedy. *South Florida Folklife*. Jackson, Mississippi: University of Mississippi Press, 1994.

Buker, George E. *Swamp Sailors*. Gainesville, Florida: University Presses of Florida, 1975.

Capitman, Barbara. *Deco Delights*. New York: E.P. Dutton, 1988.

Ceo, Rocco J. and Margot Ammidown. *Redland*. Miami, Florida: Metropolitan Dade County, 1993.

Cerwinske, Laura. *Miami, Hot and Cool*. New York: Clarkson N. Potter, Inc., 1990.

_____. *Tropical Deco*. New York: Rizzoli, 1981.

Chesney, Ann Spatch, et. al. *Miami Diary 1896*. Miami, Florida: privately printed, 1996.

Cohen, Isidor. *Historical Sketches and Sidelights of Miami, Florida*. Miami, Florida: Privately printed, 1925.

Colburn, David R. and Jane L. Landers, eds. *The African American Heritage of Florida*. Gainesville, Florida: University Press of Florida, 1995.

Confronting Racial Isolation in Miami. Washington, D.C.: U.S. Commission on Civil Rights, 1982.

Culot, Maurice and Jean-Francois LeJeune. *Miami: Architecture of the Tropics*. New York: Princeton Architectural Press, 1993.

DeCroix, F. W. *Miami and Ft. Lauderdale*. St. Augustine, Florida: Record Co., c1911.

Derr, Mark. *Some Kind of Paradise*. New York: William Morrow and Company, Inc., 1989.

Didion, Joan. *Miami*. New York: Simon and Schuster, 1987.

Douglas, Marjory Stoneman. *The Everglades: River of Grass*. Miami, Florida: Banyan Books, 1978.

_____. *Voice of the River*. Englewood, Florida: Pineapple Press, Inc., 1987.

Downs, Dorothy. *Art of the Florida Seminole and Miccosukee Indians*. Gainesville, Florida: University Presses of Florida, 1995.

DuPuis, John G. *History of Early Medicine in Dade County*. Miami, Florida: Privately printed, 1954.

Escalante Fontaneda, Hernando d'. *Memoir*. (c. 1575). Trans. by Buckingham Smith. Edited by David O. True. Coral Gables, Florida: University of Miami Press, 1944.

Fairchild, David. *The World Grows Round My Door*. New York: Charles Scribner's Sons, 1947.

Firmat, Gustavo Pérez. *Life on the Hyphen: The Cuban-American Way*. Austin, Texas: University of Texas Press, 1994.

_____. *Next Year in Cuba: A Cubano's Coming -of -Age in America*. New York: Anchor Books, 1995.

Fisher, Jane. *Fabulous Hoosier*. Chicago: Harry Coleman and Co., 1953.

Fitzgerald Bush, Frank S. *A Dream of Araby*. Opa-locka, Florida: South Florida Archaeological Museum, 1976.

Frazure, Hoyt. *Memories of Old Miami*. Miami, Florida: The Miami Herald, 1969.

Gaby, Donald. *The Miami River and Its Tributaries*. Miami, Florida: Historical Association of Southern Florida, 1993.

Garcia, Maria Christina. *Havana U.S.A.: Cuban Exiles and Cuban Americans in South Florida 1959-1994*. Berkeley, California: University of California Press, 1996.

George, Paul. *Mount Sinai Medical Center of Greater Miami, 1949-1984*. Miami Beach, Florida: Mount Sinai Medical Center, 1985.

_____. *A Journey Through Time: A Pictorial History of South Dade*. Virginia Beach, Virginia: The Donning Company, 1995.

Gonzalez-Pando, Miguel. *Greater Miami: Spirit of Cuban Enterprise*. Fort Lauderdale, Florida: Copperfield Publications, Inc., 1996.

Gifford, John C. *The Everglades and Other Essays Relating to South Florida*. Miami, Florida: Everglades Land Sales, 1911.

Guide to Miami and Environs. Works Progress Administration. Northport, New York: Bacon Percy and Daggett, 1941.

Green, Henry A. *Gesher Vakeshur: Bridges and Bonds: The Life of Leon Kronish*. Atlanta, Georgia: Scholar's Press, 1995.

Grenier, Guillermo and Alex Steppick, eds. *Miami Now! Immigration, Ethnicity, and Social Change*. Gainesville, Florida: University Press of Florida, 1992.

Hann, John H. *Missions to the Calusa*. Gainesville, Florida: The University Presses of Florida, 1991.

Harwood, Kathryn Chapman. *The Lives of Vizcaya*. Miami, Florida: Banyan Books, Inc., 1985.

Hatton, Hap. *Tropical Splendor*. New York: Alfred A. Knopf, 1987.

Hirsch, Arnold and Raymond A. Mohl, eds. *Urban Policy in Twentieth Century America*. New Brunswick, Maine: Rutgers University Press, 1993.

Hoffmeister, John Edward. *Land from the Sea*. Coral Gables, Florida: University of Miami Press, 1974.

Hollingsworth, Tracy. *History of Dade County Florida*. Coral Gables, Florida: Parker Art Printing, 1949.

Kearney, Bob, ed. *Mostly Sunny Days*. Miami, Florida: The Miami Herald, 1986.

Kent, Gertrude M. *The Coconut Grove School*. Coral Gables, Florida: Parker Printing, 1972.

Kersey, Harry A., Jr. *Pelts, Plumes and Hides*. Gainesville, Florida: University Presses of Florida, 1975.

Kinerk, Michael, Dennis W. Wilhelm and Barbara Capitman. *Rediscovering Art Deco U.S.A.* New York: Penguin Books, 1994.

Kleinberg, Howard. *Florida Hurricane and Disaster*. Miami, Florida: Centennial Press, 1992.

_____. *Miami: The Way We Were*. Tampa, Florida: Surfside Publishing, 1989.

_____. *Miami Beach: A History*. Miami, Florida: Centennial Press, 1994.

Liebman, Malvina W. and Seymour B. Liebman. *Jewish Frontiersmen*. Miami Beach, Florida: Jewish Historical Society of South Florida, Inc., 1980.

Llanes, Jose. *Cuban Americans: Masters of Survival*. Cambridge, Massachusetts: Abt Books, 1982.

Lummus, J. N. *The Miracle of Miami Beach*. Miami, Florida: Miami Post Publishing Co., 1940.

Lyon, Eugene. *The Enterprise of Florida*. Gainesville, Florida: University Presses of Florida, 1965.

_____. *The Search for the Atocha*. New York: Harper and Row, 1979.

Mahon, John D. *History of the Second Seminole War*. Gainesville, Florida: University of Florida Press, 1967.

Mahoney, Lawrence. *The Early Birds*. Miami, Florida: Pickering Press, 1987.

Martin, Sidney Walter. *Florida's Flagler*. Athens, Georgia: University of Georgia Press, 1949.

Miami Herald Staff. *Miami: In Our Own Words*. Kansas City, Kansas: Andrews and McMeel, 1995.

Milanich, Jerald T. and Charles H. Fairbanks. *Florida Archaeology*. New York: Academic Press, 1980.

Milanich, Jerald T. and Samuel Proctor, eds. *Tacahale*. Gainesville, Florida: University Presses of Florida, 1976.

Miller, Randall M. and George E. Pozzetta, eds. *Shades of the Sunbelt: Essays on Ethnicity, Race, and the Urban South*. Boca Raton, Florida: Florida Atlantic University Press, 1989.

Moore, Deborah Dash. *To the Golden Cities: Pursuing the American Jewish Dream in Miami and L.A.* New York: The Free Press, 1994.

Morrisey, Pat. *Miami's Neighborhoods*. Miami, Florida: The Miami News, 1982.

Motte, Jacob Rhett. *Journey into Wilderness*. Edited by James F. Sunderman. Gainesville, Florida: University of Florida Press, 1963.

Muir, Helen. *Miami, U.S.A.* New York: Henry Holt, 1953, 2nd Edition, 1990.

_____. *The Biltmore: Beacon for Miami*. Miami, Florida: Pickering Press, 1993.

Munroe, Ralph Middleton and Vincent Gilpin. *The Commodore's Story*. Reprinted from 1930 edition by the Historical Association of Southern Florida. Norberth, Pennsylvania: Livingston Co., 1966.

Nash, Charles Edgar. *The Magic of Miami Beach*. Philadelphia: David McKay, 1938.

Olson, James F. and Judith E. Olson. *The Cuban Americans: From Trauma to Triumph*. New York: Twayne Publishers, 1995.

Parks, Arva Moore. *The Forgotten Frontier*. Miami, Florida: Banyan Books, Inc., 1978.

_____. *Miami: The Magic City*. Miami, Florida: Centennial Press, 1990.

_____. *Miami Memoirs, A New Pictorial Edition of John Sewell's Own Story (1931)*. Miami, Florida: Arva Parks & Company, 1987

_____. *Miami Then and Now*. Miami, Florida: Centennial Press, 1992.

Patricios, Nicholas M. *Building Marvelous Miami*. Gainesville, Florida: University of Florida Press, 1994.

Perrine, Henry E. *The True Story of Some Eventful Year in Grandpa's Life*. Buffalo, New York: E. H. Hutchinson, 1885.

Peters, Thelma. *Biscayne Country*. Miami, Florida: Banyan Books, 1989.

_____. *Lemon City*. Miami, Florida: Banyan Books, 1976.

_____. *Miami, 1909*. Miami, Florida: Banyan Books, 1984.

Pierce, Charles W. *Pioneer Life in Southeast Florida*. Edited by Donald Walter Curl. Coral Gables, Florida: University of Miami Press, 1970.

Places in Time. Miami, Florida: Florida International University, 1994.

Porter, Bruce and Marvin Dunn. *The Miami Riot of 1980*. Lexington, Massachusetts: Lexington Books, 1984.

Portes, Alejandro and Alex Stepick. *City on the Edge: The Transformation of Miami*. Berkeley, California: University of California Press, 1993.

Redford, Polly. *Billion-Dollar Sandbar*. New York: E.P. Dutton and Co., 1970.

Reiff, David. *The Exile: Cuba in the Heart of Miami*. New York: Simon and Schuster, 1991.

_____. *Going to Miami*. Boston, Massachusetts: Little Brown and Co., 1987.

Sandoval, Mercedes Cros. *Mariel and Cuban National Identity*. Miami: Editorial SIBI, 1985.

Sewell, John. *Miami Memoirs*. Miami, Florida: Arva Parks & Co., 1988.

Smiley, Nixon. *Knights of the Fourth Estate*. Miami, Florida: E. A. Seemann, 1974.

_____. *Yesterday's Miami*. Miami, Florida: E.A. Seemann, 1973.

Solis de Meras, Gonzalo. *Pedro Menendez de Aviles*. A facsimile reproduction of 1567 manuscript. Translated by Jeannette Thurber Connor. Gainesville, Florida: University of Florida Press, 1964.

Stearns, Frank F. *Along Greater Miami's Sun-Sea-Ara*. Miami, Florida: Privately printed, 1932.

Taylor, Jean. *The Villages of South Dade*. St. Petersburg, Florida: Byron Kennedy and Company, 1987.

Tebeau, Charlton W. *A History of Florida*. Coral Gables, Florida: University of Miami Press, 1971.

_____. *Florida's Last Frontier*. Coral Gables, Florida: University of Miami Press, 1956.

_____. *Man in the Everglades: 2,000 Years of Human History in the Everglades National Park*. Coral Gables, Florida: University of Miami Press, 1968.

_____. *Temple Israel of Greater Miami*. Coral Gables, Florida: University of Miami Press, 1972.

_____. *The University of Miami: A Golden Anniversary History*. Coral Gables, Florida: University of Miami Press, 1976.

Weigall, T. H. *Boom in Paradise*. New York: Alfred H. King, 1932.

Willbanks, William. *Forgotten Heroes*. Paducah, Kentucky: Turner Publishing Company, 1996.

Wyden, Peter. *Bay of Pigs: The Untold Story*. New York: Simon and Schuster, 1979.

Zuckerman, Bertram. *The Dream Lives On: A History of Fairchild Tropical Garden, 1938-1966*. Miami, Florida: Fairchild Tropical Garden, 1988.

_____. *The Kampong: The Fairchilds' Tropical Paradise*. Miami, Florida: Fairchild Tropical Garden, 1993.

Photo Sources

We are indebted to the many people and institutions who shared their photographs with us. Outstanding photographers: John Gillan, Michael Carlebach and Steven Brooke went out of their way to donate their work. Other photographers and contributors are listed with the captions. The following notes those who shared multiple images.

CM   City of Miami
HASF   Historical Association of Southern Florida
MDPL   Miami Dade Public Library
MH   *Miami Herald*
MN   *Miami News*
SPA   State of Florida Photographic Archives
UM   University of Miami

About the Authors and Collaborators

Gregory W. Bush moved to Miami from New Jersey in 1983 after completing his Ph. D. at Columbia University. He has edited the *Journal of Film and History*, produced a film "Patriotic Parades: Wartime Miami 1898-1945" (1984) and authored *Lord of Attention*, a book about advertising and crowd behavior published by the University of Massachusetts Press. Bush teaches in the History Department at the University of Miami and directs its Institute for Pubic History. His first collaborative effort with Arva Moore Parks was to help found the Louis Wolfson II Media History Center.

Arva Moore Parks is a native Miamian who has been writing about her hometown for more than 25 years. She has a Master's Degree in history and is author of numerous award-winning books, films and articles on Miami including *Miami: The Magic City* named the city's official history. More than an historian, Parks is a leader, participating in many different arenas learning first hand what Miami and its people are all about. She has been widely honored for both her activism and her writing. In 1985, she was inducted into the Florida Women's Hall of Fame for helping Miami build a sense of place. In 1995, President Bill Clinton named her to the Federal Advisory Council on Historic Preservation.

Laura Pincus, a native Miamian, is a young historian with a Master's Degree in history. She is a former secondary school social studies teacher and is currently working as a research historian.

Jim Kitchens, the book designer, is a native Miamian with a degree in graphic design from Florida State University. He has designed several award winning books including *Miami Beach: A History* that won the National Association of Independent Publishers' 1994 "Book Award for Interior Design Excellence."

Steven Brooke, an internationally known photographer whose work has been highlighted in several books, did the cover photo. He was awarded the Prix de Rome by the American Academy in Rome, the first architectural photographer to be so honored; the National Institute Honor Award from the American Institute of Architects, the highest award in his field; and two Graham Foundation Grants for Advanced Studies in the Fine Arts. He has lived in Miami since 1968

Ralph Middleton Munroe, Miami's first photographer, captured the photograph of the Seminoles seen on the back cover. Munroe, an amateur photographer and noted nautical designer, came to Miami in 1877 and took his first images in 1884. His Coconut Grove home, The Barnacle, built in 1891, is a State of Florida historic site now open to the public. His book, *The Commodore's Story*, is a wonderful account of life in South Florida before the arrival of the railroad. He died in 1933 at age 82.